UML 2 For Dummies®

BESTSELLING BOOK SERIES

Knowing the Nodes

Nodes are the meat and potatoes of your UML diagrams. Each node has a symbol form that can add a rich texture to your development projects. The following table shows you all the basic ingredients that you can combine in different ways to explore, analyze, design, and document your development.

The Basic Ingredients of UML Diagrams

Node	Symbol	Node	Symbol
Class	Class Name Here	Instance or object	Instance : Class
Part	Part : Class	Port	portname
Component	ComponentName	Interface	InterfaceName
Package	PackageName	Subsystem	Subsystem
Node	Name	Artifact	ArtifactName
Action	Name	State	StateName
Activity	Name	Object node	ObjectName
Use case	UseCaseName	Collaboration	Collaboration
Pseudo States, Control Nodes		lifeline Object	Name[Select]:Class

UML 2 For Dummies®

Learning Your Lines

When you create a recipe that delights developers, you need to spice up the basic ingredients. Lines connect nodes to complete the meaning of your UML diagrams. Most of the spicy lines you need are shown in the following table.

The Spices That Connect Basic Ingredients

Line	Symbol
Association	AssociationName
Aggregation	◇———
Generalization	——▷
Dependency	- - - - - ▷
Activity edge	——▶
Event, transition	event[guard]/action ——▶
Link	LinkName
Composition	◆———
Realization	- - - - - ▷
Assembly connection	—◖——
Message	some code ——▶
Control flow	——▷

Wiley, the Wiley Publishing logo, For Dummies, the Dummies Man logo, the For Dummies Bestselling Book Series logo and all related trade dress are trademarks or registered trademarks of Wiley Publishing, Inc. All other trademarks are property of their respective owners.

For Dummies: Bestselling Book Series for Beginners

UML 2
FOR
DUMMIES®

**by Michael Jesse Chonoles
and James A. Schardt**

WILEY

Wiley Publishing, Inc.

UML 2 For Dummies®

Published by
Wiley Publishing, Inc.
909 Third Avenue
New York, NY 10022
www.wiley.com

Copyright © 2003 by Wiley Publishing, Inc., Indianapolis, Indiana

Published by Wiley Publishing, Inc., Indianapolis, Indiana

Published simultaneously in Canada

Library of Congress Control Number: 2003105654

ISBN: 0-7645-2614-6

Manufactured in the United States of America

10 9 8 7 6 5 4 3 2 1

1B/QS/QX/QT/IN

About the Authors

Michael Jesse Chonoles: An established system developer, educator, author, and consultant, Michael has done just about everything that you can do in software and system development — business, requirements, and software analysis; software, system, and architectural design; coding in many languages; testing and quality control — right through marketing, packing, and shrink-wrapping the software. His titles include Chief of Methodology for the Advanced Concepts Center (ACC), Software Development Practice Area Director, Consulting Analyst, Software Standard and Practices Manager, Test Director, Senior Software Engineer, several varieties of Team/Project Lead/Staff, and (his personal favorite) Wizard. At the Advanced Concepts Center, he was responsible for the content and direction of its Object-Oriented and Requirements-Gathering Curricula as well as its Software Development Practice. Together with his co-author, he constructed a software/system-development methodology, CADIT, which was an early attempt to combine agile techniques with aerospace discipline. He continues his quest to make the complicated simple, while increasing the professional rigor, quality, and productivity of his audience's working lives.

Michael has been involved in many aspects of UML, even before there was a UML. He's been an active member of the UML RTF (Revision Task Force) at OMG — and frequently writes, lectures, speaks, and suggests UML topics.

Michael has an MSE in Systems Engineering from the University of Pennsylvania and BSs in Math and Physics from MIT. He can be contacted at michaeljessechonoles@alum.mit.edu.

James A. Schardt: As the Chief Technologist with the Advanced Concepts Center, James provides 24 years of experience and a firm grounding in object-oriented development, data warehousing, and distributed systems. He teaches and mentors Fortune 50 companies in the U.S. and abroad. His many years of practice in object-oriented systems, database design, change management, business engineering, instructional design, systems-architecture assessment, business engineering, and team facilitation bring a wealth of experience to his assignments.

He authors papers on data warehousing and object technology and also wrote a column for *Report on Object-Oriented Analysis and Design*. James speaks at The Data Warehouse Institute's world conferences on a regular basis. He delivers a two-day presentation on collecting and structuring the requirements for enterprise data-warehouse development.

James is always looking for ways to improve the way that we develop systems and software. Clients request him by name to deliver his exceptional knowledge transfer skills, both in the classroom and as a mentor on projects. Over the years, James has managed major research and development programs, invented new systems methods, developed "intelligent" information-access systems, and provided unique insights into clients' difficult development problems.

James has an MSE in Systems Engineering from the University of Pennsylvania. He can be reached via schardt@acm.org.

Dedication

Michael dedicates this book to his wife Susann and to their son Zev, for their love, support, sacrifice, and silliness.

Jim dedicates this book to his wife Martha for her sustaining love and encouragement, and to M. R. Bawa Muhaiyaddeen as the guiding inspiration in his life.

Authors' Acknowledgments

We would like to thank all the students whom we have taught over the years for their help in shaping our ideas, and all the members of the Advanced Concepts Center, both past and present, for the chance to work with some of the best practitioners in the business of systems and software development.

Together we acknowledge the absolutely necessary help, encouragement, and moral support of our Wiley editors Terri Varveris and Kala Schrager.

Michael would like to thank a whole bunch of people who have helped him over the years, and specifically with this book: Susann Chonoles for teaching him how to write better and for help in proofreading; Zev Chonoles, for being a Test Dummy For Dummies and reading his chapters; his managers Bob DeCarli, Mike Duffy, and Barbara Zimmerman, who encouraged him even when he messed up; and his high-school buddies Joseph Newmark, Jeffrey Landsman, and Barry Salowitz, who keep on telling him what he's doing wrong. It goes without saying that he's grateful to his parents for everything.

He'd also like to acknowledge Jim Schardt for his work toward understanding UML in all its forms, and Lou Varveris for his insight, recommendations, and for access to the Popkin's System Architect tool. He's also grateful to all the members of the OMG ADTF and the UML Gurus for their technical advice, encouragement, and support over the years — especially Cris Kobryn, Jim Odell, Jim Rumbaugh, Philippe Desfray, and Bran Selic.

Jim would like to thank a number of individuals who helped him develop his knowledge and skills over the years: David Oliver for his systems perspective; Michael Kamfonas for his data-warehouse development insights; Michael Chonoles for his work toward understanding UML in all its forms; Jim Rumbaugh and Fred Eddy for their mentoring on object-oriented analysis; and Michael Blaha and William Premerlani for their guiding hand in developing database-design techniques using UML.

Publisher's Acknowledgments

We're proud of this book; please send us your comments through our online registration form located at www.dummies.com/register/.

Some of the people who helped bring this book to market include the following:

Acquisitions, Editorial, and Media Development

Project Editor: Kala Schrager

Acquisitions Editor: Theresa Varveris

Senior Copy Editor: Barry Childs-Helton

Technical Editor: Lou Varveris

Editorial Manager: Kevin Kirschner

Media Development Supervisor: Richard Graves

Editorial Assistant: Amanda Foxworth

Cartoons: Rich Tennant, www.the5thwave.com

Production

Project Coordinators: Kristie Rees, Dale White

Layout and Graphics: Seth Conley, Kelly Emkow, Carrie Foster, LeAndra Hosier, Stephanie D. Jumper, Michael Kruzil, Mary Gillot Virgin

Proofreaders: Laura Albert, Susan Moritz, Dwight Ramsey, TECHBOOKS Production Services

Indexer: TECHBOOKS Production Services

Publishing and Editorial for Technology Dummies

Richard Swadley, Vice President and Executive Group Publisher

Andy Cummings, Vice President and Publisher

Mary C. Corder, Editorial Director

Publishing for Consumer Dummies

Diane Graves Steele, Vice President and Publisher

Joyce Pepple, Acquisitions Director

Composition Services

Gerry Fahey, Vice President of Production Services

Debbie Stailey, Director of Composition Services

Contents at a Glance

Introduction 1

Part I: UML and System Development 7
Chapter 1: What's UML About, Alfie? 9
Chapter 2: Following Best Practices 19

Part II: The Basics of Object Modeling 37
Chapter 3: Objects and Classes 39
Chapter 4: Relating Objects That Work Together 61
Chapter 5: Including the Parts with the Whole 83
Chapter 6: Reusing Superclasses: Generalization and Inheritance 93
Chapter 7: Organizing UML Class Diagrams and Packages 111

Part III: The Basics of Use-Case Modeling 129
Chapter 8: Introducing Use-Case Diagrams 131
Chapter 9: Defining the Inside of a Use Case 147
Chapter 10: Relating Use Cases to Each Other 161

Part IV: The Basics of Functional Modeling 175
Chapter 11: Introducing Functional Modeling 177
Chapter 12: Capturing Scenarios with Sequence Diagrams 189
Chapter 13: Specifying Workflows with Activity Diagrams 213
Chapter 14: Capturing How Objects Collaborate 227
Chapter 15: Capturing the Patterns of Behavior 247

Part V: Dynamic Modeling 259
Chapter 16: Defining the Object's Lives with States 261
Chapter 17: Interrupting the States by Hosting Events 277
Chapter 18: Avoiding States of Confusion 293

Part VI: Modeling the System's Architecture 313
Chapter 19: Deploying the System's Components 315
Chapter 20: Breaking the System into Packages/Subsystems 339

Part VII: The Part of Tens 359

Chapter 21: Ten Common Modeling Mistakes 361
Chapter 22: Ten Useful UML Web Sites 371
Chapter 23: Ten Useful UML Modeling Tools 377
Chapter 24: Ten Diagrams for Quick Development 383

Index 393

Table of Contents

Introduction 1
   How to Use This Book 1
   Some Presumptuous Assumptions 2
   How This Book Is Organized 3
      Part I: UML and System Development 3
      Part II: The Basics of Object Modeling 3
      Part III: The Basics of Use-Case Modeling 3
      Part IV: The Basics of Functional Modeling 3
      Part V: Dynamic Modeling 4
      Part VI: Modeling the System's Architecture 4
      Part VII: The Part of Tens 4
   Icons Used in This Book 4
   Where to Go from Here 5

Part I: UML and System Development 7

Chapter 1: What's UML About, Alfie? 9
   Introducing UML 9
   Appreciating the Power of UML 10
      Abstracting out the essential truth 10
      Selecting a point of view 11
   Choosing the Appropriate UML Diagram 12
      Slicing and dicing UML diagrams 13
      Automating with Model-Driven Architecture (MDA) 16
   Identifying Who Needs UML 17
   Dispelling Misconceptions about UML 17

Chapter 2: Following Best Practices 19
   Understanding UML Terminology and Concepts 19
      Abstracting away irrelevance 21
      Encapsulating and hiding information 22
      Separating the whole from its parts 24
      Generalizing and specializing 26
      Inheriting features and performing the same
        behaviors differently 26
   Improving Your Productivity 28
      Building component-based applications 30
      Utilizing patterns in your development 31

    Using UML tools 31
    Sorting out methodology madness 34

Part II: The Basics of Object Modeling 37

Chapter 3: Objects and Classes 39

  Recognizing Classes and Objects 39
  Naming Objects and Classes 42
    Following rules for naming classes 42
    Naming objects 43
  Identifying Attributes 44
    Naming attributes and types 45
    Enumerating the possibilities 46
    Defining default values 47
    Multiplicity 49
  Performing Operations 50
    Naming operations and arguments 51
    Saying please 52
  Diagramming a System's Parts 52
    Boxing in classes and objects 53
    Differentiating between classes and objects 54
    Using arrows to indicate an object's class 54
    Using stereotypes 55
    Modeling forms 57
  Defining Visibility 58
    Marking attributes as public and private 58
    Marking static attributes ....

Chapter 4: Relating Objects That Work Together 61

  Showing Static Relationships in a Class Diagram 62
  Linking Objects Together 63
  Associating Classes 64
  Naming Your Associations 65
  Relating Many Objects (Multiplicity) 67
    Determining multiplicity 67
    Representing multiplicity 68
    Using multiplicity 69
  Understanding the Roles That Classes Can Play 71
  Associating Classes with Themselves 73
    Constraining associations 75
  Using Association Classes 75
  Qualifying Relationships 77
    Reducing multiplicity — with qualifiers 77
    Indexing with qualifiers 78
  Finding a Way — Navigation 78
  Creating a Program 79

Chapter 5: Including the Parts with the Whole 83

Representing the Whole and the Parts 83
Modeling complexity 84
Considering aggregation behavior 85
Showing Ownership: Composition 86
Showing What Can Be Shared: Aggregation 87
Deciding between Aggregation and Composition 88
Using Alternate Composite Notation 89
Showing parts as classes 90
Showing parts as attributes 91

Chapter 6: Reusing Superclasses: Generalization
and Inheritance 93

Making Generalizations 93
Specializing Classes 97
Using Generalization Sets 98
Inheriting from Ancestors 101
Making sense of inherited associations 101
Overriding your inheritance 102
Inheriting interfaces 106
Exploring the Pros and Cons of Multiple Inheritances 108
Reusing Code 109

Chapter 7: Organizing UML Class Diagrams and Packages 111

Modeling Objects and Classes on Diagrams 111
Constructing Class Diagrams 113
Drawing manageable class diagrams 113
Considering time in class diagrams 118
Using Project-Oriented Class Diagrams 119
Establishing contexts 120
Creating domain classes 121
Applying an application perspective 122
Wrapping packages 125

Part III: The Basics of Use-Case Modeling....................*129*

Chapter 8: Introducing Use-Case Diagrams 131

Identifying Your Audience 131
Casting the System's Actors 133
Finding nonhuman actors 134
Identifying the roles of the actors 136
Naming the actors 137
Exposing an Actor's Roles 137

Showing Your System's Use Cases 139
Defining use cases based on actors and goals 139
Illustrating use cases 139
Showing multiplicity with actors and use cases 140
Defining a good use case 141
Distinguishing between Internal and External 143
Documenting use-case levels 143
Treating people as design elements 144
Using Context Diagrams 145
Packaging Use Cases 146

Chapter 9: Defining the Inside of a Use Case **147**

Creating a Use-Case Specification 147
Telling the Use-Case Story 149
Describing the use case 150
Recounting the use-case narrative 151
Separating analysis from design 151
Setting pre- and postconditions 154
Indicating Alternative Courses of Behavior 155

Chapter 10: Relating Use Cases to Each Other **161**

Linking Use Cases with «include» 161
Documenting included use cases 163
Generalizing actors in included use cases 165
Using Generalization with Use Cases 166
Generalizing differing mechanisms 166
Generalizing differing agents 168
Extending Use Cases 169
Showing a new release 169
Taking alternate paths 171
Extending with optional goals 173
Misusing extends 173

Part IV: The Basics of Functional Modeling *175*

Chapter 11: Introducing Functional Modeling **177**

Modeling Functions from an Object-Oriented
Perspective 177
When use cases aren't enough 178
Describing behavior with use cases 180
Converting use cases into operations (class diagrams) 181
Writing Text-Based Behavioral Specifications 183
Writing use-case specifications 183
Writing pre- and postconditions 184
Writing general algorithms 187

Chapter 12: Capturing Scenarios with Sequence Diagrams 189

Diagramming an Interaction Scenario 190
    Choosing your interaction scenarios during analysis 191
    Examining object lifelines 193
    Creating and destroying objects 193
    Sending messages 195
    Naming your messages 196
    Designing messages and their methods 199
    Signaling by other means 201
    Choosing your interaction scenarios during design 202
Composing Interaction Diagrams 203
    Referencing and reusing interactions 203
    Adding parameters to an interaction 204
    Alternating interactions with combined fragments 206

Chapter 13: Specifying Workflows with Activity Diagrams 213

Ordering the Flow of Behavior 213
    Dissecting an activity diagram 214
    Utilizing activity diagrams 216
Working through Workflow Diagrams 220
    Diagramming use case steps 220
    Indicating the responsible parties 224

Chapter 14: Capturing How Objects Collaborate 227

Developing a Collaboration 228
    Structuring a design class diagram 228
    Preparing the participants 232
Constructing the Communication Diagram 234
    Numbering steps sequentially 235
    Outlining procedural calls 236
    Looping 238
Conquering Concurrency 241
    Looping concurrently 242
    Identifying independent threads 243
Capturing the Collaboration's Design 244

Chapter 15: Capturing the Patterns of Behavior 247

Describing Patterns with Collaborations 247
    Defining and classifying patterns 249
    Using composite structure diagrams 250
    Looking at a common design pattern 251
Applying Patterns 252
    Using the Builder pattern 252
    Showing object interaction 254
Framing Frameworks 255

Part V: Dynamic Modeling 259

Chapter 16: Defining the Object's Lives with States 261

Showing the Life of an Object 261
    Documenting object behavior and events 262
    Constructing state diagrams 263
    Exploring different types of states 266
    Transitioning from state to state 267
Programming an Object's Memory with State Attributes 270
Creating State Diagrams from Scenarios 272

Chapter 17: Interrupting the States by Hosting Events 277

Making Use of Events 277
    Operating your events 278
    Objectifying your events 281
    Parameterizing event hierarchies 283
    Holding special events 285
Indicating Order of Execution on a Diagram 289
Showing Transitions as Icons 290

Chapter 18: Avoiding States of Confusion 293

Simplifying Large State Diagrams 293
    Generalizing states 294
    Utilizing pseudostates and saving history 300
Handling Concurrency with States 303
    Diagramming concurrent states 303
    Using pseudostates with concurrent substates 305
Building Protocol State Machines 308

Part VI: Modeling the System's Architecture................313

Chapter 19: Deploying the System's Components 315

Defining Your System 316
Constructing Logical Pieces 320
    Packing up your classes 321
    Decomposing your system 322
    Developing subsystem responsibilities 323
Working with Components 325
    Showing black boxes 327
    Describing the interfaces 329
    Looking inside the box 330
Deploying Physical Pieces (Implementation) 333
    Diagramming the physical architecture 333
    Realizing your system as artifacts 336

Chapter 20: Breaking the System into Packages/Subsystems **339**

Using Packages and Subsystems 339
    Creating analysis packages 341
    Creating subsystems 343
Exploring Dependencies 347
    Diagramming dependencies 348
    Importing what you need 351
    Merging what you have 352
Patterning the Relationships 354
    Utilizing the three-tier architecture pattern 354
    Modeling architectural patterns 355
    Using other architectural patterns 356

Part VII: The Part of Tens.................................359

Chapter 21: Ten Common Modeling Mistakes **361**

Splitting Attributes and Operations 361
Using Too Few or Too Many Diagram Types 363
Showing Too Much Detail 364
Using Vague Terminology 365
Defining the Same Thing Twice 366
Linking Everything Together 366
Creating Too Many Use Cases 367
Completing One Diagram Before Moving On 368
Cycling Around Class Diagrams 368
Not Listening to the User 370

Chapter 22: Ten Useful UML Web Sites **371**

Weave a Tangled Web 371
UML Home Page 372
UML Forum 372
UML 2 Submitters 373
OCL Center 373
Magazines and Information Portals 373
Search Engines 374
Tool Sites 374
Training Sites 375
Forums and Groups 375
Miscellaneous Sites 375

Chapter 23: Ten Useful UML Modeling Tools **377**

Picking a Tool 377
Argo/UML 379
Cittera 379

Ideogramic UML 379
Objecteering 380
Rational Rose Suite 380
Rhapsody 380
System Architect 381
Tau 381
TogetherSoft 381
Visio 382

Chapter 24: Ten Diagrams for Quick Development **383**
Context Diagram 383
Use-Case Diagram 385
Domain Class Diagram 386
Sequence Diagram 387
State Diagram 388
Application Class Diagram 388
Package Diagram 390
Deployment Diagram 390
Communication Diagram 391
Activity Diagram 391

Index *393*

Introduction

<p>·····································</p>

*I*f, like us, you're a software developer or computer professional of some sort, you probably have to deal with the stereotype that developers can't express themselves among normal humans about normal things. Unfortunately, this book may not help you with that particular challenge, but it can help improve your ability to communicate with other developers about technical matters. *UML* (Unified Modeling Language) is a graphical language that is suitable to express software or system requirements, architecture, and design. You can use UML to communicate with other developers, your clients, and increasingly, with automated tools that generate parts of your system.

If you're already familiar with UML, you know how powerful and expressive it is — but don't be surprised if you're impressed all over again by the new features of UML 2. Perhaps you found some parts of UML too complicated or the apparent benefit too obscure. Well, the UML gurus have revamped UML in many areas — making easier to express yourself exactly and clearly — and they have also added fresh capabilities for the latest software- and system-development problems that you're facing.

But because your problems are complex — and your solutions are sometimes even more complex — UML is not always simple to learn. It's a large and multifaceted language, capable of helping in all areas of development, from analysis to test as well as from database to embedded-real-time. To some, it's a bewildering array of diagrams and symbols. Sometimes it might appear to you that the UML gurus purposely make it too complicated (and with UML 2, even more so) for *the rest of us* to understand.

Bottom line: You need a practical, experience-based guide to the ins and outs of this new language. Let this book be that guide. We boiled down our experiences with UML (in many environments) and our skills as educators to focus on key UML capabilities that you need *first* to be more productive.

So, with straightforward English and concrete examples, we give you a leg up on expressing yourself and being more creative on the job. (Hey, it *could* help you get a raise — just don't expect us to help you get a date.)

How to Use This Book

There's a right way and a wrong way to use this book. Luckily (like its subject, UML 2), this book is remarkably versatile. If you're a traditionalist, you can read it from cover to cover (although you'll probably stop at the index). That's a great approach if you're really new to UML. If you're familiar with earlier versions of UML, you can skip around looking for the new UML 2 stuff. You may miss our (ahem) great insights into the rest of UML, but you know why you bought the book — do what works. Using any of these techniques will get you familiar with your book so that you can count on it to help unstick you if you hit a snag with UML.

After you make friends with your book, you'll probably find yourself taking advantage of its *just-in-time* features. With just a bit of page flipping, you'll be at a section that's full of examples, tips, techniques, and warnings that will help you with your UML modeling.

There are other ways to use this book . . . and some of them are wrong ways. It's not going to work that well as a doorstop (wrong size), and it probably won't impress your date (unless you're dating a developer who's new to UML). However, it'll look great on your bookshelf — silently conveying to your boss your desire to improve — but if you never open it, you won't get the full benefit.

Some Presumptuous Assumptions

If you're reading this, we can safely assume that not only have you *already* opened the book, you're probably also a developer of software, systems, or databases, and you want to read or write UML 2 diagrams. Perhaps you're a manager or business analyst in the same boat.

We won't assume that you know any particular computer language, although knowing one will certainly help.

For the most part, we assume that you fall into one of two major categories: Either you're a modeler (with a yen to communicate requirements or how you think the world works), or you're a developer (looking to explore alternative designs or communicate your results). Either way, this book is for you.

We assume that you're capable of using a tool to draw UML diagrams — we don't care which one. If the only tool that you have your hands on is *in* your hands (as opposed to on-screen), you won't be at a disadvantage when you use this book (although your diagrams won't be quite as tidy if you're drawing with a stick on wet sand). You may even be better off doing some diagrams by hand; electronic UML tools are often expensive and may not yet be up to date with all the neat UML 2 features that we cover. If you're itching for a high-tech UML tool, take a look at Chapter 23 where we list of some of the more useful examples (in all price categories).

How This Book Is Organized

Here's your first practical hint about using UML: *Put about five to nine major elements on a diagram — no more.* Studies have shown (we've always wondered who does this type of study) that most people have a hard time comprehending more than about nine elements at a time. Likewise, when designing this book, we decided to follow our own advice and to divide the book into just seven parts.

Remember that you don't have to read this book in order. Just choose the parts and chapters that you need at the time.

Part 1: UML and System Development

If you want to know what UML is (and why knowing it is useful), this is the place to go; it covers the basics of UML and how it can be used. You'll also find some common principles for communicating or developing systems with UML. These principles guided the UML gurus when they created UML; the same principles can guide you to effective use of it. Ways to apply these principles crop up throughout the book.

Part 11: The Basics of Object Modeling

When you model by using UML, the basics are the things (or *objects*) that you draw and the relationships among them. You'll find information on classes, objects, associations, inheritances, and generalizations. No matter what type of development you do, understanding this part will probably be essential.

Part 111: The Basics of Use-Case Modeling

Use cases (detailed real-world examples) allow you to understand and communicate the purpose of a system or its components. They are great for organizing your thoughts — and your system — when you want to get a value-added product out the door.

Part 1V: The Basics of Functional Modeling

When the objects in your system get busy and you want to explain the details of their complex behavior, you'll need a technique to do so. UML supplies several to choose from — and this part explains and compares them. You'll see several different types of interaction diagrams (such as sequence, communication, and activity) in action, and discover how to combine them to create solutions, patterns, and frameworks. If you're experienced with UML, you'll find lots of new UML 2 stuff in this part.

Part V: Dynamic Modeling

Your objects are more that just clumps of data stuck together with a few functions. The objects that you develop are more like living things; they remember the past and live their lives by changing their states in response to incoming events. In this part, you can make sure that they get a life — and that you know how to explain it. Come to this part for state charts.

Part VI: Modeling the System's Architecture

Whether you're an architect, programmer, or construction worker, you build complex architectures. Computer systems and software applications distribute themselves across different hardware platforms — and spread throughout the Internet. This part outlines steps that you can use to design your systems for their mission by using system plans, packaging, and subsystems.

Part VII: The Part of Tens

Everyone enjoys making lists (and daydreaming that they'll be read aloud, backward, on late-night talk shows). Here are our top-ten lists of useful tips, tools, Web sites, and diagrams. They're likely to be your top-tens, too.

Icons Used in This Book

Appropriately for a book about graphical communication (even if it *is* software-oriented), there are signposts throughout to help you find your way.

This icon identifies the really new stuff in UML 2. Not every modified feature will get this flag, but it does alert those who are familiar with UML 1.*x* that something's really different here.

Here's a simpler way of doing something that can make it easier than the typical approach. Think of it as a shortcut to better UML.

UML can be a maze — and it can be amazing. These are gentle reminders to reinforce important points.

If you see this icon but ignore it, you'll be in good company but a bad mood.

When you see this icon, you know that we thought the associated material really interesting — but every time we tell people enthusiastically about it, they fall asleep. Skip these sections if you want.

Where to Go from Here

Okay, you're now ready to explore the world of UML 2 modeling. Relax. You've got the tools that you need in your head and your hands (one of them is this book), and it's safe to explore.

So, go ahead and *express yourself* with the power of UML 2.

Part I
UML and System Development

The 5th Wave   By Rich Tennant

"No, it's not a pie chart; it's just a corn chip that got scanned into the document."

In this part . . .

Building systems or software isn't that tough if you can communicate with your clients, co-workers, managers, and tools. Unfortunately, as your problems get harder and more complex, the risks that emerge from miscommunication become greater — and more severe when they do crop up.

Fortunately, there's a straightforward, visual language that you can use that will help promote more precise and more efficient communication about the nature of your system in all its aspects — software, requirements, architectures, designs, design patterns, and implementations. This language is *UML,* the Unified Modeling Language. The newest version, UML 2, has become more powerful and more useful than ever.

Starting here, we cover the basics of UML. You find out how it may fit your situation, how and when you can use it, and what it's good for. We give you just as much background in history, terminology, and basic principles as you'll need to take advantage of UML's highly productive features.

Chapter 1

What's UML About, Alfie?

In This Chapter

▶ Understanding the basics of UML

▶ Exploring the *whys* and *whens* of UML diagrams

So you've been hearing a lot about UML, and your friends and colleagues are spending some of their time drawing pictures. And maybe you're ready to start using UML but you want to know what it's all about first. Well, it's about a lot of things, such as better communication, higher productivity, and also about drawing pretty pictures. This chapter introduces you to the basics of UML and how it can help you.

Introducing UML

The first thing you need to know is what the initials *UML* stand for. Don't laugh — lots of people get it wrong, and nothing brands you as a neophyte faster. It's not the *Universal* Modeling Language, as it doesn't intend to model everything (for example, it's not very good for modeling the stock market; otherwise we'd be rich by now). It's also not the Unified Marxist-Leninists, a Nepalese Political party (though we hope you'll never get *that* confused). It is the University of Massachusetts Lowell — but not in this context. *UML* really stands for the *Unified Modeling Language*.

Well, maybe that's not the most important thing to know. Probably just as important is that UML is a standardized modeling language consisting of an integrated set of diagrams, developed to help system and software developers accomplish the following tasks:

- ✔ Specification
- ✔ Visualization
- ✔ Architecture design

✔ Construction

✔ Simulation and Testing

✔ Documentation

UML was originally developed with the idea of promoting communication and productivity among the developers of object-oriented systems, but the readily apparent power of UML has caused it to make inroads into every type of system and software development.

Appreciating the Power of UML

UML satisfies an important need in software and system development. Modeling — especially modeling in a way that's easily understood — allows the developer to concentrate on the big picture. It helps you see and solve the most important problems now, by preventing you from getting distracted by swarms of details that are better to suppress until later. When you model, you construct an abstraction of an existing real-world system (or of the system you're envisioning), that allows you to ask questions of the model *and get good answers* — all this without the costs of developing the system first.

After you're happy with your work, you can use your models to communicate with others. You may use your models to request constructive criticism and thus improve your work, to teach others, to direct team members' work, or to garner praise and acclamation for your great ideas and pictures. Properly constructed diagrams and models are efficient communication techniques that don't suffer the ambiguity of spoken English, and don't overpower the viewer with overwhelming details.

Abstracting out the essential truth

The technique of making a model of your ideas or the world is a use of *abstraction.* For example, a map is a model of the world — it is not the world in miniature. It's a conventional abstraction that takes a bit of training or practice to recognize how it tracks reality, but you can use this abstraction easily. Similarly, each UML diagram you draw has a relationship to your reality (or your intended reality), and that relationship between model and reality is learned and conventional. And the UML abstractions were developed as conventions to be learned and used easily.

If you think of UML as a map of the world you see — or of a possible world you want — you're not far off. A closer analogy might be that of set of blueprints that show enough details of a building (in a standardized representation with lots of specialized symbols and conventions) to convey a clear idea of what the building is supposed to be.

The abstractions of models and diagrams are also useful because they suppress or expose detail as needed. This application of *information hiding* allows you to focus on the areas you need — and hide the areas you don't. For example, you don't want to show trees and cars and people on your map, because such a map would be cumbersome and not very useful. You have to suppress some detail to use it.

You'll find the word *elide* often in texts on UML — every field has its own jargon. Rumor has it that *elide* is a favorite word of Grady Booch, one of the three methodologists responsible for the original development of UML. *Elide* literally means to omit, slur over, strike out, or eliminate. UML uses it to describe the ability of modelers (or their tools) to suppress or hide known information from a diagram to accomplish a goal (such as simplicity or repurposing).

Chapter 2 tells you more about using these concepts of *information hiding* and *abstraction* during development.

Selecting a point of view

UML modeling also supports multiple views of the same system. Just as you can have a political map, a relief map, a road map, and a utility map of the same area to use for different purposes — or different types of architectural diagrams and blueprints to emphasize different aspects of what you're building — you can have many different types of UML diagrams, each of which is a different view that shows different aspects of your system.

UML also allows you to construct a diagram for a specialized view by limiting the diagram elements for a particular purpose at a particular time. For example, you can develop a *class diagram* — the elements of which are relevant things and their relationships to one another — to capture the analysis of the problem that you have to solve, to capture the design of your solution, or to capture the details of your implementation. Depending on your purpose, the relevant things chosen to be diagram elements would vary. During analysis, the elements that you include would be logical concepts from the problem and real world; during design, they would include elements of the design and architectural solution; and during implementation, they would primarily be software classes.

A *use case diagram* normally concentrates on showing the purposes of the system (use cases) and the users (actors). We call a use case diagram that has its individual use cases elided (hidden) a *context diagram,* because it shows the system in its environment (context) of surrounding systems and actors.

Choosing the Appropriate UML Diagram

UML has many diagrams — more, in fact, than you'll probably need to know. There are at least 13 official diagrams (actually the sum varies every time we count it) and several semiofficial diagrams. Confusion can emerge because UML usually allows you to place elements from one diagram on another if the situation warrants. And the same diagram form, when used for a different purpose, could be considered a different diagram.

In Figure 1-1, we've constructed a UML class diagram that sums up all the major types of UML diagrams (along with their relationships), using the principle of *generalization*, which entails organizing items by similarities to keep the diagram compact. (See Chapter 2 for more information on generalization.)

In Figure 1-1, the triangular arrows point from one diagram type to a more general (or more abstract) diagram type. The lower diagram type is a *kind-of* or *sort-of* the higher diagram type. Thus a Class Diagram is a kind of Structural Diagram, which is a kind of Diagram. The diagram also uses a dashed arrow to indicate a dependency — some diagrams reuse the features of others and depend on their definition. For example, the Interaction Overview Diagram depends on (or is derived from) the Activity Diagram for much of its notation. To get a line on how you might use UML diagrams, check out the summary in Table 1-1.

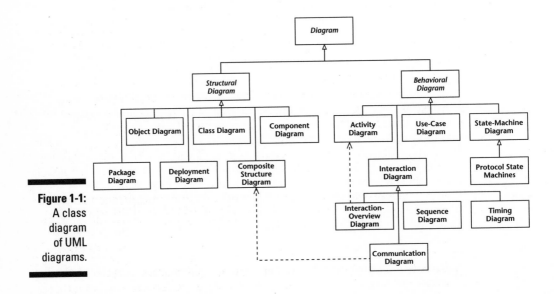

Figure 1-1:
A class diagram of UML diagrams.

Slicing and dicing UML diagrams

There are many ways of organizing the UML diagrams to help you understand how you may best use them. The diagram in Figure 1-1 uses the technique of organization by *generalization* (moving up a hierarchy of abstraction) and *specialization* (moving down the same hierarchy in the direction of concrete detail). (See Chapter 6 for more on generalization and specialization.) In Figure 1-1, each diagram is a subtype of (or special kind of) the diagram it points to. So — moving in the direction of increasing abstraction — you can consider a communication diagram from two distinct angles:

✔ It's a type of interaction diagram, which is a type of behavioral diagram, which is a type of diagram.

✔ It's derived from a composite structure diagram, which is a kind of structural diagram, which is a type of diagram.

After you get some practice at creating and shaping UML diagrams, it's almost second nature to determine which of these perspectives best fits your purpose.

This general arrangement of diagrams that we used in our Figure 1-1 is essentially the same as the UML standard uses to explain and catalog UML diagrams — separating the diagrams into *structural diagrams* and *behavioral diagrams*. This is a useful broad categorization of the diagrams, and is reflected in the categorizations in Table 1-1:

✔ **Structural diagrams:** You use structural diagrams to show the building blocks of your system — features that don't change with time. These diagrams answer the question, *What's there?*

✔ **Behavioral diagrams:** You use behavioral diagrams to show how your system responds to requests or otherwise evolves over time.

✔ **Interaction diagrams:** An interaction diagram is actually a type of behavioral diagram. You use interaction diagrams to depict the exchange of messages within a *collaboration* (a group of cooperating objects) en route to accomplishing its goal.

Table 1-1	UML 2 Diagrams and Some of Their Uses		
Category	**Type of Diagram**	**Purpose**	**Where to Find More Information**
Structural diagram	Class diagram	Use to show real-world entities, elements of analysis and design, or implementation classes and their relationships	Chapter 7

(continued)

Table 1-1 *(continued)*

Category	Type of Diagram	Purpose	Where to Find More Information
Structural diagram	Object diagram	Use to show a specific or illustrative example of objects and their links. Often used to indicate the conditions for an event, such as a test or an operation call	Chapter 7
Structural diagram	Composite structure diagram	Use to show the how something is made. Especially useful in complex structures-of-structures or component-based design	Chapter 5
Structural diagram	Deployment diagram	Use to show the run-time architecture of the system, the hardware platforms, software artifacts (deliverable or running software items), and software environments (like operating systems and virtual machines)	Chapter 19
Structural diagram	Component diagram	Use to show organization and relationships among the system deliverables	Chapter 19
Structural diagram	Package diagram	Use to organize model elements and show dependencies among them	Chapter 7
Behavioral diagram	Activity diagram	Use to the show data flow and/or the control flow of a behavior. Captures workflow among cooperating objects	Chapter 18
Behavioral diagram	Use case diagram	Use to show the services that actors can request from a system	Chapter 8
Behavioral diagram	State machine diagram / Protocol state machine diagram	Use to show the life cycle of a particular object, or the sequences an object goes through or that an interface must support	Chapter 18
Interaction diagram	Overview diagram	Use to show many different inter-action scenarios (sequences of behavior) for the same collab-oration (a set of elements working together to accomplish a goal)	Chapter 13

Category	Type of Diagram	Purpose	Where to Find More Information
Interaction diagram	Sequence diagram	Use to focus on message exchange between a group of objects and the order of the messages	Chapter 13
Interaction diagram	Communication diagram	Use to focus on the messages between a group of objects and the underlying relationship of the objects	Chapter 14
Interaction diagram	Timing diagram	Use to show changes and their relationship to clock times in real-time or embedded systems work	Rarely used, so we refer you to the UML specification

Because UML is very flexible, you're likely to see various other ways of categorizing the diagrams. The following three categories are popular:

- **Static diagrams:** These show the static features of the system. This category is similar to that of structural diagrams.

- **Dynamic diagrams:** These show how your system evolves over time. This category covers the UML state-machine diagrams and timing diagrams.

- **Functional diagrams:** These show the details of behaviors and algorithms — how your system accomplishes the behaviors requested of it. This category includes use-case, interaction, and activity diagrams.

You can employ UML diagrams to show different information at different times or for different purposes. There are many modeling frameworks, such as Zachman or DODAF (Department of Defense's Architecture Framework) that help system developers organize and communicate different aspects of their system. A simple framework for organizing your ideas that is widely useful is the following approach to answering the standard questions about the system:

- **Who uses the system?** Show the actors (the users of the system) on their use case diagrams (showing the purposes of the system).

- **What is the system made of?** Draw class diagrams to show the logical structure and component diagrams to show the physical structure.

- **Where are the components located in the system?** Indicate your plans for where your components will live and run on your deployment diagrams.

- **When do important events happen in the system?** Show what causes your objects to react and do their work with state diagrams and interaction diagrams.

> ✔ **Why is this system doing the things it does?** Identify the goals of the users of your system and capture them in use cases, the UML construct just for this purpose.
>
> ✔ **How is this system going to work?** Show the parts on composite structure diagrams and use communication diagrams to show the interactions at a level sufficient for detailed design and implementation.

Automating with Model-Driven Architecture (MDA)

Model-driven architecture (MDA) is new way to develop highly automated systems. As UML tools become more powerful, they make automation a real possibility much earlier in the process of generating a system. The roles of designer and implementer start to converge. UML provides you with the keys to steer your systems and software development toward new horizons utilizing model-driven architectures.

In the past, after the designer decides what the system would look like — trading off the design approach qualities such as performance, reliability, stability, user-friendliness — the designer would hand the models off to the developer to implement. Much of that implementation is difficult, and often repetitious. As one part of an MDA approach to a project, UML articulates the designer's choices in a way that can be directly input into system generation. The mechanical application of infrastructure, database, user interface, and middleware interfaces (such as COM, CORBA, .NET) can now be automated.

Because UML 2 works for high-level generalization or for showing brass-tacks detail, you can use it to help generate high-quality, nearly complete implementations (code, database, user-interface, and so on) *from the models*.

In MDA, the Development Team is responsible for analysis, requirements, architecture, and design, producing several models leading up to a complete, but Platform-Independent Model (PIM). Then UML and MDA tools can generate a Platform-Specific Model (PSM) based on the architecture chosen and (after some tweaking) produce the complete application.

This approach promises to free the development team from specific middleware or platform vendors. When a new architecture paradigm appears — and it will — the team can adopt it without going back to Square One for a complete redevelopment effort. The combination of UML and MDA also promises to free development teams from much of the coding work. Although the required UML models are much more specific than most organizations are used to, their use will change the way developers make systems.

With the advent of MDA and its allied technologies, UML becomes a sort of executable blueprint — the descriptions, instructions, and the code for your system in one package. Remember it all begins with UML.

Identifying Who Needs UML

Broadly speaking, UML users fall into three broad categories:

- **Modelers:** Modelers try to describe the world as they see it — either the world as is, whether it's a system, a domain, an application, or a world they imagine to come. If you want to document a particular aspect of some system, then you're acting as a modeler — and UML is for you.

- **Designers:** Designers try to explore possible solutions, to compare, to trade off different aspects, or to communicate approaches to garner (constructive) criticism. If you want to investigate a possible tactic or solution, then you're acting as a designer — and UML is for you.

- **Implementers:** Implementers construct solutions using UML as part of (or as the entire) implementation approach. Many UML tools can now generate definitions for classes or databases, as well as application code, user interfaces, or middleware calls. If you're attempting to get your tool to understand your definitions, then you're an Implementer — and (you guessed it) UML is for you.

To understand how you can benefit from UML, it will help to know how and why it was developed. It's based on successful and working techniques proposed by groups of Software Technology Vendors before the Object Management Group, and voted upon by the members.

Dispelling Misconceptions about UML

Many developers have several misconceptions about UML. Perhaps you do too, but after reading this book, you'll have the misconceptions dispelled:

- **UML is *not* proprietary.** Perhaps UML was originally conceived by Rational Software, but now it's owned by OMG, and is open to all. Many companies and individuals worked hard to produce UML 2. Good and useful information on UML is available from many sources (especially this book).

- **UML is *not* a process or method.** UML encourages the use of modern object-oriented techniques and iterative life cycles. It is compatible with both predictive and agile control approaches. However, despite the similarity of names, there is no requirement to use any particular "Unified Process" — and (depending on your needs) you may find such stuff inappropriate anyway. Most organizations need extensive tailoring of existing methods before they can produce suitable approaches for their culture and problems.

- **UML is *not* difficult.** UML is big, but you don't need to use or understand it all. You are able to select the appropriate diagrams for you needs and the level of detail based on you target audience. You'll need some training and this book (of course), but UML is easy to use in practice.

- ✔ **UML is *not* time-consuming.** Properly used, UML cuts total development time and expenses as it decreases communication costs and increases understanding, productivity, and quality.

The evolution of UML

In the B.U. days (that's Before UML), all was chaos, because object-oriented developers did not understand each other's speech. There were over 50 different object-oriented graphical notations available (I actually counted), some of them even useful, some even had tool support. This confusion, interfered with adoption of object-oriented techniques, as companies and individuals were reluctant to invest in training or tools in such a confusing field.

Still the competition of ideas and symbols did cause things to improve. Some techniques were clearly more suited to the types of software problems that people were having. Methodologists started to adopt their competitors' useful notation. Eventually some market leaders stood out.

In October 1994, Jim Rumbaugh of the Object Modeling Technique (OMT) and Grady Booch of the Booch Method started to work together on unifying their approach. Within a year, Ivar Jacobson (of the Objectory Method), joined the team. Together, these three leading methodologists joined forces at Rational Software, became known as the Three Amigos, and were the leading forces behind the original UML. Jim Rumbaugh was the contributor behind much of the analysis power of UML and most of its notational form. Grady Booch was the force behind the design detail capabilities of UML. Ivar Jacobson led the effort to make UML suitable for business modeling and tying system development to use cases.

The Three Amigos were faced with the enormous job of bringing order and consensus to the Babel of notation and needed input from the other leading methodologist about what works and what doesn't. They enlisted the help of the Object Management Group (OMG), a consortium of over 800 companies dedicated to developing vendor-independent specifications for the software industry. OMG opened the development of UML to competitive proposals. After much debate, politics, and bargaining, a consensus on a set of notation selected from the best of the working notation used successfully in the field, was adopted by OMG in November 1997.

Since 1997, the UML Revision Task Force (RTF) of OMG — on which one of your authors (okay, it was Michael) served — has updated UML several times. Each revision tweaked the UML standard to improve internal consistency, to incorporate lessons learned from the UML users and tool vendors, or to make it compatible with ongoing standards efforts. However, it became clear by 2000 that new development environments (such as Java), development approaches (such as component-based development), and tool capabilities (such more complete code generation) were difficult to incorporate into UML without a more systematic change to UML. This effort leads us to UML 2, which was approved in 2003.

Chapter 2

Following Best Practices

In This Chapter

▶ Getting to know the object-oriented principles behind UML

▶ Avoiding vendor hype

▶ Interpreting the buzzwords

*E*ver notice how buzzwords seem to sprout like mushrooms whenever experts get their hands on something really useful? The object-oriented ideas that form the foundation of UML started in the 1970s and UML itself got going in 1994, so the experts had plenty of time to come up with complex terms — like abstraction, encapsulation, and aggregation — to confuse the rest of the world. The experts think you already know these terms. Luckily, the meaning behind these words is generally quite simple.

Various vendors have developed a host of rival tools to help you with UML. The experts also went into overdrive coming up with competing *methodologies* (steps for using UML). These tools and the methodologies are supposed to make you and me more productive. Of course the vendors and the experts assume you already know how to use their tools, understand the meaning of UML diagrams, and know all the buzzwords they've come up with in their marketing brochures. In this chapter we cover the terms and other details about UML that everyone assumes you already know.

Understanding UML Terminology and Concepts

Over the years (if you're like most of us) you've learned the wisdom of such phrases as "say what you mean, mean what you say" and "get to the point." You've probably found that your best communication with other people happens when you say what needs to be said, no more and no less. The experts use their own special words to describe this common-sense principle; Table 2-1 (which uses an air-filter air exchange unit as an example) interprets what they mean.

Table 2-1	Keep It Simple: Word Interpretations	
Expert's Word	*What They Really Mean*	*Example*
Object	Refer to something useful that has identity, structure, and behavior.	The air-filter unit sitting in my living room is unique from all other air filters. It's about 3 feet tall with an 18-inch-square base. The unit behaves nicely by cleaning the air for me.
Class	A family of objects with similar structure and behavior.	You refer to my air-filter unit and the thousands of others manufactured just like it as the HEPA air-filter unit. All these similar units form a class of air-filter unit.
Abstraction	Describe the essence of an object for a purpose.	A circuit diagram of an air-filter unit describes the essence of the electrical wiring so you don't electrocute yourself when you work on it.
Encapsulation	Just tell me what I need to know to use an object.	"You turn on the air-filter unit with the external three-speed knob, and you can't get inside the unit to change the possible speeds of the motor." This statement encapsulates all the details of how the electricity flows to the motor thus turning on the motor that moves the fan, which moves the air through the filters.
Information hiding	Keep it simple by hiding the details.	Most people don't need to know the three-speed switch's part number, or the fact that it takes 120 volts AC power at 15 amperes.
Aggregation	Just tell me about the whole object *or* tell me about the parts of the whole object.	The air-filter unit (as a whole) pulls in air and expels filtered, cleaned air. The air-filter unit is composed of two filters, a fan, a fan motor, a three-speed switch, and some wire.

Expert's Word	What They Really Mean	Example
Generalization	Just tell me what is common among these objects.	Every air-filter unit has a filter to clean the air and a fan to move the air.
Specialization	Just tell me what is different about this particular object.	The HEP43x air-filter unit is unique because it has a motion sensor to speed up the fan when extra dust is flying around.
Inheritance	Don't forget that specialized objects inherit the common features of generic objects.	Since the HEP43x is an air-filter unit, it inherits the features of all air filter units — a filter and a fan.

Abstracting away irrelevance

Ignoring unimportant details is a fundamental part of your life. Most of the time you are not even aware how much you take no notice of your surroundings. If you had to pay attention to everything around you all the time, you would have no time to do anything else. When you communicate your ideas about a system or the software you are developing, you ignore the trivial and focus on the important. The experts have a fancy word — *abstraction* — for this process of distilling the "important" information (needed for some clear purpose) out of the mass of surrounding details.

You use different degrees of abstraction at different times. For example, the picture of the air-filter unit in Figure 2-1 is an abstraction; this image is not the real air-filter unit. The picture describes the *look* of the unit without details such as color, physical dimensions, and actual size.

Sometimes you need different abstractions of the same thing. For example, the electrician may need to see a wiring diagram like the one in Figure 2-2. This diagram "abstracts away" everything about the air-filter unit except its electric circuitry — and even that isn't what the actual wiring looks like. The symbols on the wiring diagram have special meanings; they indicate components or functions that would otherwise clutter up the diagram with distracting details. The symbol that looks like an upside-down triangle with three lines, for example, shows that the circuit is grounded at this point — exactly how that's done isn't important right now, and isn't shown.

UML diagrams have symbols that act as a shorthand notation. These symbols allow you to show what's important by using the principle of abstraction, just as a circuit diagram shows the electricians what's important to them.

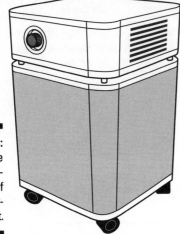

Figure 2-1:
Picture
represen-
tation of
an air-
filter unit.

When you use UML to make models — in particular, objects and classes, which are discussed in detail in Chapter 3 — they make good abstractions of the physical world. A good model contains only the important aspects of an object, such as its identity, structure, behavior, and association with other objects. (Abstracting your real world objects — paring them down to the essentials — is also a great help when you map real-world stuff into object-oriented programs.)

Don't let someone use UML to describe lots of irrelevant detail. Apply the principle of abstraction — ignore the irrelevant and model what is important to you and fellow developers.

Encapsulating and hiding information

To help you enforce an abstraction, the experts have a couple of other fancy terms:

- **Encapsulation:** When you summarize important features of your objects in one place, you are *encapsulating* them — your objects can make good abstractions of the real world by combining features such as identity, attributes, and behavior into a neat package. Everything an object needs to be itself — structure, identity, internal behavior — is close together so the object can be itself (function the way it wants to). The operations (behavior) of an object are like a wall between its internal workings and those of other objects. The wall of operations places a barrier that helps the object maintain its separation from other objects, which helps enforce the abstraction.

These walls prevent your intended abstraction from being violated. You turn an air-filter unit on and off. You cannot break the encapsulation of that object and change its internals to create a TV that you can also turn on and off.

✔ **Information hiding:** Hiding the details of how an object performs its job helps prevent overloading the user with irrelevant details. The advantage is that if you hide internal information about an object from its users, then you can tinker with that object without affecting the users.

Manufacturers of air-filter units try hard to hide how the unit works from the users of these devices. The assumption is that the user doesn't have to know anything about the operation of the unit except how to turn it on and off. If the manufacturer changes the internal workings of the unit without changing its controls — *and it performs the same function —* then its users don't have to retrain themselves to use a new unit.

Encapsulation and information hiding are used in many branches of technology. For example, computer users sometimes complain that PCs — even today — still require the user to master too much detailed knowledge. The users — all of us — still have to know a lot about the internal workings of the computer before we can change a setting or get it to do a simple task. All those details tend to get in the way of performing a job. From the user's point of view, the PC builders haven't done enough information hiding or encapsulation.

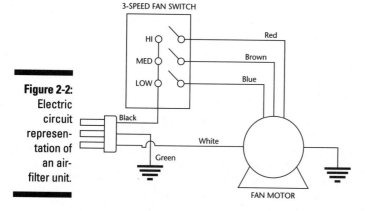

Figure 2-2:
Electric circuit representation of an air-filter unit.

A little information hiding goes a long way

During the 1990s, software developers were obsessed with Y2K — the fear that software programs worldwide would be disrupted when the year changed from 1999 to 2000. The problem boiled down to a lack of (you guessed it) encapsulation and information hiding. Two digits were customarily used to represent the *year attribute* of a date: 98 for 1998, 99 for 1999, and 00 for — what? 1900 or 2000? Programs that needed accurate dates to function properly relied on those unencapsulated two-digit year attributes — big trouble. Companies and governments around the world spent in excess of $200 billion to solve the problem.

Now, suppose those dates were encapsulated into a date object and the year representation was hidden inside the date object. The software developers could have changed the internal representation of year from two to four digits and added a wall of behavior that would, if asked, provide the date with either two- or four-digit years. When a software developer needed to see whether one date preceded another, the developer would ask two date objects to compare themselves through a simple compare operation. If early software developers had encapsulated all dates in the first place — and hidden the representation of year — then the Y2K scare would have never happened.

You use encapsulation and information hiding together when developing object-oriented systems and software. By hiding an object's structure and internal methods of behavior behind a wall of operations, you enforce your abstraction and — in effect — help keep the object intact.

Don't make the structure of your objects public. Doing so breaks the principle of encapsulation and information hiding. For openers, public attributes often attract tinkerers who make unauthorized modifications, and that makes your job of enforcing an abstraction difficult.

Separating the whole from its parts

Aggregation is, in effect, pulling together the parts of an object to make up the actual object. For example, when we say "air-filter unit" we're talking about a whole object that hides many other objects that we call its *parts*. The fan, motor, filter, switch, and wires are the internal objects/parts of an air-filter unit. You aggregate the hidden parts to form the whole air-filter unit.

You use aggregation to hide the internal parts of a complex object from the outside world. Aggregation is a form of encapsulation and information hiding. The whole or aggregate object hides many complex internal objects or parts.

If an object is especially complex, you can ignore its internals by focusing on relationships between the whole object and other external objects. We don't have to talk about the internal parts of an air-filter unit to tell you how to use it. We communicate the relationships between you, the air-filter unit, and the air that gets cleaned and moved throughout the room. In my communication with you we tell you just what you need to know.

If you must maintain the air-filter unit by replacing the filter, we tell you about that specific internal part of the unit. Nobody has to yak on and on about the unit's relationship with air, the room, and the user. Again, we tell you only what you (as maintainer) need to know.

Whenever you need to hide the internal parts of an object, use UML aggregation notation to isolate the internal complexity of a whole object from outside interactions with other objects.

Composition is another word for a strong form of aggregation. The experts needed a different word to help distinguish between two different situations:

- **Composition:** When the parts of an object are completely bound up in the life of the whole object, the whole object is *composed* of them. If you take a whole air-filter unit and crush it (end the life of the whole thing), then all its parts are crushed too (the life of each part is bound to the life of the whole).

- **Aggregation:** Some parts of a whole object exist beyond the life of the whole. For example, a subsidiary of a holding company is part of the whole company. However, if the holding company were to go bankrupt and cease to exist, the subsidiary's life would continue as a standalone company. The relationship between the subsidiary and the holding company is simple aggregation, not composition.

You manage complexity by hiding it. Suppose we build a black box and tell you how to hook up to the black box. If all you worry about is the hook up to the box and not the insides of the black box, then we have successfully hidden any complexity from you. UML classes hide complexity by forcing you to use their public operations (publicly accessible behavior). UML components with internal parts hide complexity by forcing you to use their public interfaces.

Generalizing and specializing

Like most people, UML experts prefer not to repeat themselves when communicating with others. They follow the principle of saying something once. When you hear the following words this is what they mean:

- **Generalization:** You look at a group of objects, extract the features they have in common — their attributes (structure) and their operations (behavior) — and use those features to define a generic class of objects. That way, you refer to these common features whenever you mention the class — and you only have to do so once.

- **Specialization:** Specialization is the opposite of generalization. To *specialize a* group of objects, you look at a group of objects and identify groups of objects with unique features not shared with other groups of objects. Then, you create a class for each group of objects with their own unique features.

The same is true of any object — especially of any machine. There are lots of different kinds of air-filter units, from no-frills to fancy. Figure 2-3 shows the type of air-filter unit you see above a stove. A more elaborate, whiz-bang air-filter unit, bristling with gizmos, is shown in Figure 2-4. These units share common features — internal fan, On/Off switch, replaceable air filter — that you can find in various types of filter units. When you consider all possible filter units that have these basic features, you're generalizing.

To help you see the spaghetti sauce you're cooking, the stovetop unit in Figure 2-3 has a light to illuminate the cooking surface below. None of the other air-filter units have this, so stovetop air-filter units make up a more specific class of objects.

The fancy unit in Figure 2-4 has an ultraviolet light and a motion sensor. Since we've already included it in the general class of air-filter units, we can assume that it also has an On/Off switch, an internal fan, and an internal filter — even though there's no stovetop light.

Inheriting features and performing the same behaviors differently

Okay, air filters in general have the features common to all air filters — so when we speak of a particular air-filter unit, we can focus on its specific features. By doing so, we assume you already understand that the unit has the features listed in the generic description. We're "reusing" the generic features that all air-filter units have in common.

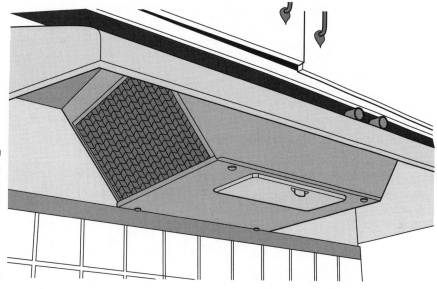

Figure 2-3:
This stove-top air-filter unit has a light so you find the oregano.

This leads us to two more terms that the experts use to confuse us:

- ✔ **Inheritance:** You notice that when we talk about a specific kind of air-filter unit, we assume you understand that the specific unit has the same features of any generic air-filter unit. The experts like to say the specific object *inherits* the features of the generic object.

  Through the principle of inheritance, you "reuse" the features of a generic object when talking about or modeling specific objects.

- ✔ **Polymorphism:** Of course, *everybody* studies classical Greek these days, right? So here it is again — *poly* meaning many, and *morph* meaning form. It's when objects have the same behavior but perform it differently. For example, all air-filter units can perform the operation of turning on — but each type of unit performs that operation differently.

  In this example, you notice there is a difference between the *operation* of the object and the *method* the object uses to perform the operation. In the object-oriented world, objects invoke the operations (behavior) of another object. The second object then performs some internal method (steps in a process) as a result. When you (the first object) invoke the operation of turning on the air filter unit (the second object), the air filter unit performs an internal method (it passes electricity through a switch to the fan).

  The idea of polymorphism is to hide the exact method of operation behind the operation itself. You *invoke* the operation of an object without worrying about how the operation is performed. So when you step up to an air-filter unit, you just turn it on. The method inside the unit does the rest.

Figure 2-4:
Air-filter
unit with
ultraviolet
light. (Do
dust motes
glow in
the dark?)

When you use UML to describe general and specific objects, use the Principle of Least Surprise. You place an attribute or an operation in whatever class — generalized class or specialized class — is least likely to surprise the user.

Improving Your Productivity

Developing software is a hard job, made harder because the product has to be easy to use, loaded with additional functionality, and usable even when distributed over complex Internet environments. Software must continually be better, quicker, and faster than ever before. To help you achieve these goals, software development has gone object-oriented. Instead of writing functions, you create little software objects that send messages to other software objects. Unlike functions, these software objects allow you to hide the details of internal operations in tidy programming objects. Now, to go along with this new direction in software development, you encounter a whole bunch of buzzwords. You can use Table 2-2 to translate the slew of new buzzwords when UML pros want to talk shop (or vendors want to sell you methods and tools for UML modeling).

Table 2-2	UML Buzzwords and Their Interpretations	
Expert's Word	*What They Really Mean*	*Example*
Component	A real-world object or unit of software code that is so self-contained that it can be swapped out and replaced by another object, without the user knowing the difference.	You can replace one DVD player in your entertainment system with another DVD player of equal or better capability; you can replace one module of code with another that works better.
Component-based development	Building your system out of modular/replaceable units of code.	Develop your system using Enterprise Java Beans, .Net, or CORBA components.
Interface	A contract that specifies what the object must do (but not how to do it).	A DVD player must accept audio and video signals through specific connectors (for example, RCA-type).
Pattern	Description of how developers solve a frequently occurring problem.	Use the adapter pattern to adapt an existing class interface to a new interface you can handle.
Framework	A large-scale pattern that dictates the architecture of your application.	You could implement a hotel reservation application using an event-driven framework using GUI screens, or an auction framework over the Internet.
UML Modeling tool	Software that allows you to create UML diagrams — and generate code based on the diagrams.	Chapter 23 lists some vendors of Modeling tools.
Life cycle	A sequence of generic steps from beginning to end that everyone on the team has to follow for developing a system or software.	For many software projects, the life cycle (Waterfall, for instance) starts with the analysis step, followed by the design step; all steps are sequential.
Methodology	A prescribed detailed approach to the task of developing a system or software.	These are the steps prescribed by industry experts for the development of systems and software. These steps often involve the use of a modeling language like UML, RUP, OMT, Booch, and Agile.

Building component-based applications

You've seen manufacturers assemble hardware from groups of components. Each part of a device (for example, a disk drive) is created first. Then the parts sit in bins, waiting to be picked at the right time in the assembly process. One instance of a part like a power supply or disk drive is exactly like another; each part is a replaceable unit. The assembly-line approach to building hardware is more productive than building things by hand; object-oriented programming applies the same principle to software development.

Building software by assembling prefab pieces is faster and more productive than creating each program line by line from scratch. This is what the experts call *component-based development*. You can think of components as units of code that can be plugged into the software (as if into a circuit board) to form an application.

To develop applications from groups of components, you need to perform the following tasks:

✔ **Create components:** Write units of software as groups of cooperating objects, which you can reuse from application to application.

✔ **Separate what a component can do from how the component does it:** You must declare interfaces to your components. Each interface specifies the name of the operation and any parameters needed by that operation. When one component invokes the interface of another component, it should not have to know anything about how the operation is performed.

For example, if we build a streaming-video component in software that provides a run interface, you should be able to simply ask any of our streaming-video components to run. You shouldn't have to know anything about the internal type, structure, or format of the video to run it. Thanks to this separation of concerns (external interface from internal code), you can replace our component with another component that provides the same run interface and your assembled application will continue to work. It's like replacing one power supply in a disk drive with another.

✔ **Provide a common standard for communication among components:** To make your components replaceable, you have to standardize on the exact way one component talks to another. The Object Management Group's CORBA and Microsoft's COM are two established communication standards that offer this sort of consistency.

✔ **Allow your components to exist in a standard environment:** Your components must be able to create instances of other components, find out which interfaces other components provide, and register themselves so other components can find them and invoke them. Enterprise Java Beans (EJB) is a good example of a component environment. EJB provides standard ways to create, register, find, interface with, and delete components.

Use UML component diagrams to describe an assembly of parts for your application. Use class, composite structure, sequence, and communication diagrams to describe how the insides of your components work. (Class diagrams show the attributes and operations of each object making up your component. Composite structure diagrams show the internal parts that make up each component. Sequence diagrams show interaction among the components over time. Communication diagrams show complex internal interactions of the parts of a component.)

Utilizing patterns in your development

One way you can become more productive is by reusing solutions to common development problems. Why reinvent the wheel every time you have a design problem? During the 1990s, many developers got together and documented common solutions to common system and software problems. They called the resulting documents *design patterns*. Each pattern has a name, a description of the problem it solves, a standard solution, and the documented trade-offs you encounter if you apply the pattern.

For example, the *proxy* design pattern allows you to have one object take the place of another. This pattern allows all objects to interact with each other across different computers. Your object on a client computer invokes a *proxy object* on the client computer; and that object is the one that contacts the real object on the server computer. Your original object knows nothing about how to contact the server object — and doesn't have to (that's what the proxy is for). This approach can make object development easier.

Here the terminology gets confusing. *Patterns* describe a common way of making objects work together. Some experts use the word *framework* to describe larger-scale patterns used to create applications. Other experts use that same term — framework — to describe an existing group of objects that you customize for your own purposes. When the experts sort it out, we're sure they'll let us know.

You can use UML collaborations and collaboration occurrences to model patterns and frameworks. For more information on diagramming collaborations and collaboration occurrences, see Chapter 15.

Using UML tools

UML is easy to draw; artistically challenged experts designed it that way. But, keeping track of many different kinds of diagrams — on many pieces of paper — is especially tedious when you have to make changes during development. Using UML to model and build today's complex software systems requires something more than a white board, lots of paper, and pencils with big erasers.

What you need is a UML modeling tool, formerly known as a CASE (Computer-Aided Software Engineering) tool. A modeling tool aids the development of software by keeping track of all the software engineering symbols (such as those in UML), and it helps you do the following tasks:

- **Drawing UML diagrams:** This can include class diagrams (see Chapter 7), use case diagrams (see Chapter 8), and sequence diagrams (see Chapter 12).

- **Drawing UML notation correctly:** The tool draws a UML class as a box and a UML state as a rounded rectangle. You don't have to fool with getting the icon to look right.

- **Organize the notation and the diagrams into packages:** With large projects, as the number of classes increase you need help organizing your diagrams. Modeling tools help you organize by packages. (For more information on package organization see Chapter 7 and Chapter 19.)

- **Searching for specific elements in your diagrams:** This is very helpful when you have a lot of diagrams with many classes, objects, associations, states, and activities.

- **Reverse engineering:** Some of the tools read your object-oriented programming code and convert it into simple class diagrams. This saves you time when you're modeling existing software.

- **Model reporting:** You can disseminate information about your models to other developers by asking the tool to generate a report.

- **Generating code:** The big payoff of a UML modeling tool is the fast creation of some, but not all, of the code you need for your software.

Over 120 different modeling tools support UML modeling. (Chapter 23 in this book describes ten such tools.) You can even get some of them free. Whatever the outlay, choose a UML tool that fits the kind of system you're building and that makes you the most productive.

Think carefully about the kind of system you're building before you buy a UML modeling tool. Consider the following system categories:

- **Information systems:** You want to build software applications that process information. Look for a tool that is well rounded in that it provides you with all the UML diagrams.

- **Real-time and embedded systems:** You concern yourself with strict timing and sizing issues in these systems. Get a tool that is especially good at state diagrams (see Chapter 16), timing specifications, and real-time simulation of event handling (a special program that directly implements a state diagram).

- **Database systems:** In this case, you design databases to handle transactions online or serve as data warehouses. Consider the tools that support conceptual, logical, and physical models, and that can generate the code to query and extract data from your chosen database-management system.

✔ **Web-based systems:** Here you concern yourself with scripting languages and Web services; you have to generate XML data structures, create client-side code, and specify server-side operations. You need a tool that allows you to diagram all the different components in a Web-based application.

The primary reason you buy a UML tool is to improve productivity. Look for a tool that gives you the automated support you need on the job. Don't listen to vendor hype; look first at what the modeling tool can actually do for you. The best tools have capabilities like these:

✔ **Shell generation:** The tool generates header files for your code according to a class diagram, but doesn't generate any actual method code.

✔ **Code generation:** Now we're talking. These tools generate basic code for setting and getting the attributes of a class. They also generate simple constructor methods.

✔ **Language-development support:** You find some tools support the whole application development process. These tools integrate requirements management, UML modeling, and an interactive visual development environment. A good tool that supports your language development parses your code in the UML model for correctness. You should be careful to choose a tool that fits your language needs and supports the development tools you use. These tools also reverse engineer code into simple UML models, helping you with integrating legacy code.

✔ **Database generation:** These tools allow you to specify logical and physical data models as different class diagrams. The tool generates *Data-Description Language* (DDL) statements such as `create table` and `create index`. Make sure the UML tool generates the DDL you need for the relational database-management system (RDBMS) you use.

Some UML tools don't generate DDL directly. The tool vendor supplies you with an export facility. You export your UML class diagram into a more traditional entity-relationship modeling tool. That tool generates the DDL.

✔ **OCL support:** The *object-constraint language* (OCL) provides you with a powerful way of expressing business rules beyond the UML diagrams. OCL allows you to declare pre- and postconditions for your operations. A *precondition* is a statement of truth before an operation can work properly. A *postcondition* is a statement of what is true after an operation executes successfully. If you use OCL heavily, look for tools that parse OCL and generate partial code from OCL.

✔ **Support for collaboration on large projects:** Many UML tools place your diagrams in a file on your computer. If you work with others, then you have to send them copies of the file with your diagrams. On very large projects (with 50 or more developers), that approach leads to disaster — the files get changed, no one knows which file is the latest and greatest, and mistakes proliferate. When you work big projects, look for tools that store their models in an industrial-strength database instead of a file. Large projects also require lots of documentation. Look for a tool that generates reports in HTML, XML, and hard copy.

Sorting out methodology madness

UML is just a notation. UML does not tell you when to use which diagram. The experts had plenty of time to create lots of suggestions about when, what, where, why, and how to use UML. They call this advice a *methodology*.

Most experts use their own obscure terms to describe their specific methods. You may find their jargon very confusing — especially when different experts use the same word to mean different things, or different words to mean the same thing.

Every method for developing systems and software starts with the following basic steps:

1. **Planning:** Organize your project.

2. **Analysis:** Find out *what* your application does or needs to do.

3. **Design:** Specify *how* your application works.

4. **Implementation:** Just build the application.

5. **Testing:** You make sure the application works properly.

6. **Deployment:** Launch the finished application onto servers and the users' computers.

Any good engineer will tell you about the basic steps for developing a system. But you need to know which UML diagram to use during each step. You must have a sense of how to order the steps, and how long you should take to perform a step for your project (for example, some complex software requires a longer requirements-gathering period). That's where the experts come in with their life cycles and their methodologies.

Riding multiple life cycles

A system or software development life cycle tells you what to do (process steps) and when to do it (the sequence of process steps). When the experts give you just a life cycle, they don't tell you how to perform the actual steps.

Fortunately, life cycles come in recognizable types. Here are the ones you're most likely to come across:

✔ **Waterfall:** This life cycle is one of the oldest and one of the simplest. Each basic step (planning, analysis, design, and so on) follows the others in a strict sequence. First you perform your planning. When that is done, you gather your application requirements during analysis. Only after you have all the requirements can you move on to design. This life cycle is not very flexible.

- ✔ **Spiral:** The Spiral was originally a way to make the Waterfall life cycle more flexible. Think of this cycle as a sequence of mini-Waterfalls. Your project progresses in smaller steps. At the end of each spiral (a whole sequence of risk assessment, analysis, design, and prototyping), the team assesses how well the project is doing. The next spiral then addresses these issues to build a larger prototype. Eventually the prototype becomes the full, delivered system.

- ✔ **Iterative Development:** The Spiral is thorough, but developers needed a life cycle that didn't take so long. When they recognized they could perform groups of steps in parallel iterations, they had the key to speeding up the process.

  First, high-level requirements are gathered. Then the project is broken up into small bit-size pieces of customer-oriented capabilities that meet those requirements. Small project teams work on each iteration at the same time to deliver each piece. (An *iteration* involves building, testing, and providing a small functional part of the overall program.) You get the project done faster because your team works on different parts of the project at the same time.

Adhering to multiple methodologies

A methodology tells you how to perform a sequence of steps to get the job — completing an application — done in the time available. When you read experts' prescriptions for building an application you may get the impression they're really saying, "Do it my way or else face disaster."

Don't be confused by the lingo. What some experts call a methodology is just a life cycle. Look for a method that's well enough thought out to tell you what to do, when to do it, how to do it, and how long to do it.

No one follows the experts all the time. Every project is different and yours is no exception. Read what the experts have to say — and then create a customized methodology that fits your company culture, your type of project, your team dynamics, and your path to success.

If you want some useful starting points, you can find methodologies like the following by using your favorite search engine on the Web:

- ✔ **OMT, Booch, Objectory:** In the old days (pre-1995), these were the leading object-oriented methodologies. Each method had its own notation. UML came along and replaced the different diagram symbols with one unified notation. But you can't get a complex project done using just a notation — look deeper at the overall approach.

✔ **Rational Unified Methodology:** During the mid-1990s, the Rational software tool company hired (or had access to) the methodologists of OMT, Booch, and Objectory fame. These folks (known to developers as the Three Amigos) came up with a unified method to go along with the unified notation. Rational called its new method RUP for the Rational Unified Process. (See www.rational.com.)

✔ **Catalysis:** During the mid- to late 1990s, component-based development became fashionable. Desmond D'Souza and Alan Wills developed a methodology they called Catalysis that describes how to perform development using components. (See www.catalysis.org.)

✔ **Agile, eXtreme Programming / eXtreme Modeling:** After the turn of the current century, a number of developers came together to address the continuing failure of methodologies. Older methodologies like RUP seemed bloated and overbearing, resulting in projects that generated lots of diagrams and documents but still failed. These developers wanted something more agile than RUP. The result — the Agile method — encouraged developers to tailor their methods to meet their specific needs. Agile modeling using UML is geared toward small development projects with tight deadlines, like building Web front ends. (For agile development see www.agilealliance.org. For eXtreme Programming see www.extremeprogramming.org.)

Use risk as your guide. Each step of a methodology is intended to mitigate some risk you might face on a project. Every project is different because every project faces a different group of risks. Typical risks include lack of communication among developers, not enough money in the budget, not enough time on the schedule, and failing to meet user requirements. Review your project to identify the high-priority risks that could kill your development effort. Then you should find the process steps, methods, and UML diagrams to help you mitigate those risks.

No matter what method you choose, successful projects happen because teams learn to work together. Don't worry about the fancy words; get everyone on the team focused and excited by the project. You can use UML diagrams to communicate, exchange ideas, build consensus, and document for others what your project, application, system, or software is going through on its way to completion.

Part II
The Basics of
Object Modeling

The 5th Wave   By Rich Tennant

EARLY DEVELOPMENTS IN THE BUTTERFLY KEYBOARD

THE SPIDER KEYBOARD   DUNG BEETLE KEYBOARD   PRAYING MANTIS KEYBOARD

LARVA KEYBOARD

THE CATERPILLAR KEYBOARD

"WHERE'S THAT FLAKE TEMPLEMAN? HE'S SUPPOSED TO BE HELPING US WITH THIS."

In this part . . .

This part introduces you to the everyday notation at the heart of modeling objects and developing object-oriented programs. Whether you're a modeler or a programmer, we familiarize you with objects, classes, associations, generalizations, aggregations, and packages. We cover the important details of UML's object-modeling notation and give you tips on how to develop good modeling practices. We also warn you of problem areas and show you how to avoid them.

Chapter 3

Objects and Classes

· ·

In This Chapter

▶ Choosing key objects and classes

▶ Nominating good names

▶ Attributing the attributes

▶ Getting openness with operations

▶ Building the boxes

▶ Allowing for privacy

· ·

*J*ust as you take time to get to know a friend, you need to take the time to get to know the important objects and classes of your system before you start doing UML modeling. With this chapter as your guide, you can identify these key classes and objects in your system and give them useful names. By spending quality time with classes and objects, you get a good idea of what attributes a class has, what operations it can do, and even what parts must remain private or may be shared.

In this chapter, we offer useful tips for identifying and naming classes and their parts, and then we help you start organizing all these parts into a model that everyone on your development team can easily understand and use.

Recognizing Classes and Objects

Before you can go about modeling objects and classes with UML, get familiar with the entities in your system that match the definition of an object or a class:

> ✔ **Object:** An *object* can be any useful item that has identity, structure, and behavior. When an object-oriented software system is running, the items in the system are interacting software objects. When a real-life physical enterprise is in operation, the individual interacting entities in the enterprise system are the business objects.

✔ **Class:** A *class* is a family of objects. If several objects have similar structure, behavior, and meaning, then you can group the objects into a class — in effect, a template (or even a factory) you can use to create uniform individual objects. When you develop an object-oriented system, the system is described as being made up of classes — and that's even true of a real-life enterprise system. Some examples of classes might be the `Crash Dummy` class, `Lease` class, `Client` class, or `Owner` class. Each class provides a generic scheme for one or more objects, and a class can be a template for many objects or only one.

There is often (and should be) a strong parallel between a software system and its underlying physical enterprise: The system's software objects should parallel the enterprise's *business objects* (actual, tangible things that the software objects represent). Imagine that you are constructing the software for a *Rent-A-Crash Dummy* business enterprise. As you walk through the enterprise in your mind's eye, you recognize business objects: a particular Crash Dummy, a specific lease document, and a particular client. All these objects are useful, can be recognized, have structure, and have behavior. A well-designed system shows a parallel between the business and the software; every business object has a software object. There is a software object for each Crash Dummy, each document, and each client.

Even so, some additional software objects are necessary parts of the design and implementation of an object-oriented software system — even though they're not strictly parallel to the business system. If you were to walk through your software system as a virtual traveler, many of the sights you could point out would be such objects: individual pieces of data such as records, software structures such as queues, working bits of code such as instance variables. These are the *construction elements* of the object-oriented software world; no less than the business objects, they too have identity, structure, and behavior. When you first start modeling your system, don't include these design or implementation objects; they get added in later activities.

You can use many techniques to choose your objects and classes. Because your project will be using these objects and classes for a long time to come, thinking a bit about your choices is worthwhile. One of the most common techniques, called *Underlining the Nouns (and Words That Relate to Nouns)*, can help you identify which classes and objects to use. You start by describing the system (or the system's behavior). Then you examine each noun in the description and consider whether it meets the following criteria:

✔ It's a thing or family of things

✔ It's part of a problem to be solved

✔ It's not part of the implementation details

✔ It's not an event or occurrence

✔ It's not a property of a thing

After you underline all the nouns and related words in your system description, you can start weeding out the ones that might make good classes or objects. Table 3-1 can help you sort through these words.

Table 3-1	Sorting the Nouns (And Noun-Related Words)	
Type of Noun	*Example*	*It's Likely to Be a(n)...*
A family of things	Person, Crash Dummy	Class
A proper noun (name)	Max	Object
A property of something	Age, Color	Attribute (see the section "Identifying Attributes" later in this chapter)
A value or data	27 years, Red	Attribute's value
A condition of a thing	Adult, New	State (see Chapter 16)
An occurrence, event, or time	Birthday Party, Telephone Ring	Operation (see the section "Performing Operations" later in this chapter) or event (see Chapter 17)
Part of the implementation	Database, Table, EJB	Leave for design (see Chapter 19)

Set up a list for the nouns that make the cut. Be generous: If you're not sure whether something is a good candidate, add it to the list anyway. After you identify a noun as an object, look around for the class that this object is an instance of.

Don't completely discard the nouns that don't qualify as objects. You'll find that they may serve as attributes, states, operations, events, and so on — all of which have value later.

As mentioned earlier, the input to this technique is a description of the system or of the system's behavior. If no description is available, construct your own. Sometimes the description of the system's behavior is best organized as a set of outside entities, called *actors,* pursuing their individual goals, called *use cases,* which are invoked whenever they use the system. You can find actors and use cases covered in Chapter 8.

Naming Objects and Classes

After you identify the classes and objects you want to use in your system, you can start thinking about what to call them. In this section, we provide some UML naming guidelines. (For general naming tips, see the sidebar, "Perfecting your names.")

Following rules for naming classes

Every project may have its own guidelines for naming classes, but your class names also need to follow some commonly obeyed rules associated with UML. If you made a list of possible names (as we discuss in the section "Recognizing Classes and Objects"), you can start with a name from the list and whip it into shape by following the refinement process illustrated in Table 3-2.

Follow your organization's rules and style when naming your classes. You may want to use different style names during different phases of your projects. It's common to put spaces between terms in the names during analysis but to make the names more code-like by dropping the spaces as you enter the design phase.

Table 3-2	Refining Names to Be Good Class Names
A good class name . . .	*Revised example*
Uses a noun or noun phrase	`my modern crash dummies`
Is singular not plural	`my modern crash dummy`
Avoids possessives	`a modern crash dummy`
Doesn't contain irrelevant adjectives	`a crash dummy`
Is bold and is centered in its box	`a crash dummy`
Uses initial capital letters	`A Crash Dummy`
Doesn't have spaces between words	`ACrashDummy`
Doesn't contain articles (a, an, the) pronouns	`CrashDummy`

Perfecting your class and object names

Since the goal of a good name is to convey information quickly and accurately, avoid anything that could be confusing or that might slow down interpretation. It's good policy to avoid using any abbreviations in any name and make sure your spelling is correct.

Almost all abbreviations have multiple meanings and can be momentarily bewildering. Even a one tenth of a second delay adds up to be significant lost time over the life of a project. If you must use acronyms, make sure they come from a limited central list of allowable abbreviations. Likewise, avoid puns and *double entendres*. (Impress your fellow modelers with your UML skills, not your humor.)

Also remember that spelling counts. Don't think for a moment otherwise. Misspelling a word brands you as careless, and even worse, interferes with the rapid recognition of the name. Models are made for accurate and quick communication, which won't happen if your audience is laughing. Proofread carefully and correct all spelling and grammar mistakes.

Okay, some of you may say you entered the field of software because you loved math and hated Language Arts (especially spelling). Unfortunately, most UML tool support doesn't provide diagram spell checking, but all is not lost. One approach is to export your diagrams or class definitions into a word processor, such as Microsoft Word, and *then* run the spell checker. While you're there, run the grammar checker, too. Your output need not be literary, but it should definitely be literate.

Naming objects

Naming objects is just as easy. When an object is modeled, it's typically a specific object that we know a lot about. If the object is one of our friends, a name like Max will do. Alternatively, you can use a noun phrase that describes a specific object. If the Rent-A-Crash Dummy system found it useful to name their dummies in order of acquisition, for example, some good names might be CrashDummy001 and CrashDummy002.

During the design or implementation phases, you'll find that some objects require more generic names. This approach is appropriate when you're dealing with an object that is really just a variable — a slot that's waiting for someone to put one object in it at one time and a different object at another time. Name such objects with the class name preceded by a pronoun, adjective, or article prefix, as in the following examples:

```
myCrashDummy
currentCrashDummy
aCrashDummy
thisCrashDummy
```

If the code loops over all the dummies to check their status, you can give the variable dummy a name to indicate that it's holding the current object under consideration.

Identifying Attributes

After you become familiar with your classes and learn how to name them, you need to consider their properties. To be an interesting and useful class, instances of the class (objects) should have some interesting and useful properties. UML calls these properties *attributes*.

Finding these attributes is usually not difficult. You can often identify attributes by considering how you would describe the objects within a class and how you could differentiate among them. For example, the color of an object might be interesting and may differ, so *color* could be an attribute. The *weight* of an object might be interesting and may differ, so weight could be an attribute.

Depending on your background, you may feel comfortable thinking about attributes as member variables or data slots. Each data slot has a data value placed inside it. Either way you look at it, attributes are the specific features or values that an object of a class may have.

If you have a background in using or designing databases, you may find it helpful to match UML terms with database terminology. They're not exactly equivalent, but seeing the parallels in Table 3-3 will give you a head start to understanding. Don't be enamored too much with this comparison. It works well for the data aspects of a class, but a class is a larger concept than just a table because the class encompasses both data and behavior.

Table 3-3	Parallel UML and Database Terms
UML Term	*Parallel Database Term*
Class	Table
Object	Record
Attribute	Field or Column

After you identify an attribute, you may want to indicate the attribute's type. (A *type* specifies what kind of data that attribute can hold.) When you do supply it with a type, place the type's name after the attribute's name as follows:

```
attribute:Type
```

The type of an attribute can be the taken from your programming language's possibilities — or (since UML allows it) you can develop your own. UML also defines several intrinsic data types:

- ✔ **Integer:** This includes all positive and negative whole numbers, as in the following list:

  . . . , _2, –1, 0, 1, 2, . . .

- ✔ **Boolean:** *Boolean* values specify a state of logical truth, such as True or False.

- ✔ **String:** A *string* is a sequence of characters and spaces in code (as in the example "A Typical String").

Ultimately, it's going to be necessary to specify the type of all the attributes to produce an executable system. However, you can delay *typing* (specifying the type) until you know it and wish to share it with your model readers. Many UML tools provide a default type for attributes as you add them to the model.

Naming attributes and types

Attributes follow the same naming conventions that object's names follow (see the section "Naming Objects and Classes" earlier in this chapter), but they don't usually begin with an article *(a, an, the)* because they're only properties. The following are some attributes of a Person class:

- ✔ name: String uses an Intrinsic UML type.
- ✔ age: Integer uses an Intrinsic UML type.
- ✔ weight: Double uses a Language Defined type.

Some attributes of a Lease class could be as follows:

- ✔ date: Date uses a Language Defined type.
- ✔ duration: Integer uses an Intrinsic UML type.

Sometimes an object may need to have an attribute borrowed from another class — or refer to an object of another class. You can show this situation by using a class name in the Type field. For example, on a Lease class, you might want to indicate a particular Crash Dummy being leased and the person renting the Crash Dummy. You could set it up as follows, where CrashDummy and Person are classes:

```
hiredDummy: CrashDummy
renting: Person
```

You can find much more about referencing objects of other classes in Chapter 4.

When you name types, generally follow the same conventions that you would follow when naming classes. (See the section "Following UML rules for naming classes," earlier in this chapter.) To distinguish classes from types, end your user-defined type names with the word Type. It is also standard convention to prefix Boolean attributes with the word is. For a Person class, some additional attributes could be as follows:

- ✔ phoneNumber: PhoneNumberType uses a user-defined type.
- ✔ streetAddress: AddressType uses a user-defined type.
- ✔ isSingle: Boolean uses a Boolean attribute.

Enumerating the possibilities

If you find that an attribute has a value that's taken from a (usually small) fixed list of discrete, possible values, you want to construct what is called an *enumeration data type*. It's good modeling practice to clearly identify these types by ending their names with the word Kind, as in the following examples:

- ✔ GenderKind could have the values Male or Female.
- ✔ TrafficLightColorKind could have the values Red, Yellow, or Green.
- ✔ SuccessKind could have the values Succeed or Fail.

You may ultimately want to expand a data type such as GenderKind to include every single esoteric possibility. But as with all typing (and all modeling, for that matter), too much detail may be counterproductive.

Defining default values

When your system is up and running, slots for the attribute values are created every time an object is created, but the contents of the slots are undefined. You probably want to determine default values to initialize your attributes, and may do so when you define them at modeling time, as follows for a member of the Person class:

```
attributeName: AttributeType = default value
```

```
name: String = ''
age: Integer = 0
weight: Double = 0.0
gender: GenderKind = male
phoneNumber: PhoneNumberType = 000 000-0000
isSingle: Boolean = true
```

These default values are used only when a new object is created at runtime, and the type of the default value has to be compatible with the type of the attribute.

UML is constantly improving. Occasionally, the UML gurus change things that probably don't really need changing. In UML 1.4, the value assigned to an attribute when an object is first created was called the *initial* value. In UML 2, the gurus changed this to the *default* value — less precise (but more common) terminology.

Multiplicity

In normal situations, you want your objects to have one attribute value for each attribute you've identified. UML allows for more. Perhaps your friend has two telephone numbers, or more than one name. UML enables you to indicate exactly how many values an attribute has (called the *multiplicity*) and even allows for a range. You place the multiplicity in square brackets after the attribute's type, as follows:

```
attributeName: AttributeType [Multiplicity]
```

You can express the multiplicity by following the examples in Table 3-4.

Table 3-4	UML Multiplicities or How Many Do We Have
UML Multiplicity	**Meaning**
1	Exactly 1 (the default)
2	Exactly 2
1..3	From 1 to 3 (inclusive)
3, 5	Either 3 or 5
1..*	At least one, and at most, unlimited
*	Unlimited (includes 0)
0..1	Either 0 or 1

Attributes and analysis

During the early phases of development, it's often premature to consider low-level features (such as data types, slots, or fields). Instead, concentrate on the *knowledge responsibilities* that an object might have. Ask yourself, *What questions could be directed to the object that the object should be expected to reply to?* Questions about the object's state, status, or condition are all natural knowledge responsibilities; typically all are treated as attributes.

In early development steps (such as analysis), you also need not compress and eliminate spaces in the attribute names. Keeping the names normal-looking helps you spell-check the names — and also helps show that your early-stage attributes are merely conceptual, not meant to be directly implemented.

Similarly, consider using the conceptual approach to units of measurement (such as `Degrees Celsius`) instead of *implementation data types* (such as `int` for integer) in the early stages of developing your model. The reviewers of your models are likely to be users and business analysts. They're not expected to know what `double` or `int` means, but can catch on to standard units. If you're modeling a `thermometer` class for a domain expert (for example), and want to convey that you've got a handle on the subject, `current Temperature: Degrees Celsius` makes the point better than `currentTemperature: Double`. For the `Lease` class, the analysis step would probably benefit more from `duration: Weeks` than from `duration: Integer`.

The default multiplicity for an attribute is 1, so you shouldn't bother to indicate it explicitly unless the fact that the multiplicity is 1 is surprising. If an attribute value may be omitted, perhaps because its value is not always defined or known when the object is created, allow for zero in the multiplicity. Such attributes are commonly described as having *nulls allowed.*

Look at the follow attributes on a Person class. A person must have at least one name, but may also have a nickname. The second name is only created when needed, so only initialize the first.

```
name: String [1..2] = "Michael"
```

If a person's age were optional, you should include zero in the multiplicity. As a person cannot have more than one age, the upper limit on the multiplicity should be one.

```
age: Integer [0..1]
```

On the other hand, if you decide that it might be better to always have an age attribute for every Person, use a multiplicity of one. You should also consider whether you need a default value, as in the following example:

```
age: Integer [1] = 0
```

If you have a high-multiplicity attribute and you want to initialize several of its possible values, you can do it as follows:

```
phoneNumber: PhoneNumberType [2]
          =(000 000-0000, 000 000-0000)
```

This initializes both possible `phoneNumber` values to the default value of 000 000-0000.

Performing Operations

As you get to know your classes and get to know their properties (attributes), you also get to know their behaviors. UML uses the term *operations* to refer to the possible behaviors of a class what the objects of the class can do *or have done to them*. Consider what can you ask objects of the class to do — or what can cause them to change their states — when you create the basic syntax for an operation. A typical example follows:

```
operationName (optional argumentList): ReturnType
```

So if you wanted to ask a `Person` object to rent out a crash dummy, the operation would look something like this.

```
rentOutDummy (): SuccessKind
```

An operation is usually called (asked to be performed) because the caller wants something in return. Specify the `ReturnType` as an attribute-like *type identifier*. If nothing is returned when this operation is performed, either use `Null` or omit the `ReturnType` altogether. In the previous example operation, a success indicator is returned.

But before something can be returned, something must usually be given — and generally requires information before it can do something. The *argument* of an operation specifies a piece of information needed by the object to perform this operation.

Specify the information needed by the operation in an optional `argumentList` of comma-separated arguments or parameters — the specific things the object needs to perform this operation. Here's how the arguments go together:

```
operationName (argument1, argument2, . . . ): ReturnType
```

Each argument must have a `type` declaration so that the kind of information that is needed can be determined. Each argument in the `argumentList` above looks like a mini-attribute, as shown below:

```
argumentName: ArgumentType [Multiplicity] = default value
```

So our example operation might be more completely shown as follows:

```
rentOutDummy (aDummy:CrashDummy[1],forClient:Person[1]): SuccessKind
```

In this example, the operation `rentOutDummy` has two arguments. The first argument is a singly valued argument named `aDummy` and is of the `CrashDummy` type. The second argument is also a singly valued argument, which is called `forClient` and is of the type `Person`. When called, the operation returns a value that is of the enumeration type `SuccessKind`.

As with attributes, if you don't specify a multiplicity for an argument, it will default to 1. And as with attributes, you may also specify a default value if you want.

```
rentOutDummy (aDummy:CrashDummy,forClient:Person): SuccessKind
```

Besides a type, a multiplicity, and a default value, each argument can also have a *direction*. If you need to set the argument before the operation is called, the argument is an `in` argument. If you set the argument by calling the operation, then the argument should be an `out` argument. If the argument must be set before the operation is called and is changed by calling the operation, it's an `inout` argument. The direction precedes the name of the argument. (The default is `in`.)

Here's the syntax and an example of an operation with the direction included:

```
direction argumentName: ArgumentType [Multiplicity] = default value
```

```
rentOutDummy (in aDummy:CrashDummy, in forClient:Person): SuccessKind
```

The complete specification of the operation name, arguments, and return for an operation is called the operation's *signature*. As people have their own signature, each operation has one also. However; more than one person can have the same name, and more than one operation can have the same signature, whenever there is more than class in question, it's best to precede the operation with the owning class name:

```
Class::operationName (argument list): ReturnType
```

```
Person::rentOutDummy (in aDummy:CrashDummy, in forClient:Person): SuccessKind
```

Naming operations and arguments

Name operations in the same format as attributes (start with a lowercase word, compress blanks, and capitalize all successive words), but operation names should be verbs or verb phrases. Though not technically required, follow the operation name with ( ) to emphasize the visual distinction from an attribute. When naming the operation, name it from the point of view of target object, the object performing the operation, not from the point of view of the requestor. If the requestor also performs an operation to make the request, then there are two parallel operations. We show some examples in Table 3-5.

Try to choose active verbs whenever possible; you don't want your readers to fall asleep or drown in those passive helping verbs.

Table 3-5	Operation Naming
Requestor's Operation	*Recipient's Operation*
`hireDummy (aDummy, fromPerson)`	`rentOutDummy(aDummy, toPerson)`
`borrowTool (aTool, fromPerson)`	`lendTool (aTool, toPerson)`
`offerProposal ()`	`acceptProposal ():Boolean`

Saying please

One trick to help name the operations correctly from the target object's point of view is to place a virtual "Please" before each operation. When you want a person to lend you a tool, you ask them, "Please, *lend* me that tool" and not "Please, *borrow* me that tool."

When naming arguments, consider that the argument name has four purposes. The name is supposed accomplish the following:

- ✔ Make it clear to the *reader* what the argument does.
- ✔ Make it clear to the *caller* what needs to be supplied.
- ✔ Make it clear to the *caller* what the argument is going to be used for.
- ✔ Make it clear to the *coder* what the incoming argument is.

The most useful approach is to make the whole operation signature read like a sentence. Remember to place a logical "Please"(replacing the two colons) right before the operation name and right after the class name. For example, consider the following operation:

```
Person::rentOutDummy (thisDummy:CrashDummy, toThatPerson:Person):SuccessType
```

It could be translated this way: *"Person, please, rentOutDummy, thisDummy of type CrashDummy toThatPerson of type Person, returning a SuccessType"*

Diagramming a System's Parts

UML is primarily a diagramming language. In this section, we show you how to take the classes and objects, along with their attributes and operations and to graphically represent them on diagrams. By capturing the elements on diagrams, you can depict and solidify your understanding of the static structure of your system, as well as communicate it to others for comment and buy-in.

Boxing in classes and objects

The UML symbol for both classes and objects is the *box*. Its solid nature makes it a good foundation for building our knowledge of UML. If you're a frustrated artist and really care about how it looks, try to draw it with a width-to-height ratio of about 1.6:1, as you can see in Figure 3-1. This ratio is the Golden Ratio (Φ) and proportions close to it are generally considered pleasing to the eye. (The actual value of $\Phi \approx 1.618$.) Of course, you should conform the proportions of the box to the text within.

Figure 3-1:
UML's class
box.

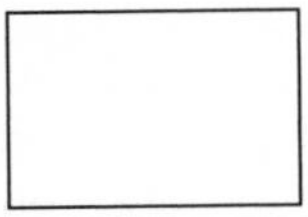

To show a UML class box, just place the chosen class name in the center of the box, or perhaps about one third of the way from the top of the box, as shown in Figure 3-2.

Figure 3-2:
A class
box with
a name.

CrashDummy

TECHNICAL STUFF

What's in an icon?

The UML gurus argued for a long time on what shapes to use for the UML notation. For classes, one of the UML Three Amigos, Grady Booch, argued for an amorphous cloud-like figure (as shown in the figure) — based, of course, on his own Booch notation. Another Amigo, Jim Rumbaugh, argued for a box (based, of course, on his own Object Modeling Technique notation). Others argued for a variety of shapes, one of which was a tombstone-like icon. For a while, they even toyed with pentagons. Ultimately they settled on the rectangle box for objects and classes. Their key reasons: Objects and classes have crisp boundaries and need a crisp, solid, stable icon. And it had to be something simple to draw, not only for the developers, but for the UML tools too.

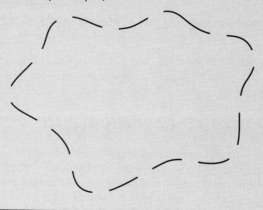

Differentiating between classes and objects

UML always tries to make similar things have similar shapes. Although this simplifies remembering the form, it can make them hard to tell apart. Objects also use boxes, just as classes do. To differentiate them, the UML gurus decided that object names must be underlined and then followed by the class name, with the two names separated by a colon.

When you show an object on a diagram, you can omit the class part of the name if its class is clear from the context (or if it's still unknown and must be left unspecified). When you omit the class part, you're allowed to omit the colon as long as you keep the underline. Alternatively, the object name may be omitted when you want to emphasize that any anonymous object of the class would do under the circumstances. Figure 3-3 shows several sample objects with different name forms.

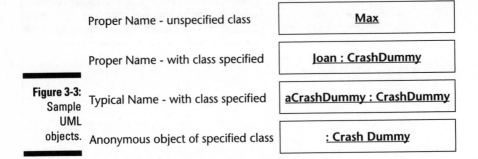

Proper Name - unspecified class   <u>**Max**</u>

Proper Name - with class specified   <u>**Joan : CrashDummy**</u>

Figure 3-3:
Sample
UML
objects.

Typical Name - with class specified   <u>**aCrashDummy : CrashDummy**</u>

Anonymous object of specified class   <u>**: Crash Dummy**</u>

Using arrows to indicate an object's class

Sometimes UML has more than one way of showing the same information. This doesn't mean that you have to use them all. Even though redundancy can often improve communications, it usually makes the diagram more complicated. UML has another way of indicating that an object is an *instance* of a specified class — by drawing a dashed arrow from the object to the class. Avoid this arrow technique unless there is some reason to strongly emphasize that the object is a member of the class — and even then, it's still probably better to drop the redundant class name from the objects. Figure 3-4 shows the use of an arrow to indicate the object's class.

Figure 3-4:
An object
pointing to
(instanti-
ating) its
class.

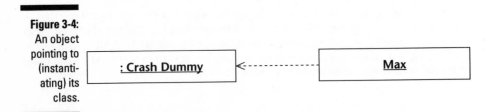

<u>**: Crash Dummy**</u>   <u>**Max**</u>

Using stereotypes

UML has lots of different kinds of dashed arrows that look identical. Luckily, UML allows you to label a model element to indicate exactly what kind of element it is. UML calls this label a *stereotype*. You show the stereotype next to the element (preceding the name of the element if there is one). UML has several predefined stereotypes or you can define your own to indicate a special kind of element for your own purposes

The syntax for a stereotype is as follows.

```
«stereotype name»
```

A stereotype can appear before any UML element. You could label the kind of dashed arrow we used in Figure 3-4 as «InstanceOf» as the arrow indicates that the object is an instance of the class it points to.

The special characters surrounding the stereotype name are called *guillemets*. If you're typographically challenged, you can use the double angle brackets << and >>, but the « and » are used in the UML standard.

Modeling forms

Following the object-oriented principles of encapsulation and co-location (as explained in the Chapter 2), UML displays each class along with its properties and behaviors together. Each type of information (class name, attribute, and operation) has its own *compartment* in a class-box symbol. And following the object-oriented principles of encapsulation and information hiding, the compartments may be hidden if desired. Figure 3-5 demonstrates the standard arrangement of the three compartments, and the following list describes them:

- ✔ **Name compartment:** The name of the class goes in the Name compartment.

- ✔ **Attribute compartment:** Place those attributes that you've already identified for the class in the Attribute compartment. When you look over all the attributes, you may find that there are some redundancies. It's almost always good advice to eliminate duplication, but sometimes, there's an attribute whose value can be calculated from some of the other attributes yet you still want the attribute to be kept. The calculated attribute is called a *derived attribute* and is flagged by a slash (/). For example, consider the following attributes of a Rectangle class:

```
height: LinearUnits
width: LinearUnits
/area: SquareUnits
```

In this case, the `height` and `width` are considered *base attributes* and the `/area` is the *derived attribute*. The base attributes are those whose values are needed to calculate the derived attribute. (See the sidebar "Derived attributes" for more on — you guessed it — derived attributes.)

✔ **Operation compartment:** The operations of the class go in the `Operation` compartment. But don't model all operations; some of them are automatically implied. Whenever there is an attribute on the class, there is likely to be an operation to `SET` the attribute's value and an operation to `GET` the attribute's value. Because these `GET`/`SET` operations *(accessor operations)* are relatively obvious, most UML tools generate such operations for you. If you write your own `GET` or `SET` operations, you may confuse the tools — and you'll certainly crowd the `Operation` compartment.

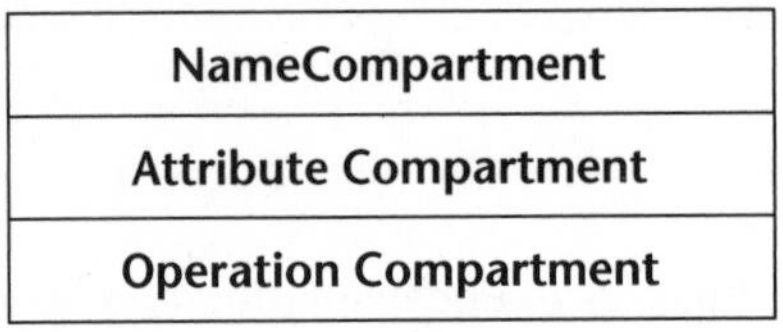

Figure 3-5:
A class's compartments.

NameCompartment
Attribute Compartment
Operation Compartment

Derived attributes

Why might you keep a derived attribute if it's really a duplicate? There are two basic reasons.

✔ During analysis, you may find that a key customer concept, something from the customer's basic vocabulary, is really derivable. If you eliminate that concept, you'll have to spend a lot of effort in explaining why the customer can't find the concept in your model. You run the risk of seeming either ignorant or arrogant if you leave it out. So leave it in — but mark it *derivable*.

✔ During design, derived attributes have another purpose — efficiency. Suppose some calculated value is needed often, and quickly. If you plan ahead, you might want to precalculate the value and store it so it's available when you need it. (Just remember to recalculate the derived attribute when the base attributes change.)

Unless it's obvious, flag each derived attribute with the formula needed to recalculate it, as in the following example:

```
height: LinearUnits
width: LinearUnits
/area: SquareUnits    {/area =
    height × width}
```

These brackets — { } — indicate a constraint and may contain any information that limits the values of an attribute.

```
height: LinearUnits    {height >
    0.0}
width: LinearUnits    {width >
    0.0}
/area: SquareUnits    {/area =
    height × width}
```

Defining Visibility

If you really get to be friendly and know your classes well, you'll be able learn some private secrets about them. When you make your models and design your classes, you'll be able to define what's visible and what's not. Typically, all the attributes are private so that only the owning object can see the values of the attributes. Thus, each `person` object can see his or her own age, because you own and control your own attributes.

Each attribute — and each operation — of a class should have its visibility determined. You model the visibility by preceding the feature definition with a typographical symbol, as defined in Table 3-6.

Table 3-6		Symbols for Modeling Visibility
Symbol	*Visibility*	*Meaning*
+	Public	Any object can use the feature.
-	Private	Only the owning object can use this feature.
#	Protected	Only the owning object or descendants of the owning object can use this feature.
~	Package	Only objects in the same package as the owning object's package can use this feature.

The object-oriented principle of information hiding should be guiding you to avoid exposing any details. Keeping the details hidden allow you to change them later, whenever you want to. To give yourself this freedom to change, make all the attributes *private*. You don't want anyone to get to them without going through the *accessor* (GET/SET) operations where you can control the access.

On the other hand, most operations are public. You want the objects to be useful, so they need to be accessible to be told do their stuff.

You can find more details on information hiding and other principles of object orientation in the Chapter 2.

Marking attributes as public and private

Many UML tools enforce the information-hiding concept of *attribute privacy* strictly. Even if you mark an attribute as *public*, it is still generated as *private*. How do the UML tools get away with ignoring your requests, after all, you're the modeler and should be in charge?

Most tools generate the attribute as private, but generate *accessor operations* with your requested visibility. This surprising trick puts up a wall that enables you to control the details of the access.

If you modeled it as +name:String, you'll probably automatically have the following generated:

```
- name:String
+ getName():String
+ setName(toNewName:String)
```

But what should you do, if you really want to have an attribute that's mostly private, but not to everybody? In many programming languages, it's possible to mark some classes as friends. Only close friends can get to see the private parts; these friends can break the encapsulation rules. (For more about encapsulation see Chapter 2.)

Marking static attributes

Every object in a class has its own attributes and keeps track of its own data. Sometimes, however, members of the same family have to share information. They do this through by flagging the attributes representing the shared information as *static* attributes. This indicates that the attribute has *class-scope*. Once flagged, every object in the class has the same value for that attribute. Change it once, and every object's value is changed. You mark these attributes as static by underlining them. Operations that set or get these static attributes should also be marked static.

Normally, when a regular (non-static) operation is called or an attribute is referenced, you start with the object name, as follows:

- aCrashDummy.name indicates the name of the aCrashDummy object.
- myNeighbor.borrowTool() indicates the borrowTool operation on the myNeighbor object

With a static attribute, you refer to the class as a whole — so you precede the operations and attributes with the class name, like this:

✔ `CrashDummy.nextID` indicates the `nextID` used by the whole `CrashDummy` class

✔ `CrashDummy.getNextID()` also indicates the operation to get the `nextID` value used by the whole `CrashDummy` class

If you want to define a static attribute or operation for a class, include it in the class box, but flag it as static by underlining it. Figure 3-6 shows an example.

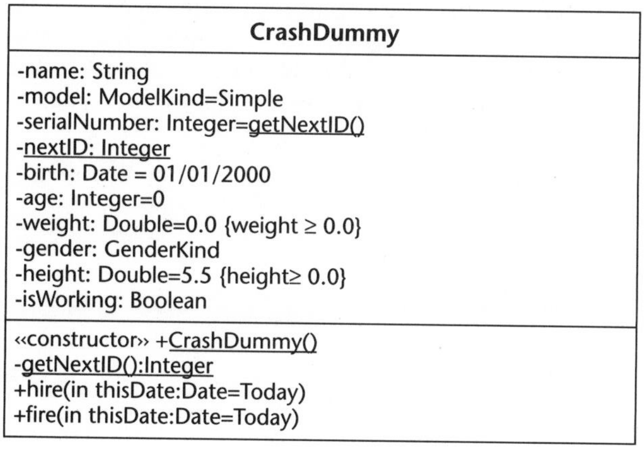

CrashDummy
-name: String -model: ModelKind=Simple -serialNumber: Integer=<u>getNextID()</u> <u>-nextID: Integer</u> -birth: Date = 01/01/2000 -age: Integer=0 -weight: Double=0.0 {weight ≥ 0.0} -gender: GenderKind -height: Double=5.5 {height≥ 0.0} -isWorking: Boolean
«constructor» +<u>CrashDummy()</u> -<u>getNextID():Integer</u> +hire(in thisDate:Date=Today) +fire(in thisDate:Date=Today)

Figure 3-6: A class with many features.

The `CrashDummy` class in Figure 3-6 illustrates some of the features that are discussed in this chapter. The attribute compartment has several private attributes and the operation compartment has several public operations:

✔ The `birth` attribute captures the construction date for the Crash Dummy.

✔ The `age` attribute captures the targeted age that `CrashDummy` mimics.

✔ You use the `gender` attribute of the dummy to capture the gender that the `CrashDummy` mimics.

✔ Use the `weight` and `height` to capture physical properties of the dummy. Each has their own default value and a constraint governing their values.

✔ You can see a Boolean isWorking attribute, which reflects whether the dummy is need of repair.

✔ The nextID attribute is a static (also known as a class-scope) attribute, whose value is available to the class as a whole.

✔ The nextID attribute is used with the static operation getNextID().

✔ The CrashDummy() operation is also considered a static operation; although it makes a CrashDummy object, it operates on the class to do so.

✔ The CrashDummy() operation is also flagged with the stereotype «constructor» to remind the reader or tools that this operation will make up new objects.

Most of these attributes capture constant properties of a CrashDummy object. After you set them, you can forget them, as they don't change over the life of the object. However, make you shouldn't forget that objects typically have attributes that reflect the state of the object and may change over time.

Chapter 4

Relating Objects That Work Together

In This Chapter

▶ Showing how objects and classes relate

▶ Figuring out how many objects relate to each other

▶ Indicating which objects play multiple roles

▶ Adding attributes to associations

▶ Partitioning your objects

▶ Implementing associations

*U*ML allows modelers and programmers to show static relationships between classes and objects. If you're a modeler, you describe relationships between objects that communicate with each other in the real world so you can better understand these objects and their classes. If you're a programmer, you specify which objects interact with each other so you know how to define classes in your program. This chapter tells you about two types of relationships — links and associations — and shows you the UML notation for modeling these important relationships between objects and between classes.

You must resolve a lot of issues as you define and depict relationships between objects and classes. You need to figure out how to show an association and what makes a good association name. You also need to decide how many objects can link together. Then, you need to think about the details of associations, such as names at each end of an association, association classes, and qualifiers. These issues can be tricky, but we break them down for you. We also give you some pointers to help you accurately model various associations and take the mystery out of what modeling associations mean for your programs.

Showing Static Relationships in a Class Diagram

There is a lot more to this world than just objects. Relationships between objects are just as important as the objects. In UML these relationships are defined using *associations* and *links*. To give you a concrete sense of these relationships, we use several different examples. Our first example involves a company that rents crash dummies to clients for tests. Consider this the *Rent-A-Crash Dummy* example. You have to relate the crash dummies to the clients who rent them — and show that a specific crash dummy named *MAX* was rented to a client named *Safety 'R Us*.

An instance of a class is an object. We use the words *object* and *instance* interchangeably.

Links are instances of associations. Associations relate classes, whereas links relate instances of those classes (objects). So a link would connect an object in the Client class with an object in the CrashDummy class.

You show a simple association by drawing a line between the two classes you want to relate. Likewise, you show a link by drawing a line between two instances of two associated classes.

After you have specified that two classes are associated, think about a few details for depicting the association. Here's a quick list (which we discuss further later in this chapter):

- **Name:** Normally an association has a name — placed along the association line — that describes the relationship between the classes. Older versions of UML specified italics for the association name so it would stand out. UML 2 doesn't require italicized association names — but it's not a bad idea. A good practical rule is to use the form that your UML modeling tool uses.

  Names of associations are not underlined, but the names of links are. Use associations to connect classes; use links to connect objects.

- **Multiplicity:** Use multiplicity to specify how many instances of one class can be linked to a single instance of another class. The multiplicity is shown as a number (or numbers) indicating the lower and upper bounds on the number of links at each end of an association.

- **Roles:** Here you name the class on one end of an association by indicating how the class participates in that association. The name is placed at the end of the association closest to the participant class it is identifying.

✔ **Constraints:** Employ *constraints* on an association if its underlying links must follow some rule(s). Place a constraint in curly brackets { } close to the association.

✔ **Qualifiers:** Use *qualifiers* to show that navigation from an instance of one class to a partitioned set of instance(s) of another class must be based on an attribute of that other class. Place a qualifier in a box appended to the class from which the navigation begins.

✔ **Directional navigation:** Utilize a *navigation arrow* on the association line when one class can communicate one way with another. Show directional navigation with an arrowhead at one end of the association, indicating the direction of allowable communication.

Well, yes, there are a lot of details here, but the chapter takes you through them. Fortunately, you don't have to place all these details on each and every association in your diagrams. Usually the name of the association and the multiplicities are all you need.

Linking Objects Together

When you want to show that a relationship exists between two objects, you create a link in your UML class diagram. That is, a *link* is the device you use in a UML diagram to indicate that two objects communicate with each other. The link appears as a line connecting two boxes representing the objects and may have a name showing somewhere along the line.

Remember these characteristics of links when creating or reading a UML diagram:

✔ A *link* relates two objects that communicate.

✔ A line connecting two object boxes represents a link.

✔ Naming the link is optional. We name a link only if it helps clarify what we mean to others who look at our diagrams.

So say that Safety 'R Us is a company that rents a dummy called MAX for testing. Figure 4-1 shows an object called SafetyRus (an instance of the class Client) renting MAX, an instance of the class CrashDummy — and rents is the name of the link between these two instances.

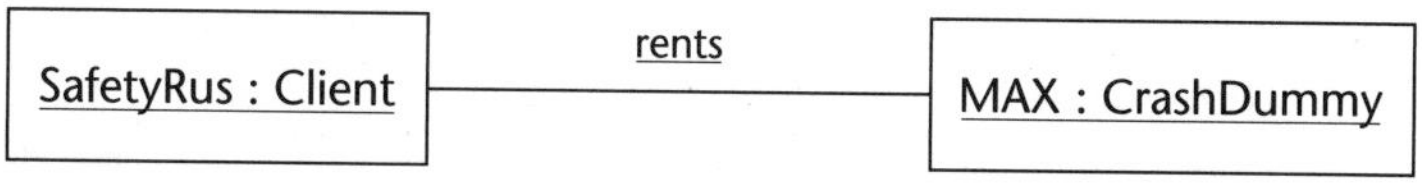

Figure 4-1:
Two linked
objects.

| SafetyRus : Client | rents | MAX : CrashDummy |

Only when two objects are linked together can they communicate. In UML, the link notation allows the modeler to specify that SafetyRus is linked to MAX, and therefore SafetyRus can rent MAX. The link notation allows the programmer to specify that the instance SafetyRus is linked to the instance MAX, and therefore SafetyRus can invoke MAX's operations. Still confused? Well, try looking at links like the strings on a marionette. If you want to invoke the behavior of the puppet, you must be linked to it via the strings.

Associating Classes

You show meaningful relationships between classes with an association. It's called an association because you are indicating that instances of certain classes *associate* — that is, communicate with each other — and thus work together. The definition of an association sounds a lot like the definition of a link.

Keep in mind:

- ✔ Links relate *objects*.
- ✔ Associations relate *classes*.
- ✔ You give the association a name to help others understand the nature of the relationship between two classes.

Figure 4-2 shows a simple rents association between the Client class and the CrashDummy class. Clients do not purchase or make crash dummies; clients rent crash dummies. So we want to use UML associations to indicate what the instances of these classes do when they get together. The link shown in Figure 4-1 is an instance of the rents association shown in Figure 4-2.

Figure 4-2:
Two associated classes.

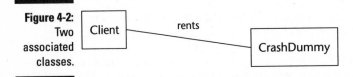

Because a link between two objects carries the same name as the association between the objects' classes, the link name is often omitted. This is a fancy way of saying, *Name your associations, but don't worry about link names.*

Naming Your Associations

When you name an association, use a verb phrase that best describes what these two classes do with (or to) each other. If you consider the classes at either end of an association along with the association name, then the whole thing can be read as a sentence, such as, "A client rents a crash dummy."

Try to find an active verb phrase that relates the two classes. This enables others to understand your diagrams more easily.

Although associations have meaning in both directions, the name you choose should be readable from left to right or from top to bottom when someone is looking at your diagram. When you build class diagrams with many classes and associations, however, you cannot avoid having some of your association names running in the wrong direction. If you must use an association name that reads from right to left or bottom to top, then use a small arrowhead — the *name-direction arrow* (as in Figure 4-3) — to help the reader. Considered as a sentence, the association in Figure 4-3 reads like this: "Test equipment monitors a crash dummy."

Figure 4-3:
Use of
arrowheads
for reading
association
names.

Some *UML modeling tools* (software that helps you draw UML diagrams and may generate code as a result) don't have the directional-arrowhead feature that UML requires. In such cases, we use the keyboard symbols in Table 4-1 as substitutes for the arrowheads. If possible, however, we recommend using name-direction arrows (if your UML modeling tool provides them) to help other developers know exactly what you mean.

Table 4-1	Substitutes for Association-Name Arrowheads	
Symbol	*Keyboard Keys*	*Purpose*
<	Shift+, (comma)	Read association from right to left
^	Shift+6	Read association from bottom to top
>	Shift+. (period)	Read association from left to right
v	Lowercase *v*	Read association from top to bottom

We highly recommend that you name your associations. Names emphasize relationships instead of data flow (more about that in the sidebar, "Noname associations"); they also increase the readability of your diagrams by leaps and bounds. After all, UML is all about effective communication with other developers. When we return to a class diagram months after we put it together, the association names help us remember what we had in mind months earlier.

Noname associations

Watch out for class diagrams with lots of classes and associations that have no names. This indicates the modeler is not thinking about objects interacting together — and may be trapped in thinking about getting data from one place to another.

When they program, many expert developers use a functional mindset — worrying about the data that must be poured into each function, constantly working to get data from one function to another. They speak of "data flow." When these *functional programmers* start using object-oriented techniques and languages, they want the data to flow from one *object* to another just as if it were moving from one *function* to another.

So why does someone create a class diagram with "noname" associations? Well, some developers start by drawing a few classes with attributes and operations. Then they focus on one of the classes and think about the data it needs. Next, they see that another class has an attribute with the right data. Finally, they draw a line (association) from the class with the data to the class that needs the data — but they don't bother to *name the association.* If you ask them to read the association in the recommended way (class name, verb phrase, class name) so it describes how the two classes relate, they can't come up with a good verb phrase. They haven't really thought about the nature of the

interaction between the two objects — just the data flow.

For example, suppose we need to route the data about a crash dummy after a bumper test — say, from the test equipment to a TV monitor. But object-oriented programs are about *getting objects to interact* in different ways to accomplish particular tasks or functions — they're not about data flow. The crash dummy is not really associated with the TV monitor; the *test equipment* has that association. The test equipment *monitors* the data about the state of the dummy; the TV *receives* the summarized results from the test equipment. We would model this situation by drawing one association between the crash dummy and the test equipment, and another association between the test equipment and the TV monitor.

Remember, one object can ask another object for information. The second object can in turn ask a third object for that information, and then return the result to the first. This is done all the time in the real world. For example, our bosses are always asking us for stuff. We just turn to the Internet, get an answer, and turn it around to the boss — who has no direct relationship to all the things we used to get the information.

So, to avoid getting stuck in the functional mindset, associate classes that really interact — and give those associations accurate, natural-sounding names. Don't worry about data flow.

Relating Many Objects (Multiplicity)

As in the real world, you can link one object to many instances of another class. Surely, if you want to have a successful business renting crash dummies to clients, your clients should be able to rent more than one dummy at a time — and a dummy should be rentable to more than one client over time. Specifying how many instances can be linked together is called *multiplicity*.

When showing multiplicity on your association, remember to do the following:

✔ Position the multiplicity numbers above or below the association line, close to the class.

✔ Place multiplicity numbers at both ends of an association.

✔ Use multiplicity to show how many things at either end of an association are potentially linked together.

Notice the 1..* symbol close to the CrashDummy class in Figure 4-4. This symbol tells you that a client rents at least one or more crash dummies. In other words the appearance of 1..* represents the idea of having one or more instances of CrashDummy that a Client rents. The 1 in the 1..* means that a client *must* rent at least one crash dummy. The * in 1..* indicates that a client can rent more than one crash dummy, and does not place an upper limit in the number that can be rented.

Because associations have meaning in both directions, you also place a multiplicity symbol on the association line next to the Client class. In Figure 4-4, you see that a CrashDummy can be rented by zero or more instances of Client (0..*).

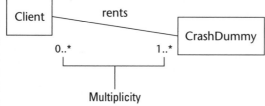

Figure 4-4:
Association with multiplicity.

Determining multiplicity

When you specify the multiplicity of an association, you must determine the value to place at each end of the association line. Follow these steps to make your determination:

1. **Establish the classes that form the endpoints for the association.**

   In this example, the classes are `Client` and `CrashDummy`, connected by the `rents` association line.

2. **Examine the characteristics of the association from the perspective of one class.**

   In this example, we look at the `Client` class and ask ourselves the following questions:

   - Can a client rent zero crash dummies and still be a client? (No.)
   - Must a client rent at least one dummy? (Yes.)
   - Can a client rent many dummies over time? (Yes, many.)

   The answers to these questions tell us that the multiplicity must be `1..*` because the client must rent at least one crash dummy, and can rent many.

3. **Place the multiplicity symbol that represents the answer to questions in Step 2 at the proper point on the UML diagram.**

   In this example, we place `1..*` at the opposite end of the association from the `Client` class.

4. **Repeat Steps 2 and 3 from the perspective of the other class.**

   To complete this example, we look at the association from the perspective of the `CrashDummy` class. We ask ourselves the following questions:

   - Is it possible for `MAX` to never be rented? (Yes, poor `MAX`.)
   - Must at least one client rent `MAX`? (No.)
   - Can more than one client rent `MAX` over time? (Yes, although not at exactly the same time.)

   The answers to these questions tell us that the multiplicity must be `0..*` because a particular crash dummy may never be rented by a client, but could (over time) be rented by many clients.

   Finally, we place `0..*` at the opposite end of the association from the `CrashDummy` class.

Notice that we first look at the association from the client's perspective — as if we had only one client. We decide to use `1..*` as the multiplicity symbol and place it at the opposite end from the client class. Then we consider the multiplicity from the crash-dummy perspective. The chosen multiplicity is `0..*` and we place it at the opposite end of the association from the `CrashDummy` class.

Representing multiplicity

Table 4-2 lists the various symbols that can use for multiplicity. To understand the table, consider the multiplicity symbol at the crash-dummy end of the `rents` association in Figure 4-5. You can then replace the *??* in the figure with a symbol from the table to see what that multiplicity means.

Figure 4-5:
Choosing
multiplicity.

Table 4-2	Multiplicity Symbols
Multiplicity Symbol	**Meaning**
1	A `Client` instance must be linked with exactly one instance of `CrashDummy` no more and no less.
*	A `Client` instance may be linked with zero or more instances of `CrashDummy`.
0..*	A `Client` instance may be linked with zero or more instances of `CrashDummy`. This is just like using * for the multiplicity.
0..1	A `Client` instance may be linked with either zero or one instance of `CrashDummy`. This is known as the *optional multiplicity*.
1..*	A `Client` instance must be linked with at least one or more instances of `CrashDummy`. This is the multiplicity we chose for Figure 4-4.
5..9	A `Client` instance can be linked to at least 5 instances of `CrashDummy` but not more than 9 instances.
3,5,7	A `Client` instance can be linked to (and thus rent) 3 or 5 or 7 instances of `CrashDummy`.

Using multiplicity

The multiplicity you end up with on your diagrams varies depending on the application you develop. For instance, suppose you build an application that keeps track of all clients who ever rented dummies, whether they are renting some now or not. You would have to allow a multiplicity of zero or more for the `CrashDummy` class (as shown in Figure 4-6). In this situation, you have the possibility that an instance of `Client` rents zero crash dummies.

If your application is a simple order-entry system, you may require that a client rents at least one dummy. However, if your application is keeping track of all clients, you need to show that a client rents zero or more dummies.

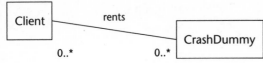

When you start thinking about the multiplicity of your associations, you uncover hidden assumptions about how many objects can be linked together. When you talk with users, often they're vague about associations and don't consider every possible way of linking the instances of one class with the instances of another class. For example, thinking about objects that invoke each other's behavior in a program can easily make a programmer forget to consider all the different situations. It's left to you to discover whether an instance of one class must be linked to another — or perhaps doesn't always require a link. Consider these details when you gather requirements and analyze the situation; it pays dividends later, when you start programming.

Some time ago, we were writing a simulation program that associated airplanes with their location on a simulated map. The location was called a cell — the map was composed of cells, and each plane was placed in a cell. As the simulation progressed, a plane would move from cell to cell. Figure 4-7 shows a UML diagram of the associations between plane and cell. A plane is currently located in exactly one cell and a plane moves through one or more cells during the simulation.

Figure 4-7:
Multiplicity
example
with cells
and planes.

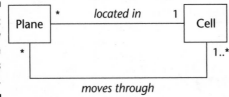

What we didn't properly appreciate at programming time was the fact that a plane *had to* be in a cell. We created the plane class but did not enforce any multiplicity. So, when we started to use instances of the plane class, they were not automatically assigned to a cell. When another object in our program asked a plane, *Where are you?* the program blew up — that's because it was chasing a null pointer to a nonexistent `cell` object. (A *null pointer* is a program variable that is set to zero instead of to a valid address in a computer's memory. This one was a real nuisance.) If we'd used UML, we would have discovered the need to code a link from plane to cell, right from the start, instead of having to debug and rewrite it after the fact. This is just another example of why considering the details of multiplicity is a good habit to get into.

Understanding the Roles That Classes Can Play

When objects get together, sometimes they behave differently in different relationships. You could say they have multiple personalities. We use the term *role* to describe in a single name how a class behaves in association to another class.

For example, consider one of your authors as if he were an object (he won't mind): He plays the role of `Husband` in the relationship with his wife — and in quite a different relationship to his job, he plays the role of `Chief Technologist`. (Sometimes he plays the role of `Crash Dummy`.) He plays many roles, depending on who or what he's associating with. The same is true of objects in UML.

When adding roles to your association, consider the following:

- ✔ A name is shown on the association line next to the class that plays some role in relationship to another class.

- ✔ You use roles to help clarify the nature of the behavior that an instance exhibits when it's linked to an instance of another class.

In versions of UML previous to UML 2, the name at the end of an association was called a *role*. In UML 2, the word *role* has disappeared, replaced by *association end name*. To be precise, a name at an "association end" indicates what kind of behavioral participation the instances of one class (at that end) perform in relationship to instances of the class that occupies the other end of the association. That specific kind of behavioral participation is, in effect, a role — so the idea that objects play roles in relationship to other objects still makes sense to us. Therefore, as a practical matter, we use the word *role* instead of "association end name."

The `Cell` class in Figure 4-8 has two different roles in relationship to the `Plane` class. An instance of a cell may play the role of "current cell" in association with one plane, and a "route element" in relation to another plane that has already moved through that "current cell" to another cell.

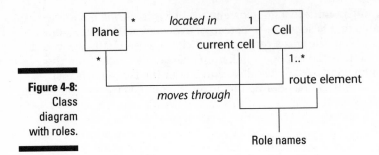

You can think of a role as the name of an attribute belonging to the class on the opposite side of an association. The role "current cell" is an attribute of the class Plane. Even though the diagram doesn't show it, the class Plane has attributes currentCell and routeElement (as in Figure 4-9). The data type for each of these attributes is the class Cell.

Association names are important to the readers of your diagrams. Role names are important to the code generators of your UML modeling tools. We recommend you provide role names on your class diagrams whenever you can; it makes for better code generation.

Figure 4-9:
The Plane
class with
role-name
attributes.

Plane
-currentCell : Cell -routeElement : Cell[1..*]

Diagrams for modeling objects and classes come in two flavors — class diagrams and instance diagrams. The *class diagram* shows the static structure of classes and their associations. The *object diagram* shows objects (that is, instances) and their links. You use class diagrams most of the time — but now and then an instance diagram helps clarify a class diagram by providing an example. You build class diagrams to communicate the structure and behavior of each class. To show which classes can interact, you associate them together. When other developers have trouble understanding the meaning of your class diagram, use a instance diagram to show specific objects linked together. The instance diagram illustrates your class diagram.

When we put together the class diagram in Figure 4-8, for example, some developers didn't understand what we meant. So we built a sample instance diagram (shown in Figure 4-10). Note that Figure 4-8 shows a Plane class associated with *(located in)* a Cell class — and the Cell class plays the role of currentCell. Figure 4-10 illustrates the meaning of these associated classes by showing an instance of Plane (p12) linked to only one instance of the Cell class (c45-23). Here cell c45-23 plays the role of the current cell, showing where plane p12 is at this point in time.

Figure 4-8 also shows a Plane class associated with *(moves through)* a Cell class. Here the Cell class plays a different role, that of routeElement. Again, Figure 4-10 illustrates the meaning of the association (moves through) by showing the p12 instance linked to three instances of the Cell class — c45-20, c45-21, c45-22. Each of these three Cell instances plays the role of routeElement, showing which other cells plane p12 has visited on its route.

Thus an instance diagram can help you clarify the meaning of a class diagram by illustrating it with a specific example of linked objects.

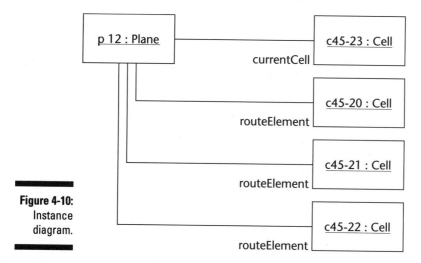

Figure 4-10:
Instance
diagram.

Associating Classes with Themselves

You may need to show that two instances of the same class can be associated with each other. In certain tests, for example, crash dummies are lined up in a row with one dummy as the leader and the rest as followers. During the test, the lead dummy blocks the dummies lined up behind it. Each dummy then has an association — block — to the next dummy behind it. Such an association relates instances of the same class — and is known as a *reflexive association.*

When diagramming reflexive associations, remember to do the following:

1. Draw an association.

   You need an association that comes out of a particular class and goes back into the same class.

2. **Name the association.**

   Make sure you name the association so it reads like a sentence.

3. **Add multiplicity.**

   Consider the multiplicity at each end of the association.

4. **Provide roles.**

   To lend clarity to the diagram, add role names to describe what different instances of the same class do in the association.

You would read the diagram in Figure 4-11 as follows: "A crash dummy blocks zero or more instances of CrashDummy in the role of follower. Further, a crash dummy may be blocked by one crash dummy in the role of leader."

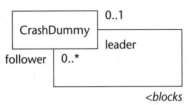

Figure 4-11:
A reflexive
association.

To read the blocks association shown in Figure 4-11, you would read in the reverse direction, like this:

"A crash dummy *(class name)* is blocked by *(association name in the reverse direction)* zero or one *(multiplicity)* instances of CrashDummy *(class name)* in the role of leader *(role name)."*

Reading reflexive associations

Reflexive associations can be tricky to diagram, which can also make them tricky to read. Here's how to keep them focused:

✔ For the sake of clarity, always use at least one role name in the diagram.

✔ Be careful when you read the role names in reflexive associations: They have to be read in both directions. We use the following template:

"*(A* or *One) (class name) (association name) (multiplicity)* instances of *(class name)* in the role of *(role name)."*

We always start the reading of associations with the word *A* or *One.*

✔ Don't read the multiplicity close to the starting class, only the multiplicity at the *other* end of the association.

Notice we did not use the role name of *follower* or the multiplicity of 0..* in this example. Why, you ask? Because it's not true in every case that a crash dummy in the role of follower is blocked by the one crash dummy in the role of leader. The other dummies can be blocked, but only by dummies other than the leader. So, because there can be only one leader dummy, the multiplicity is 0..1 rather than 1.

Constraining associations

Under some special circumstances, you may want to say more about the association than just its name, roles, and multiplicity. For instance, suppose you want to say that the association must be an ordered set of instances instead of an unordered set — that a reflexive association shall not have cycles. You can do so by using UML to specify any constraints that must be imposed on the links of an association. As with all constraints in UML, you place the text that names the constraint or limitation in curly brackets { }.

For example, Figure 4-12 shows that the follower dummies are ordered in relation to the leader dummy. That means there is a first follower, a next follower, and on down the line to the last follower. Notice that the word {ordered} is surrounded by the curly brackets used to indicate a constraint.

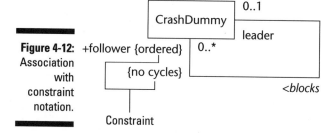

Figure 4-12: Association with constraint notation.

Figure 4-12 shows another important constraint called no cycles This is especially useful for reflexive associations. The no cycles constraint means you cannot have a dummy in the role of leader that is also in the role of a follower. We don't want a circle of dummies.

Using Association Classes

When you model the real world you find attributes that do not seem to fit in any one class. For instance, in our rental example you have two classes, Client and CrashDummy. Further, you know that clients rent crash dummies.

Now you want to model the attribute `dayOfRental`. The value of that attribute is the day a particular client rents a particular dummy. Where does the attribute belong?

Well, for openers, the `dayOfRental` attribute does *not* belong in `Client`; the client may rent dummies on different days. You could create attributes for `client` called `dayOfRental1`, `dayOfRental2`, and `dayOfRental3`. But if you create multiple attributes, how do you know which crash dummy was rented on `dayOfRental1`? On the other hand, `dayOfRental` doesn't belong in `CrashDummy` either; any given dummy can be rented on many different days, to different clients. The solution to this dilemma: Recognize that `dayOfRental` is an attribute of the `rents` association and *not an attribute of a class.*

If you find an attribute whose value depends on more than one class instance, you need a third class that holds that attribute. For example, the `dayOfRental` attribute depends on the specific instance of `Client` and the specific instance of `CrashDummy` that were linked in the `rents` association on that day. You would designate the needed third class — an *association class* — by using a dashed line to connect the new class to the association.

Figure 4-13 shows the UML notation for showing such special attributes. The figure shows your two classes — `Client` and `CrashDummy` — in the `rents` relationship. It then shows another class (`Rents`) that contains the special attribute `dayOfRental`.

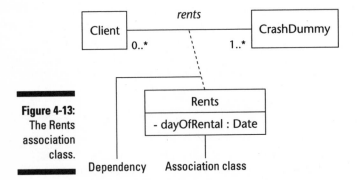

Figure 4-13:
The Rents
association
class.

In UML, a dashed line means *dependency;* Figure 4-13 shows dependency between the `Rents` class and the association named `rents`.

The name of the association class must be the same name as that of the association — because they are really two different aspects of the same association. Association classes are, however, classes in their own right — so they can have operations as well as attributes. You can even associate your association classes to other classes — but this can get complex in a hurry. Our recommendation is to keep your modeling simple and easy to read.

Qualifying Relationships

People often partition the objects of a class into groups based on the value of an attribute in that class when they describe the real world. This grouping of objects may be an important aspect of an association between two classes. In our rental example, we group crash dummies by their size — and it turns out that size *is* an important attribute of a crash dummy. When clients place orders for crash dummies, they always specify the size of the dummies they want. When placing orders, the client "qualifies" the order with a value for dummy size. They ask for two 72-inch dummies and three 52-inch dummies. It helps the order processing to group the orders according to the sizes requested. Thus the `orders` association between client and crash dummy is known as a *qualified association*.

Modeling this situation requires the use of something the UML gurus call a *qualifier,* a notation that qualifies — that is, partitions into groups — navigation from an instance of one class to the instances of another. Figure 4-14 shows a qualified association where the qualifier occupies a small box between a class and an association. The qualifier goes at the opposite end of the association from the class of which it's an attribute.

Say what? In Figure 4-13, `size` is an attribute of `CrashDummy`. When a `Client` instance orders zero or more instances of `CrashDummy`, they must specify the size they want. (The qualifier `size` goes at the opposite end of the `orders` association, away from the `CrashDummy` class.) So Figure 4-14 means that if we take an instance of `Client` and a value for the `size` qualifier, then we have zero or more `orders` links to instances of the class `CrashDummy`. So, given a specific client, the particular crash dummies rented are of a certain size.

A *qualifier* is an attribute in the instances at the far end of the qualified association. Any attribute can have a datatype. In Figure 4-14, for example, the `size` qualifier has the `inches` datatype.

Figure 4-14:
Qualifying
an
association.

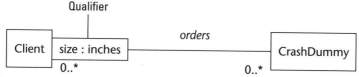

Reducing multiplicity — with qualifiers

Often you find qualifiers reduce the multiplicity of an association. The `rents` association between the `Client` class and the `CrashDummy` class (for example) is a many-to-many association. If we recast the association as a *qualified* association (as in Figure 4-15), the multiplicity is reduced. Figure 4-15 has the following meaning: "Given an instance of `Client` and the value for a `CrashDummy serialNum`, the `Client rents` zero or one instance of `CrashDummy`." (This is true because each crash dummy has a unique serial number.) Using qualifiers to reduce multiplicity is like tossing a lot of similar things into a bin, where the bin name describes the contents. If bin name is a unique attribute (like serial number), you get one thing per bin. If the bin name is descriptive attribute (such as size), you can get lots of things per bin — but less than the whole drawer.

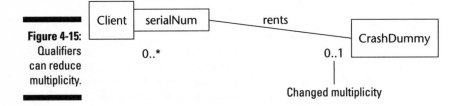

Figure 4-15:
Qualifiers
can reduce
multiplicity.

Indexing with qualifiers

During design, you may want to tell the programmer to use an index when invoking the methods of an object at runtime. An *index* is a way of quickly looking something up; it works like a card catalog at the public library: You look up a book by its title, author name, or keyword. The card catalog provides an index for looking up books quickly rather than searching each shelf for the book. We've often found that qualifiers are a good way to show indexing in UML.

As a designer, you're often concerned with performance — and if you need to execute a fast lookup to find a particular crash dummy by its serial number, then the diagram in Figure 4-15 does the trick. To show the programmer you want a fast way of looking up crash dummies by serial number, use the qualifier notation in your class diagram.

Finding a Way — Navigation

Whenever you associate two classes, you are indicating that instances of these classes can "see" and communicate with each other. That means you can navigate from one side of an association (the *source*) to the other side (the *target*). An association is navigable in both directions if the objects involved invoke *operations* (in which an object sends a message to another object to ask the second object to perform some specific behavior) on each other. If you have objects involved in an association and they can navigate in both directions, then each object can serve as both a source *and* a target.

You may only need to navigate an association in one direction during runtime. To show this navigation constraint, you place an arrow on the association line to indicate the direction of the invocation — from the source object toward the target object. We generally use navigation arrows during design time. If an association has no arrow, then (normally) it's okay to implement the association in both directions. If an association has an arrow, then you program the association only in the direction of the arrow — and not the other direction.

In Figure 4-16, the arrow on the `rents` association line indicates that an instance of `Client` can invoke methods of `CrashDummy` objects at runtime. However, an instance of `CrashDummy` cannot see (and thus cannot navigate to) instances of the `Client` class, as it would have to do in order to invoke behavior on instances of `Client`.

Figure 4-16:
Using the navigation-arrow symbol.

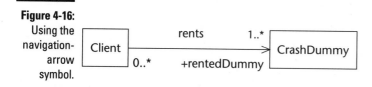

Creating a Program

Suppose you want to implement your program by specifying an association between classes in a UML diagram. We want to show you how a UML diagram with associations is turned into code. Refer to the class diagram in Figure 4-17, the following bulleted list, and Listing 4-1 to see how this simple model of client and crash dummy becomes program elements implemented in Java programming code:

- **Classes:** The `Client` and `CrashDummy` classes become classes in the Java code in statements such as the following:

```
public class Client
```

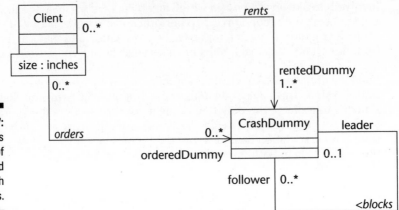

Figure 4-17:
Class
Diagram of
clients and
crash
dummies.

✔ **Associations:** The `rents`, `orders`, and `blocks` associations become combinations of attributes. For example, you implement the `blocks` association in both directions by declaring the attributes `public CrashDummy leader` and `public CrashDummy follower[]` within the `CrashDummy` class. The diagram shows you can only navigate from `Client` to `CrashDummy` (and not the other way around); the `rents` and `orders` associations are implemented only in the `Client` class, as follows:

```
public Btree orderedDummies;
public List rentedDummy;
```

✔ **Roles:** Notice that we use the role names as the names of the attributes used for implementing an association. So the role of `leader` is implemented as the name of the reference attribute `leader` by making the following declaration:

```
public CrashDummy leader.
```

The `orderedDummy`, `rentedDummy`, and `follower` roles are also handled as attributes, along the following lines:

```
public Btree orderedDummies;
public List rentedDummy;
public CrashDummy follower[];
```

✔ **Qualifier:** The `size` qualifier is implemented as `Private Integer Size` so it is an attribute of `CrashDummy`. The qualification aspects are implemented using a `Btree` class named `orderedDummies`. The `Btree` class allows you to associate a value for the `size` qualifier with an instance of `CrashDummy`. Then, the `Btree` is used to lookup a `CrashDummy` by its `size`.

> ✔ **Multiplicity:** Finally, the multiplicity is handled by using the following:
>
> - A simple reference pointer, as in `Public CrashDummy leader` where multiplicity is to `0..1` or `1`.
>
> - An *array* as the default for handling multiplicities of more than one, as in `Public CrashDummy follower[]`.
>
> - A designer-defined container, such as `List` or `B-tree`.

What would the diagram in Figure 4-17 look like in a programming language such as Java? Well, if you convert classes to classes and associations to references, then you generate code that looks similar to Listing 4-1.

Listing 4-1:   Java Code for Simple Associations

```
public class Client
{
    public B-tree orderedDummies;
    public List rentedDummy;

        public Client() {
    }
}
public class CrashDummy
{
    public CrashDummy leader;
    public CrashDummy follower[];
    Private Integer Size;

    public CrashDummy() {
    }
}
```

Chapter 5

Including the Parts
with the Whole

In This Chapter

▶ Modeling the whole and its parts

▶ Differentiating between aggregation and composition

▶ Programming considerations for aggregates

▶ Showing parts within class boxes

*W*hen you model associations between classes, you find that UML treats one kind of association with special reverence. This particular association embodies the "whole-or-part-of" relationship that UML modelers call aggregation. *Aggregation* is just a fancy way of talking about a group of distinct objects (parts) gathered together to form some whole. In this chapter we define aggregation and its stronger form — *composition*. We demonstrate the UML notation for aggregation and explain why it holds a special place among associations in the world of object-oriented modeling and programming.

Representing the Whole and the Parts

If you have a class such as car and you want to model the car and its parts (such as the engine, brakes, chassis, and wheels), you use aggregation. In UML, *aggregation* shows the relationship between the whole and its parts. Using the notation is simple; just follow these steps:

1. **Decide which class is playing the role of the whole and which classes play the role of the whole's parts.**

2. **Draw an association line between the class that is playing the whole (car) and each of its parts (engine, brake, and so on).**

3. **Place a small diamond shape on the association line, right up against the class that is playing the role of the whole (car).**

   We show an example of this diamond shape in Figure 5-1, later in this chapter. (We also talk about when to fill in the diamond as in Figure 5-1 and when not to as in Figure 5-2 later in the chapter.)

4. **Consider the multiplicity of this special association that is now an aggregation.**

   Usually the whole has multiplicity of one.

5. **Consider the multiplicity of the each of the parts in relation to the whole.**

   For example, the engine has a multiplicity of one, and the wheels have a multiplicity of four (or five if you count the spare tire).

Modeling complexity

For the modeler, aggregation is important because it hides complexity. Objects are like black boxes: We can see the outside of the box but not what is inside. If an object is really an aggregation of parts, then the inside of the box may be complex. A car, for example, is a complex object — and (as with a black box) we don't have to understand all its internal parts to use it. The aggregation notation helps the modeler handle complexity by building two diagrams:

✔ **External associations of the aggregate:** On this class diagram, place the class playing the whole, and show classes outside the whole that are associated with the whole. This first diagram shows the external context of the whole class.

   This diagram hides the complexity of the internal parts. In other words, just look at the external aspects of the complex whole.

✔ **Internal structure of the aggregate:** On this second class diagram, place the class playing the role of the whole at the top and show all of its parts underneath. Then consider the associations between the parts and show those on this diagram.

   This diagram only shows the classes involved in the aggregation and does not show any classes outside the aggregation. The modeler can focus on the internal workings of the aggregate without the complexity of what is outside the aggregate. In other words, just look at the internal aspects of a complex whole.

Considering aggregation behavior

A whole and its parts form a special bond. The whole object usually invokes the behavior of its parts to accomplish its own behavior. When you start a car, you use an interface (the ignition-key slot) that is *part* of the car. After turning the ignition key, various *parts* of the car (wires, battery, ignition coil, engine, and so on) are invoked in the right sequence to start the engine. From a programming perspective, the whole (car) invokes behavior on the aggregated parts to achieve its requested behavior (to start running).

For programmers, aggregations have a special meaning beyond just allowing instances of one class to invoke the behavior of instances of another class. Because the whole controls its parts, use the following when designing operations for the whole and its parts:

- **Constructor:** Think about the *constructor* operation (the operation invoked to create instances of the class) of the whole. Ask yourself what parts must be available as soon as the whole object is created at runtime. Be sure to create them in the constructor's method (the actual code for the constructor operation).

- **Life cycle:** Consider the life cycle of the whole. You need to think about the state changes the whole goes through during its life — and for aggregates, this can be quite complex. During the life of an aggregate, its parts are created and deleted at specific times, and the aggregate invokes the behavior of each part at specific times in specific order. You may want to consider building a state diagram for the class that plays the role of the whole. (You can find more information on state diagrams in Chapter 16.)

- **Cascading operations:** For each major stage in the life cycle, consider what behavior the whole is performing. Further consider which parts get involved to assist the whole. For example, when the car is asked to accelerate, the accelerator, throttle, engine, transmission, axes, and wheels get involved. When the car is asked to stop, the brakes, wheels, axes, transmission, and engine are involved. Think of how requests of the whole object are passed down to requests on the parts.

- **Handling errors:** Consider how you handle errors. If a part is having a problem, the natural place to handle the problem is within the part. However, if the part can't deal with the error, you can throw the error over to the whole and let it deal with it. Often the whole object "knows" enough about the internal workings of itself and all its parts that it can rectify the problem.

- **Destructor:** Don't forget the *destructor* operation (the operation that contains behavior to delete instances of a class) of the whole. You should consider what happens when the whole is asked to destruct. Take the time to think about the life cycle of the whole's parts. Reflect on whether any parts are left over — are they all destroyed along with the whole? Program your destructor operation on the whole accordingly.

The following are some quick guidelines for specifying aggregation:

- ✔ Don't worry about naming this special association. All aggregations are also associations. Aggregations are a special kind of association because they associate a whole with its parts. So, all aggregations are implicitly named "part-of." You can name them if you want to, but you don't have to.

- ✔ Consider naming the part end of the association only if it plays some special role in relation to the whole.

- ✔ On the class representing the whole, add operations that control the parts.

- ✔ Create a state diagram for the whole, indicating its dynamic life cycle. (See Chapter 16 for more on state diagrams.)

- ✔ Carefully consider the constructor and destructor operations on the whole.

Showing Ownership: Composition

If you have a part instance of some whole instance which belongs to one and only one whole, then you have a special case of aggregation known as *composition*. With composition, parts can't be shared with other objects. The life of the part is completely within the life span of the whole. If you think of a VCR, it is a composite. Take a look inside your VCR through the door that accepts the videotape. It is composed of all those internal parts — such as circuit boards, a power supply, and a tape-transport mechanism. If the VCR is destroyed, then all the parts within it are destroyed as well. When you have a part whose life is within the life of the whole, then you have *composition*, which is a strong form of aggregation. To indicate composition in UML, simply fill in the diamond that appears next to the class playing the role of the whole, as shown in Figure 5-1.

A typical real-world example is a client who needs to build a reporting system. Imagine such a system including a `GenericReport` class — a composite that contains several other classes. Figure 5-1 illustrates a simplified version of the class diagram that describes this composition. A `GenericReport` is composed of four parts — `Header`, `Column`, `Body`, and `Footer`. The diamonds are filled in with a solid color to indicate composition. Because composition is a kind of aggregation, and aggregation is a special form of association, you can place association names, multiplicities, role names, and qualifiers on the line between the classes. Notice that the body plays the role of detail. The multiplicity at the `GenericReport` end is 1 because these parts belong to one and only one instance of the composite object (`GenericReport`). Given a `GenericReport` there are zero or more instances of `Header`, one for each page of the report. A `GenericReport` has one or more `Column` instances, one or more `Body` instances, optionally a `Footer`.

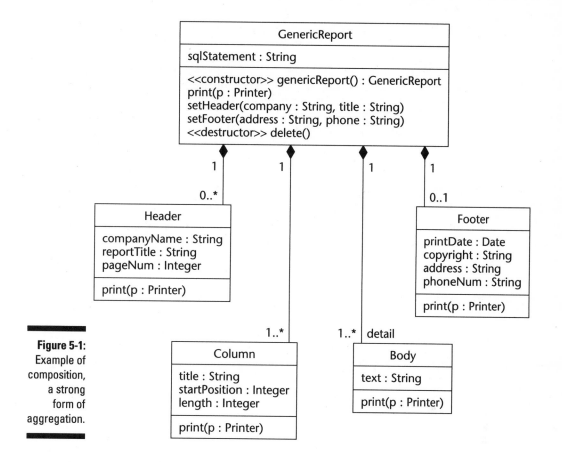

Showing What Can Be Shared: Aggregation

There are times when you want to show that a part can be shared among more than one aggregate. This is known as the weak form of aggregation. A part such as a computer can be shared among different networks at different times. The part's life is not strongly tied to the life of the whole. The computer as part of the network maintains a separate existence from that of the network. You don't fill in the diamond in the case of this weaker form of aggregation.

The relationship between a class playing the role of the whole and its parts in known as aggregation. When the life of the parts are tied up in the life of the whole, then you call the aggregation relationship *composition*. When a part is sharable among different wholes, then you simply call the aggregation relationship *aggregation*.

Figure 5-2 uses the weak form of aggregation to model a common business object called `SalesRegion`. A sales region contains one or more offices, may or may not contain a wholesale warehouse, and does contain one or more retail outlets. Here the `SalesRegion` class is playing the role of the whole. Nevertheless, the association is not a composition because the parts are not necessarily destroyed if the sales region goes away.

Here's a closer look at the multiplicity in the direction from the parts to the whole: An office is contained within zero or more sales regions, which means some offices belong to more than one sales region at the same time. A single wholesale warehouse services zero or more sales regions. A retail outlet belongs to at least one or more sales regions. The respective parts are potentially shared among sales regions.

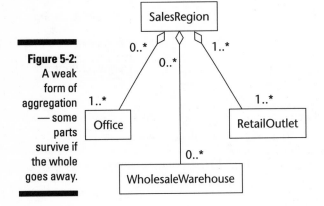

Figure 5-2:
A weak
form of
aggregation
— some
parts
survive if
the whole
goes away.

Deciding between Aggregation and Composition

You might find it difficult to decide between modeling a relationship as an association, an aggregation, or a composition. Here are a few clues to look for when you're modeling relationships:

- ✔ If you hear words like "part of," "contains," or "owns," then you probably have an *aggregation* relationship.

- ✔ If the life-cycle of the parts are bound up within the life-cycle of the whole, then you have a *composite*.

- ✔ If the parts are shared, then it's an *aggregation*.

- ✔ If the parts are not shared, then you may have *composition*.

Aggregations (and composition) also have two other identifying properties: they're not symmetric but they are transitive. Hang on, these are fancy terms for a couple of simple ideas. An association is *symmetric* if it is the same thing in both directions. Think of the relationship between a generic report and one of its columns. Although it's true that the column is part of the generic report, it's not true that the generic report is also part of the column. (Seems obvious, doesn't it?) When you're deciding about whether you have a part-of relationship, ask the symmetry question. The transitive property is a fancy way of saying: If *A* is a part of *B*, and *B* is a part of *C*, then *A* is also a part of *C.*

Here's a down-to-earth way to say that again: If a filament (*A*) is a part of a light bulb (*B*), and a light bulb (*B*) is part of a lamp (*C*), then the filament (*A*) is also part of the lamp (*C*). If you can apply the transitive property, then chances are you have an aggregation.

Table 5-1 summarizes these criteria to help you decide whether you have an aggregation, composition, or association.

Table 5-1	Aggregation Versus Composition: Clues
Decision Result	*Criteria*
Aggregation or Composition	Part-of, contains, owns words are used to describe relationship between two classes
Aggregation or Composition	No symmetry
Aggregation or Composition	Transitivity among parts
Composition	Parts are not shared
Composition	Multiplicity of the whole is *1* or *0..1*
Aggregation	Parts may be shared
Aggregation	Multiplicity of the whole may be larger than 1
Association	Relationship does not fit the other criteria

Using Alternate Composite Notation

UML allows you to place a class diagram inside a class. When we're talking about composites, this isn't as strange as it may seem. Since the second compartment of a class shows structure, and a composite has complex structure within itself, then you can show the parts of the composite inside as a mini class diagram.

UML 2 has a new diagram name for this alternative notation: composite structure diagram.

The UML notation for class has three major compartments:

- ✔ The first compartment names the class, describes its stereotype and lists its properties.

- ✔ The second compartment shows the *structure* of the class as a list of attributes.

- ✔ The third compartment is where you place the class's behavior specification.

This compartmentalization was allowed as an interesting idea in the previous version of UML 1.4. Most of the CASE tools, however, didn't pick up on this idea. But that is changing with UML 2.0.

Showing parts as classes

Modeling the strong form of aggregation — composition — often results in a class diagram with lots of confusing lines. You have lines between the class playing the role of the whole and classes playing the role of the parts. You also have lines showing the associations between individual parts internal to the composite. With all these lines, the diagram can be difficult to read. UML 2 allows you to model composites and their parts as a class diagram within a class (composite structural diagram). This reduces the clutter and allows you to be clear about what you mean.

You can show the parts of a composite inside the structure compartment of a class by putting a box around the part and providing a name for that part: part name, then a colon, then a class name for the part. If you have more than one part of the same type in the composition, then you can show its multiplicity in square brackets. For example the `Body` part of a `GenericReport` would be surrounded by a box with `detail:Body[1..*]` inside, as in Figure 5-3.

Parts can also be connected by (you guessed it) *connectors* — lines that indicate links between instances of parts within a composite — so those parts may communicate with each other. UML 2.0 provides for two kinds of connectors — assembly and delegation. An *assembly connector* allows one part of the composite to supply services that another part needs. On the other hand, use a *delegation connector* to show the whole composite forwarding some external request for behavior to one of its internal parts. The assembly connector connects two parts like an association. The delegation connector connects the whole with one of its parts. The delegation connector is shown as a line from the edge of the composite class to one of the parts inside the composite class.

Figure 5-3 illustrates just such a diagram. The GenericReport class is playing the role of the whole or composite. The parts are anonymous parts with classes named Header, Column and Footer. One of the parts is named detail which is of the class Body. The parts are connected using lines that can be named just like associations. Indeed you can place multiplicity, role names, and qualifiers on these connections. Each of the connections shown in Figure 5-3 are assembly connections. For instance the Header will invoke the print service of Column.

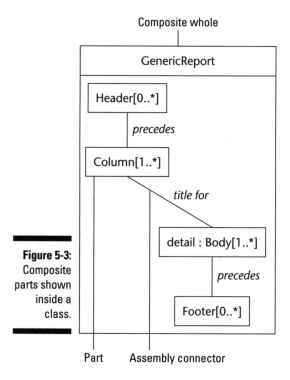

Figure 5-3:
Composite parts shown inside a class.

Showing parts as attributes

This section ties together composites, part diagrams (those class diagrams inside of a class), and attributes. Figure 5-4 shows the class for GenericReport and its attributes. Notice the correspondence between the attributes in Figure 5-4 and the classes in Figure 5-3. The class definition in Figure 5-4 hides the internal structure of the GenericReport class by simply listing the major parts as attributes. The sqlStatement is not a part — rather, it's one of the attributes of the GenericReport class.

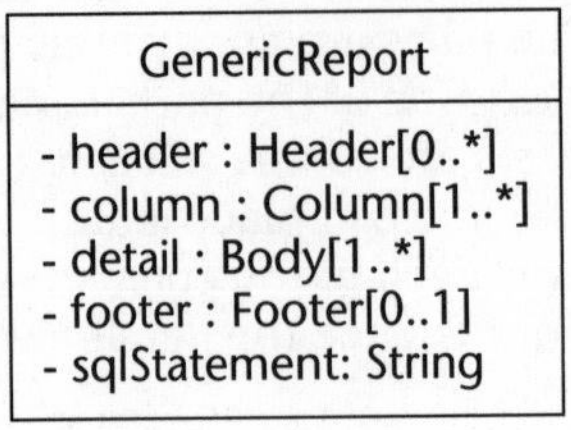

Figure 5-4:
Showing
composite
parts as
attributes
inside a
class.

GenericReport
- header : Header[0..*] - column : Column[1..*] - detail : Body[1..*] - footer : Footer[0..1] - sqlStatement: String

If you want to convert a simple class into a composite structure diagram, you can use Table 5-2 as a guide. The table shows the correspondence between attributes in a simple class diagram and the elements of a part diagram inside of a composite class. For instance the detail attribute of the GenericReport becomes a part with the same name in the composite structure diagram. The Body datatype becomes the name of the detail part's class. The [1..*] multiplicity is carried forward to the multiplicity of the detail part.

Table 5-2   Attribute Correspondence to Composite Parts

Attribute Feature	*Composite Structure Feature*
Attribute name	Part name
Type	Part's class name
Multiplicity	Allowable number of connections between part instances

Chapter 6

Reusing Superclasses: Generalization and Inheritance

In This Chapter

▶ Reusing common attributes and operations

▶ Defining generalization and specialization

▶ Providing steps to show generalization

▶ Adding discriminators to inheritance hierarchies

▶ Weighing the pros and cons of multiple inheritance

*I*t's natural to classify objects in categories and to organize categories into subcategories. If you look for a place to live, you find yourself categorizing a dwelling unit as a house, apartment, townhouse, condominium, mansion, and so on. Houses can, in turn, be further organized by styles such as ranch, split-level, colonial, and saltbox. UML provides you with notation to capture these types of classifications — also known as generalization and specialization — and make use of them as a modeler and a programmer. This chapter covers generalization — and how it leads to inheritance. (Specifically, subclasses that inherit the attributes and operations of a superclass. For more on superclasses and subclasses read on.) We show you the UML notation for inheritance and how to take advantage of it.

Some of us object-oriented developers will go to great lengths to save ourselves a little work. When we can model something once and reuse it, we're interested. If we can write a method (the program code for an operation) for a class only once and use it many times, then sign us up for higher productivity. If you want to save yourself time by specifying attributes and operations once and then reusing them many times, read on.

Making Generalizations

As you define classes, you may notice that some classes have the same attributes or the same operations. When this is the case, you place these common features (attributes, operations, and so on) in a more generic class called the *superclass*. The classes that share the common features are known as *subclasses* of the superclass. For example, the length of recorded material on a videotape, audiotape, compact disc, or movie film is an attribute of all four kinds of recorded media. These classes can share other attributes as well, such as their physical dimensions and the date each one was used to make a recording. In this case the *superclass* would be `RecordedMedia`, the subclasses would be `Videotape`, `Audiotape`, `CompactDisc`, and `MovieFilm`, and some shared attributes could include `recordedLength` and `totalLength`.

This process of finding similar attributes or operations across classes is known as *generalization*. For example you generalize the attribute `recordLength` into a more generic class called `RecordedMedia`. The process for showing a generalization in UML is simple:

1. **Identify the subclasses.**

   Locate classes that have the same attributes and/or operations. These classes are your subclasses.

2. **Create a superclass.**

   Provide a superclass to hold the common attributes and/or operations of the subclasses. Give the superclass a name that categorizes all the subclasses. We recommend placing the superclass above the subclasses in the diagram. (You don't have to, but it does make it easier to read.)

3. **Add common features to the superclass.**

   Remove the common attributes and operations from the subclasses and place them (once) in the superclass.

4. **Draw a generalization relationship.**

   You draw a generalization line from each subclass to the superclass. In UML the generalization line is represented as a solid line with a hollow arrowhead at the superclass end. In UML, a line with the hollow arrowhead that connects a subclass to a superclass is known as a *generalization relationship*.

After you create a superclass with the common features such as attributes and operations, the subclasses *inherit* those features from the superclass. This way you only have to write the common features once in the superclass instead of many times in each of the subclasses.

You can tell whether you have a generalization by looking at the language you (or others) use to describe the relationship between classes. Notice that in describing recorded media and its various types such as videotape earlier in this section, we used the phrase "four kinds of recorded media." If you find yourself using phrases such as "kind of" or "type of," then chances are you have a generalization on your hands.

One of our clients is concerned with keeping track of materials in an archive. This client has accumulated different *kinds of* recorded media such as video-tapes and audiotapes. As modelers, we need to capture the differences between these media as well as their similarities. The diagram in Figure 6-1 shows the beginnings of several generalizations, arranged in an *inheritance hierarchy.*

Developers use the term generalization or inheritance to refer to the same concept of reusing shared attributes and operations that you show in a superclass and reuse in subclasses. Generalization refers to the concept of generalizing from specifics (the subclasses) to the generic (the superclass). Inheritance refers to the effect of generalization on the subclasses.

In Figure 6-1 RecordedMedia is the superclass. The hollow arrowhead is just below (and right up against) the superclass. Lines from the arrowhead indicate that Videotape, Audiotape, CompactDisc and MovieFilm are all subclasses or "kinds of" RecordedMedia. Each subclass inherits the common attributes of recordedLength, totalLength, height, width, depth, and form. Each of the subclasses also has the operation recommendPlaybackMachine as an inherited common feature from the superclass. Each subclass has its own attributes as well. For example, CompactDisc has two unique attributes (recordedTracks and errorRate) that the other classes don't share.

When you see a *generalization* relationship between classes, its meaning is very different from that of an *association* relationship between classes (as discussed in Chapter 4). An association is ultimately a relationship among many *objects* — some instances of one class have a relationship (link) with instances of the other class. In a generalization relationship among *classes*, the relationship is really about the classes. The best you can say is that an object created from a subclass contains all the features of the subclass and of the superclass.

You only have one object from a class in a generalization relationship. Even though you show two classes, the subclass and the superclass, you only have one object that gets created. You can think of an object of the Videotape class also being an object of the RecordedMedia class because of inheritance. Figure 6-2 shows an object created from the Videotape class with all its attributes. (The instance of a class is represented as an object symbol.) You don't have two different objects (one for RecordedMedia and one for Videotape), just one object. When the object vtu83-1023 was created, we set all its attributes' values. The recording on the tape is 57 minutes. The total length of the physical tape is 60 minutes. The tape is a Umatic videocassette with a height of 10 inches, a width of 7 inches, and a depth of 1.5 inches. The recording is analog, and a log of tape contents is attached to the tape for the archivist to reference.

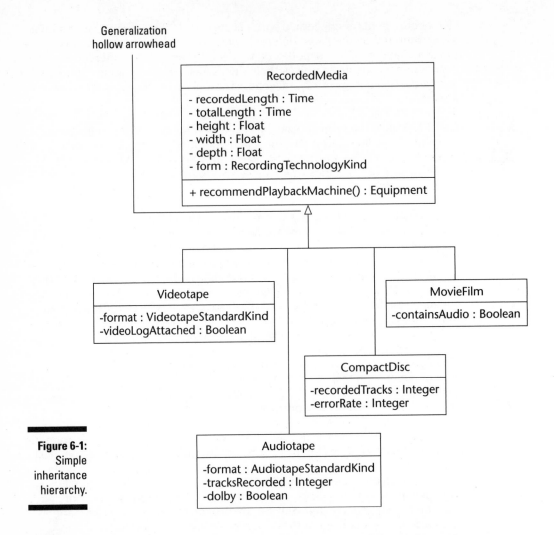

Generalization
hollow arrowhead

RecordedMedia

- recordedLength : Time
- totalLength : Time
- height : Float
- width : Float
- depth : Float
- form : RecordingTechnologyKind

+ recommendPlaybackMachine() : Equipment

Videotape

-format : VideotapeStandardKind
-videoLogAttached : Boolean

MovieFilm

-containsAudio : Boolean

CompactDisc

-recordedTracks : Integer
-errorRate : Integer

Audiotape

-format : AudiotapeStandardKind
-tracksRecorded : Integer
-dolby : Boolean

Figure 6-1:
Simple
inheritance
hierarchy.

You only have one instance defined by a subclass and its superclass. The subclass and the superclass may have a constructor operation (to create the instance) and a destructor operation (to destroy the instance). When your software runs, and you create an instance of a subclass, the constructor of the superclass is executed first, followed by the constructor of the subclass. When it comes time to eliminate the instance you created, the destructor of the subclass is called first, followed by the destructor of the superclass. If things are more complex because you have subclasses of subclasses, just remember: Constructors are invoked from the top of the inheritance hierarchy to the bottom; destructors are called in order from the lowest subclass up to the highest superclass.

vtu83-1023 : Videotape
recordedLength = 57 totalLength = 60 height = 10 width = 7 depth = 1.5 form = analog format = Umatic videoLogAttached = True

Figure 6-2:
An instance showing all inherited attributes.

Specializing Classes

You might hear some experts talk about specialization. *Specialization* is just the opposite of generalization. Instead of taking common features from subclasses and creating a generic superclass, you create specialized classes from a common superclass. In the archive we have "print media." It turns out there are two kinds of print media – books and transcripts. So print media is a superclass. Books and transcripts are specializations and thus subclasses of print media. While we started with the idea of having a class called PrintMedia, we recognized there were special forms of PrintMedia in the archive.

When you generalize, you start with some subclasses and develop a superclass. When you specialize, you start with a superclass and develop some subclass.

For specialization, we start with PrintMedia and use UML to show PrintMedia as a superclass and it's "specialized" subclasses. Figure 6-3 shows the inheritance hierarchy for PrintMedia. The Book class holds its own unique attributes of isbn, author, title, publisher, and publishDate. Transcript (on the other hand) has typist, editor, and transcribed attributes.

We may have specialized from the class PrintMedia instead of generalized, but you notice that we still have an inheritance hierarchy with a superclass and a couple of subclasses. So, the Book and Transcript subclasses both inherit sheetWeight, paper and needsBinding from PrintMedia.

Generalization and specialization are just two sides of the same coin. Whether you generalize or specialize, the UML diagram ends up having superclasses connected to subclasses — an inheritance hierarchy. A developer looking at your diagram might focus on the superclass and think of the subclasses as specializations. Another developer looking at your diagram might focus on the subclasses and think of the superclass as a generalization. You can look at inheritance diagrams either way no matter what technique (generalization or specialization) you used to create the diagram.

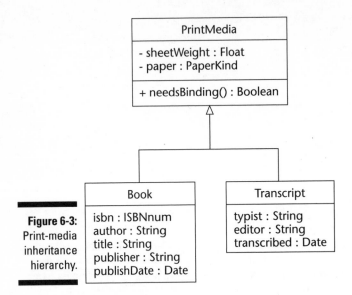

When doing practical development of systems, you'll find that you're doing a fluid dance with generalization and specialization. Sometimes you'll be seeing how things look the same, comparing them and generalizing the results. Sometimes you'll be seeing how things look different, contrasting them and specializing the results. If you work hard at it, and dance with everyone, you'll find the order of your dancing doesn't make that much difference to the final generalization hierarchy. You'll have gathered together the commonalities, separated out the differences, and made a robust hierarchy.

Using Generalization Sets

Each generalization relationship is known as a *binary relationship* because the generalization relates two classes: the superclass and a subclass. When you create an inheritance hierarchy, you also create a *generalization set* — a concept that helps you discriminate among the subclasses that inherit general characteristics from a common superclass. For example, the basis for distinguishing among the subclasses of `PrintMedia` is the material form of each printed medium — whether a book, magazine, or transcript.

In our example of `PrintMedia` there are two generalization relationships, one between `Book` and `PrintMedia` and the other between `Transcript` and `PrintMedia`. These two generalization relationships then form a generalization set (known in earlier versions of UML as a *discriminator*), which is a characteristic that distinguishes individual specializations of a class into subclasses. The basis for this particular generalization set is the physical form of the printed material.

You can show the basis for discrimination among subclasses in UML. Just place the name of the generalization set (discriminator) close to the hollow arrowhead. Figure 6-4 shows the name of the generalization set to be physical form.

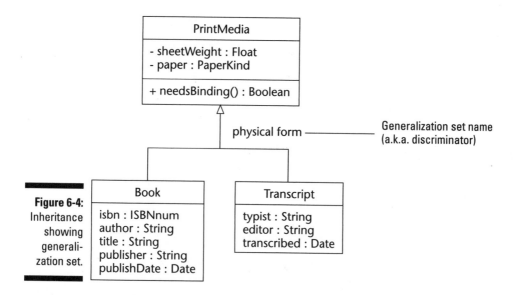

Figure 6-4: Inheritance showing generalization set.

You should use named generalization sets when you have large inheritance hierarchies. This will make it easier for others to know the basis for each part of your large hierarchy. If you ever have to add a class into your hierarchy at a later time, you can make the right decision as to what part of hierarchy the class belongs so your inheritance hierarchy remains consistent.

We experienced just such a problem with the materials in the archive. Figure 6-5 shows just the superclasses and subclasses for archive material and their basis for discrimination into generalization sets. (We've hidden the attributes and operations to make the diagram easy to read.) The ArchiveMedium are classified by the mechanism used to create them (creation mechanism). RecordedMedia are created using some recording device. PrintMedia are created using a machine that places ink on paper such as a printing press, photocopier, or typewriter. Videotape and CompactDisc are types of RecordedMedia based on their physical form.

Okay, now we have a nice inheritance hierarchy — everything fits. Then, someone remembers that some old photos are also part of the archive. Photos are not made using a recording device, nor are they created putting ink to paper. Photos have a different creation mechanism and they are a different physical form from the classes in the hierarchy. However, because we have names for our generalization sets, we can see where to place the new class in the hierarchy.

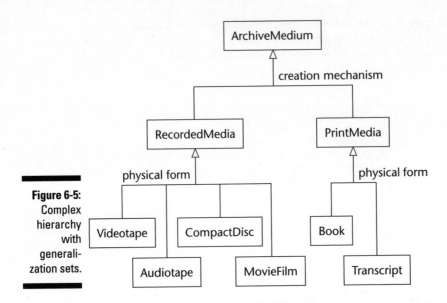

Figure 6-5:
Complex hierarchy with generalization sets.

In order to solve the problem, we need add a new class, so we add PhotoMedia as a kind of ArchiveMedium and Photograph as a kind of PhotoMedia. You create PhotoMedia with a camera and film, and then develop the film to reveal a picture. Understanding the basis for discriminating between the subclasses of ArchiveMedium helps place the Photograph class into the complex inheritance hierarchy, as in Figure 6-6.

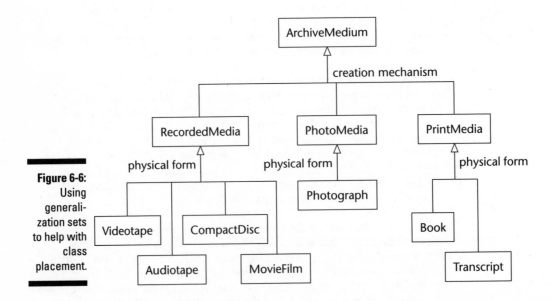

Figure 6-6:
Using generalization sets to help with class placement.

Inheriting from Ancestors

Generalizations are a great way to inherit common attributes and operations, but a class inherits much more from a superclass, namely associations, constraints (limits), methods (code for an operation), interfaces (specification of an operation), and composite parts (the parts internal to a class).

Think about an instance of a generic dwelling unit (a superclass) and its associated instance of an address. Now think of a particular kind of dwelling unit, say a ranch style house (a subclass). The ranch unit is also *associated* with an address because it is a kind of dwelling unit. The ranch unit subclass inherits the dwelling unit's association with the address class. If you constrain the definition of any dwelling unit's size attribute to be no smaller than six square feet, then that ranch unit's size could not be any smaller than six square feet. The ranch unit inherits any constraints of the superclass dwelling unit. You could reuse the dwelling unit's *method* for calculating its own resale value based on size and location for calculating the ranch houses resale value based on the same formula. You also inherit the *composite parts* of a dwelling unit such as the kitchen, living room and bedroom in any type of dwelling like the ranch-style house.

You should be careful when inheriting from a superclass. The regulations for using inheritance are a little complex, but we'll show you the rules that you use most often. When your superclass is associated with other classes, then the subclasses (being special cases of the superclass) are also associated with those same classes. Even so, you should be aware that only certain aspects of an association are inherited. (See the next section, "Making sense of inherited associations," for more information.) When your subclass specifies constraints, they must be the same as — or more constraining than — those of the superclass. Operations and their methods may be simply reused, or redefined.

Making sense of inherited associations

In the archive example that we used earlier in this chapter, it turns out that storage space — like shelves and file cabinets — store all manner of archive media. Videotapes are stored on special movable shelves. Transcripts are stored in file cabinets of various sizes. To demonstrate this connection, we modeled this situation as an association between the class StorageSpace and the class ArchiveMedium.

All the subclasses of ArchiveMedium inherit this association and so RecordedMedia is associated also with StorageSpace. However, the subclasses of ArchiveMedium only inherit certain features of the association.

You inherit the role name, multiplicity and constraints on the far side of an inherited association. For example, RecordedMedia inherits the multiplicity at the StorageSpace end of the association between ArchiveMedium and StorageSpace. You inherit any constraints and qualifiers on the near side of an inherited association. The near side of the association would be the ArchiveMedium side of the association between ArchiveMedium and StorageSpace.

Figure 6-7 illustrates the far-side features that the subclasses RecordedMedia, PhotoMedia, and PrintMedia inherit from ArchiveMedium in the stores association: 0..1 multiplicity and mediaLocation role name. The subclasses are also forced to be ordered because the stores association has the near-side constraint ({ordered}).

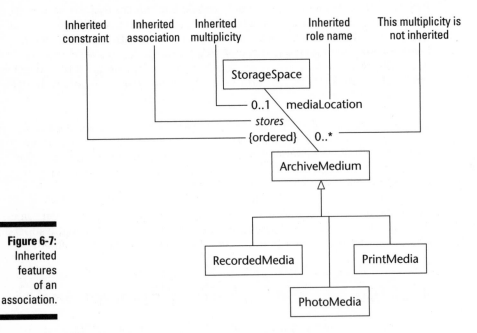

Figure 6-7:
Inherited
features
of an
association.

Overriding your inheritance

You can override inheritance — change aspects of inherited attributes, constraints, and the methods used for operations. For example, an attribute of a subclass can redefine an attribute inherited from the superclass. Additionally the method used to implement an operation in a subclass can be a refined version of the operation inherited from the superclass. For example, all types of vehicles (the superclass) can move (the superclass operation). However, each type of vehicle like a sailboat and a car (subclasses) move in very different ways (different subclass methods for the inherited move operation).

Overriding attributes

When overriding attributes inherited by a subclass keep the following in mind with examples illustrated in Figure 6-8:

- ✔ **Redefined name:** An attribute in a subclass can redefine an attribute in the superclass by showing a constraint with the word `redefines` followed by the name of the redefined attribute from the superclass.

  The class `ArchiveMedium` has an attribute defined as `inventoryID: Text`, and the subclass `Book` inherits that attribute but redefines it as `isbn: String {redefines inventoryID}`.

- ✔ **Datatypes:** The datatype of an inherited attribute must be the same as or a specialization of the inherited attribute's datatype in the superclass.

  In the superclass `ArchiveMedium` the `inventoryID` has the datatype `Text`. The subclass `RecordedMedia` defines the datatype for `inventoryID` as `String`. `String` being a specialization of `Text`.

- ✔ **Default value:** The default value of an attribute in a subclass may override the default value of that same attribute in the superclass.

  The `generation` attribute in the class `ArchiveMedium` has a default value of one because it is assumed that most of the material in the archive is an original and not a copy. However, all the photos in the archive are copies from a private collection. So, the `generation` attribute of `PhotoMedia` has a default value of 2.

- ✔ **Derived attribute:** The subclass may have a derived attribute that was not a derived attribute in the superclass.

  `ArchiveMedium` has a `weight` attribute that is not a derived attribute. However, the `Transcript` subclass inherits the `weight` attribute from `ArchiveMedium`, and inherits the `sheetWeight` attribute of `PrintMedia`. The `weight` attribute of `Transcript` is a derived attribute because it can be calculated using the `sheetWeight` and the `numPages` attributes. (`Transcript` inherits both `sheetWeight` and `numPages` from `PrintMedia`.)

Overriding constraints

Inevitably, you deal with business rules that constrain the objects in your system. For instance, the archivist must follow the rule that no material (`ArchiveMedium`) may be borrowed from the archive for longer than thirty days. You recognize this as one of those rules people have to follow, and you have to make sure your software doesn't violate that rule. The archive-system software must warn the archivist when any instance of `ArchiveMedium` is out for a period close to (but not more than) thirty days.

This case illustrates an important principle: If the superclass has a constraint or limitation, then all of its subclasses have that constraint too. When you use inheritance, your subclasses must not loosen any constraints placed on the superclass. Therefore `Books` and `Transcripts` cannot be borrowed for more than thirty days.

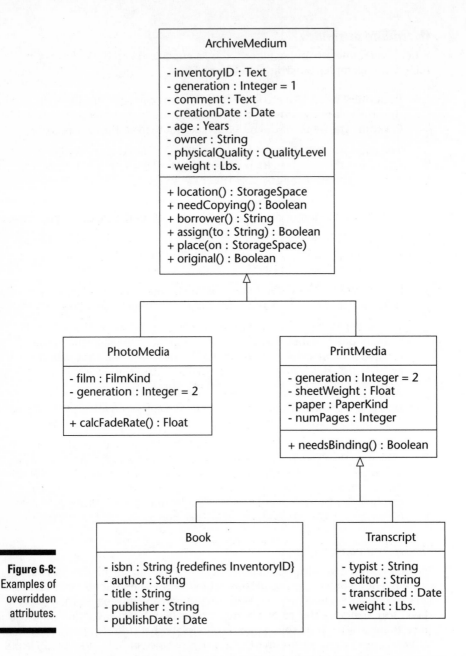

Figure 6-8:
Examples of
overridden
attributes.

Although you can't loosen the constraint for subclasses, you can tighten it. One example is the rule that `Videotapes` can't be borrowed for more than a week.

Overriding operations and methods

One thing we like about inheritance is being able to reuse the method for an operation defined in a superclass. Often the method code for a superclass operation has to be written no more than once; all the subclasses then have that operation. No need to write the method code again (once for each subclass). The `original` operation of `ArchiveMedium` has a simple method that works the same for every subclass. The method (using the Java language) looks something like this:

```
public Boolean original() {
    if (generation == 1) then
    return True;        //first generation means original
    else
    return False;
}
```

Although you can reuse your inherited operations and their methods, you can do more than simply reuse the method code. You can extend, restrict, or optimize your methods. For a concrete idea of these different ways to override methods in the superclass, consider `ArchiveMedium` and its `place` operation:

```
private StorageSpace mediaLocation; //attribute to implement
            // the association to an instance of StorageSpace

public void place (StorageSpace on){
if (on.spaceAvailabe())   //check to see if there is space
    if (on.add(this))      //add media to storage space
    mediaLocation= on;      //set pointer to our media loca-
                tion
}
```

Now let's look at what it means to extend, restrict, or optimize a method:

- ✔ **Extend:** Reuse the method code you inherit from the superclass and then add some code that extends the method to deal with specialized attributes of the subclass. For example the `Transcript` classes' `place` operation must make sure the editor of the transcript has access to the place where the transcript is stored. So the `place` operation is extended to check that condition:

  ```
  public void place (StorageSpace on) {
  if (on.userAccess(editor))   //extension is here
  super.place(on);              //then reuse superclass method
  }
  ```

- ✔ **Restrict:** Your method code in the subclass must account for some additional constraint that is placed on the subclass. In the archive example, a videotape must not be placed in a crowded storage area. So the `place` method of the `Videotape` class must be restricted to storage spaces that are no more than 80 percent full:

  ```
  public void place (StorageSpace on) {
  if (on.percentUsed() <= 80) //check for enough space
  super.place(on);              //then reuse superclass method
  }
  ```

✔ **Optimize:** You optimize the method code for a subclass because you can take into account the specialized extra attributes or constraints in the subclass. It turns out that photographs are so thin that we almost never have to worry about whether there's enough storage space available. So, to optimize the code for the place method a little, you can remove the statement that first checks to see whether space is available. The resulting code looks like this:

```
public void place (StorageSpace on) {
if (on.add(this))        //add media to storage space
mediaLocation= on;  //set pointer to our media location
}
```

Inheriting interfaces

Classes have *public operations* that you invoke from instances of other classes. You can think of each one of these public operations as being an interface between you and the internal workings of the class. Each operation is defined by its name, parameters, and return-result type. This definition is known as the operation's *signature*. For instance the signature for the `assign` operation on the `ArchiveMedium` class includes the name `assign`, the `to` argument and its datatype `String`, as well as the `Boolean` return result type. In UML the signature for `assign` looks like this:

```
assign(to:String): Boolean
```

Your subclasses inherit this signature as well as the method code for that operation. When you invoke the `assign` operation on any subclass of `ArchiveMedium`, your subclasses must all have the `assign` operation with one parameter — and the operation will return a `Boolean` value, no matter how you write the method code for the subclasses.

Normally you create instances of classes. Each class has methods defined for each operation. A method must follow the rules laid down by the operation's signature. The classes used to create instances are known as *concrete classes*. Most examples of classes in this book are concrete classes. However, suppose you have a superclass operation with no method code for that operation. Such an operation — without method code — is known as an *abstract operation*. In UML, abstract operations are shown in italics. If an operation is abstract (has no method), then you can't create instances of that class. The runtime environment wouldn't know what to do if you invoked an operation that had no method code. In this situation, any of your classes with abstract operations are known as *abstract classes*. Any class for which you cannot create instances is an abstract class. In UML, abstract classes have their class names shown in italics.

Abstract classes are a great way to enforce interface inheritance. If you specify an abstract operation in a superclass, then all of its subclasses must conform to the signature of that operation. So anyone who inserts a new subclass into the inheritance hierarchy must write method code for the inherited abstract operation to create a concrete subclass.

You cannot create instances of abstract classes. You can only create instances of concrete classes.

In Figure 6-9, you see that `recommendPlaybackMachine` is an abstract operation and `RecordedMedia` is an abstract class. We don't have enough information in the superclass to define a method that could recommend what equipment to use to play back recorded media. On the other hand, we have that information *in each of the subclasses.* Given (for example) an instance of the `VideoTape` class and a value for its `format` attribute, we have all the data we need to make a recommendation.

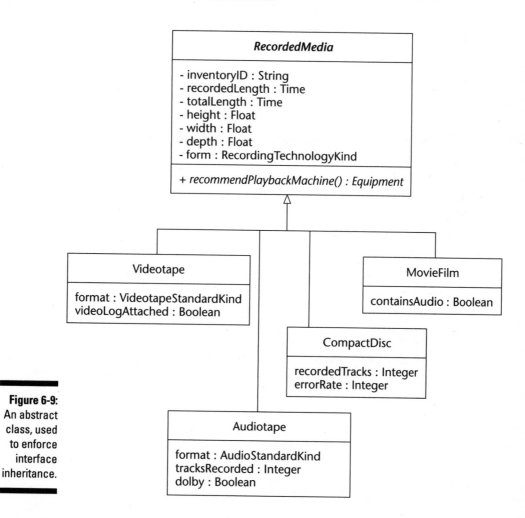

Exploring the Pros and Cons of Multiple Inheritances

You categorize classes in many different ways. A `person` class could be categorized by `age`, `income`, `job role`, or `location`. You use inheritance as a way to categorize your subclasses. If a subclass can inherit from one superclass, why not from two or more superclasses? Well, it can; UML allows you to show such multiple inheritance. For example, the `MovieFilm` class is an instance of `RecordedMedia` and of `PhotoMedia`. It should have all the attributes and operations of both superclasses, as illustrated in Figure 6-10. You show multiple inheritance in UML by connecting the subclass to each of its superclasses with a generalization relationship.

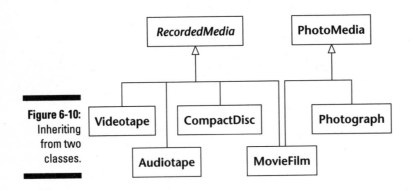

Figure 6-10:
Inheriting
from two
classes.

Ah, but does the use of multiple inheritance make our programs richer? Sometimes. There are both advantages and disadvantages to using multiple inheritance. First, the advantages:

- ✔ You categorize classes in many different ways. Multiple inheritance is a way of showing our natural tendency to organize the world. During analysis, for example, we use multiple inheritance to capture the way users classify objects.

- ✔ By having multiple superclasses, your subclass has more opportunities to reuse the inherited attributes and operations of the superclasses.

Now for the disadvantages:

- ✔ Some programming languages (such as Java) don't allow you to use multiple inheritance. You must translate multiple inheritance into single inheritance or individual Java interfaces. This can be confusing and difficult to maintain because the implemented code for categorizing objects is quite different from the way the user organizes those objects. So, when the user changes their mind or adds another category, it is difficult to figure out how to program the new subclass.

✔ The more superclasses your subclass inherits from, the more maintenance you are likely to perform. If one of the superclasses happens to change, the subclass may have to change as well.

✔ When a single subclass inherits the same attribute or operation from different superclasses, you must choose exactly which one it must use. For example, the MovieFilm subclass inherits the place operation from both the RecordedMedia superclass and the PhotoMedia superclass. Remember, the RecordedMedia and PhotoMedia classes inherit the place operation from their superclass — ArchiveMedium. So now you must choose which method code for place to use for MovieFile — the one from RecordedMedia or the one from PhotoMedia. These choices can get very complex with multiple inheritance hierarchies. Be careful.

During analysis, we use inheritance hierarchies to capture the way our users think about their world. During design, however, we try to stay away from multiple inheritance. In the long run, its disadvantages outweigh its advantages.

Reusing Code

The really great thing about inheritance is the productivity you get through reuse of code. We've shown you an example of code reuse earlier in the chapter with the following method from the Transcript classes place operation:

```
public void place (StorageSpace on) {
if (on.userAccess(editor))  //extension is here
super.place(on);           //then reuse superclass method
}
```

Notice the third line says super.place(on);. We are reusing the place method that is located in the ArchiveMedium superclass.

Creating an inheritance hierarchy of classes helps you simplify your programming code. Object-oriented programs can loop through a set of objects that are from the same generalization set (based on the same superclass) without knowing which object of which subclass is being invoked. The object-oriented program simply invokes an operation defined on the superclass. The program does not have to worry which object is being invoked because they all share a common superclass and all subclasses inherit the superclass operations.

For example, if our program has a list of objects created from the Videotape, CompactDisc, MovieFilm, and Audiotape subclasses and these objects were all mixed up on the list, we could write a program to retrieve each object from the list and invoke the recommendPlaybackMachine operation on that object. Since each object inherits the recommendPlaybackMachine operation from the RecordedMedia superclass the right behavior will be invoked.

The real payoff for you is when you want to extend your software. You can add new subclasses to an inheritance hierarchy and not have to change code in other parts of your program. For example, suppose we added a DVD subclass to the RecordedMedia inheritance hierarchy. We would have to program the subclass to handle the recommendPlaybackMachine operation. Even though we added a whole new class to the software, we would not have the change that part of the object-oriented program that goes through that list of objects described in the previous paragraph. If we added an object created from the DVD subclass to the list the program would still just invoke the recommendPlaybackMachine operation just as before. No code changes in the existing program.

Chapter 7

Organizing UML Class Diagrams and Packages

In This Chapter

▶ Avoiding confusing class diagrams

▶ Showing the right number of classes on a single diagram

▶ Building top-level and second-level diagrams

▶ Showing the context of your system

▶ Handling multiple time periods

▶ Diagramming classes and instances

▶ Modeling foundation classes

▶ Considering application classes

▶ Grouping classes into packages

*U*ML diagrams such as the class diagram are quite versatile. You use class diagrams to express the static structure of the objects and classes you want to model and the static blueprint of the program you want to build. In this chapter we give you some tips for constructing class diagrams. We also show you several different kinds of class diagrams that you can use when modeling systems or developing software.

Modeling Objects and Classes on Diagrams

You have two main types of static diagram in UML — class diagrams and object diagrams. *Class diagrams* show classes and associations, aggregations, and generalizations. Pure *object diagrams* just show instances of classes and their links to other instances. Of course, you can also show classes and objects on the same diagram, but this is rarely done. We use these different diagram types for specific purposes.

If you use a UML modeling tool, take a close look at the different types of diagrams that it supports. If you do not see an object diagram, then the modeling tool probably lets you place objects on class diagrams.

Most of the time you use class diagrams; they provide the broadest way of showing what you're modeling. They're also the most useful diagrams you can produce, because the code that UML tools generate is based on the class diagram.

Pure object diagrams simply show instances and links — the objects and the connections between objects. (For more on links see chapter 4.) For complex modeling, you have to show many instances and links on a single diagram. But, the class diagram would be quite simple. Figure 7-1 shows you just what we're saying. An instance of the Supplier class called ace1 links up with two instances of the Invoice class, a1 and a2. Both instances a1 and a2 are bills that were sent out in the past because they play the role of pastBill. These two invoices were paid from an instance of the SupplierAccount class called aceAcc. Another instance of the Supplier class, generalAirF, is linked to a different set of invoices. From the diagram you see that the instance b4 of the Invoice class plays the role of the currentBill.

The diagram in Figure 7-1 illustrates two different cases for suppliers and their invoices. In one case the supplier ace1 has no current bill. In the other case generalAirF has a current bill. This object diagram is an illustration of the class diagram shown in Figure 7-7, later in this chapter.

Pure object diagrams are good for showing a simple example of what you mean by a class diagram. We sometimes have one or two pure object diagrams for a software project; they help give managers an idea of what's going on.

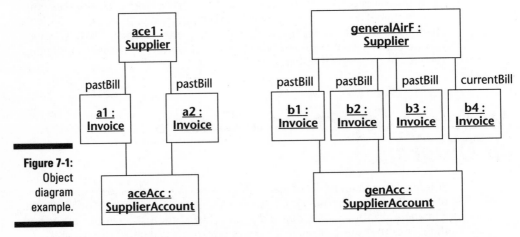

Figure 7-1:
Object
diagram
example.

You can also build a *hybrid class/object diagram*. You'll find this most useful when you want to show your classes — and also show one or two example instances of no more than a few of those classes.

Table 7-1 helps you choose when to use each type of diagram.

Table 7-1	Choosing a Diagram Approach
Diagram Type	*Purpose*
Pure class diagram	Show classes, associations, aggregations, and generalization.
	Arrange classes for code generation in a UML tool.
Pure object diagram	Show management a specific example.
	Consider what instances you have at runtime (also use a communication diagram).
	Describe pre- and postconditions of a piece of behavior (what is true before and after some behavior is performed).
	Show a setup for test runs.
Hybrid class object diagram	Show examples of specific classes that are hard to understand.

Constructing Class Diagrams

Your class diagrams show the fixed structure of classes, objects, attributes, operations, associations, generalizations, and aggregations. (See Chapters 3, 4, 5, and 6 for more on these items.) If you're engaged in a large modeling or development project, building one large class diagram for the whole project isn't helpful — classes get lost, the diagram becomes confusing and difficult to read — break that diagram up into manageable pieces. You want to be consistent in your diagrams as well. A class diagram should have the same time period reflected in each association. (You may also find it helpful to build diagrams that have only instances of classes, but this is rare.)

Drawing manageable class diagrams

We have seen many developers draw impossibly large diagrams using the development notation of the day. Some of these diagrams fill entire walls.

These diagrams can be difficult to understand because the important information was buried in amongst hundreds of unimportant details. To make our diagrams comprehensible we break them up into smaller more understandable pieces.

It's more effective to use a simple process to get more bite-size diagrams. To illustrate this process we use the example of a company that's in the business of selling air-filter units to customers and buying stock from their suppliers. The process is as follows:

1. **Build one top-level diagram with up to 15 key classes.**

   The *top-level diagram* provides developers with an overview of the most important classes. It avoids showing details. The *key classes* are those groups of objects that are most important to your business; they may include classes such as `customer`, `air filter`, and `supplier`.

2. **Build second-level diagrams with one of the key classes in the center of the diagram surrounded by 5 to 10 supporting classes and their association with the key class.**

   Now you choose one of the key classes from the top-level diagram. Add in details showing attributes, operations, other supporting classes, and associations that directly relate to the chosen key class. For example, build a class diagram with `customer` at the center, showing supporting classes such as `coupon`, `customer account`, `credit card`, and `club card`.

3. **If you have a significant aggregation, show the aggregate and its parts on a separate diagram.**

   The class playing the role of the whole (aggregate) should appear on the top-level diagram or on one of the second-level diagrams. For example, you show the air filter and its parts on one diagram.

4. **When you have a significant inheritance hierarchy, place the superclass and its subclasses on a separate diagram.**

   See Chapter 6 for more on inheritance.

   From our running example, you have many types of coupons. On a separate diagram, show the generic coupon as a superclass and the different types of coupons as subclasses.

5. **If any of your second-level diagrams are too complex with more than ten supporting classes, consider creating a third level of class diagrams.**

When you follow this process, you get a hierarchy of class diagrams; each diagram has a specific focus. Stakeholders and users who want a quick overview look at your top-level diagram. Figure 7-2 shows just such a diagram for a simple retail system that handles customer orders. Notice that the top-level diagram just shows the most important classes, without specifying their attributes or operations. The top-level diagram should be simple, without much detail to clutter it up.

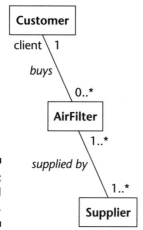

Figure 7-2:
A top-level
diagram.

Each class diagram should have a single major theme — and should have no more than 15 to 20 classes. People have a hard time remembering more than a half-dozen things in their short-term memory. So if you put 20-plus classes in one diagram, most people will find it confusing and difficult to work with. We talk about a top-level diagram followed by a second-level diagram. If a class on the second level also has a lot of supporting classes, you can create third-level diagrams. Try to keep the number of classes on any one diagram below 20 classes.

You see a second-level diagram in Figure 7-3 with the focus on a Customer class. All the classes that relate to Customer are shown. Developers interested in all aspects of Customer turn to this diagram to see the details. Users and developers in a specific area of your business should be able to review the diagrams that focus on their areas of expertise. They should not have to look over every class in your system to find those that interest them.

Notice that the second-level diagram in Figure 7-3 shows details such as the attributes and operations for Customer and all its supporting classes — ClubCard, CreditCard, CustomerAccount, and Coupon. Sometimes we place other top-level classes on a second-level diagram because other developers need to see how the details of a key class fits into the big picture shown in the top-level diagram. For example, the second-level diagram shows the Customer class associated with the AirFilter class so you can understand the context of the customer focus diagram and its relationship to the higher-level diagram. The AirFilter class is shown without attributes and operations. To account for them, we would provide another, second-level diagram with AirFilter at the center, and show its supporting classes.

Figure 7-4 shows you the details of the AirFilter class. This diagram focuses on the internal parts of the air filter. You notice that the diagram isn't cluttered with other classes outside of the AirFilter class.

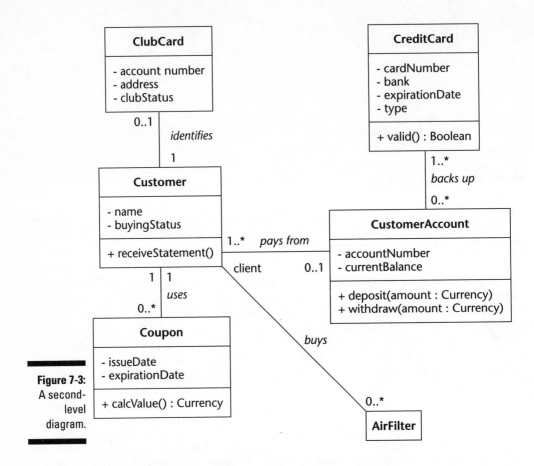

Figure 7-3:
A second-level diagram.

The class diagram in Figure 7-5 gives your developers a way of focusing on an inheritance hierarchy without having to wade through the complexity of other classes and associations.

Keep the following in mind when deciding what to put in a class diagram:

- Don't try to put every class on one diagram.

- Create a top-level diagram with your 5 to 15 key classes.

- Think of each class diagram as having a theme — all the classes in the diagram support that theme.

- Provide second-level diagrams. Each second-level diagram focuses on one or two of the key classes shown in the top-level diagram.

- Create separate class diagrams that show only an aggregate and its parts

- Put inheritance hierarchies into their own class diagrams.

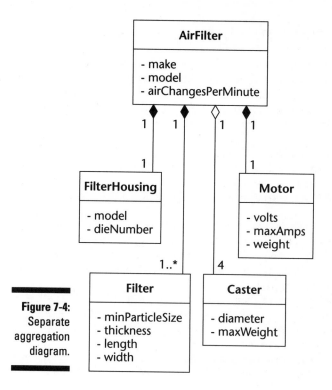

Figure 7-4:
Separate
aggregation
diagram.

Figures 7-2, 7-3, 7-4, and 7-5 begin to capture the language of an air-filter order system. Users of that system understand what a coupon is. They can look at Figure 7-4 and tell you whether you have captured all the different kinds of coupons. These four figures are known as a *domain diagrams* because they describe the domain of ordering air filters in a retail setting.

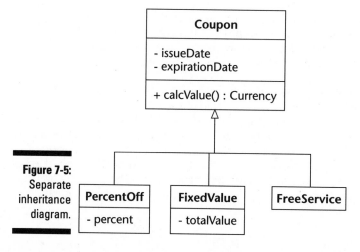

Figure 7-5:
Separate
inheritance
diagram.

Considering time in class diagrams

When you draw a class diagram with its classes and its associations, the diagram is tied to a time period. This sounds odd because of the static nature of these diagrams. But, when you think about the multiplicity of an association you must specify it for some time period. Check your diagram to see that all the multiplicities are for the same time period.

You might create a class diagram with hidden assumptions about time period. All the multiplicities on a class diagram should reflect one time period. If you draw a diagram with more than one time period, you create confusion about what you mean — which leads to poor programming down the road.

Figure 7-6 shows a class diagram with two different time periods, and the multiplicities used in the diagram are tied to that fact. The supplier may or may not send an invoice according to the `sends` association, and to represent that, we have used the `0..1` multiplicity. It's certainly true that a single supplier sends many invoices over a long period of time, say five years. We chose the `0..1` multiplicity because we're focused on a very short time period — today — with a current outstanding invoice that must be paid. The diagram in Figure 7-6 also shows that invoices are paid from a supplier account. It shows that a supplier account pays for zero or more invoices. The `paid from` association also has a time period — for all time or for a very long time period. The `paid from` association isn't focused on just the outstanding invoice from a specific supplier.

The problem with the diagram in Figure 7-6 is that it uses two different time periods. Readers of the diagram would not necessarily catch that — and would become confused. The diagram could be interpreted as meaning that a supplier only ever sends one invoice.

Assign each of your class diagrams a time period. Then check the multiplicity of each association to make sure it conforms to your chosen time period.

If you can't avoid showing different time periods on the same diagram, you can use role names on your associations to help keep the time periods distinct. Create an association for each time period you plan to use, and then add a role name to indicate the time period for that association.

Figure 7-7 shows the two time periods that were hidden in Figure 7-5. The supplier sends an invoice that plays the role of the current bill. We show this with a `sends` association connecting the `Supplier` class with the `Invoice` class and a `currentBill` role name. The supplier is also associated with all past sent invoices. This second association adds the second time period of the past to the diagram. We associate the `Supplier` class with a second association to the `Invoice` class and a `pastBill` role name. The `paid from` association between the `SupplierAccount` class and the `Invoice` class remains unchanged.

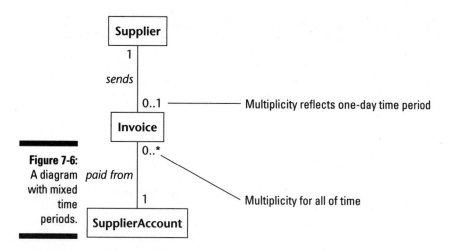

Figure 7-6:
A diagram with mixed time periods.

If you make an assumption about the time period for a class diagram, you should add a comment to the diagram. That way you tell other developers exactly what to expect when reading the multiplicities of the associations between the classes.

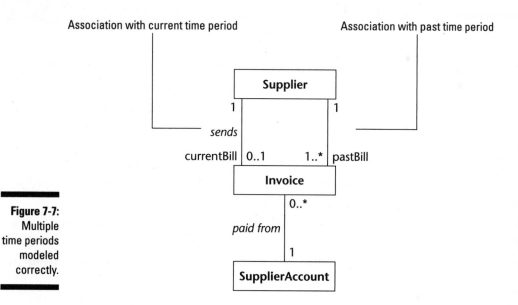

Figure 7-7:
Multiple time periods modeled correctly.

Using Project-Oriented Class Diagrams

Class diagrams are also used to pull together key aspects of your project —
during analysis, and again during design. Accordingly, it can be helpful to
create class diagrams that represent the context of the system, its problem
domain, application requirements, and the design of each subsystem.

Establishing contexts

There are two kinds of context diagrams you show with class diagrams:

- ✔ **External context diagram:** This type of diagram shows a central class
  and the classes to which it's related. An external context diagram doesn't
  show the internals of the central class but instead illustrates the boundaries of the central class.
- ✔ **Internal context diagram:** This type of diagram shows the opposite of
  the external context diagram. You see the internals of a central class but
  none of the externally related classes.

Use external context diagrams to scope your system (to put a boundary
around your system). We use the following steps to se up an external context
diagram for our system:

1. **Create a class and give it the name of the system you're developing.**

   Don't show any attributes or operations on this class.

2. **Think about all the actors and other systems that you expect to interact with your system — and add a class to your diagram for each such
   interactor.**

   These are your external classes.

3. **Draw an association between each interactor and your** system **class.**

4. **Consider the multiplicity of each association.**

   Ask yourself, *How many instances of these actors/systems will my system
   interact with?*

5. **Add an operation to any external class if your system must invoke its
   behavior.**

6. **Add an attribute to any external class if that class must have some
   knowledge important to your system.**

Internal context diagrams allow you to show internal structure. If you have a
complex aggregation, then use this kind of context diagram to show the internal parts of the class. For this diagram, simply inflate the size of the class
box. Place a mini-class diagram where you normally show the attributes of

the inflated class. Figure 7-8 shows just such an internal context diagram for a generic report. See Chapter 5 for a detailed description for showing the internal parts of a class as a strong form of aggregation. For information about context you show using use case diagrams see Chapter 8.

UML 2 has a new diagram called the *composite structure diagram*, discussed in Chapter 5. You use composite structure diagrams to show internal context.

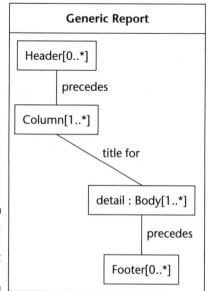

Figure 7-8:
Internal
context
diagram.

Creating domain classes

As you develop your system or software application, you'll notice that you use some classes over and over again. These highly reusable classes are based on the real world and represent things in your business. In our air-filter example, classes such as `Customer`, `AirFilter`, and `Coupon` are found in the business world. When you talk to users, these are the very words they use when discussing their business. We call these words the *domain language* or the *language of the user*. We capture and model this user language for two reasons:

✔ **Reusability:** As a developers, you use domain classes — classes that reflect the domain or language of the user — in several different ways, and each way they are used is known as a *use case*. (For more on use cases, please read Chapter 8.) For example a manager uses the retail order system to track the sales of air filters to customers and to find out which supplier has the best price for air filters. In both cases different parts of your application software will use instances of the same `AirFilter` class. These reusable domain classes become the foundation for many of your applications.

✔ **User verification:** Many of the classes in your software represent things in the real world. It's easier to talk with a user about a problem (and the software you have to build to solve that problem) if your diagram shows classes that are familiar to that user. The user can see the words you have in the diagram and tell you whether it's right or wrong because you have built a diagram that only includes words from their language — words they are familiar with.

As we mention in the section "Drawing manageable class diagrams," Figures 7-2, 7-3, 7-4, and 7-5 begin to capture the language of an air-filter order system. Users of that system understand what a coupon is, and they can look at Figure 7-5 and tell you whether you have captured all the different kinds of coupons. These four figures in this chapter are examples of *domain diagrams* because they describe the domain of ordering air filters in a retail setting. Your classes that capture the language of the user are known as *domain classes.*

Domain class diagrams that capture the user's language are good for the following purposes:

✔ Defining a common vocabulary between the user and the developer

✔ Capturing the most stable classes in your system

✔ Staying the same from application to application

✔ Removing vagueness from the definition of your real world classes

Develop your domain model during the requirements-gathering phase of your project. Capture in domain class diagrams what the user means as they describe what they do. Refine the domain class diagrams when the user talks about what they want your system to do for them. The very nouns the user says become classes or attributes. The verb phrases from the mouth of the user become associations.

Applying an application perspective

There comes a point in your software development when you want to show which classes come together to bring a use case to life. Remember, object-oriented software contains nothing but objects interacting together. The functionality described in a use case arises from this interaction. You need to show which objects interact to make each use case come to life. To show this relationship, use an *application class diagram,* which shows which classes work together to perform the job of a use case. The diagram will include a few classes from your domain diagrams as well as special classes known as application classes. *Application classes* have the attributes and behavior necessary to make your software live up to the description written for a use case.

The following is a list of some application classes that will help you get your project done:

- ✔ **Controller class:** These are classes that manage the interaction between the user and the internal domain classes in your application. Controllers know when to ask a domain class to make the application work. We usually add a controller class for each use case in our applications. The responsibility of this use case controller class is to ensure that user interactions with the system defined in the use case description are done properly, in the right sequence over time.

- ✔ **View class:** A view class has the responsibility to manage the user interface boundary between a person and your application. Users want to see the information or objects in your system in a variety of ways. Each view class knows how to interact with the underlying domain classes to show the user a specific view of those domain classes.

- ✔ **Boundary class:** Boundary classes are similar to view classes because they sit on the boundary between your application and an actor outside your application. Boundary classes interact with other systems, databases, and external devices that interact with your application. For instance, we use boundary classes to separate our application from a database. If any objects within our application require data from a database, they ask a boundary class to go get it for them. That way if the database changes (or the database-access mechanism changes), we only have to change the internal workings of the boundary class. The boundary class hides the complexity of the world outside of my application.

These classes encapsulate the attributes and operations of your application that are "visible" to the user. The controller encapsulates what the user can do and when they can do it for your application. The view classes show things to your users. Boundary classes hide the external interactions of your application from its internal classes.

Figure 7-9 illustrates one of the application class diagrams used in an air-filter order-handling system. The attributes and operations of each class are not shown, making the diagram easier to read. You notice Figure 7-9 actually has two diagrams separated by a thick line. At the top of the figure is a use case diagram showing the review accounts use case. At the bottom of the figure is an application class diagram showing the classes that must perform the `Review Accounts` use case for the `Order Clerk` actor. (An *actor* is a person outside your system that interacts with your system.) The `AccountReviewer` knows when to access the database via the `DatabaseAccessor` to retrieve instances of the `Customer`, `CreditCard`, and `CustomerAccount` classes. The `Account Reviewer` also knows when, at the users request, to create instances of the view classes (`CustomerView`, `CCView`, `AccountView`, and `ComplexAccount View`) and when to ask a view to show itself to the order clerk user.

Notice that we do not draw all the associations between all the classes in Figure 7-9. The `AccountReviewer` controller class has associations with all the view classes because it must create them, but drawing association all of these lines clutters up the diagram and does not add anything surprising for the developer. Another reason why we may not draw the line between the `AccountReviewer` class and the other classes is that associations are often reserved for those situations where one class needs to continually know about another class. The more temporary the knowledge of the other class is, the more likely we don't bother modeling it. When we use a UML modeling tool, we add these extra associations to the diagram just before we ask the modeling tool to generate code.

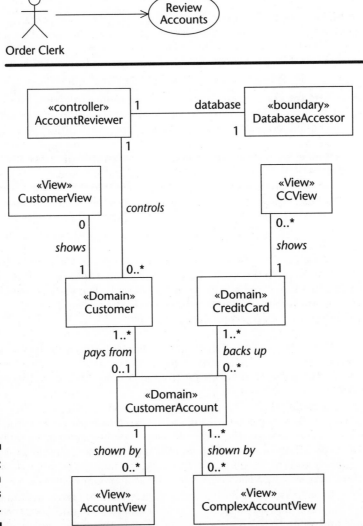

Figure 7-9:
Application
class
diagram.

All you find in object-oriented software is (you guessed it) *objects*. It's the objects — not functions — that get together at runtime, collaborate, send messages to each other, and get the job done. Each use case is realized by a group of cooperating objects. Both application objects and domain objects must work together to get a use case to work.

Wrapping packages

At some point in a project, you may find that the modeling you perform to gather requirements, analyze those requirements, and develop software to meet those requirements is getting out of hand. You probably have different levels of class diagrams as well as domain class diagrams and application class diagrams. You might well be wondering how to keep it all under control. We have faced this same problem many times — and each time we used packages. You can wrap up groups of classes and even groups of diagrams into a UML package.

A *package* is a way of grouping classes together. A UML package looks like a tabbed file folder. You think of the package as containing certain diagrams and/or certain classes. There are several ways of organizing packages for your system:

 ✔ **Development phase:** Create a package for each development phase — for example, Analysis, System Design, and Detailed Design. Place the classes in each package as you find them during each phase. (Classes discovered during analysis go in the Analysis package.)

 ✔ **Diagram type:** Create packages to hold the classes and the major types of class diagram. We mention some of those diagrams in this chapter — and we often create Domain, Application, System, and Subsystem packages. We place domain classes and domain class diagrams into the Domain package.

 ✔ **Version control:** Create packages to represent each version of your system as you develop it. The packages would be named Alpha Version, Beta Version, Release One, and so on. This way all the classes for a particular version are available in one place.

When your development becomes really complex and large, you can put packages inside packages.

To keep track of all those packages, use a *package diagram*. This diagram simply shows the packages as tabbed folders, with the name of each package on the front of each folder. You can also show any dependencies among your packages by showing a dashed line with an arrow at the end of the line up against the package some other package depends on.

The package diagram is now an official diagram in UML 2. In previous version of UML we used a class diagram to show packages and their dependencies because there was not official package diagram separate from the class diagram in the UML modeling tool.

Packages *own* their content. You can't put the same class into two different packages. Place each class in one — and only one — package. You can use the class in other packages, but some package has to own the reused class, and that's the only one it should occupy. See Chapter 20 for more details on organizing classes into different packages.

Figure 7-10 is a package diagram showing some of the packages you might have for the retail air-filter order-handling system. The Review Account, Handle Order, and Setup New Clients packages contain classes and diagrams that are specific to use cases by the same name. The Air Filter Domain package just contains other packages. Finally, the Client, Product, and Vendor packages contain groups of classes that are important to each of those major parts of the user's language.

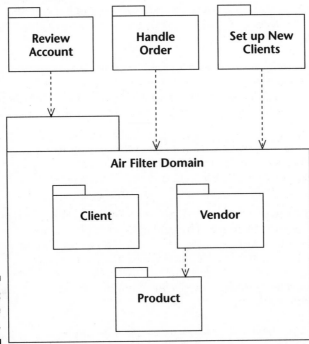

Figure 7-10:
Package
diagram.

Dependencies are also shown here. You see a dependency line from the `Review Account` package to the `Air Filter Domain` package. The `Review Account Package` is dependent on the `Air Filter Domain` package; to review an account, you must also use some of the classes in the `Air Filter Domain` package.

Packages are a great way to group important stuff together so your complex models don't get out of hand.

Part III
The Basics of Use-Case Modeling

The 5th Wave By Rich Tennant

"NIFTY CHART, FRANK, BUT NOT ENTIRELY NECESSARY."

In this part . . .

This part covers some of the most important stuff in software and system development: Who's your system for? What must it do? Why build it in the first place? Here we cover the basic techniques that help you find answers to those questions: *use-case diagrams,* which capture and present how the basic users (called *actors*) call upon the system in their typical situations (called *use cases*). We explain how to document the contents, flow, and alternate courses as the use cases unfold, making the big picture easier to grasp for narrative or specification purposes.

For advanced use-case modeling, we detail the possible relationships — inclusion, extension, and generalization — among multiple use cases, and help you avoid common problems in this tricky area.

If your use cases start to multiply and get unruly, we show how to corral them in packages so they stay manageable. And we offer advice on how use cases can not only help you create a better understanding of your system's goals and requirements (so your stakeholders buy in with minimum fuss), but also benefit the process of design and implementation.

Chapter 8

Introducing Use-Case Diagrams

● ●

In This Chapter

▶ Determining who will use your system

▶ Showing your system's uses in terms of use cases

▶ Indicating system context

▶ Partitioning your system into use-case packages

● ●

*U*ML has lots of pretty pictures and diagrams. Some focus on harnessing the power of object-oriented theory and techniques to analysis and design — and some focus on the meat-and-potatoes of detailed design and construction. In both cases, these diagrams help you accomplish a task or communicate with your peers in your organization.

However, practical development isn't just an internal activity, especially in the current climate of competition and shrinking budgets. If you want to stay in business, you have to capture and understand your customer's requirements and needs, and make a product or system that they want. Use cases and use-case diagrams are the UML features that support the gathering and analysis of user-centric requirements by starting with your users' goals.

Use cases can keep you focused on your users' goals and on producing practical systems that deliver value to your customers, whether they're paying external customers or paying internal customers (those with the money inside your company).

Identifying Your Audience

A *use case* is a particular purpose that a user can actually use the system to accomplish. Use cases achieve their great power primarily by simplicity and organization: When you identify and organize use cases, you can paint a clear picture of what the system has to do. You can show this clear picture to your customers, users, management, and peers — which can help you get invaluable, focused feedback on your ideas for the system early in its process of development.

Consider the stakeholders

Considering the needs of the clients and their customers and workers is a good start, and although the use case's focus on actors does help you consider their needs, it's not enough. We recommend that you also acknowledge the existence of *stakeholders* (the many individuals and organizations that have a vested interest in the success of your project). Every system has a set of these potential stakeholders — individuals or organizations affected by the operation of your system (or who may affect the operation of your system). The stakeholders are the sources of your funding, your requirements, and your opposition. They are your fans and opponents. Even within these groups, subgroups whose opinions matter must be identified.

As an example, if you examine the workers, the stakeholders include those who will use your system and those who have used the previous system. Also, consider those workers whose jobs you automate, change, or eliminate. If you examine your own organization, the different types of developers have their own stakes in the project.

Anyone who cares about the success of your system or who can derail it is a stakeholder. The authorities (legal, regulatory, industry, political, trade, and so on), lobbies, and special-interest groups are also stakeholders.

Are hackers and terrorists also stakeholders, then? After all, they can certainly derail your system. Well, not normally. Some companies do explicitly treat the bad guys as stakeholders — and sometimes even model them as actors — but that's a part of threat analysis. For a normal assessment of stakeholders and their needs, concentrate on identifying individuals, teams, and groups who represent political and economic forces that have legitimate vested interests (stakes) in your system.

During the process of gathering the requirements for your system, you'll be spending most of your time with the actors — but you must consider all the stakeholders. Diagram the actors with their use cases, but examine the stakeholders also. Prioritize them by their potential impact on the system as you evaluate their needs. The more you satisfy your stakeholders' needs, the smoother sailing your system will have, and acceptance and follow-on will be high.

To get an accurate picture of your system's purpose, you must identify whom the system is for (your customer) and who uses the system (the users).

The users and the customers are generally not the same group of people. Even when they *are* the same people, it's beneficial to think of *user* and *customer* as different roles.

- ✔ **Your customers:** Your customers — sometimes called *the clients* — are the people or organizations that ultimately fund and task your team. They must be satisfied for you to get paid. Your team may have a contractual relationship with them (external customers), or they may be part of your own management structure (internal customers). When you're in an in-house development organization, consider your parent organization as your client.

- ✔ **The client's customers:** When you talk about *the customers* (as opposed to *your customers*), you typically are referring to the customers of your client. These are the people or organizations that buy things from your client. If your system doesn't make them happy, your client is unhappy, and that means you're unhappy.

✔ **Users:** When you refer to *users* of a system, they may be your clients' customers, or they may be the *workers* in your client's organization who have a hands-on relationship with the system. Many systems have users of all types — clients, their customers, and their workers. Users get the closest feel for the system — and get the strongest impressions. The tasks of the users are what the system must automate; the needs of the users are what the system has to meet.

UML has a special term for the users, whether they're clients, customers, or workers: *actors*. The actors initiate behaviors in the systems and receive information from the system.

Imagine you're building a hotel registration system to be used by both potential guests from home (via the Internet) and by registration clerks at the hotel when the potential guests phone them. Table 8-1 lists the main stakeholders on this project. (The nearby sidebar "Consider the stakeholders" provides more information on stakeholders.) In the table, Potential Guest appears as twice as a stakeholder — once in the role of customer (when the actor is Registration Clerk), and once as an actor who uses the system directly via the Internet. Such duplication happens often when there are optional intermediary workers (such as Registration Clerk).

Table 8-1	Main Stakeholders
Stakeholder Group	*Example*
Client	Hotel Chain
Customer	Potential Guest
Actor (Worker)	Registration Clerk
Actor (Customer)	Potential Guest

Casting the System's Actors

It's easy to start identifying the main groups of actors (refer to Table 8-1) by taking a high-level view of the workers and customers who *act* as end-users. Evaluate these main actors to see if there are subdivisions with special privileges and capabilities. For example, in the hotel registration system, special types of Potential Guests represent large parties for conferences or affairs — typically they want to reserve blocks of rooms at a special price, and may also be reserving other hotel facilities. These Event Organizers are another type of actor for this particular system. Identifying these subgroups helps you construct an evolving list of actors for your system.

Many systems have paired sets of actors. For every *customer* actor type, (for example) there is often a parallel *worker* actor type. The system allows the customer-actor to work directly with the system or through a worker-actor intermediary — which gives you *two* actors with paired roles. You might be able to treat both actors as only *one* actor if their user interface is identical (as it would be when their privileges are exactly the same) — but typically these paired actors use the system in different ways. In the hotel registration system, the customer-actors of Potential Guest and Event Organizer have paired worker-actors of Registration Clerk and Event Consultant.

When classifying actors, you have to consider all sources of input to the system. For example, a system typically needs input to define the evolving configurations. In the Registration system, someone — perhaps the Hotel Manager — must define configurations for the rooms, their prices, checkout policies, and the like.

Finding nonhuman actors

In UML, human end-users aren't the only actors in the system. The term *actor* also includes everything that passes information or events directly to or from the system. Such actors include other systems/subsystems, other databases, hardware, and devices.

Incorporating system and database actors

You have to consider these nonhumans as actors even though they aren't stakeholders — or (really) users of the system — for several reasons. Each external system that interacts with your system has its own stakeholders and actors. By modeling the external system as an actor, you capture it as a *proxy* — a symbol for the collected goals and requirements of these stakeholders and actors. The Hotel Reservation system must deal with an external Credit Card Authorization system. The Credit Card Authorization system, considered as an actor, works for you as a proxy for its clients, customers, and workers. Another such actor might be an external database (such as external Frequent Traveler database).

Ignoring internal components (databases and systems)

When considering databases and other systems, you should only consider and model the external ones as actors. If they're an internal part of your own system, you can just leave them off the diagram.

Adding an internal component to the list of actors doesn't really add any value, because that component's clients, customer, and workers are just a subset of your own system's actors — not a source of *new* requirements or information. Even so, don't just ignore the internal components; be sure to check whether any of them qualify as actors that must be added to your total list of actors.

Telling internal databases from external databases

If a database is external, it should be modeled as an actor; if it's an internal component, then it shouldn't be modeled as an actor. Sometimes it's hard to tell whether a database is external or internal; you have to look at the list of clients, customers, and workers who deal with the database. If the actors for the database are vastly different from the other actors of your system, don't add them to your list; instead, treat the entire database as an external actor. If the actors for the database are mostly the same as your actors, then you probably have control over the database — and you can probably treat it as an internal component without flinching. For another way of looking at this criterion, consider that the more you think of a system component as under your control and design, the more likely it is to be internal. If you think of it as outside your control, then it's most likely external, and best modeled as an actor.

Incorporating device actors

Input and output devices must also be considered potential actors:

- **Input Devices:** Input devices (sometimes called sensors) have to be considered because they report on some condition or events in the outside world. A sensor typically serves in one of two roles:

  - **Proxy for the causer of the events:** For example, a TV remote control acts upon the TV system to change the channel as an agent of the person using the remote control.

  - **Proxy for the setter of the sensor threshold:** For example a thermostat in a refrigeration system. It reports when the temperature increases over a preset level. The thermostat is an actor because it acts for the person(s) who set the temperature threshold.

- **Output Devices:** You should consider *output devices* because (by definition) they produce an effect or output for some stakeholder to use, or to comply with a stakeholder's wishes. The compressor in a refrigeration system (for example) is an actor because it acts upon the system's contents to satisfy the wishes of the person who wants the contents cold.

Consider the card reader in an ATM system. It reads the card to get identity and account data of the patron. As such, it acts for the person as a way of getting his or her data into the system — therefore it should be considered an actor. The display in an ATM system is an actor for much the same reason because it outputs data to the user. When the whole unit is essentially one device, you can combine the card reader, display, keyboard, and so on into one (complex) actor for your system.

Ignoring transparent actors

Don't treat *all* sensors and devices as actors. Most devices are so ubiquitous that you deal with them transparently. Consider the standard keyboard, display screen, and computer mouse. These hardware elements can often just pass data or events from your system to its actors so easily that you consider its direct actions as your own. Standard computer hardware provides examples of internal design elements that are so well understood or easy to use that you need not (typically) consider them as sources of system requirements. They are *transparent* to the system.

Incorporating clock actors

An actor starts every thread of activity in your system. To complete the identification of the actors, you may have to include a device — in this case, a clock — as an actor to initiate internal scheduled activities. The clock-actor stands in for the stakeholder who scheduled the activities. In the Hotel Reservation system, the Clock automatically cancels room reservations if the Guest hasn't arrived by some cutoff time.

Identifying the roles of the actors

As you look for actors for your system, consider that an actor isn't a specific person, but rather, a role in which a person may act. Don't use individuals' names. (They may be stars, but from the system's viewpoint, they're only instances of roles.) Individuals often serve as different actors, depending on what part of the job they're doing. The same person may act as a Registration Clerk and then later as an Event Consultant, depending on the job flow.

Also, consider that job titles alone may not be sufficient to distinguish actors. A particular job title such as *hotel manager* may encompass several separate roles — you may have to define several actors, one for each role. In your diagram, reserve the *actor* Hotel Manager for the role that only a hotel manager can play.

One way you may try to distinguish the different roles an employee may play is to construct a class diagram around the employee, where each employee is considered a class. (Class diagrams with roles are discussed in Chapter 4.) If there are several different relationships (associations) connecting the employee to the other system elements, then there is a separate role for each association the employee participates in. Usually each of these roles would be a separate actor. You can see an example in Figure 8-1, where an employee with the job title of Hotel Desk Clerk acts in at least two roles — Reservation Clerk and Check-In Clerk — and these are the true actors of the system.

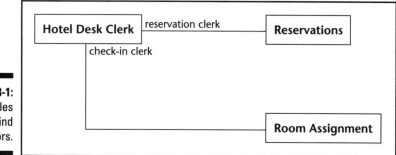

Figure 8-1:
Using roles
to find
actors.

Naming the actors

Actors are very much like classes, so you should use nouns to name your actors. Generally, the names of human actors should be singular-agent nouns formed from an active verb. In English, many of these end in *-er* or *-ant,* though they may end in *-or, -ee,* or *-ar* (Customer, Organizer, Consultant, Debtor, Professor, Employee, Registrar). Be sure to examine the role names that come from association roles in the class diagram (as discussed in Chapter 4). These often contribute such standard names as Reservation Clerk, Check-In Clerk, Guest, Student, or Patron, which identify specific types of relationships between actor and system. If an employee who has a particular job title acts in only one role, you can use the job title as the actor's name.

When naming the nonhuman actors, you can use the name of the role that the hardware or external system performs relative to your target system. Or, you may find it convenient to use the given name of the system to simplify identification. For example, if there is an external system to authorize the potential guests' credit cards, it is acting in the role of CreditCardAuthorizer, and that's not a bad name for it as an actor. But if it's already well known by a specific name such as *credit card authorization system,* then that might be a better name for the actor.

Exposing an Actor's Roles

Actors are not shy; they have to be shown to their public if you want to get their value. Within UML, the notation for an actor is traditionally a stick figure, as you can see on the left of Figure 8-2. You can also use a class box (as shown on the right of Figure 8-2) to indicate an actor — you label the box with the string «Actor». This is called *stereotyping,* and each « and » mark is a *guillemet.* You may use double angle brackets (<< and >>) if you're typographically challenged (as are many UML tool vendors). Stereotyping is the common UML way of distinguishing similarly drawn figures of different types.

The box form for an actor is similar to a class box (discussed in Chapter 3), but actors and classes are treated differently — and the stereotype «Actor» helps you recognize which is which.

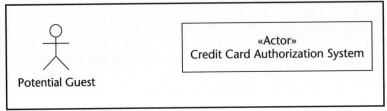

Figure 8-2:
Exposing
actors on
diagrams.

Potential Guest

«Actor»
Credit Card Authorization System

We recommend using the stick figure form for all the human actors and the box class box form for non-human actors (other systems, databases, and devices). This little visual convention will help you distinguish them quickly.

Sometimes you'll find it possible to generalize your actors — especially when an *"is-a" relationship* ("*x* is a *y*") exists among some actors. You can use the UML generalization notation to capture this relationship. You may also find this same type of relationship among classes. (Chapter 6 discusses the generalization relationship.)

Figure 8-3 shows an example of generalized actors. In this case, we started with looking at the actors, `Potential Guest`, and `Frequent Traveler`. We recognized that some of the essential activities of each could be generalized as those of a `Reserver`, as they both make reservations. As we feel that a `Potential Guest` "is a" `Reserver` and a `Frequent Traveler` "is a" `Reserver`, we use the generalization symbol to reflect the relationship.

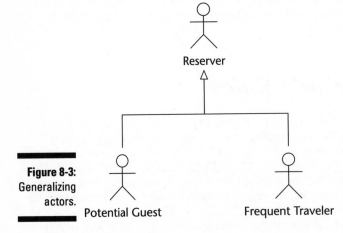

Figure 8-3:
Generalizing
actors.

Reserver

Potential Guest

Frequent Traveler

Showing Your System's Use Cases

Finding and categorizing the stakeholders and identifying the actors will certainly help you determine the sources of requirements for your system and help you get critical feedback early. However, to get full value from UML use-case diagrams you have to show how the actors use the system. Each distinct use of the system — or purpose for which the system can be put to use — is called a *use case*. Each use case must be initiated by some actor, whether human user, device, clock, or other system.

Defining use cases based on actors and goals

Put yourself in the place of each actor in turn. Consider the goals that each human actor has when using the system. Determine the job the actor performs while using the system you're developing. You need to recognize and understand how your system helps the actor meet job goals or personal goals. If using the system returns some observable or measurable value to the actor that moves the actor toward the goal, then that use is a good candidate for a use case. For example, making a reservation returns a reservation to the actor; checking in returns a room assignment and a key; checking out returns an end-of-room assignment and a bill. For the non-human actors, consider the goals the actor's stakeholders have when it initiated interaction with your system.

All actor-and-system interactions are part of some use case. For each set of interactions with the system, examine the goals or purposes of the initiating actor, sometimes called the *primary actor*. If more than one actor participates in the use case, then the actor who starts the behavior (or contacts the system) is the primary actor. The system contacts other actors as it attempts to meet the primary actor's goals. You can call these other actors the *secondary actors*. Often an actor may be primary for one use case and secondary for another.

Illustrating use cases

UML has a simple way of indicating the relationships between actors and their use cases. You draw a line from each actor to each use case he or she (or it) participates in. (An example of a use-case diagram appears in Figure 8-4.)

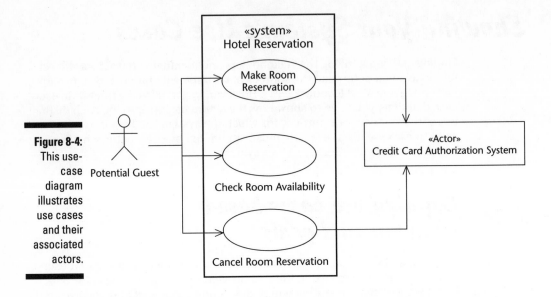

Figure 8-4:
This use-
case
diagram
illustrates
use cases
and their
associated
actors.

Show the use case by drawing an oval, which is UML notation for a use case (and other such behaviors). The name of the use case is supposed to be placed inside the oval, but this is rarely seen. Some tool vendors find it difficult to redraw diagrams when the text is inside the oval, so they put the use-case name on the outside, near the bottom of the oval. UML accepts either location for the name. Our Figure 8-4 shows both ways of drawing use cases.

If there are multiple actors participating in a use case, it's sometimes convenient to show who is in charge and who is just along for the ride. We recommend that you indicate the actor who initiates a use case — the primary actor — by drawing an arrow from the actor to the use case. Other actors, who might just participate in the use case, you show as the targets of arrows that start at the use case. We demonstrate this convention in Figure 8-4.

When you draw the use case yourself by hand, you'll find it easy to put the name inside the use-case oval if you remember the simple rule for using your hand as a UML tool: *Draw the words first, and then draw the container.* If you draw the oval first, the name will rarely fit inside.

Showing multiplicity with actors and use cases

In many of your systems, the concurrency of each use case is useful to capture. The concurrency of a use case is the number of instances of the use case that the actor can communicate with at the same time. You can use the multiplicity value (see Chapter 4 for the complete details of how multiplicity is indicated) to show concurrency as well. If an actor can participate in more than one running of a particular use case — at the same time — then the multiplicity of the use case should be 0..*. In the normal situation (one-at-a-time participation), you can use 0..1 as the multiplicity, or just don't bother to indicate it. In Figure 8-5, we show that the Credit Card Authorization System can work with many instances of the Make Room Reservation running at the same time, but a Potential Guest can only try one Make Room Reservation with our system at a time.

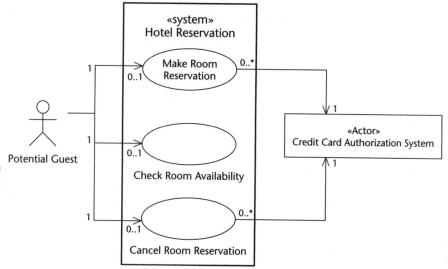

Figure 8-5:
A use-case diagram with multiplicity.

Don't get too confused over arrowheads or multiplicity. The lines from the actors to the use cases can be adorned in many ways, all of which are optional. All you need is the basic core line to indicate that the actor participates in the use case. If a use case has only one actor, it's obviously the initiating actor. If there is more than one actor, you can distinguish this *primary actor* by showing that it initiates the use case (do so by making the arrowhead point to the use case). You can also try the convention that places the primary actors on the left of the diagram and *secondary* (non-initiating) actors on the right. Of course, you can use both conventions on the same diagram.

Defining a good use case

A use case is an actor-initiated, complete, system behavior that brings value to the actor. Sometimes it may be difficult to identify the set of use cases that our system offers. The following list provides several helpful hints for defining a good use case:

✔ **Choose a good name:** A use case is a behavior, so you should name it with a verb phrase. To make it more precise, you should add a noun to the name to indicate the class of objects that the action effects. To help you choose the verb-noun phrase for the use case name, going back to the class diagrams that helped you find the actors (see Figure 8-1) may help identify the objects and the associations created by the use cases. Look at a possible good name for your use case, by examining the name of the relationships of the actor to the system's objects.

✔ **Illustrate a complete behavior:** A use case must be a complete behavior that starts with the initiating event from the primary actor and ends with the actor normally reaching his/her goal. If a proposed use case is only a step along the way to the goal, don't treat it as a use case unless you can consider it a goal in itself. For example, `Specify the Bed Size` (such as *king, queen,* or *double*) is an activity that you have to perform to reserve a room — but it's only a *part* of the `Make a Room Reservation` use case because it never really stands alone and doesn't (by itself) return a useful result. It's not really a goal for the actor to use the system. However, you may consider `Check Room Availability` important enough to be a use case. It returns a value and could stand alone.

✔ **Identify a completable behavior:** To achieve a goal and produce value for an actor, the use case must complete. When you name the use case, choose a verb phrase form that implies completion or ending. For example, use `Reserve a Room`, rather than `Reserving a Room`, because the *"ing"* describes an ongoing behavior.

✔ **Provide "inverse" use cases:** Whenever you see a use case that accomplishes a goal that is to change a state in the system, you probably need a use case to *un*-accomplish that goal. For example, the use case `Make a Room Reservation` is undone with `Cancel Room Reservation`. Use cases that just obtain information don't need an undo. (For example, you don't need an undo for `Check Room Availability`.)

✔ **Limit each use case to one behavior:** Sometimes you might be tempted to have a use case achieve more than one goal or do more than one activity. To avoid confusion, keep the use case focused on only one thing. For example, the potential use case `Check-in and Check-out` is unfocused; it attempts to describe two different behaviors. If a proposed use-case name has an *and* or an *or* in the name, it's probably too unfocused to be one activity.

✔ **Represent the actor's point of view:** Write the use case from the actor's point of view, *using the terminology of the actor,* not that of the system. Doing so allows the actors to review their use case properly without having to learn your system's terminology. In addition, it helps keep you and your team learning — and using — your *user's* terminology, making you more responsive to their needs. For example, you would allow a `Guest` to use the system to help `Reserve a Room` (using common `Guest` terminology), but you would not name that use case `Schedule Room Assignment`, because that's a Hotel's terminology and not the Guest's.

One hint that can help you find good names for your use cases is to put the name in the conversational words of a typical actor — for example, "System, please help me to *<verb> <noun> <phrase>*." When you use this form, you automatically force the use-case name to adopt the actor's point of view.

Distinguishing between Internal and External

Taken together, the use cases of your system cover all the services that your system offers to the totally of actors. Every service, every behavior, every interaction with the outside world must be covered. You may enclose all the system's use cases in a box (representing the entire system) if you want to emphasize that your system is what's offering these services. Label this box with the name of the system under construction (refer to Figures 8-4 and 8-5). Of course, this box is optional — and not all tools support this kind of notation — but it will help make the ownership of use cases clearer (at least it helps when the use cases can fit in the box).

Documenting use-case levels

Though it's (technically) optional to do so, you should also stereotype the box in which you're offering the use cases as «system». Other entities (such as subsystems or even classes) can offer use cases within UML, so using the stereotypes can help the reader understand who is offering these use cases as services.

We also recommend the use of «business» or «enterprise» when you want your use cases to be offered by the entire business, whether they're automated or not. Depending on your methodology — and the size of the system you're building — you may need «business», «system», «subsystem», «class», and even «component» stereotypes to identify different levels of use-case diagrams. Doing so helps you understand, explore, develop, and document your system — one iteration at a time.

When you do document your use cases at the «business» level, don't consider the internal workers of your system as actors. Instead, consider them internal parts of your business system — essentially transparent. You ignore the workers at the business level because your model should assume they're internal entities — under your complete control, like a database or other internal subsystem. (You can read more about this approach in the section on "Defining a good use case," earlier in this chapter.) Similarly, when you're diagramming at a business level you should ignore "transparent" devices (discussed earlier); instead, indicate the ultimate actors that use those devices.

For that matter, ignore *all* internal subsystems when you're showing use cases at the «system» level. You can — provided you're building a large enough system — decompose the system into several interacting subsystems. Then you can find use cases for each subsystem, each with its own use-case diagram (focused on itself). From the point of view of the subsystem, its actors are the other interactive subsystems of the system — including (if the subsystem interacts with the outside world) one or more actors of the system as a whole. Figure 8-6 shows an example of use-case levels.

Treating people as design elements

If you model the Hotel as a Business, the registration clerks and other employees show up in the model as internal design elements. Perhaps you could automate their jobs completely. Consider the recent trends in libraries and supermarkets; it's now possible to check out your own books and check out your own groceries. *From the model's point of view,* clerks or cashiers are designable elements, not actors; in effect, the business doesn't exist for the employees; the employees exist for the system.

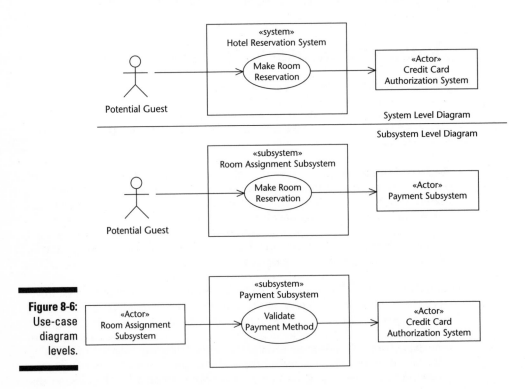

Figure 8-6:
Use-case
diagram
levels.

Using Context Diagrams

Use-case diagrams are very powerful, but in most systems, the number of use cases you have will be larger than you can conveniently show on one diagram. A popular form of the use-case diagram may help summarize the interaction of actors with the system. This diagram is called a *top-level use-case diagram,* but as it's very similar to a type of diagram that predates UML; often you'll see it called by its traditional name: *context diagram.* This type of diagram, shown in Figure 8-7, displays the system of interest and all its actors — but it hides the use cases themselves.

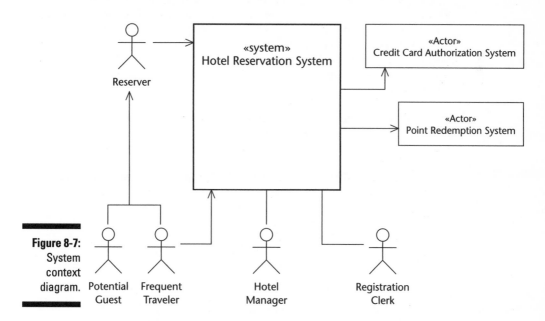

Figure 8-7: System context diagram.

When you draw these context diagrams, you don't have to worry about the arrows. If an actor is always the initiator in all its use cases, you can have the arrow pointing to the system. If an actor is never the initiator, you can have the system pointing to the actor.

You can draw these context diagrams right after you identify the actors — and before you take a crack at the use cases — so a good guess is probably sufficient. To be safe, don't use the arrowheads if you're not sure.

As with the regular use-case diagrams, context diagrams can be subdivided into levels. To minimize confusion, focus your diagram on the subsystem, component, or class of interest — and use stereotypes to indicate what the diagram elements are doing.

Packaging Use Cases

Context diagrams are popular because they can show the entire picture at one shot. In complicated systems, you couldn't show all use cases on one diagram anyway. Therefore, what you want to do is to produce a use-case diagram for each initiating (primary) actor. If you make the actor names on the context diagram into hyperlinks, then your context diagram becomes a graphic table-of-contents that refers to a set of use-case diagrams.

This organizational structure is probably the most efficient for you anyway. If you produce artifacts based on the use-case structure, you'll want to organize them actor-by-actor so the actor community can review the diagrams more easily. The real-world actors (supervisory personnel, for example) can give you focused feedback and input if they can narrow their view — which means looking only at their own sections. This approach works for identifying requirements, as well as for the stages of analysis, design, implementation, and delivery.

When you use this approach to structure part of your system, you put your initiating actor and its use cases in a separate package. (You can find more about using packages in Chapter 7.) A *use-case package* has an optional, special icon (a tabbed folder with an oval in the center) that you might want to use (as shown in Figure 8-8). Although use cases themselves are behaviors — which you name with verb phrases — use-case *packages* are *things,* so you name them with noun phrases. We recommend creating a package called `Actor Uses` for each primary actor you can name. If you find that you have too many use cases within a single package, you can make lower-level packages. In fact, you may need several levels of packages if you're planning a large system.

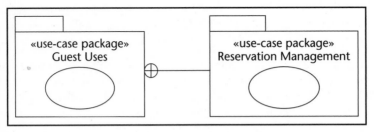

Figure 8-8:
Gathering use cases into packages.

«use-case package»
Guest Uses

«use-case package»
Reservation Management

Chapter 9

Defining the Inside of a Use Case

In This Chapter

▶ Describing the use case's theme and plot

▶ Narrating the use-case story

▶ Pouring use-case flows into tables

▶ Showing alternative flows

Simple UML use-case diagrams clarify how you expect your system to satisfy the needs of its actors. That's fine, as far as it goes. Identifying or naming the services your system offers is often a good start — but more details of the use case are needed before you can get on with development. This chapter lays out some common approaches to defining the inside of a use case.

Creating a Use-Case Specification

A use case is one way of using the system. You identify the actors (the users of the system) and their use cases — placing them on a use-case diagram — in order to understand and organize your thoughts about the system, and as a useful way to organize the system's requirements, analysis, design, and potential artifacts (documents, diagrams, and so on).

You can also consider a use case as a behavior that the system offers to the actors to help meet the actors' goals. (For more on identifying actors and their use cases, and drawing them in use-case diagrams, see Chapter 8.)

UML tells you to draw use cases as named ovals, and to connect them to their actors (stick figures and boxes), but it doesn't say much about how to supply details of how the system performs behaviors needed to meet the actors' goals. Though use-case diagrams are helpful, without more information on how the system is to do this work, your development effort will stall.

So you have to supply information on how the use case is to work — and put that information somewhere. Where? Somewhere close by and available when you need it, but not anywhere that clutters up the simplicity and effectiveness of your use-case diagrams. Figuratively we place these details *inside* the use case — not on the diagram, but behind the scenes. Often a textual document or form is the place to put these details; it may be reached (perhaps by hyper-linking) easily from the use-case oval.

This set of needed details placed inside a use case is sometimes called the *use-case specification* because you use it to *specify* (spell out in detail) how the system behaves when triggered by actors to meet their goal(s). (The format of the specification isn't standardized in the industry — each development organization develops or modifies its own standard — but we've based the discussion that follows on the common features of the most popular approaches.)

Filling in this specification isn't difficult if you step through the following tasks:

1. **Identify and name your use case.**

   See Chapter 8 for more on this process.

2. **Draw a diagram indicating the use case, as well as its primary (triggering) and secondary actors.**

   See Chapter 8 for more on drawing use-case diagrams.

3. **Describe the use case briefly.**

   Give a sentence outlining the purpose of the use case.

4. **Narrate the story of what happens in this use case.**

   The use-case narration should be a written story. Usually it starts with the phrase, "This use case starts when the actor *<does something>* . . ." and then describes what the actor and system do in the normal course of events. Often this description takes the form of alternating steps: The actor does this, and then the system does that, and so on, until the story ends with: "This use case ends when the system *<does something>* and *<the actor's goal> <is satisfied>*." If there are some major plot variations to the story (that is, alternate paths the use case might take), you should include them in the narration as well. You don't have to be exhaustively complete — and certainly don't be formal. Go for a few paragraphs that get the idea across.

5. **Describe the main course (sometimes called the *main flow*) of events in your use case.**

   When you and your customers are satisfied with your narration, you can take the main story — the typical interchange of events — and capture this *flow of events* (what the actor does and then what the system does, and so forth) more formally. Later in this chapter, we give various popular techniques for capturing a flow of events.

6. **Define appropriate pre- and postconditions for this flow of events.**

   As part of making the flow of events more formal and precise, we specify the conditions that must be true to enable this version of the story to occur — the *preconditions*. We also specify the conditions that will be true after this flow of events finishes — the *postconditions*.

7. **Identify alternative, error, and exception scenarios.**

   Now we look at the alternate plot lines we indicated in the narration. We identify all the alternative paths, possible errors (and their consequences), and exceptional situations that the use case might encounter.

8. **Describe each scenario's alternative course with a flow of events, adding pre- and postconditions.**

   Using the same techniques used in Step 5 (to describe the flow of events for the main course), describe each alternate course identified in Step 7. Then identify the pre- and postconditions, as in Step 6.

9. **Add to the use case any requirements that must be obeyed, or any implementation notes.**

   Document any usual business rules and data validations that the use case must enforce. Capture any guidelines on design and implementation that might be helpful.

Remember, every use case must have a specification constructed. How much of the specification you ought to fill out depends on the formality of your project and where you are in your project.

Telling the Use-Case Story

In Chapter 8, we give a basic definition of a use case as an actor-initiated, complete, system behavior that brings value to the actor. Chapter 8 also presents some techniques to help you find and identify these use cases, culminating in naming your use cases and placing them on use-case diagrams, as shown in Figure 9-1. However, just naming the behavior does not tell the whole story; you need more.

Figure 9-1:
A use-case diagram for the use case Make Room Reservation.

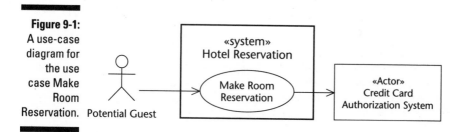

All approaches to defining a use case's behaviors are more or less the same as detailing how the system responds to actor-initiated triggers — and ultimately delivers the value back to the actor. That plot and theme bind the use case together.

Describing the use case

The simplest way to describe a use case (and normally the first one tried) is to identify the theme of the use case in a simple sentence or two — the *use-case description*. Given the use case `Make Room Reservation`, you might describe the plot and theme as follows:

> **Use-case name:** `Make Room Reservation`
>
> **Description:** The actor `Potential Guest` uses a Web browser to specify desired room features and dates, in order to obtain from the system a confirmed room reservation.

The use-case description you write is, in essence, a simple synopsis or abstract of the use-case story. It explains the goals, plot, and theme of the use case when just the use-case name will not. But, it is not the full story; an abstract needs a body. An abstract may stand for the body under some circumstances. As with any abstract, the use-case description may stand in lieu of the use-case story when there is no room for the full version — or during iterative development (before the full story has been written) — but the full story must also be done.

Use cases are not just descriptions

While there are many templates and guidelines that give overall good sample formats of the use-case description, they often suggest a simple miswording that may lead you down the wrong path. You may see samples that start something like, "This use case describes how the system . . . ."

This leads you to think that a use case is a document as it *describes* a behavior. I believe that this is confusing on several levels. In a typical iterative development, you have several different documents that describe the same use case — each made at a different level of detail. The documents describe the use case; they are not the use case itself.

This simple confusion between the *use case* itself and the *use-case description* sometimes leads to a more fundamental error. Use cases are primarily artifacts of analysis and discovery. By looking at your system, you can discover or uncover the existing use cases — the ones that are there whether you notice them or not. However, when you talk about them as documents or descriptions, they may lead you to think that use cases are artifacts of design, subject to the arbitrariness of ingenuity and creativity and convenience, and that any use-case arrangement will suffice. A word to the wise: While there is certainly room for leeway in naming and organizing your use cases, it doesn't justify *sloppy* use cases.

Recounting the use-case narrative

You have many choices and techniques to capture the full behavior of the use cases. Most developers use a combination of approaches to show all the aspects of the required behavior in the use case, and do so incrementally, starting with less formal textual approaches and iteratively use more formal specification approaches. You can choose a mix of formal statements-of-requirements (such as, "The system *shall* provide the capability to reserve rooms up to one month in duration") or employ UML functional modeling techniques (such as the interaction diagrams and textual behavioral specifications outlined in Chapter 11).

The level of formality you stop at depends on the level of formality that your development needs or wants. Not every organization needs the full treatment (which can, after all, be time-consuming).

The most basic approach you can take to capture the use-case behavior is a narrative paragraph form where you describe the interaction between the actor and the system as if it were a story.

First, identify the actor's triggering behavior, and then describe the system's response. Repeat this for every future action by the actor and follow it by the system's response. Describe alternatives or exceptions as they can occur, though significant variations can be described in other paragraphs. End the narrative when the actor achieves his/her goal.

Separating analysis from design

Most developers use use cases as artifacts of analysis. Use cases should be used to specify the required behaviors of your system not to capture design of your system. Design decisions change often; implementations change even oftener. By separating the requirements from the design, you allow the use cases to be a stable definition of what your system must do to be successful. They become part of your agreement with your stakeholders — that if you produce a system that delivers these use cases, they will be happy (and pay for it). You can then do whatever you want to design and implement the system — knowing that if you make the use case *work,* you're okay. Putting design details in the use case, however, means that if you change your mind about the design, you have to change the use case — and go back to your stakeholders for approval.

Separating analysis from design also frees your test team to start developing their test plans directly from the use cases — knowing that the use case will be (relatively) stable, knowing that they will be able to test the functionality of the system directly from the use case.

To concentrate on the required visible, testable behavior of the system, we recommend you follow these guidelines in your use cases:

- Tell *what* happens and *when*, but ignore the *how.*

- Use the actor's terminology and perspective.

- Don't describe any internal workings of the system, unless they are ultimately visible to an actor. Treat the system as a black box whose inside is hidden.

- Cover the major alternatives, exceptions, and looping in activity of the interaction with the actor and system.

- Start with "This use case starts with the actor performs X," where X is the triggering action.

- End with "This use case ends when the actor is satisfied with the behavior of the system or is unable to continue."

You should have the goal to describe the required behavior of the system without saying *how* it is to be done, as in the following use-case narration:

Use-case name: Make Room Reservation

Description: This use case allows the actor, Potential Guest, to use a Web browser to specify the desired room features and dates and to obtain from the system a confirmed room reservation.

Narration: This use starts when the actor, Potential Guest, visits the opening Web page. The system responds by prompting for the span of reservation days and the room type. The actor identifies the type of room that is desired (bed size, is-smoking allowed) and the desired reservation day span. The system validates the inputs and prompts for re-entry if incorrect. The system then checks to see if a room matching the actors request is available during the day span specified and returns this to the actor. If several different classes of rooms are available, they are all returned to the actor. If none match the actor's criteria, the actor may re-specify or may exit the use case. If one or more rooms meet the actor's criteria, the actor selects the room desired. The system prompts for payment information. The actor supplies name, billing address, credit card number, and expiration date. The system contacts the other actor, Credit Card Authorization System, to validate the credit card and available credit. If the credit card transaction is rejected, the System informs the Potential Guest, who may then change the card or cancel the use case. If the credit card transaction is accepted, the System marks the room as reserved over this time period to prevent subsequent reservations, calculate a unique reservation number, and informs the Potential Guest. The use case ends when the actor reviews the successful reservation and leaves the System. If the actor cancels before submitting acceptable credit card information, the use case ends without a successful reservation.

This narration form is often the first approach used to specify the behavior of a use case. However, many ultimately prefer an approach that breaks the flow of events into individual numbered actions so that they are easier to see and refer to when necessary. A typical approach that works this way is called the *use-case flow of events*. This approach allows you to clarify whether an event is actor- or system-initiated, using indentation or numbering. The top-level statements describe the actions that the actor performs. The indented, lower-level statements describe the responses of the system. The following is a partial example of this technique:

Use-case name: Make Room Reservation

Description: This use case allows the actor, Potential Guest, to use a Web browser to specify the desired room features and dates and to obtain from the system a confirmed room reservation.

Main course:

1. This use case starts when the actor visits the opening Web page.

    1.1. The System prompts for the span of reservation days and room type.

2. The actor identifies type of room (bed size and smoking or non-smoking) and reservation day span.

    2.1. The System validates inputs.

    2.2. The System determines available matching room classes.

    2.3. For each available room class, the System determines reservation costs.

    2.4. The System displays possible reservations.

    2.5. The System prompts for actor selection.

3. The actor identifies type of room (bed size and smoking or non-smoking) and reservation day span.

    3.1. . . .

We generally recommend writing the narration first — and having that reviewed by your stakeholders before you construct the flow of events. Afterward you may be able to discard the narration.

One important consideration using this flow of events approach is that a flow captures only one path throughout the system. As you use the numbering and indentation to convey order and initiator, they are not available to you to indicate looping or decision. Therefore, when using the flow of events approach to documenting a use case, you will need to use multiple different flows or courses to document the entire use case. You start with documenting the *main course.* This is the course of events that is the most common and straightforward approach to achieve the actor's goals with the use case. (You may also hear the main course called the *main flow* or *main path* through the use case.)

Setting pre- and postconditions

Most use case specification templates will ask you to supply pre- and post-conditions for the course of events. The *preconditions* specify the state of the world that must hold before the course can be triggered. The *postconditions* specify the state of the world the will hold after the course has been success-fully completed.

When documenting the main course of most use cases, we have found that the preconditions are often simple as they just tell where the actor must be to start the use case. Likewise, the postconditions of the main course may also be simple if they are just statements that the actor's goals have been reached. However, sometime the conditions can be very complex, especially when describing the conditions for alternate or error flows. You can see some examples of not-too-complex pre- and postconditions in the section "Indicating Alternative Courses of Behavior."

We normally use natural language statements to capture constraints on the world, but we often find it useful to be more formal if the English could be ambiguous. In these circumstances, you might use Object Constraint Language (OCL) to indicate formal relationships among objects and attributes from the domain model. (You can find more about using OCL in Chapter 11.) For even more clarity, you may consider drawing object diagrams. We discuss these diagrams as the underpinning of collaboration diagrams in Chapter 14.

Avoid the Happy Path

Occasionally people will refer to the use-case main course as the Happy Path. We believe that the term *Happy Path*, despite its popularity, is often inappropriate and should be avoided. The adjective *happy* is a matter of opinion and has to do with interpretation of whether the actor's *desired* goal is also *desirable.* There are many circumstances in which *happy* will be incongru-ous, such as `Cancel Reservation`, `Close Hotel`, or (more darkly) `Execute Prisoner`. Generally, you will be more professional if you avoid value judgments in your terminology.

Indicating Alternative Courses of Behavior

As the main course is just one possible course through the use case, if there are other ways of reaching the actor's goals, you need to construct other courses for each way. Each possible path through a use case is called a *scenario*. Consider a scenario as an instance of a use case, which you may diagram as shown in Figure 9-2. The use-case instances use the same oval notation as the use cases, but have their instance name, in the standard underlined format, as follows:

```
scenario name: use-case name
```

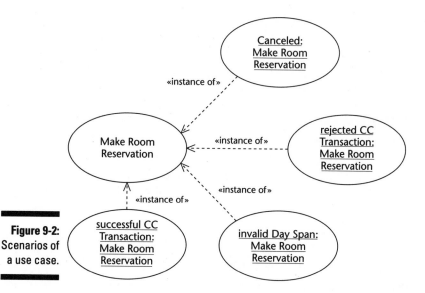

Figure 9-2: Scenarios of a use case.

The modeling notation shown in Figure 9-2 is similar to that of classes and their instances, objects, which is covered in Chapter 3. Name each scenario so that they are easily distinguished using the format for object instances.

There are often infinite potential instances of use cases, each of which is a slightly different path through the use case, with different values for user input, or different number of errors occurring in different orders. However, don't bother to even try to identify all of these. You should just identify the ones that yield quantitatively different results. For example, identify different ways of meeting the goals or different error messages. Construct scenarios that span all errors, exceptions, or variations of flow. Ultimately, the set of scenarios that you identify should exhaust all the logic of the use case.

Each scenario you identify has to be a possible path through the use cases. Thus you'll probably have to construct a separate flow of events for every scenario you've found. Each of these additional flows is usually called an *alternate course*. Document the alternate courses in the same way as the main course.

This might seem a bit redundant. The scenario in which the credit card is accepted is very similar to the scenario in which the credit card is rejected, at least, up to the point of rejection. Luckily, it's not necessary to duplicate steps mentioned in previous courses. When you start an alternate course, indicate the step from which it branches off and the conditions that cause the branch off.

When you end an alternate course, it has several possibilities:

- ✔ The use case ends because the goal is reached in an alternative way. Write a postcondition to indicate the results of this course.

- ✔ The use case ends because it's not possible to reach a successful conclusion. Write a postcondition to indicate the results of abandoning the use case.

- ✔ The use case resumes at a previous step to re-attempt a failed behavior. Indicate the next step in the original course that follows.

- ✔ The use case accomplishes a subgoal in a different way so that it skips a group of steps and rejoins at a latter step. Indicate the next step in the original course that follows.

Here's an example of an alternate course

> **Alternate course #1:** Invalid reservation day span.
>
> **Precondition:** At Step 2, the actor enters an invalid reservation day span (more than 1 month, or less than 1 day).
>
> > 2.1 The System validates inputs but the reservation day span fails validation.
> >
> > 2.2 The System displays an error message indicating the problem to be fixed.
> >
> > 2.3 The System prompts for correct reservation span.
> >
> > Processing continues with Step 2.1 of the main course.

You may become tempted to use control syntax, such as IF, ENDIF, DO, FOR, or CONTINUE AT, to minimize the number of alternate flows in a use case, but it's best to avoid such things altogether. If you yield to temptation, you'll find in hard to stop and the flow would quickly become unreadable.

When you describe use cases to specify requirements for your system, you want to *use the language of the user.* That way, your users will be able to clearly understand what the system does for them — and they can better review and critique your use cases.

Another common approach to capturing the courses or flow that you might use is table-oriented steps. The following example shows how a main course and a few of the possible alternate courses could be captured using the table-oriented steps:

Use-case name: Make Room Reservation

Description: The actor Potential Guest uses a Web browser to specify desired room features and dates, and to obtain from the system a confirmed room reservation.

Main course of events: Successful credit card transaction.

Precondition: Actor reaches the hotel's home Web page wanting to make a reservation.

Successful postcondition: Actor has a confirmed room reservation.

Potential Guest	*System*	*Credit Card Authorization System*
1. This use case starts when the actor visits the opening Web page.	**2.** Prompts for span of reservation (in days) and room type.	
3. Identifies type of room (bed size and is smoking allowed) and span (in days) of reservation.	**4.** Validates inputs using Data-Validation Rules 1 and 2.	
	5. Determines available matching room classes.	
	6. For each available room class, determines reservation cost. (See Business Rule 1.)	
	7. Displays possible reservations.	

Potential Guest	System	Credit Card Authorization System
	8. Prompts for a choice.	
9. Selects desired room.	**10.** Prompts for billing information.	
11. Supplies name, billing address, credit card number, and expiration date.	**12.** Validates the inputs, using Data-Validation Rules 3 through 6.	
	13. Sends transaction to Credit Card Authorization system.	**14.** Reports transaction is accepted.
	15. Marks room as reserved by `Potential Guest` over the specified time period (to prevent subsequent reservations).	
	16. Calculates unique reservation number. (See Business Rule 2.)	
	17. Informs `Potential Guest` of success.	
18. This use case ends when the actor, satisfied with the reservation, leaves the system.		

Alternate course #1: Invalid reservation day span.

Precondition: At Step 3 of the main course, the actor enters an invalid reservation day span (more than 1 month, or less than 1 day).

Potential Guest	System	Credit Card Authorization System
	1. Fails Reservation Day Span validation.	
	2. Displays error message, indicating problem to be fixed.	

Potential Guest	System	Credit Card Authorization System
	3. Prompts for corrected reservation span (days).	
4. Use case continues with Step 3 of the main course.		

Alternate course #2: Credit card authorization fails.

Precondition: At Step 14 of the main course, the Credit Card Authorization System rejects the transaction.

Potential Guest	System	Credit Card Authorization System
		1. Rejects transaction.
	2. Informs Actor of transaction rejection.	
	3. Prompts for corrected or different credit card.	
4. Use case continues with Step 11 of the main course.		

Alternate course #3: Reservation canceled.

Precondition: At any of Steps 3, 9, or 11 in the main course, the actor desires to cancel the reservation.

Postcondition: This use case ends with no reservation made.

Potential Guest	System	Credit Card Authorization System
1. Indicates Cancel or leaves Web page.	**2.** Cancels ongoing transaction.	

In this example, we occasionally refer to Business Rules (for example, Step 6) and Data-Validation Rules (Steps 4 and 12). Some use-case authors place the details of the field validations and algorithmic calculations in line with the steps. This is acceptable, but we prefer to refer to the rules, and place them somewhere else, usually at the end of the document. If you place the rules right inside of the steps, the steps can get very long and difficult to read. Readability should be one of your most important goals when you write use cases, because you are attempting to get agreement and buy-in from your stakeholders and other developers. In addition, business rules and data validations tend to change often — so it's best to take the ones shown here out of your final steps so the steps don't have to change.

Here are some examples of the business and data-validation rules that we referred to in our example. The business rule helps calculate the room prices; the data-validation rules prevents reservations of less than one day or more than one month. Here's what they look like:

```
Business Rules:
1.  DoubleOccupancyPrice = 1.75*BaseRoomPrice
```

```
Data-Validation Rules:
2.  Day Span: Date1 -- Date2
  Format:  MM/DD/YY -- MM/DD/YY
a Date2 > Date1
b Date2 - Date1 α  1
c Date2 - Date1 ' 31
```

As we write out use cases, we need to be aware of situations that may cause problems with the design — or the implementation — of the use case. Here's an example of a typical design note that would apply to our use case:

Design note:

If more than one `Potential Guest` could be running this use case at the same time, there is the possibility that they may be attempting to reserve the same room(s). This can cause inconsistent results. The design must consider *locking* (preventing another actor from selecting) the offered rooms until one is selected, and then locking the selected room until the reservation is confirmed or canceled.

Chapter 10

Relating Use Cases to Each Other

In This Chapter

▶ Using «include» relationships to extract common flows among use cases

▶ Generalizing and specializing use cases to show common goals

▶ Showing optionality with extended use cases

*N*o one likes to do redundant work — and normally your use cases shouldn't require it. In this chapter, we show you some techniques to help you keep duplicate work to a minimum, using two general approaches:

✔ **Extracting areas of commonality** with included or generalized use cases can save you work (you only have to document the common parts once).

✔ **Extracting and emphasizing optionality** — that is, identifying variations (as with extended use cases) — lets you simplify your work.

Linking Use Cases with «include»

You'll often run into *déjà vu* as you document your use cases — especially when several of them show an identical sequence of events exchanged between an actor and the system. This is more than coincidence; multiple use cases often have common subsequences. Usually (for example), some common setups or prerequisites must be established before work even begins — and common subgoals have to be reached on the way to accomplishing the actor's goals.

Recognizing this commonality is good — because if you don't recognize it, you can end up doing your use-case work twice. Doing the same thing over again is bad enough, but the consequences to your project can be worse. If you document your use cases twice, you'll likely document them differently — which leads to designing, implementing, and testing them differently. Such systems are also costly because such a lack of reuse adds complexity — and your users may easily get lost in a system that shows no cohesion. They'll have to learn and remember different techniques *to accomplish the same goals* in different contexts.

To save everyone some hassle, it's worth looking for opportunities to reuse common pieces of use-case interactions between an actor and the system.

In the Hotel Reservation system diagrammed in Figure 10-1, the actor Potential Guest may trigger the use case Make Room Reservation — and another actor, Event Organizer, may trigger the use case Make Facility Reservation. Both use cases involve an additional actor, the Credit Card Authorization System, to guarantee a reservation.

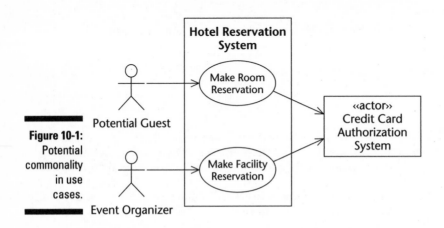

Figure 10-1:
Potential
commonality
in use
cases.

After a little thought, you may notice a set of interactions that Make Room Reservation and Make Facility Reservation have in common: the process of verifying the credit card. This common set of interactions begins with the actor requesting to pay by credit card, and the system responding with prompts for credit-card information (such as type, number, date, and name). After the actor fills in the fields, the system validates their values, and passes the information to the Credit Card Authorization system, along with an estimate of cost for the room or event. Here the information is verified; if it's acceptable, the system puts a hold on the credit card for the estimated cost. There are several alternate paths to this result — for example, validation errors, insufficient credit, card reported stolen, and so on. (You can see the Make Room Reservation use case, which includes these flows, documented in Chapter 9.)

You can add such sets of common interactions to a new use case of their own — which you can then *include* wherever you need it.

In Figure 10-2, for example, you can see that we pulled out the common interactions of two use cases and placed them in a new use case called Guarantee Reservation. We show the relationship by drawing a dashed arrow between the *base use cases* (the ones doing the including because it needs the common behavior) and the common (included) behavior, labeling the arrow with the stereotype «include». The resulting *include relationship* points from the base use case to the *included use case,* indicating that the included use case is a necessary part of the base. This included use case is a real use case; you document it in the same manner as a base use case.

Though it uses a different notation, the «include» relationship is similar to the aggregation relationship discussed in Chapter 5.

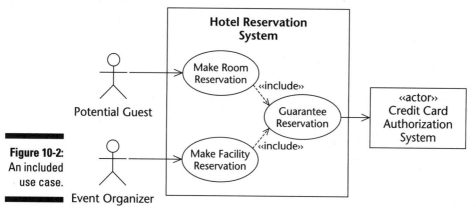

Figure 10-2:
An included
use case.

An included use case is often handy (and needed) when several use cases share a secondary actor, such as Credit Card Authorization System. Often these secondary actors are dealt with in common ways (share common exchanges of events) from a number of different use cases. If the interactions with the actor are the same and significant, it's worth your time to make a new use case for those interactions so you can simply «include» them.

Documenting included use cases

You may have one difficulty when you attempt to document the included use case: How do you identify the primary actor? After all, three different actors are involved with the Guarantee Reservation use case — and at least two of them are potential primary actors. In fact, you should consider *both* Potential Guest and Event Organizer as primary actors (yes, there can be more than one). Any primary actor for any base use case is also a primary actor for the included use case. You must document the included use case in a way that allows any primary actor to interact with the system being built. You can see one way of doing this in the following example, which is the beginning of the documentation for the Guarantee Reservation use case.

There's also a bit of controversy about how to document these included use cases. If you look at the following, you can see that we have a spot in the header to list the base use cases (Make Room Reservation and Make Facility Reservation). Normally, object-oriented principles guide us to hide the identity of the *callers* from the *called*. This bit of information hiding allows us to change the identity and number of callers (that is, the base use cases) without requiring us to rework the called (that is, the included use cases). When you implement your use cases, however, it's often worthwhile to ease up on the information hiding when you're doing the documentation. As you may expect, too much information hiding makes it hard to communicate well. (For more about object-oriented principles of information hiding, see Chapter 2.)

Use-case name: Guarantee Reservation

Description: This use case allows the actor, either Potential Guest or Event Organizer, to guarantee a reservation using a credit card.

Base use cases: Make Room Reservation, Make Facility Reservation

Main course of events: Successful credit card guarantee.

Precondition: Actor is ready to guarantee the room or facility reservation with a credit card. The system already knows the expected cost of the reservation.

Successful post condition: Actor has guaranteed the reservation.

Potential Guest or Event Organizer	System	Credit Card Authorization System
1. This use case starts when the actor is ready to guarantee the reservation.	**2.** Prompts for billing information.	
3. Supplies name, billing address, credit card number, and expiration date.	**4.** Validates inputs data validation rules X through Y.	**6.** Reports transaction is accepted.
	5. Sends transaction to Credit Card Authorization system.	
	7. This use case ends when the guarantee is accepted by the system.	

Generalizing actors in included use cases

You may also generalize the potential actors and refer to them in their generalized form. In Figure 10-3, we've generalized Potential Guest and Event Organizer into a new actor named Reserver. In this situation, the Potential Guest actor and the Event Organizer actor — for as long as they're participating in the Guarantee Reservation use case — share common goals and purposes. Thus, when you document the included use case, you can refer to Reserver as the actor. This is an especially good technique when you have many base use cases, each with its own primary actor. If you don't have to explicitly refer to each individual actor, you improve readability, save some documentation costs, and produce more change-tolerant documentation.

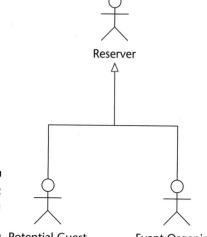

Figure 10-3:
Generalizing
actors.

Potential Guest   Event Organizer

These advantages come with a caveat: When you produce the use-case diagram, don't connect the included use case directly to the generalized actor. That way lies confusion; primary actors of an included use case are implicitly the actors of the base use case(s). Adding a connection to the generalized actor just adds another actor to the use case — one actor too many. This common diagramming error indicates that another actor instance is required to execute the use case — when it isn't.

Use-case diagrams are, by and large, graphically simple. With only a few actors and a few ovals per actor, you can convey lots of information about your system (such as its users and services). Adding «include» relationships can complicate the diagram slightly, but you gain clarity by highlighting areas of commonality and regularity. It's comforting to understand a system deeply enough to identify areas of uniformity — and practical, because it enables reuse and predictability.

Using Generalization with Use Cases

Sometimes there's more than one way to reach a goal. When you find common purposes or goals in UML, you have an opportunity to use *generalization* — the object-oriented technique of specifying common features in a more general way to enable the reuse of objects. (For more about generalization, check out Chapter 2; for more about the UML notation for generalization, see Chapter 6.)

There are two common circumstances where you'll find opportunities to generalize use cases:

- **Differing mechanisms for the same goal:** If there's more than one alternative technique or approach that the system uses to help the actors get their goals accomplished, they may share only a little implementation in common. If they meet the same goal, however, then the approaches will be still be sharing quite a bit: requirements, business rules, and data validations. With generalization, we can make this sharing explicit and save on duplications, by putting the common stuff in a single use case.

- **Differing agents for the same goal:** If there is more than one actor trying to accomplish the same goal, you may be able to generalize the actors as we explain in the section above on generalizing actors in included use cases, However, you will find that often the actors have separate privileges, capabilities, or user interface. This is especially common when one actor acts as an agent or intermediary for the other. Generalizing the actors might still help, but now we want to explain how the use case works differently for each type of actor. Instead of generalizing the actors, generalize the use cases, placing in the generalized use case the common documentation, requirements, business rules, data validations, and perhaps implementation that they share. Using generalization will help you corral this common stuff and put it in its place (in a separate single use case).

Generalizing differing mechanisms

As technology evolves, your systems evolve as well. But it's rare that you can completely eliminate legacy (pre-existing) solutions to long-standing needs. This can mean that at any one time, there are often several different ways to achieve the same goal.

Sometimes it's not a question of retaining legacy approaches; you may just be hedging your bets with two different solutions to the same problem. Perhaps it's because of uncertainly about what will become the dominant technology, or a desire to cater to diverse user populations with different preferences.

We show a typical example of such use-case generalization in Figure 10-4. The actor Potential Guest connects to the generalized use case Make

`Room Reservation`. You place the common requirements, business rules, and even most of the flow description inside that use case. Then, in your lower-level *(specialized)* use cases, you have to document *only* the specific behavior required for their implementation mechanisms — that is, only the differences. In the figure, we show that we have to implement the same Make Room Reservation using modern HTTP Web technology, old-fashioned, VT100 technology, and IVR (Interactive Voice Response) pushbutton telephone technology.

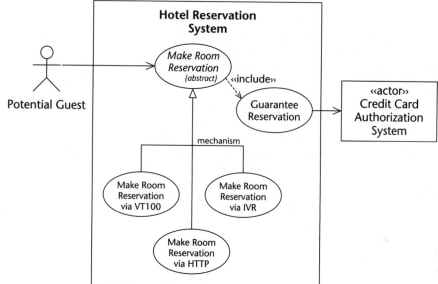

Figure 10-4: Generalizing use cases by mechanism.

You'll find that when you generalize a use case in this manner, what you get is typically an *abstract use case* — one you can't implement directly (because the details are missing) and that you can only put into action by implementing the specialized *concrete use cases* that specify the detailed mechanism. (UML indicates that a use case is abstract by italicizing its name and adding the {abstract} property tag.) There's a discussion on abstract and concrete and how to indicate them in Chapter 6.

As part of the generalization notation, you can label the generalization (this label is called a *discriminator*) to clarify the basis or reasons for the generalization. We use the discriminator `mechanism` when we separate the implementation mechanisms in the diagram.

If your use cases are only for identifying requirements and documentation, generalizing by mechanism can actually work against you. Instead, try putting the requirements, common business rules, and field validations in the generalized use case — don't bother creating the specialized use cases at all (if you already created them, you can delete them). Unless you have to mention requirements that arise from the mechanism, specialized use cases may not offer much new to say. For many organizations, however, use cases serve purposes other than just gathering requirements — for example, they can help with scheduling and document organizing, or serve as a powerful explanatory tool. In such circumstances, generalizing by mechanism can still be valuable.

Generalizing differing agents

In the traditional model for service-oriented business, a customer contacts the business and requests some service. A worker — a cashier, library-circulation clerk, or hotel phone-reservation agent — performs the service for the customer. However, in our increasingly technological world, the customer may be able to interact directly with the system without using an intermediary (worker). Improving technology enables this trend toward *disintermediation* — in effect, losing the middleman — as a major thrust for Internet growth.

Your systems may have to support both *direct* (without an intermediary) and *indirect* (with an intermediary) usage — and traditionally you would construct a separate use case for each approach. Generalizing offers you an alternative. Figure 10-5 (for example) shows two different approaches to making hotel reservations — one direct (by Potential Guest over the Internet), and the other indirect (Potential Guest contacts a Reservation Clerk to do the work of making the reservation).

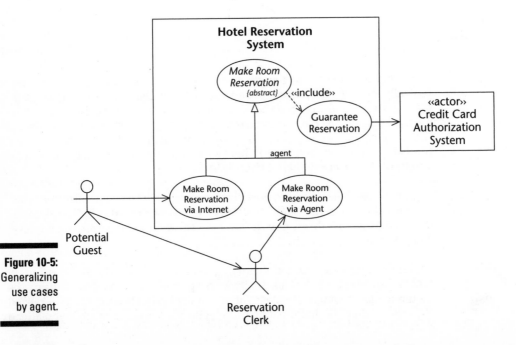

Figure 10-5: Generalizing use cases by agent.

When you generalize your use cases, you also add complexity to the diagrams — but what you get back is thoroughness: You can diagram the generalized use cases, which map to the essential goals of the actors, as well as the different specialized variants on the themes.

Extending Use Cases

Your use-case diagrams can convey lots of information packed into a simple form — but most information developed in the analysis stage ends up inside the use case, serving as its specifications (discussed more fully in Chapter 9). In practice, use-case flows get much of their true complexity from the entanglement of multiple alternate courses and paths.

When you draw use-case diagrams, you're practicing the good object-oriented principles of *abstraction* and *information hiding* (as described in Chapter 2) to simplify the tangle — communicating the essence without the distraction of suppressible details.

Hiding complexity is generally good, but sometimes you have to expose some details to gain clarity somewhere else. With UML, you can depict important alternate flows graphically by making them into their own use cases. Then you can connect these new use cases to their base use cases by establishing an «extend» relationship. Thus, you can emphasize otherwise-hidden information when the reviewers of your use-case diagram want to see it. Some reasons this might be desirable are as follows:

- **Changed capability:** If you have changed a use case significantly — perhaps because of a later release — you may find it useful (and perhaps politic) to emphasize that the change has occurred, rather than burying it in the use-case specification.

- **Major variation:** If you have a major alternative path in the use case, and it's complex enough to have its own alternative paths, then placing it on your diagram will honestly expose the complexity — which is helpful in costing, assignment, and scheduling.

- **Optional subgoal:** If you have parts of the use case that would be optional to implement (or even optional to execute) to meet the actor's goals, put those parts into their own use case. Doing so clarifies the relationships between actors and their goals. It also emphasizes that you may deliver these optional goals in later releases.

Showing a new release

When you have significantly changed a capability in a *new release* (a new delivery of code to the users), it's often best to create a new extension use case that extends the existing use case. Figure 10-6, for example, shows `Make Room Reservation V2.0` as an *extension use case* of the original `Make Room Reservation`. The «extend» relationship uses an open-headed, dashed arrow that points from the extension to the base use case.

When you document the changes in such an extension use case, you save yourself the work of changing any existing documentation. In fact, it's considered incorrect for a base use-case specification (the textual description discussed in Chapter 9) to mention that it's extended (except for listing extension points, as discussed in a moment). This prohibition supports encapsulation — so you can extend at whim without having to change any existing use cases. As an added bonus, you shield your existing use cases from extra review or criticism.

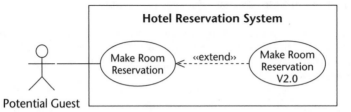

Potential Guest

When you use extensions to indicate additional releases of a use case, you may find yourself in a common methodological quandary: The extension use case is only *supposed* to capture any *differences* from the base use case. The idea is to avoid duplicating things unnecessarily. On the other hand, documenting a second-release use case without duplication is sometimes difficult, especially if lots of small changes have cropped up within the use case.

Using extension to show a new release also introduces a maintenance problem. After a while, you may end up with a chain of extended use cases — `Make Room Reservation 3.0` extending `Make Room Reservation 2.0` and so on. No subsequent use case can then be understood without understanding the previous use case. This situation will undoubtedly cause problems.

And no, there are no ideal solutions to those problems. Therefore, we generally recommend that you document subsequent releases as shown in Table 10-1.

Table 10-1	Documenting New Releases
Extent of New Release	*Documentation Approach*
Very small (or small diffuse changes), throughout the use case.	Modify your existing use-case documentation. Use change bars (or equivalent) to indicate new requirements or approaches for the next release.

Extent of New Release	Documentation Approach
Small, compact changes.	Use alternate flows or courses to indicate new requirements or approaches for the next release.
Large, compact changes.	Create an extension use case to indicate alternative flows found in the next release.
Large, diffuse changes.	Create generalized use case for common behavior, and then create specialized use cases for current and future releases.

Taking alternate paths

You'll often have situations in which a use case takes an alternate path or course (based on some circumstances or condition) but still attempts to reach the original goal. In Chapter 9, we explain that an alternative course is a variation in the path of the use-case flow caused by some condition. For example, when a Potential Guest Makes a Room Reservation, the user who wants the room may come to the point at which the system prompts for any *affinity plans* (such as frequent-traveler, hotel, or airline-mileage plans) in which the user participates. Not only may extra points be available for each stay, but also a Potential Guest enrolled in the right plans can get a room upgrade.

This activity of upgrading the reservation is an alternate path on the way to reserving a room that only happens at a specific point in the use case — while the actor is entering the affinity plans, and only under specific conditions — the plan being entered is the right (eligible) plan. It's also a complex alternate path — there are usually restrictions on how and when an upgrade may be obtained, and usually a guest must have (or trade) a certain minimum number of points for the upgrade. Thus upgrading has its own alternate paths.

Not only is it complex, this path is not really necessary to achieve the main goal of Make Room Reservation. This makes it a good candidate to pull it out of the Make Room Reservation use case and document it as a separate use case. This new use case that we pull out, Upgrade Reservation, UML calls an *extension* use case, because it extends the original (or base) use case with new capabilities or flows.

The place in the original (base) use case where the extension use case was inserted (or as you may think of it, where the extension use case came from), is called the *extension point.*

A dashed arrow pointing from the extension to the base connects the base use case and extension use case. Label the arrow with the stereotype of «extend». Figure 10-7 shows the ongoing example.

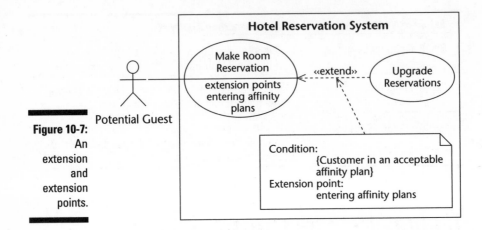

Figure 10-7:
An
extension
and
extension
points.

Almost everyone is initially confused about the direction of the «extend» arrow. It points from the new extension use case to the base, in the opposite way from that of the «include» relationship discussed earlier. In Figure 10-7, you should read the relationship as, "Upgrade Reservation extends Make Room Reservation", or if you prefer reading in the other direction, "Make Room Reservation is extended by Upgrade Reservation".

Besides the basic notation for the «extend» relationship, there is some optional UML notation that you may find useful. In the lower section of the oval that represents the base use case, you can list the *extension points* — places where extension use cases may be inserted. Each of these identifies a step (or range of steps) in the flow of events in the base use case shown in Chapter 9. The numbering techniques given in that chapter to identify the location of an alternate course can be used to identify the location of the extension points (for example, *Main Course Step 5; Alternate Course 2, Steps 3-6*). To avoid exposing the inner details of the step numbering (which would require the diagram to change too often), we recommend that you use a easily remembered name for each extension point. This name should be mapped to the step numbers in the specification for the base use case. In Figure 10-7, for example, the extension point is identified as Entering Affinity Plans.

Another way of identifying an extension point is to refer to the name of the activity that the use case must be executing when the extension is inserted. Check out Chapter 13 for using UML activity diagrams to diagram the steps of a use case.

The figure also shows how you can attach to the «extend» relationship a comment indicating the condition under which the extension applies. To completely read the diagram with the optional UML notation, it would go something like this: "Upgrade Reservation extends Make Room Reservation when the condition {Customer is in an acceptable affinity plan} is true at the point the Make Room Reservation reaches the extension point Entering Affinity Plans".

Extending with optional goals

Believe it or not, you may have to add an activity to a use case that's not needed to achieve its goal. For example, you may want to request that any `Potential Guest` answer a marketing survey when making a room reservation (as in Figure 10-8). This may become a mandatory insertion, but it's optional to the actor's goals — you could, in theory, eliminate it — so it's best modeled as an extension.

Figure 10-8:
Mandatory
use case
with
optional
goal.

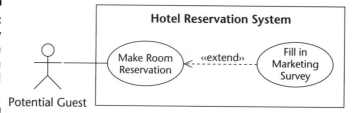

Misusing extends

You may have problems determining when to employ extensions (as opposed to other techniques such as inclusion or generalization discussed earlier in this chapter). Unfortunately, the advice typically given isn't sufficient to end controversy. You're usually told that the extension use cases *must be optional* when invoked from their base use cases — and that the extension use cases *cannot depend* on their base use cases.

One problem with such pronouncements is that the term *optional* isn't well defined. There are at least two possible meanings here. An extension use case could be *optional to implement* or *optional to execute at runtime*. Most practitioners prefer the second approach because it seems easy to see whether a use case has a condition to test before it executes. For many use cases, however, it's hard to define whether something is truly optional to execute. For example, if the runtime test is always `true`, is the use case *really* optional to run? And if you can't decide which course is the main course and which is an alternative course, would a use case be an *extension* if it's used by the alternative course — but considered *included* if it's used by the main course?

Okay, we do have some subtle reasons to believe it's better to interpret *optional* to mean *optional to implement*. For openers, we believe that UML directed arrow requires that base use case not depend on extension use cases, but a base use case can depend on included use case. If you follow this guideline, your use-case diagram can (and should) determine required implementation order. This approach leads to two other clear requirements:

- ✔ You *must* deliver any *included* use case *along with* its base use case.
- ✔ You *may* deliver any *extended* use case *later* than its base use case.

Not only is this information valuable for scheduling work, it's easy to understand visually.

On the other hand, we've seen civilized discussions on whether a use case should be an extension or an inclusion become disagreements, then arguments, and ultimately — well, they can cost your project a lot of time, money, and good will. You're probably best off if you don't take a hard line on such issues; this chapter's three guidelines for extending use cases (listed earlier) will steer you in an effective direction.

Part IV
The Basics
of Functional
Modeling

The 5th Wave   By Rich Tennant

"WELL, SHOOT! THIS EGGPLANT CHART IS JUST AS
CONFUSING AS THE BUTTERNUT SQUASH CHART
AND THE GOURD CHART. CAN'T YOU JUST MAKE
A PIE CHART LIKE EVERYONE ELSE?"

In this part . . .

*W*hen you're specifying use cases or designing operations, you are doing functional modeling — and
UML has some tools for you. The chapters in this part get
you started with the notations and techniques that make
up your toolkit for functional modeling.

We cover several different ways of representing the details
of your system's functionality and behavior: *sequence diagrams* (which show the event exchange among objects),
activity diagrams (which show workflow and decision-
making), and *communication diagrams* (which show collaboration among objects to accomplish some behavior).
We even cover some UML-based ways to use text that are
sure to come in handy.

Chapter 11

Introducing Functional Modeling

In This Chapter

▶ Realizing your use cases

▶ Modeling the details of behaviors

▶ Choosing the best functional modeling approach

▶ Harnessing the power of OCL

▶ Writing text-based specifications

*U*se cases (discussed in detail in Chapters 8, 9, and 10) capture your system's behavior as seen by the actors of the system. However, use cases are services your system offers to the outside — before the system can deliver results to the outside, *you* have to deliver the insides, that is, you must specify, design, and develop the inside parts of the system that accomplishes these use cases. This is the point at which you have to worry about *use-case realization* — how to realize (accomplish) the use cases.

This chapter introduces some UML capabilities available for designing and capturing the details of behavior — and offers guidelines on how to model behavior.

Modeling Functions from an Object-Oriented Perspective

Before object-oriented analysis and design methodology captured the imaginations of software developers, the primary methods they used to ply their trade either emphasized the functions (the behavior*)* or emphasized the structure (the data).

Actually, the most common technique was (and still is) *hacking* — in effect, a mostly undisciplined, unrepeatable approach — but styles of hacking continue to evolve, influenced by fashionable programming languages, concepts, and other fads of the day.

The predominant style then separated out functional development (analysis, design, and implementation of the behaviors) from that of structural development (analysis, design, and implementation of the data). That is, people designed their *behaviors* (the things the system does) independently from that of their *data structures* (the values, fields, records, and database that contain the data of the system).

These approaches worked, but they tended to result in fragile, hard-to-maintain systems. Someone always wanted to change a behavior (which was on one set of models), or change a data structure (which was on another set of models) — without seeing both views — and with no encapsulation or information hiding to limit complexity, the system usually broke. Every change propagated ripple effects that could change everything else. (For more about encapsulation, information hiding, and other good development principles, review Chapter 2.)

Object-oriented techniques help you address these problems by keeping an eye on some aspects of the functional view (seeing the operation in terms of behavior and control) and the structural view (focusing on objects) at the same time.

UML tries very hard to prevent this dangerous decoupling of behavior and data. Because UML arose from the principles of object-oriented development (such as described in Chapter 2), it presents a unified view of behavior and the objects that do the behavior. Each diagram type may emphasize one or another aspect of the system, but no diagram type is exclusively functional. In Table 11-1 (in the next section), we show some of the modeling techniques you can use when you need to concentrate on the details of a behavior.

You can't get away with ignoring the objects that *do* the behavior and considering only the objects that the behavior works on. There is no pure functional diagram in UML.

When use cases aren't enough

Often your use cases will be simple behaviors of your system. The text-based approach to their documentation, as explained in Chapter 9, will be sufficient to document their externally visible behavior. Your use-case courses — the main course and the alternate course(s) — describe a set of interactions between an actor and the system. It's simple when there are only two objects. However, you may have secondary actors involved, in which case your interactions can get complicated with three or more participating objects. You also may have many alternate courses, or alternate courses of alternate courses. You may find the simple text-based main and alternate course approach sufficient for requirements understanding, but you will be challenged to use it to help in design.

UML has several possible approaches that might help you in explaining the details of behavior. We outline the different approaches in Table 11-1 and give you some idea of their domain of suitability. You might use any of them to capture the use-case flows graphically, which can help you in designing them — and understanding them. Often you need more than one modeling approach to properly clarify the behavior of interest. These techniques are available for exploring the details of any behavior, so you can apply them to use cases as well as operations in your work.

Table 11-1	Functional/Behavioral Modeling Techniques	
Technique	*Indicates . . .*	*You'll Find more Info . . .*
Use case diagrams	Externally visible behavior from actor's point of view. Covers all scenarios at the same time, may call out some variations graphically. Good for high-level overview and understanding and specifying requirements.	Chapter 8, 9, and 10 (and later in this chapter)
Operations (Class diagrams)	Name, signature, arguments. Good for simple presentation and showing how to call behaviors on objects.	Chapter 3 (and later in this chapter)
Sequence diagrams	Participating objects, exchanging events. Usually a single scenario at a time. Good for application analysis and system design.	Chapter 12
Activity diagrams	Ongoing activities, concurrency, data flow. May cover several scenarios at a time. Good for capturing and designing repeating or concurrent activities, or finding target objects for lower-level behavior.	Chapter 13
Communication diagrams	Detailed operation design playing out over static structure. Usually a single scenario at a time. Good for capturing and designing complex operations, algorithm design, and design patterns.	Chapter 14
State diagrams	Response to complex events. Usually covers all scenarios at the same time. Good for capturing and designing event driven behavior or state machines.	Chapters 16, 17, and 18
Text-based specifications	Flows and scenarios. Constraints, pre- and postconditions. Usually covers all possible scenarios. Good for requirements specification, mathematical algorithm design, language-independent programming. Often used along with other techniques.	Later in this chapter

One reason that you will find these techniques useful for all sorts of behavior is that use cases may describe behavior offered up by any class-like entity in UML. For our purposes, the subject of a use case may be a system, subsystem, class, or a component.

Describing behavior with use cases

As we explain in Chapter 8, use cases describe the behavior of the system as seen from the actors, who are outside of the system. The actors consider the use cases as the system's operations. Figure 11-1 shows part of a use case diagram for the Hotel Reservation System. Any model element in UML that exhibits behavior can be the subject of a use case, so you can describe the behavior with use cases at any level.

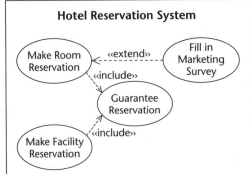

Figure 11-1:
Use cases
of a system.

We recommend that you draw use case diagrams for the system as a whole. We also recommend that you draw use case diagrams whenever you find you have a complex subject that needs to be treated as a *black box,* where the external and visible behavior needs to be specified, but the internal behavior is hidden. You'll find that this will apply to all systems, because you need to distinguish the testable, required (visible) behaviors that the users want from the designable (hidden) insides that you want to develop.

In larger systems, this need for use cases will also apply to subsystems. As you decompose the system into subsystems, these subsystems can be treated as use-case subjects. Their actors will be those entities that are external as you look at each subsystem in turn. For example, the top part of Figure 11-2 shows a piece of the Hotel Reservation System context diagram — emphasizing the system and its surrounding context. They are good for quick communication of what in and what's out of the system. The bottom part of the same figure shows the results of portioning the complex system into three simpler subsystems (User Interface, Business Logic, and Persistent Store).

When you do this type of partitioning, treat these subsystems as the subjects of their own use cases with their own actors. The actors of the `User Interface` subsystem are the original `Potential Guest` and the neighboring `Business Logic` subsystem. From the `Business Logic` subsystem point of view, you would treat as actors the `User Interface` subsystem and the `Persistent Store (DB)` subsystem. (By the way, the tuning-fork symbol in the upper-right hand corner is the optional UML icon for the «system» or «subsystem» stereotype — some tools will use it and some won't.)

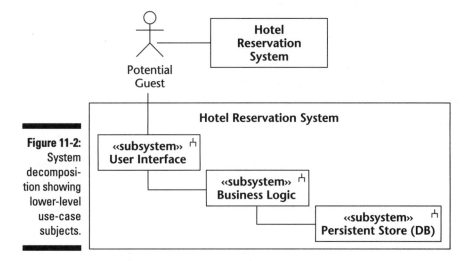

Figure 11-2:
System decomposition showing lower-level use-case subjects.

As with the subsystems, you may find that documenting with use cases would even apply to lower-level decompositions, either to the behaviors of lower-level subsystems or to the behaviors of large components or classes. This is most useful for you in the larger development efforts where different development teams may be assigned these large components and classes. You'll be taking advantage of the suitability of use cases for separating requirements from internals, when you use them to *spec out* (specify) the requirements for each development team. For another look at this sort of leveled decomposition, see Chapter 8.

Converting use cases into operations (class diagrams)

To map use cases directly to system level operations, you can start by converting all directly actor-accessible use cases to *public operations on a class representing the system*. Remember, operations are behaviors that a class may be asked to perform. They must be public because they are visible to the actors.

You typically convert other use cases — such as included use cases (connected by an «include» relationship) or extended use cases (connected by an «extend» relationship) — to *private operations* — while they are behaviors the system needs to perform, they can't be invoked directly by an actor. If you were to convert the use cases from Figure 11-1 into and use the UML notation for operations and visibility that we explain in Chapter 3, you would arrive at the system as shown in Figure 11-3. Remember that the + sign indicates public visibility, and (you guessed it) the - sign indicates private visibility.

Figure 11-3:
Use cases
as system
operations.

«system»
Hotel Reservation System

+ makeRoomReservation()
+ makeFacilityReservation()
**– guaranteeReservation(estPrice:Money,
        aCard : CardInfo) : Boolean**
– fillInMarketingSurvey()

Converting the use cases to operations is really one of the first steps you can do to design your system. It's simple, but it's a start at identifying the operations. The next step for each operation in Figure 11-3 would be to add the operation's return type and arguments, and the arguments' types, directions, and default values.

Figure 11-3 shows these details for the guaranteeReservation operation indicated in bold. From the description of the use case in Chapter 10, it is clear that this operation needs to be passed a price and card information for use by the Credit Card Authorization system. We choose estPrice:Money and aCard:CardInfo as the arguments and their types. They are shown in the argument list of the guaranteeReservation operation in the figure. We also determined that the including use case, Make A Reservation, would need to know if the guaranteeReservation use case was successful, so we indicated a Boolean (True/False) success flag to be returned from the operation.

If you continued with this design, you would define the details of CardInfo, which includes, at least, HolderName, CardNumber, and ExpirationDate, in a separate class box called CardInfo using the techniques of Chapter 3. We won't do that here. You might also find that the operation needs other information or returns other information — if so, capture them as input or output arguments to the operation. When you do this design, you may come up with slightly different results, but go ahead, it's your design.

Writing Text-Based Behavioral Specifications

One of the most common ways to capture the details of a behavior is to use *text-based specifications* — using text in a semiformal way to express what the behavior does. You have several different forms to choose from, based on what you exactly want to accomplish, your tools, and your organization's standards. For example, you may have to type these text-based specifications directly into your UML tool after opening up the use case ovals or you may need to place them in separate documents. You may have strict templates to follow or you may have considerable freedom. And, you may use a different approach when documenting use case behaviors than when documenting operation behaviors. With whatever restriction you have, keep the following considerations in mind when using text-based approaches:

- ✔ **Don't descend to pure functional thinking.** Pay attention to the objects that are performing the behavior or the behavior is being performed on.

- ✔ **Consider your audience.** Text-based approaches can easily become exercises of codelike complexity or pure expressions of logic and set theory. Unless your audience will understand what you are writing, you're wasting your time.

- ✔ **Choose the right level of abstraction.** Keep away from lower-level details unless you need them to explain the intent of the behavior. Object-oriented approaches tend to have many small behaviors that collaborate to accomplish larger goals. Sometimes you'll be documenting those small behaviors; sometimes you'll be documenting how they collaborate. The description of the behaviors should be consistent with the current level of abstraction — which you have a chance to bring lower when you write the code itself.

- ✔ **Maximize cohesion.** Follow this traditional advice for any design of behavior. When you trigger a behavior, the effects should be all working together to a common goal. If a part or piece of behavior seems extraneous, drop it or move it somewhere else. If the parts and behaviors work together well, and all of them are needed, then you have high cohesion. If the name of the behavior, operation, or use case requires an *and,* reconsider if the behavior is properly focused on a single coherent behavior. For example, if the use case were called `Reserve Room and Order Room Service`, you'd know pretty quickly that the use case is trying to do too much.

Writing use-case specifications

The traditional documentation approaches for use cases (discussed in Chapter 9) are possible choices for behavioral specification. Although there are several different ways of documenting use cases, they typically describe one main course (flow), with alternatives described afterwards, without disturbing the main flow.

I recommend using this main-and-alternate-flow approach whenever the requirements for a behavior seem unclear, and when the complexity of seeing too many scenarios at once starts to boggle your mind. It's very good for documenting externally visible behavior and requirements — but this technique isn't quite as good for capturing algorithmic, design, or implementation ideas.

Writing pre- and postconditions

One common and very useful style of documenting behaviors of all sorts that you may use is the establishing of pre- and postconditions. These may be used along with other text-based approaches, or with the graphical approaches:

- **Precondition:** A *precondition* is a statement that must be true about the world before a behavior is started. Its existence serves to guarantee that the behavior proceeds as planned. For example, before you can cancel a room reservation, there must be an active room reservation, and you must be the reserver or a representative.

- **Postcondition:** A *postcondition* is any statement that must be true about the world after the behavior successfully completes. For example, after you cancel a room reservation, the room is marked as free and any credit hold on your card is dropped.

- **Invariants:** Besides pre- and postconditions, you must guarantee your *invariants* — conditions that must be true *both before and after* a behavior executes. For example, the number of occupants for a room on a given day is never, never less than zero.

Invariants are really conditions that must be true any time another object queries (or looks at) the object executing the operation. In the presence of multithreading, where an object can do more than one thing at a time, it's possible for an object to be executing an operation while reporting on its condition. This means that the invariant can't be violated even temporarily while the operation is running.

When you supply a complete set of preconditions and postconditions for a behavior, you define that behavior *without implying a design*. Any caller or invoker of a behavior or operation tries to guarantee that the preconditions are met before the behavior is called. Then the object offering the operation guarantees that the postconditions are met — after the behavior finishes. This approach is sometimes called *design-by-contract*. It allows the designers to do whatever they want as long as the contract is upheld.

Writing OCL constraints

Though you can write constraints in any language, you may use a special language that is part of UML when writing these constraints. The *Object Constraint Language (OCL)* was built upon the underlying concepts of UML and can refer explicitly to the objects, attributes, and links within your own class diagrams. By using OCL, you can be sure that your constraints are unambiguous.

OCL is a very complex and complete language. If you use OCL for complex expressions, you tend to sacrifice readability for precision. However, with some of the UML tools, the OCL may be formally processed and verified. If you can properly construct the OCL constraint, it means that you have enough information in your models to enforce the constraint. When you write in a natural language such as English, you can easily write a constraint that just cannot be enforced *because there is missing information in the model.* Of course, knowing it's possible to enforce a constraint doesn't mean the enforcement is easy.

When you use OCL constraints, you refer directly to features that appear on the class diagram — for example, classes, attributes, roles, and operations. This direct reference prevents you from divorcing your functional definition from the objects the behavior actually operates on.

Harnessing OCL constraint syntax and applying the OCL dot operator

When you're writing an OCL constraint, you usually attach it to an operation in a note box (see Figure 11-4). Here's the basic syntax for OCL constraints for operations:

```
context Type::behaviorName(para1:Type1, . . .): ReturnType
pre ConstraintName: OCLExpression
post ConstraintName: OCLExpression
inv ConstraintName: OCLExpression
```

The following list details the syntax used in OCL constraints for operations:

- ✔ `context`: The keyword that starts up the OCL constraints. It precedes the definition of the constraint context, where the applicability of the constraints is indicated.

- ✔ `Type`: The subject of this behavior. It's the name, the system, subsystem, class, or type where you're defining the behavior.

- ✔ `behaviorName`: The name of the operation or use case.

- ✔ `para1:Type1, . . .`: The parameter list for the behavior.

- ✔ `ReturnType`: The type of any return value from the behavior.

- ✔ `pre, post, or inv`: Keywords that indicate the type of constraint. They indicate precondition, postcondition, and invariant respectively.

✔ `ConstraintName`: An optional name for the constraint so that it can be referred to again.

✔ `OCLExpression`: A logical expression that must evaluate to true or false.

We show an example in Figure 11-4, using both pre- and postconditions on the operation `Reservation::cancel()`.

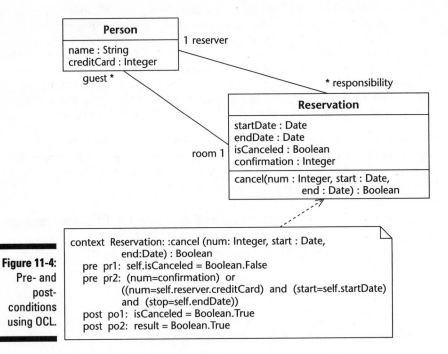

Figure 11-4:
Pre- and post-
conditions
using OCL.

In this example, the `Reservation::cancel()` operation has three parameters: a number (`num`) and two dates (`start` and `end`). There are also two preconditions and two postconditions.

First, the `context` keyword establishes that this set of constraints is for the operation `Reservation::cancel()`, that is, the operation `cancel` defined in the class `Reservation`. The `context` also defines the object that owns the operation. You can refer to the owning object (the object of the class `Reservation` that is running the operation) by using the keyword `self`.

The first constraint in Figure 11-4, the precondition named `pr1`, refers to the `isCanceled` attribute of the `self` object and requires it to have the value of the enumerated literal `False`, as defined in the `Boolean` type. (An *enumerated literal* is one of the possible values of finite-valued type where all the possible values are listed when the type is defined.) What it's saying is that you can't cancel an already-canceled reservation.

The dot (.) operator in OCL has several possible meanings, as shown in Table 11-2.

Table 11-2	OCL Dot Operator
A.B	*Refers to*
`object.attribute`	The attribute(s) B of the object A
`object.queryOperation`	The results of calling the query operation B on the object A. Query operations return values but doesn't change any values.
`Class.staticAttribute`	The static attribute B of the class A. Static attributes are owned by a class as a whole and not by individual objects.
`object.rolename`	The set of object(s) playing the role B across the association from A
`EnumeratedType.literal`	The value represented by the literal B of the enumerated datatype A

The dot operator has one more property that is interesting; you can successively apply it to the results of a *previous* dot operation. In practical terms, A.B.C is the same as (A.B).C.

You might take advantage of some common ways of reading complex OCL dot expressions, such as A.B.C can be read as "A's B's C" or "the C of the B of the A".

The second constraint in Figure 10-4, the precondition named `pr2`, requires the input parameter `num` to match either the confirmation number or the credit number of the reserver. Using the approach discussed above to read these complex statements. The expression `self.reserver.creditCard` refers to `self`'s (current object) `reserver`'s `creditCard`, or the `creditCard` of the `reserver` of the current object (`self`). If the `creditCard` number is used the correct `startDate` and `stopDate` must also be supplied.

Finally, two postconditions are shown in Figure 11-4. The first requires the operation to leave the `isCanceled` flag set to `true`. The second indicates that the `result` of the operation is also set to `true`.

Writing general algorithms

You may have occasion to specify a mathematical, scientific, or computer-science algorithm. This is rare for most developers, but if you find yourself in these situations, it's usually best simply to refer to a document where the algorithm is predefined.

You may define an algorithm with *pseudocode* — codelike sequences of characters that describe an operation. The purpose of pseudocode is to describe an algorithm in sufficient detail so (technically oriented) non-programmers can understand it, without forcing the use of a particular programming language.

When using pseudocode, describe the essence of the algorithm — don't go too deep by writing nearly pure code. You may find this goal hard to achieve. We generally recommend utilizing alternative graphical techniques other than writing pseudocode. You can see some of these techniques in Chapters 12, 13, and 14.

UML developers forced to use pseudocode (whether by corporate standards or because the operation uses lots of algorithms) often base their pseudocode on OCL. Unfortunately, OCL is only a *constraint language;* it can't actually change the value of anything. In addition, OCL has only limited control structures. The common strategy uses two different syntaxes:

- ✔ You can adopt the syntax of your current programming language for assignment and control statements.
- ✔ When you need to refer to elements in the class diagram, use the OCL dot notation as your navigation syntax.

Using this approach for writing OCL-based pseudocode can help you design and write creditable algorithms.

Another approach may soon be commonly possible. Recently added to UML, and formally incorporated into UML 2 are the *Action Semantics*. The Action Semantics define a *metamodel* (a model made up of models) for specifying behavior independent of implementation — that is, suitable for automatic machine translation into various implementations for various architectures. This is part of OMG's *Model-Driven Architecture* (MDA) allowing developers to skip writing code in programming languages. By constructing very complete models and formally defining the behaviors, developers can target implementation on different platforms or architectures without changing the models.

Several syntaxes for the Action Semantics are possible. Different tools support MDA differently — for different types of problems and different ranges of architectures. Tool support is already available in the embedded and real-time development areas.

Chapter 12

Capturing Scenarios with Sequence Diagrams

● ●

In This Chapter

▶ Seeing your object's lifelines

▶ Sending messages to other objects

▶ Capturing scenarios in sequence diagrams

▶ Composing interactions from fragments

● ●

*W*henever you need to understand how some objects interact, you should consider creating some type of UML *interaction diagram*. UML has a rich assortment of these diagrams to choose from, such as sequence diagrams, communication diagrams, activity diagrams, and timing diagrams, all of which are designed for the specific purpose of helping you express the details of how objects interact and collaborate to accomplish a behavior. And UML even allows you to mix these diagrams together. Don't be bewildered. Following the guidelines given in Chapter 11 and the techniques of this chapter, you'll come to rely upon sequence diagrams as your first choice in many circumstances.

Sequence diagrams, especially in their basic form, simply display the lifelines of participating objects as they exchange messages in a single scenario. (A *lifeline* represents the evolving life of the participating object by showing relevant events that are important to the object.) Of all available UML interaction diagrams, the sequence diagrams are usually the best suited to exploring the scenarios or flows of a particular use case. Not only are they easiest to draw, they are also easy for developers and clients alike to understand.

In this chapter, we introduce the features of sequence diagrams and help you depict interactions among your objects.

Diagramming an Interaction Scenario

All interaction diagrams capture at least one *interaction,* which is the interplay of messages sent between objects over time for a specific purpose. Usually the most important interactions you document are the major use-case *scenarios.* In this context, we use the term *scenario* as defined in Chapter 9 — an instance of a use case. As discussed in Chapter 9, each use case has a generalized description of its most common scenario — its *main course* or *main flow.* In such a flow, you describe the interaction of participating objects as an ordered set of steps or actions that an actor (or system) takes as the flow plays out.

A participating object takes a set of actions, communicating the results of one or more of these actions in a message to another participating object — which (in turn) takes its own set of actions and communicates. Sometimes the participating object needs help from other object, so it requests a service in a message to another participating object, which (in turn) takes its own set of actions and communicates. When you draw an interaction diagram, you emphasize the message sequences among the participating objects, as shown in Figure 12-1, and (usually) hide the internal actions.

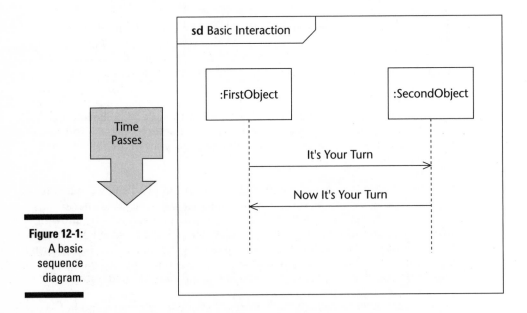

Figure 12-1:
A basic
sequence
diagram.

In the sample diagram in Figure 12-1, you can see the basic features of a sequence diagram. You diagram the participating objects as vertical lifelines. These lifelines consist of an icon indicating the type of participant (such as an object or an actor instance) at the top of a dashed line where you can indicate the messages sent and received by the participating object. Show the messages among the objects as directed arrows from sender to target object.

In this diagram, the FirstObject informs the SecondObject that It's Your Turn, and later, the SecondObject informs the FirstObject that Now It's Your Turn. The convention is that time passes as you read down the page, though you can turn the diagrams so time runs from left to right. As is typical in these diagrams, the messages alternate.

Place the interaction in the contents area of a frame, and then place the diagram interaction's title in the odd-shaped heading area (a rectangle with a cut-off corner) in the upper-left corner. The heading contains a prefix that describes the type of interaction you've placed in the frame. The sample diagram shows the interaction as a sequence diagram, so the descriptive prefix can be sequence diagram (for which the typical abbreviation is sd).

The frame and heading, new in UML 2, are applicable to all UML diagrams. Because UML 2 must be backward-compatible with previous work, the frame and heading are optional, and for the most part, you don't need to use them. However, we recommend using them with interaction and behavioral modeling as they form the basis for behavioral decomposition (as shown later in this chapter).

In Figure 12-2, we've diagrammed the main course from the Make Room Reservation use case discussed in Chapter 9 (and added a bit more detail for illustrative purposes). In this diagram, you can see how we used the sequence diagram to extract and show specific instances of communication among interacting entities. You don't show details of what must be done, just the messages — which makes it easy to see what's going on. This is an example of how UML uses abstraction to make your work understandable by hiding the details of internal behavior.

Choosing your interaction scenarios during analysis

You probably notice that the basic sequence diagram doesn't add much more than the textual approach to use cases (discussed in Chapter 9). Of the two techniques — textual use cases and graphical sequence diagrams — textual use cases actually contain more information. Sequence diagrams just extract and show the messages that move among the objects; the use case tells more about what the system has to *do* — which makes for a fuller picture of the requirements it must meet.

So, if you fully document a simple use case in text (using the techniques of Chapter 9), you probably won't need to draw additional sequence diagrams to account for every flow. On the other hand, pictures are worth thousands of words — and sequence diagrams are *very* communicative. Often the quickest way to get a team to understand a scenario is to put a sequence diagram on a whiteboard, extracting the essence of the scenario. This is an application of the principle of abstraction to improve communication.

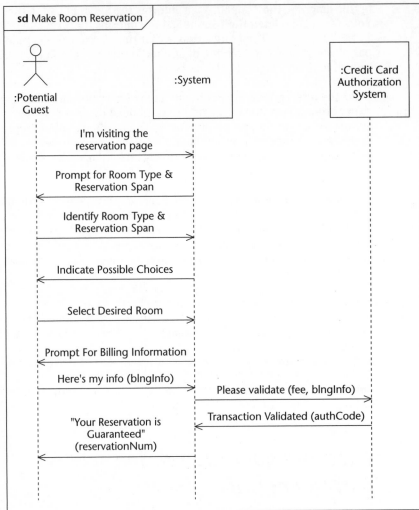

Figure 12-2:
A sequence
diagram for
the Make
Room
Reservation
use case.

Our practical advice — for initial analysis, anyway — is that you draw
sequence diagrams for only those scenarios that need better explaining or
supplemental communication. Drawing up the main course and one other
illustrative scenario would suffice for a typical complex use case. (Even that
might be too much for some simple use cases.)

If you need to draw other scenarios of a particular use case, abstract out the
essences of those scenarios and draw only the differences — that is, capture
the alternate flows, not entire alternate scenarios. Try to avoid getting yourself bogged down with redundant diagramming.

Examining object lifelines

Figure 12-2 shows the lifelines of three interacting participants: the actor Potential Guest, the system being built, and another actor — the Credit Card Authorization System. You can have your sequence diagram contain any UML entity that can exhibit behavior. Normally, these will be actors (see Chapters 8 and 9), systems or subsystems (see Chapters 9 and 20), objects (see Chapter 2), parts (see Chapter 5), and components (see Chapter 19). For sequence diagrams done during analysis (that is, before you do the design) that you use to diagram a use-case flow, you will normally be restricted to actors and systems. As you move into design, additional participants (usually objects) will start to appear. These will be the objects added to realize the scenario. At an even lower level, if you use a sequence diagram to diagram an operation's method, you can show lifelines for parameters and return values. Whatever type of participant you have, place its representative symbol at the top of the diagram and extend its dashed line to the bottom of diagram.

As the messages play across the lifelines, they tell the reader a story of the scenario. In my example, the actor, Potential Guest, visits the appropriate Web page, which notifies the system of his/her presence. The system displays prompts for necessary information, to which the actor responds. This alternates until the actor enters his/her billing information. Then, the system forwards the billing information to the external Credit Card Authorization. As authorization is granted, the system tells the Potential Guest that the reservation is guaranteed and the scenario ends.

Creating and destroying objects

Not every participant exists throughout the entire interaction. Although the external participants may be out of your scope, every internal object you must *create somewhere* and you must *destroy somewhere*. Before you finish design, you should find out those *wheres* for each major internal object. In Figure 12-3, for example, the object Reservation is created in this interaction (as indicated by a dashed line directly into the object's box), and the lifeline starts down from that point.

You can also indicate that you want to destroy an object in an interaction. In Figure 12-4, we show that the object Reservation is destroyed if the Potential Guest cancels his reservation. You can indicate this graphically by ending the lifeline with a large graphic X. In this diagram, we also show that one can use a selector or qualifier to indicate which specific object is participating. You can do this yourself by putting the selector in the qualifier brackets before the class name of the object.

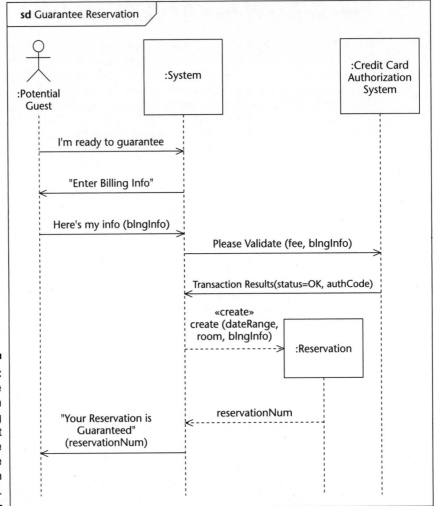

Figure 12-3:
Guarantee
Reservation
and creating
an object
within the
Guarantee
Reservation
system.

The basic notation for a participating entity's name includes such parts as
qualifier, selector, and class name, ordered as follows:

```
roleName [qualifier/selector] :ClassName
```

Place the name in the participant's box (or under it) on top of its dashed line.
In Figure 12-4, the rightmost lifeline represents the participating
Reservation object. Though we didn't bother giving it a specific role name
(it's optional), it's not just any Reservation object that gets destroyed. (We
use resNum as the selector to choose the correct Reservation object.) As
the figure indicates, the Cancel Reservation interaction requests a reservation number from the Potential Guest and uses the input resNum to
identify and delete the correct Reservation.

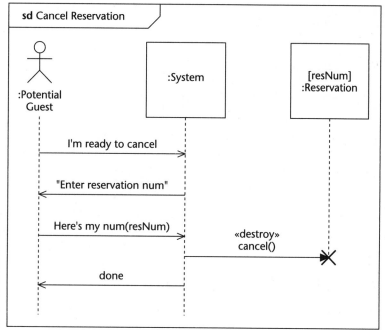

Figure 12-4:
Destroying
an object in
the Cancel
Reservation
system.

You may flag the creating message with the stereotype «create» (as we did in the Figure 12-3) and the destroying message with the stereotype «destroy», (as we did in Figure 12-4), but such redundancies often clutter up diagrams. Use them only if your UML tool requires them for code-generation purposes.

Sending messages

The lives of objects would be very boring if they didn't get messages from other objects. Each incoming message may stimulate it to calculate a result, to start a behavior, to create another object, or to die. The arrows from life-line to lifeline indicate one object sending a message to another object to stir up some activity or response.

When you have an object receive a message, it's a big event in the life of the object. It's called a ReceiveEvent and it occurs at the tip of the arrowhead where it touches the lifeline. (As you can imagine, the sending of an object is called a SendEvent, but those are less useful.) ReceiveEvents are important because they are the primary way an object gets to change its state. If you go to your state diagrams for the target object, you should find an incoming event for every possible ReceiveEvent and a corresponding *state transition* (a change of state caused by an incoming event) or *internal transition* (a response to an event without changing the state). By examining and combining all sequence diagrams that an object of a particular class participates in, you can complete the state diagram for that class. (You can find more about state diagrams, transitions, and using sequence diagrams to construct state diagrams in Chapter 16.)

You use the directed line to show the sending of messages from one object to another. While you do requirements and analysis work, or are early in your project, you'll probably be using the plain "V" arrow ($\rightarrow$) to show messages. (You can see several examples to this type of arrow if you refer to Figure 12-1 through 12-4.) When you use this arrowhead shape, you indicate that the message is sent and received in an unspecified manner, by some undefined signaling technique. That is, the sender may tap the shoulder of the receiver, pass a note, call on the receiver's telephone, or call on the receiver's operation. During design or later in the project, you need to be more precise. At that point, the $\rightarrow$ arrow indicates *asynchronous messages,* which we discuss in the section "Going on without an answer (asynchronous call)" later in this chapter.

Naming your messages

When you diagram a message, center the name of the message above the arrow to indicate what the sender wants the receiver to know. You can choose any of several message-naming styles. We generally recommend a naming approach that's informative or interrogative, but not procedural. (If the message tells the receiver that something happened, it's *informative*. If the message tells the receiver that the sender wants something, it's *interrogative*. But if the message doesn't tell the receiver what to do about the situation, then it's *procedural*.)

Good examples appear in Figure 12-3, where the `Potential Guest` tells the `System`, `I'm Ready to Guarantee`, and in Figure 12-4 the `Potential Guest` tells the `System`, `Here's my num(resNum)`. The sender tells the receiver that some information is available, and that an event has happened, is happening, or has stopped happening. Grammatically, these message names are declarative and are in the present or past tense. This naming approach is the most flexible because it assumes nothing about the nature of the relationship between sender and receiver. By using it, you support the good practice of *decoupling,* which entails encouraging flexibility by limiting dependencies between the participants.

Using parameters and arguments with messages

Messages can have parameters or arguments if you want to indicate data or an object being passed along with the message. The syntax for an argument (in a message or an operation) is as follows:

```
direction argumentName: ArgumentType [Multiplicity]
          = defaultValue
```

The direction is either `in`, `out`, or `inout`, indicating whether the argument is input to the message, output from the message, or both. If you don't specify the direction for argument, it defaults to `in`.

If there's a particular argument in the list that you don't need to specify because it's not relevant to your flow, you should replace it with a hyphen (`-`).

Use the `defaultValue` to show any explicit value that the argument takes in this scenario. By doing this, you make the story explicit and easy to follow. When you need to develop test scripts (later in the process of development), you'll find it convenient to use these sequence diagrams as a source if they have the values indicated. The following example of this technique also appears in Figure 12-3; here the result from the `Credit Card Authorization System` is a `status` of `OK`:

> *Transaction Results* `(status=OK, authCode)`

Early in your project's development, avoid getting too formal about your arguments; often the reader of the diagram can infer an argument from the name of a message. We recommend that you use actual message arguments for only the most important information you want the system to pass. Concentrate on the following tasks instead:

✔ **Keep your use case consistent:** There is often information you need to track for use-case purposes. Use high-level argument names and document them as classes in your class diagrams and/or in tables of text in your use-case specifications. By using the arguments in this way, you allow the use case's reader to track the information flow and check for completeness. Later, you should decompose these arguments into detailed components as they help the user-interface designer to determine what fields need to be included in the interface.

✔ **Documenting workflow:** A common pattern to these sequence diagrams is where the sender passes an object to receiver, who might do some work with it, but then passes it along to another receiver. This is an example of workflow, which might best be documented with a UML activity diagram (described in Chapter 13). However, you'll often find workflow illustrated in a sequence diagram. When you do, show the passed object as an argument in the messages as they go back and forth among the objects. Figure 12-3, for example, uses the argument `blngInfo` (short for `BillingInfo`) to stand for the information that the actor `Potential Guest` passes to the `System`, which passes it on to the `Credit Card Authorization System`.

Don't forget to consider drawing a state diagram (as discussed in Chapter 16) for the passed object if it changes state as other objects take turns dealing with it. And (of course) document the passed object in an appropriate class diagram.

As you start doing detailed design, replace any informal argument descriptions with complete definitions. Doing so allows your UML tool to check for consistency and automatically generate code.

Quoting a message

Another common approach is to put the message name in quotes when you mean that there is a literal error message or screen message that needs to be displayed. Even if the text is not meant to be the literal message text, using the quotes flags to the reader that a literal message needs to be written or a screen displayed. You might think of the quotes around `"Enter Reservation Number"` as shorthand for the wordier `I've Sent To You(msg:String="A Literal Message")`.

Designing a message name

During design and implementation, you should make the message names and their arguments match your intended implementation. If you implement your messages with an operation call (as most messages are), their names and their arguments should match your standard for writing operations. You can still use the informative and interrogative forms (described earlier in this chapter in section "Naming your messages"), but you may find it more useful to use imperative forms to the messages. For example, instead of `System, I'm Ready to Guarantee`, you're more likely to use something like `System Guarantee My Reservation` or `System.guaranteeReservation(res : myReservation)`.

Pressing a button

Another shortcut — used in naming messages and their parameters — you can apply when the argument of the message is a *button* name. This is the case when an actor sends the message by pushing a real physical button on the hardware (or by clicking a visual button on-screen). For example, instead of naming the message something like

```
buttonSelected(buttonName : ButtonNameType="Submit")
```

we recommend

```
selected Submit or submit Selected
```

or the even the simplest: `submit`.

We use the underline to replace the whole rigmarole of indicating the operation name, argument name and value. Yet it makes the message clearer to the reader and more likely to fit above the very small arrows that volley across typical sequence diagrams. For an example of how this looks in a diagram, you can refer to Figure 12-12 later in this chapter; it uses a `cancel` to indicate that the actor presses the Cancel button.

Your use-case specifications and their sequence diagrams typically shouldn't be so detailed that they contain user-interface button or key names. However, as you do more design, this shorthand allows you to be brief but precise in the more design-focused sequence diagrams that capture the details of the user-interface.

Designing messages and their methods

Using the plain, unadorned "V" arrow (→) during analysis indicates that you plan to use an unspecified signaling method to send a specified message. This approach may be acceptable while you're doing requirements and analysis, but it won't cut it when you're trying to implement the system. In-between the analysis and implementation phases, you have the chance to state exactly what you want to happen and how it should be done. This phase is called *design*.

Calling on a neighbor object

The most common mechanism for sending a message between objects is an *operation call* that uses standard software techniques. (Examples include a Java method, a C++ member function, and sending a message to a Smalltalk object.) You indicate that you want to use a standard call by using the solid triangular arrowhead (→) pointing in the direction of the call (that is either left or right, as the case might be). In Figures 12-3 and 12-4, we use standard calls to create and cancel the reservation.

Returning from a call on a neighbor

In these standard calls, control of the process transfers from the sender to the receiver. The sender pauses until the receiver finishes and returns. You may want to indicate the *return* (that is, the result you get) from a standard call as a message as well. Why? Because the return may bring in important values, information, or an object that you need to use. Or the return itself may be the significant event that transfers control. Returns are optional to indicate, but when you do so, you use a dashed V-headed arrow (←− −). For example, when the System creates a Reservation object (as in Figure 12-3), it returns the reservationNumber to the System for later use.

In Figure 12-5, we diagram a fragment of an interaction diagram in which an actor selects a hotel from a hotel chain and then prints out the information about the hotel. Because we've decided to make this a design-time diagram, we have dropped the actors from the diagram and have replaced them with *design-time boundary objects* (system components that act as the interface or boundary to the actor) we have chosen as part of our design. This is common step in moving to the details of the design-time modeling. Although actors are important to understand when you're modeling domains and requirements, they're usually not under your control when you're designing, so they're less important during this phase.

In Figure 12-5, we've chosen a common architectural design pattern in which a centralized controller maintains detailed, serialized control of the use case in a tightly scripted Kiosk environment. Here the `Controller` calls each input boundary device in turn, and waits until it gets a response. Messages such as these — going to the boundary objects from the central controller where the central controller has to wait for a response — are indicated with a solid triangular arrowhead (→). You indicate explicit returns with the ←—— and place the return value on top of the arrow.

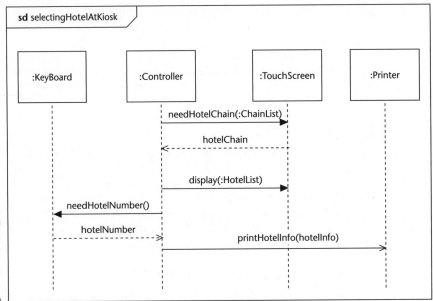

Figure 12-5:
Centralized
pattern
architecture.

You need not always mark the return message explicitly. If the message expression uses the operation form and indicates the return type (or if nothing of interest is returned), you can drop some clutter by dropping the return message. For example, in Figure 12-5, both the needHotelChain(:ChainList) and the display(:HotelList) messages are sent as calls from the Controller to the TouchScreen boundary object. The Controller waits for a reply from the TouchScreen for the selected HotelChain, but does not wait on the TouchScreen for a reply for the display(:HotelList) call, so we decided to skip the explicit return arrow. The Controller does need to know the selected hotel, but we designed that to return via a separate call to the Keyboard.

Going on without an answer (asynchronous call)

Sometimes you don't want to transfer control — or don't want to wait at all. You want the sender of the message to keep on going. This situation is called an *asynchronous call* and it's where you use the V-shaped arrow (→) during design.

Although the use of asynchronous calls is becoming more common, technically you may use them only if there are multiple threads of control in your system (physically or logically), that is, only if the sender can remain running while the receiver is working. In Figure 12-5, the `Controller` call to the `Printer` is an asynchronous call — which is logical because you rarely want to wait until the printer is done before you go on to the next task. Most systems allow spooling of the print job to the printer and concurrent printing and computing.

Signaling by other means

You may find it useful to choose other specific mechanisms for sending a message. Every operating system has several underlying message communications techniques. While they are rare to be used directly for most object-oriented developers, if you need to use them and don't mind breaking portability you can indicate the mechanism by stereotyping the message with the mechanism, such as «`interrupt`», «`spin-lock`», «`semaphore`». If you use a particular mechanism often, you may want to create a specialized graphic adornment to indicate your mechanism. In Figure 12-6, we list the standard adornments, plus a few common ones we've used that are not currently part of the base UML 2 standard.

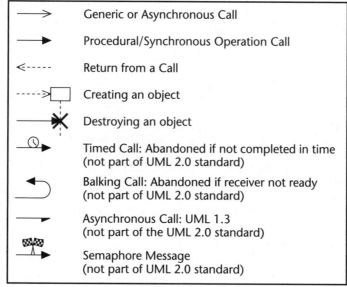

Figure 12-6: Some possible message adornments.

Choosing your interaction scenarios during design

Using interaction diagrams (such as sequence diagrams) during your design activity is very different from using them to gather requirements or assist in analysis. Interaction diagrams can approach the detail and specificity of code. If you are a programmer, you're likely to be reluctant to be so precise without obvious gain.

There are three primary reasons to consider using sequence diagrams for design:

✔ **Improved understanding before coding:** While you're likely to be more familiar with coding (and therefore more comfortable with it), UML diagramming — whether with a good-quality tool or a whiteboard — is actually easier to do. It's worth investing your time to do it well. Once it becomes second nature to you, you'll find that you can see the general outline of your design in advance — before you even start coding — and you can check it out to make it better, safer, and more complete. To get a visual handle on complicated interactions, you can draw UML interaction diagrams of them before coding them.

✔ **Improved communication:** If you're a designer responsible for leading several people's implementations or tests, you'll find that communicating a design is a lot easier when you use diagrams. The way you want a behavior to work is a lot easier to explain (especially when it involves several objects) if you use UML interaction diagrams. Showing someone a pile of code won't do much to convey the big picture, nor offer much insight into the way multiple operations work together. Draw UML diagrams to communicate your design for prototypical interactions — and to communicate the sense of how similar interactions are to work.

✔ **Improved testing and execution:** Increasingly the UML tools can test the logic and generate complete code from diagrams such as the interaction diagrams. When using such tools, you won't need to be thinking as much in a code-specific or language-specific manner unless performance considerations become paramount. Visual modeling and visual testing increasingly eliminate the need for much of the implementation phase — and its associated costs. Of course, reaping that benefit requires near-codelike specificity in the diagrams, but the result is a design that can operate independently of any particular implementation — which saves money and time. If you're modeling with a tool capable of generating quality code and/or tests, plan on modeling sufficient scenarios to exercise all the logic.

Composing Interaction Diagrams

We discussed the basic parts of a sequence diagram earlier in this chapter: the participating objects and their lifelines, events, and messages. But a problem that occurs with sequence diagrams, as with any sort of scenario-based documentation or diagramming is that they can become complex as well as redundant. The scenario and its corresponding sequence diagram, for a Potential Guest making a successful online reservation is very long, and the scenario for failing to so (because of a rejected credit card) is just as long and mostly the same. If you run into this problem while constructing use cases, simply capture one scenario as the main flow, abstract out the essential differences between the scenarios, and document the differences in an alternate flow,(as described in Chapter 9).

In sequence diagrams, you do almost the same thing. Instead of documenting the essential differences somewhere else, you use the power of graphical representation to display the variations side by side. (Remember, however, that you can suppress details for readability's sake, and present them later.) In this section, we cover some ways you can use UML to document complex scenarios.

Referencing and reusing interactions

The most common problem with sequence diagrams — or, for that matter, with any interaction diagram — is that you can't quite avoid redundancy with another sequence diagram: Often two scenarios overlap. The solution here is to make (and document) an interaction occurrence that you can refer to in several other diagrams. The technique is easy and pretty slick: Any named interaction diagram can be referred to by name and inserted into another diagram.

Earlier in this chapter, we provided a sequence diagram for the scenario of guaranteeing a reservation (shown in Figure 12-3). Suppose that diagram contains an interaction that we want to reuse elsewhere — or from which we want to extract the details for encapsulation. To refer to this interaction, we use what UML 2 calls an *interaction occurrence,* which is a reference to a reusable piece of an interaction defined elsewhere.

In Figure 12-7, we first define the sequence diagram for Validate Credit Card. Here the interaction is simple, consisting of two objects and two messages, but it could be very complex.

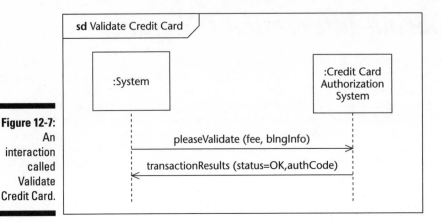

Figure 12-7:
An
interaction
called
Validate
Credit Card.

In Figure 12-8, we refer to our defined interaction by using a UML frame with the operator in the label box, ref, and the title of the interaction in the body section of the frame. This reference is an occurrence of the interaction Validate Credit Card, hence the name interaction occurrence. You can use a reference like this anywhere in an interaction diagram. In typical use, it just means inserting the referenced behavior into the larger diagram. This approach is a suitable way (especially for use cases) to eliminate redundant diagramming.

Adding parameters to an interaction

You can use this sort of reference anywhere in an interaction diagram. In the typical use, it just means that there is an insertion of the referenced behavior into the larger diagram. However, you often find that the behavior has some slight differences in each occurrence. You need to be able to tailor the inserted sequence diagram to the current situation.

You can be more explicit about how the inserted behavior works while making it more reusable if you add *input and output parameters* to the interaction. In Figure 12-9, for example we've redefined the inserted sequence diagram to indicate that it needs fee and blngInfo as inputs and that it returns status as a return value and authCode as an out parameter. The syntax for indicating the input and output parameters is the same as shown for operations in Chapter 3.

Figure 12-10 shows how these returned values are now used. You indicate where you want to assign the returned values in the reference to the interaction. In the reference to the Validate Credit Card interaction of Figure 12-10, the System.Transaction.Status attribute is assigned the return value from the interaction (the use of the equal sign indicates the assignment), and the System.Transaction.AC is assigned the value of the out parameter authCode. When the Validate Credit Card interaction finishes, both output parameters (the return value status and authCode) are assigned to some attribute of the Transaction object that is part of the System object.

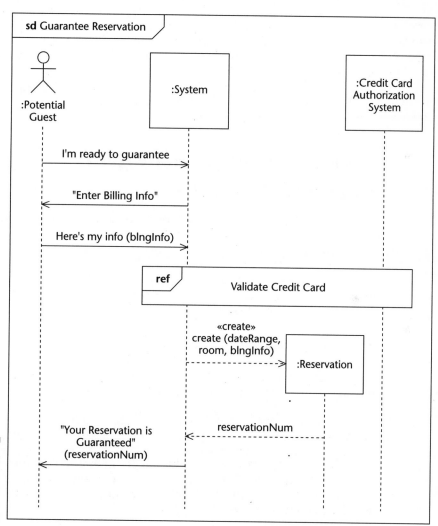

Figure 12-8:
Incorpo-
rating a
reference.

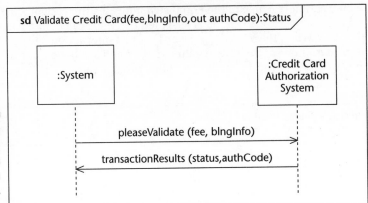

Figure 12-9:
Adding
arguments
to an
interaction.

Alternating interactions with combined fragments

One common difficulty occurs when the main path splits into several paths and depends on the return from a message (or some other condition) before it can proceed.

UML 2 gives you several different operators to use in this situation; you can indicate whether a sequence may be optional (opt), may be repeated (loop), or may have an alternative (alt).

Taking an optional path

You can use a frame with the opt operator to indicate that it may not be used under some circumstances. Usually you place an explicit *guard* (that is, a test) in square brackets to indicate such a condition.

In the example shown in Figure 12-11, we've changed the reference to the interaction occurrence of Validate Credit Card to return a generic Status from the previous example of Figure 12-10, where we set the Status to OK. This is followed by a frame with the opt operator. The whole interaction fragment contained in the frame is optional — and can only occur if the guard [status=OK] is true. You can also put the guard in the label along with the operator opt [status=OK].

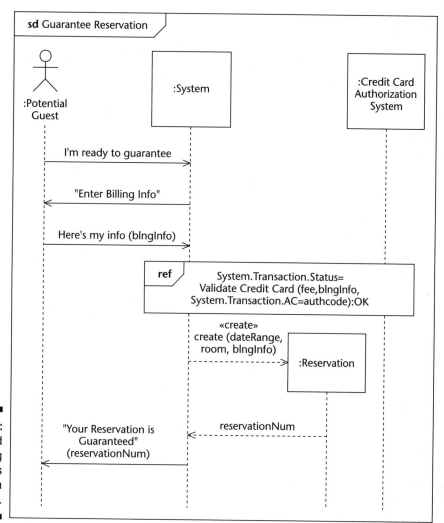

Figure 12-10:
Passing and
returning
arguments
from an
interaction.

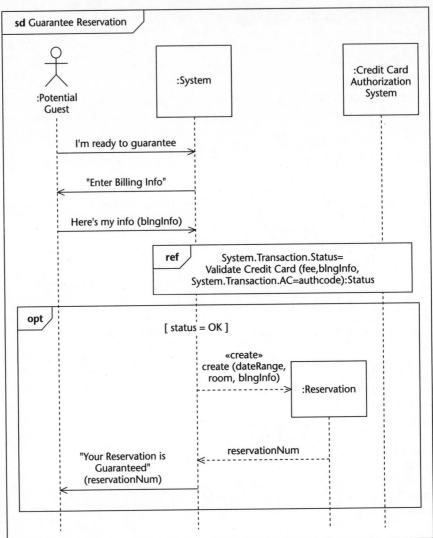

Figure 12-11:
An optional
interaction.

Looping around a path

In some situations, instead of an interaction occurring zero times or one time, it may be repeatable multiple times. That's when you use the loop operator, which looks like this:

```
loop minint, maxint, [guard]
```

You replace *minint, maxint, guard* with actual values as follows:

- ✔ *minint*: Must loop at least this number of times.
- ✔ *maxint*: This parameter is optional. The interaction may not loop more than this number of times. If not given, `maxint` = `minint`.
- ✔ *guard*: A guard is an optional condition shown in square brackets. After the first `minint` iterations, the condition is tested before each additional loop iteration. If the condition is false, then the loop is abandoned. If the `guard` is not specified, it is assumed to be true, so the loop continues to iterate until the `maxint` iterations are performed.

An example of a loop is shown in Figure 12-12. We allow the `Potential Guest` three tries to find a credit card to be good. By setting the `minint` to 1, we're requiring the loop to be executed at least one time. By setting the `maxint` to 3, we're requiring the loop to execute no more than three times. The loop exits early if it tries to start the second or third iteration and the guard, `[status=bad]` is false, which will be the case if the card's status is good.

Breaking out of a loop

Loops can be sticky, and often you'll find you need a way of escaping from them. UML supplies the `break` operator for that purpose; you can use it to indicate the scenario that causes escape from a loop (or from any enclosing segment) and that processing continues with the first message after the loop. In Figure 12-12, we show that if the actor selects the Cancel key/button, the loop is immediately escaped.

Making a decision on the path

If you have two more choices for the path to take, you can set yourself up with the `alt` operator. Divide your frame into sections with interactions inside each of the sections. Place a guard to control whether the section is entered. You can use `[else]` as the guard to the last section — it will be entered if none of the above sections are entered (because all the other guards are false).

The `alt` operator is the construct to use if you're thinking of including an `if` or `case` statement in your code. In the example shown in Figure 12-12, the top section of the `alt` operator is executed if `status=OK`. If the `status` is not `OK` — say, because the loop executed three times without success or because the actor hit the Cancel key/button — then a warning message is issued instead.

Choosing advanced operators

UML 2 gives you many operators to use if you want to compose complex interaction diagrams. The operators indicate which of several interactions would be executed (such as `alt`), how many times to execute a particular interaction (`loop`, `opt`, `break`), how to interpret the interaction (`assert`, `neg`), and the relationship of the interaction with other ongoing interactions and events (`par`, `region`). Table 12-1 shows some of these operators and how you can use them. For the programmers among you, we give some idea of the programming statements that correspond to some of these operators.

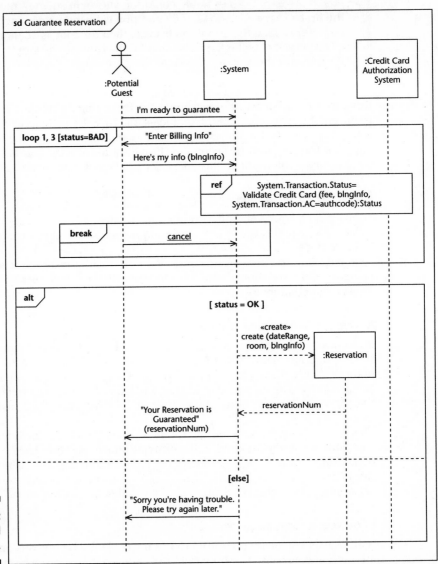

Figure 12-12:
Looping and
alternatives.

Table 12-1		Operators in an Interaction Diagram
Operator	*Keywords*	*Description*
alt	[guard1] ... [guard2] ... [else] ...	Selects one interaction to execute from a set of interactions. The selected interaction follows a true guard condition or an [else] condition if none of the guard conditions are true. In programming, this corresponds to statements like case or if] ... then ... else ... endif.
assert		The selected interaction must occur exactly in the way indicated. If it doesn't, you have an invalid interaction.
break		If the selected interaction occurs, the enclosing interaction (usually a loop) is abandoned. You may be familiar with this as the programming statements of break or escape.
loop	minint, maxint, [guard]	Execute the interaction minint times, then execute the interaction up to maxint times as long as the [guard] is true. This corresponds to programming statements such as do ... until, while, or for ....
neg		This interaction is invalid and can't occur.
opt	[guard]	This interaction only occurs if the [guard] is true. This corresponds to the programming statement if...endif .
par		This operator indicates several interactions that may run concurrently (overlapped in time). For example, several threads of the interactions Make Room Reservation and Canceling a Reservation may be running in parallel.
ref		Refers to an interaction defined elsewhere. This corresponds to the programming concepts of call or invoke or the use case concept of «include».
region		The enclosed interaction is a *critical region*. No other messages can interleave. A critical region is needed when a shared resource is updated to prevent the updates from overlapping and producing inconsistent results. You would typically use this within parallel interactions. For example, many threads of the Make Room Reservation may be running in parallel, but a critical region is needed when you seize the room, or else several Potential Guests may wind up reserving the same room.

Chapter 13

Specifying Workflows with Activity Diagrams

··

In This Chapter

▶ Defining activities

▶ Documenting business processes

▶ Ordering operations

▶ Controlling object flow

··

Sometimes, when you are modeling a system or developing software, you need a good old-fashioned dataflow diagram, workflow diagram, or behavior flow diagram. UML has a sort of updated version of the dataflow diagram — called an *activity diagram* — to help you out in just such a situation. Class diagrams show you who (which class or classes) is related (associations and generalizations) with whom (other classes) — and what each can do (each class's operations). Sometimes even all that isn't enough. In this chapter, we show you how to use activity diagrams when you want to emphasize the order of behavior and not necessarily who does the behavior. We give you some tips for modeling complex operations, intricate use-case interactions, and business workflows.

Ordering the Flow of Behavior

When you want to explore the flow of behavior across classes, use an activity diagram. Although your class diagrams (see Chapter 3 and Chapter 7) tell you who performs what operations, they don't show a valid sequence of operations across classes. If you build a state diagram (see Chapter 16), you show a sequence of operations — but a state diagram limits you to the operations within a single class. The activity diagram, on the other hand, allows you to show the flow of behavior across *multiple* classes. Use activity diagrams whenever you want to show object flow, dataflow, or the flow of control across different classes.

Dissecting an activity diagram

All activity diagrams have a few basic elements. Normally you use the following pieces to diagram the flow of behavior:

- **Action:** A simple piece of behavior is called an *action*. An action cannot be further decomposed into smaller actions. You can specify pre- and postconditions for an action — defining what must be `true` before the action can execute and what must be `true` after the action executes. An action could be any of the following:

  - Getting or setting an attribute value

  - Invoking the operation of another class

  - Calling a function

  - Invoking an activity that contains actions

  - Sending a signal or notification of an event to a group of objects

  You show an action in UML notation as a rounded rectangle. Place the name of the simple behavior as text inside the rounded rectangle.

- **Activity:** Activities contain sequences of actions and/or other activities. You use activities to group sequences of actions together. At the level of an object-oriented class, you can use an activity to represent the method of an operation. You can also use activities to represent the tasks that make up a business process.

  You diagram an activity as a rounded rectangle with the name of the activity inside (as with an action). You can also show activities in a large rounded rectangle containing complex sequences of actions, activities, object flows and control flows. The complex form of an activity also allows you to show parameters, preconditions, postconditions, and properties of the activity.

- **Control flow:** Think of control as moving like a stream that connects actions and activities together; shows the sequence of execution.

  Connect your activities and actions with a line that has an arrowhead to indicate the direction in which control is flowing. For example, you draw a control flow from an activity like `Browse Book` to an activity such as `Make A Note`.

- **Object node:** Your classes' operations take in parameters and generate return results. Activities modify objects or transform objects into other objects. You use an *object node* to show these objects as they move from activity to activity.

  You use a class box with the name of the object's class to show an object node. You can also describe the state of the object by including the name of the state in between square brackets underneath the name of the class.

✔ **Object flow:** In the old days, this was known as *"data flow."* Now the experts call the flow of objects, *object flow*. You use activity diagrams to show this flow of objects from one activity or action to another.

✔ You place an object node between two activities or actions to show object flow. Connect the first activity or action with a line and an arrowhead in the direction of the object node. Then connect the object node to the second activity or action with a line and an arrowhead in the direction of the second activity or action.

✔ **Control node:** You use *control nodes* to guide the flow of control (and the flow of objects) through a group of activities and actions. Control nodes come in a variety of forms, depending on what you need; they serve as traffic cops for the flow of control and flow of objects. The control nodes are as follows:

- **Initial:** You start a sequence of activities or actions with an *initial node*. An initial node is shown as a large dot.

- **Final activity:** When you want to end all control flows and object flows in an activity, use the *final-activity node*. Show final activity with a bull's-eye symbol.

- **Final flow:** If you want to end some — but not all — flows inside an activity, use the *final-flow node*. You show a final flow as a small circle with an X inside.

- **Decision:** A *decision node* uses a test to make sure that an object or control flow goes down only one path. Use this node when you want to construct an *if-then-else* selection for an execution path. You indicate a decision node with a large diamond shape. Connect the diamond with each downstream activity or action by drawing a control-flow arrow. Place decision criteria for each path in square brackets on the control flow line.

- **Merge:** You bring separate decision paths back together with a merge node. Show your merge using a large diamond shape. This is the same shape as a decision node. Decision nodes create divergent control paths through an activity diagram. The merge node allows you to bring those divergent paths back together again following a decision node. Merge nodes do not have any decision criteria in square brackets.

- **Fork:** Sometimes you need activities or actions to work in parallel. To split behavior into concurrent operations, use the fork node. A fork looks like (you guessed it) a fork. You show a fork with one line going into the fork and multiple lines coming out the other side.

- **Joins:** A join is the opposite of a fork. When you want to bring parallel flows of operations back together, use the *join*, a symbol that looks like the mirror image of a fork.

- **Connector:** If you run out of room on your diagram and you need to continue the flow of control to another page, use a *connector* —

a small circle with a label inside. The connector indicates that the flow picks up at another location in the diagram or on another page where you find a connector with the same label.

Older versions of UML had activity diagrams, but UML 2 takes this diagram to a new level. Previously, activity diagrams were a special kind of state diagram. You could show flow of control across classes — from one operation to another — but the diagram limited the kinds of flow you could show. UML2 provides activity diagrams that act like a *Petri net* — a flow that works kind of like a pinball machine: Instead of silver balls, objects known as *tokens* (which represent other objects or the presence of control) can bounce from node to node (that is, flow from activity to activity). In UML 2, activities and actions *consume* tokens and *produce* tokens — so now you can construct pure flow diagrams that pass the tokens around.

Utilizing activity diagrams

We recommend using activity diagrams in several different situations:

- ✔ **High-level operations:** When you have a class with a complex operation that involves many steps, use an activity diagram to show those steps as a sequence of activities.

- ✔ **Use-case details:** If one of your use cases is really a *group* of steps performed concurrently, use an *interaction-overview diagram* — a form of activity diagram that shows the flow of interaction between the main success scenario and any alternative scenarios. We show you an example interaction overview diagram a little later in this chapter.

- ✔ **Workflow or business-process flow:** Activity diagrams are great for modeling business processes, not just software operations. You show who performs activities, which decisions must be made, and what documents the business process generates.

- ✔ **Process modeling:** Since activity diagrams are the latest form of the good old data-flow diagram, you can use them to model any process. You model the steps in a process as activities and show sequencing with control flows and control nodes.

- ✔ **Summarize many sequence diagrams:** If you find yourself generating lots of sequence diagrams for a use case — usually to make sure you capture all allowable orderings of events — then consider creating an activity diagram to summarize those sequence diagrams. The complex behavior of your use case — with its concurrent sequences — may be easiest to grasp as an activity diagram.

Avoid the function trap. If you use the activity diagram as a way to pick apart functions into subfunctions (and the subfunctions into subsubfunctions), then beware — you may have fallen into the "functional decomposition" trap that lies in wait for anyone who builds object-oriented systems and software. After all, your system or software is composed of *objects, not functions*. Each object has a responsibility to perform certain behavior when asked. Functionality emerges from the collaboration of objects invoking behavior on each other. To avoid the functional trap, keep in mind *who* performs each action and *who* is responsible for each activity.

Figure 13-1 and Figure 13-2 illustrate the basic use of activity diagrams to document a high-level operation. This example focuses on the planTrip operation of the Person class. The operation takes one parameter — travelBooks : Book[0..*]. When you invoke the planTrip operation, you pass in zero or more instances of objects called travelBook — instances of the class Book. When planTrip completes, it returns an instance of the Itinerary class. The Person class has the needs attribute with the NeedKind datatype. NeedKind is a datatype that enumerates the different needs a person may have. Those needs are shown in the NeedKind class stereotyped with «enumeration».

Figure 13-1:
The Person
class with a
high-level
operation:
planTrip.

Person
notes: Travel Note [*] needs: NeedKind
planTrip(travelBook : Book[0..*]) : Itinerary

«enumeration» NeedKind
vacation eat sleep work pay taxes

Suppose a person like you needs a vacation (no challenge there). To plan a trip, you get your hands on several travel books and browse each book. If you have an interest in the locations discussed in one of the books, you take some notes, look into the location in more detail via the Internet, and call some friends. After you settle on a place to go, you make reservations and end up with an itinerary. Figure 13-2 captures your behavior for planning a trip in an activity diagram.

The name of the complex activity — Plan Trip — is shown in the large, rounded rectangle in the upper-left corner. You show parameters underneath the name of the activity. In this example, the travel-book parameter is shown as travel book: Book. You show pre- and postconditions in an activity close to the name of the activity, in the form of text preceded by a stereotype of the right type. Figure 13-2 shows the need vacation as a precondition and complete itinerary as the postcondition.

You name activities with a verb phrase. Your activities express some behavior that an object or objects will perform. Just like use case names (see Chapter 3), activity names are best stated as an action verb followed by a noun or simple noun phrase.

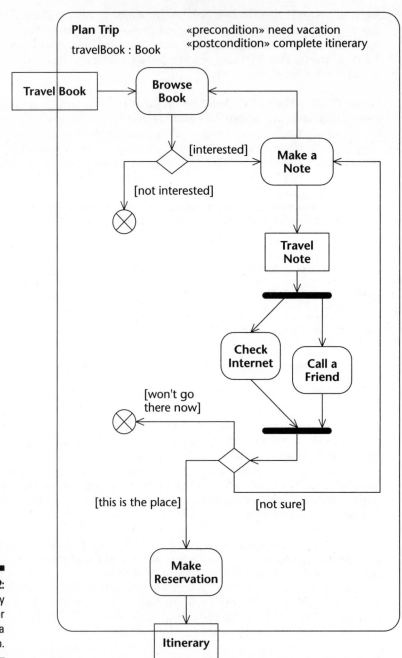

Figure 13-2:
Activity
diagram for
planning a
trip.

Whenever you have a complex operation, declare the pre- and postconditions for the operation. *Preconditions* describe what must be true before the operation can execute. *Postconditions* express what is true after the operation completes successfully.

After you determine which objects(s) flow into an activity (you identify them via parameters) and the object(s) that an activity returns (you identify them via operation result types), place them on the outside contour line of the rounded rectangle. Diagram incoming objects as object nodes inside a class box. The Plan Trip activity has an incoming Travel Book object node on the contour line of the activity. Any outgoing objects are also shown as class boxes. The Itinerary object node is also shown on the contour of the Plan Trip activity.

As a modeler, you can reveal activities, actions, flow, and control nodes inside the border of a complex activity, as we did in Figure 3-2. In the example, you see a sequence of steps — Browse Book, Make a Note, Check Internet, Call a Friend, and Make Reservation — in order to plan a trip. You show each step in a rounded rectangle. Flow of control passes from activity to activity along the lines in the direction of the arrow. For example, control flows from Make a Note to Browse Book after the Make a Note activity finishes.

In this example, we use several control nodes to further guide the flow of objects and the flow of control. For instance, a diamond-shaped *decision node* directs flow of control according to whether the person planning a trip is interested in the contents of a travel book he or she has finished browsing. If the person is interested, then control flows onto the Make a Note activity. If the person is not interested, then control flows to a final flow node — the X in a circle.

As you look at an activity diagram, visualize objects flowing down a path like balls in a pinball machine. For example, a travel-book flow begins as follows:

1. Into the Plan Trip activity.

2. Moves to the Browse Book activity.

3. When the Browse Book activity finishes, the travel book is passed on to the decision node:

   • The decision node tests the interested condition. If the condition is true, then the book moves on to the Make a Note activity. If this condition is false, then the decision node tests any other conditions attached to it.

   • The decision node tests the not interested condition. If the condition is true, then the book moves on the *final flow node* — where it disappears. The job of a final flow node is to remove any objects that flow into it.

From here, the flow continues on through the rest of the complex activity.

Your activities can generate new object nodes. For example, Make a Note generates instances of the Travel Note class. These travel notes are passed on, like balls in a pinball machine, to other activities.

If you have activities that happen concurrently, use a combination of fork and join control nodes. In the example, Check Internet and Call a Friend are activities that happen at about the same time but are independent of each other. Above these two activities is a *fork control node* — a thick horizontal line with one control flow line coming into it and two control flows coming out the bottom. The flow of control comes back together into a single path with the use of a join control node shown below these two activities.

Concurrent does not mean *simultaneous*. Concurrent activities may occur at the same time, but they are always independent of each other; one concurrent activity could start before other concurrent activities and end before they are complete.

Working through Workflow Diagrams

Your specific needs for modeling workflow can come in many shapes and sizes. The example in Figure 13-2 illustrates the use of an activity diagram at the level of a complex operation on a class. You can also use UML for more than developing software. We use it to model business processes, document flow, and employee responsibilities. The activity diagram is very useful when you want to illustrate work flowing through a business process. You can also document complex use cases with what is known as an interaction overview diagram.

Be careful not to use the activity diagram at too low (that is, detailed) a level. Activity diagrams can potentially specify the line-by-line code for a method — but (alas) today's UML tools don't generate code from activity diagrams. So if you find yourself thinking, "I could have already written the code in the time it took me to draw this activity diagram," then you're definitely modeling at too low a level.

Diagramming use case steps

Some of your use cases are likely to be complex enough to have a main success scenario, many alternative flows, and error flows. UML 2 has come to the rescue by making possible a special kind of activity diagram: the *interaction-overview diagram*.

In an interaction-overview diagram, you show *interaction occurrence nodes* connected by control flows instead of showing action and activity nodes. An interaction occurrence is some notation for referencing a full-fledged sequence diagram. You draw an interaction-occurrence node as a rectangle with a small thumbnail in the upper left-hand corner. The thumbnail contains the keyword ref. The rest of the box contains the name of the interaction. See Chapter 12 for more details about interaction occurrences.

You can help others to understand complex use cases by giving them an overview of how the interaction sequences flow. For example, Figure 13-3 shows a simple use-case diagram for the process of making a room reservation in a hotel reservation system.

Figure 13-3:
A use-case
diagram for
Make Room
Reservation.

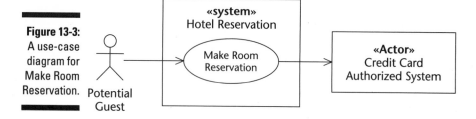

Figure 13-4 shows an interaction overview diagram, looking suspiciously similar to an activity diagram. Instead of enclosing the diagram with a symbol for complex activity (a rounded rectangle), you use a sequence-diagram frame in a regular rectangle.

Use interaction occurrences instead of activities when you need to show alternative flows. Use decision/merge nodes and fork/join nodes to indicate the flow of control through the use case.

To construct an interaction overview diagram for your complex use cases, follow these steps:

1. **Place the name of the use case in the upper-left corner just after the sd keyword.**

    In the example in Figure 13-4, the name is Make Room Reservation.

2. **Start your interaction with an initial node, a large dot.**

3. **Draw a control flow that starts at the initial node and goes to the first interaction occurrence.**

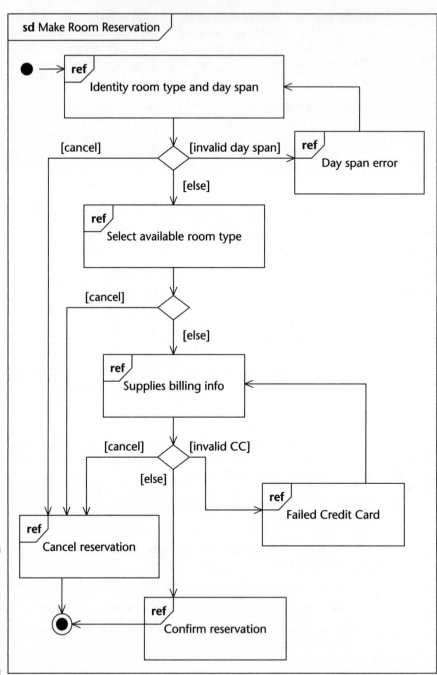

Figure 13-4:
Interaction
Overview
diagram for
making a
room
reservation.

4. Break up your main success scenario into groups of interactions.

Draw your main success scenario, breaking it up into groups of interactions. To make a reservation our actor, `Potential Guest`, must pick a room type and day span for the reservation, select an available room type, supply billing information, and confirm the reservation.

5. Each group of interactions becomes an interaction occurrence.

You show each interaction occurrence as a box with the `ref` keyword in the upper-left corner and the name of the occurrence in the middle of the box. For example, `Identify room type and day span` is a small interaction between the `Potential Guest` actor and the system. You show this referenced interaction in another sequence diagram. If the interaction is simple, you can show a mini-sequence diagram instead of an interaction occurrence.

6. Connect the main success scenario interactions with control-flow lines to show the correct sequence.

The `Select available room type` follows the `Identify room type and day span` interaction occurrence.

7. When you have an alternative flow, break the control flow between interaction occurrences and insert a decision node or a fork node.

If the alternative flow or flows are concurrent to the main success scenario, then use a fork to indicate it; otherwise use a decision.

In the reservation example in Figure 13-4, a decision must be made between the `Identify room type and day span` and the `Select available room type` interactions. If `invalid day span` is true, then control flows to the `Day span error` interaction occurrence. If `cancel` is true than control flows to the `Cancel reservation` interaction occurrence. Otherwise, control flows normally to the next part of the main success scenario.

Repeat this step as needed to encompass all the alternative flows for your use case.

8. Use merge or join nodes to bring any alternative paths that pass through the interaction diagram back together (if necessary).

This is the same technique used in an activity diagram. The example illustrated in Figure 13-4 doesn't require any merge or join nodes.

9. You must use the activity final node in your interaction overview, because all use cases must come to an end.

In the reservation example, the interaction ends after the `Confirm reservation` interaction or the `Cancel reservation` interaction. To indicate this situation, you place a bull's-eye at the bottom of the diagram with control flow lines coming from those two interaction occurrences.

Indicating the responsible parties

UML 2 lets you show who is responsible for an activity or an action in two ways:

- ✔ **Swim lanes:** You can divide up your activity diagram into rows or columns, called *swim lanes*. To understand the concept of swim lanes, think of placing your activity diagram in a large pool. At the head of the pool you place each person involved in the business process, each in his or her own swim lane. Each person who dives into the pool then swims over the various activities for which they are responsible.

  You show swim lanes as parallel lines across or down the page. At the top or side of the lane put the name of the person, job role, or organizational unit that is responsible for performing the activities in that lane. Place the activities or actions for that party inside the lane.

- ✔ **Partition names:** When you can't use swim lanes, you can just place the name of the responsible party in parentheses inside the rounded rectangle above the name of the activity or action.

When you model a business process, it's necessary to show each part of the process and each individual responsible. With UML, you show business processes as an activity diagram with swim lanes. Figure 13-5 shows the process of getting through an airport to board a plane. This business process involves four participants: Passenger, Ticket Agent, Airport Security, and Boarding Agent.

We chose to place the swim lanes in vertical swim lanes because they fit the page better, but we could have used horizontal swim lanes. Each lane has the name of one participant. Each participant is responsible for performing the activities in his or her lane.

You notice the Ticket object changes state as it moves through this activity diagram. When the Ticket Agent performs the Generate Pass activity, the Ticket object has the valid state. After the Boarding Agent performs the Stamp Pass activity the Ticket changes to the used state.

 Use a connector when you run out of space in an activity diagram. For example, we ran out of room at the Receive Pass activity that the passenger performs. So, we placed a connector with the label A. Then we drew a control-flow line from Receive Pass to the A connector. Using the same technique, you can pick up the control-flow path at the connector with the same label A at the top of the Passenger's swim lane, and then proceed to the Wait in line activity.

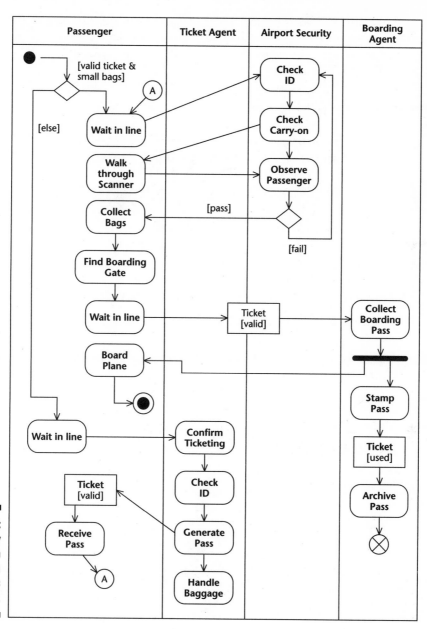

Figure 13-5:
Activity
diagram
showing a
business
process.

Figure 13-6 shows two examples of partition names placed inside the activity's rounded rectangle. Instead of using swim lanes, you can show that the `Passenger` is performing the `Wait in line` activity and `Airport Security` performs the `Observe Passenger` activity.

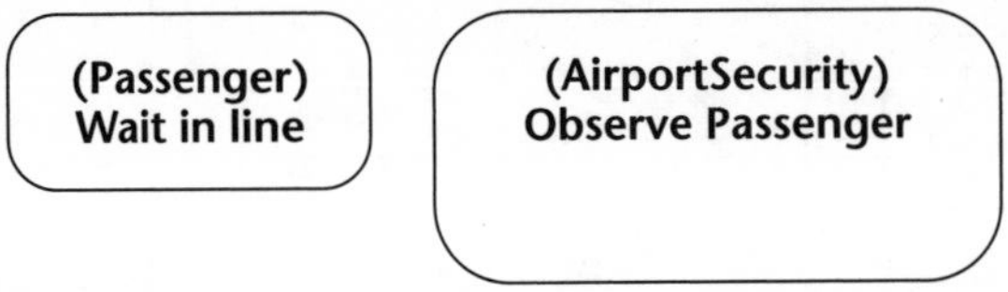

Figure 13-6:
Showing
who's
responsible
with names
placed
inside an
activity.

(Passenger)
Wait in line

(AirportSecurity)
Observe Passenger

Chapter 14

Capturing How Objects Collaborate

··

In This Chapter

▶ Structuring a communication diagram

▶ Numbering your messages

▶ Conquering concurrency with communication diagrams

▶ Capturing the design of a collaboration

··

*T*o get a job done, you design interactions among a set of participating objects so that they can work together to achieve your goal. UML gives you several tools to work out the details of these interactions, such as sequence diagrams, communication diagrams, activity diagrams, and timing diagrams. If you follow the diagramming guidelines given in Chapter 11 (along with the techniques of this chapter), you'll be using communication diagrams when it's necessary to design the details of an interaction.

Communication diagrams are not really new to UML 2, but their name is new. In the previous UML 1.*x* versions, these diagrams are called collaboration diagrams, because they show how objects collaborate to meet a goal. While this was a good name, UML also uses collaboration to mean something else. In UML 2, a *collaboration* is a specification of how a set of objects and associations playing specific roles realize an operation or use case. Therefore, with the old terminology, a collaboration diagram was just *one* way of indicating the details of *one* scenario that a collaboration was realizing. Confusing? You bet. So, the UML gurus finally decided to change the name to *communication diagrams.*

In UML 2, when you attempt to design a collaboration (the set of classes and associations that realize a use case or an operation), you'll need to specify the participating objects and links. Then, for each possible scenario that the use case or operation has, you must specify the interaction of messages among the participating objects and links in the collaboration.

To do this, you'll need one or more interaction diagrams to capture these scenarios. Sequence diagrams will probably suffice for many circumstances, but as you move into detailed design, you may find the capabilities of communication diagrams more suitable to your needs.

While the new UML 2 communication diagrams look a lot like the old UML 1.x collaboration diagrams, they seem to be significantly less complicated, and unfortunately, less expressive and powerful. In this chapter, we offer advice on how to regain some of the lost expressiveness, while still keeping you from drowning in details. We've asked the UML 2 team at OMG to re-insert some of the features they've taken out for the sake of compatibility and power. You'll need to keep track of future revisions to UML 2 (perhaps UML 2.1) to see exactly how they've done the corrections.

Developing a Collaboration

In the following sections, we outline the design of a `GenerateBill` use case using some of the communication diagram features. This process starts with the analysis class diagram for the classes that must participate in this use case, which we change by adding some specific design features to help accomplish the use case's behaviors.

As the class diagram evolves to incorporate the design of the use case and appears to stabilize, you construct a communication diagram that walks through the designed interaction, showing the step-by-step interchange of message over the objects and links participating in our use case.

As you make decisions in the communication diagram, go back to the class diagram to ensure consistency. You need individual communication diagrams to capture different scenarios of the use case. This suite of communication diagrams and the class diagram evolve to capture the design details of the dynamic behavioral view and static class view consistently.

Structuring a design class diagram

When you construct a communication diagram, you need to identify the participating objects and lay them out in a static structure diagram, such as a class diagram. You can find more about the typical features of these diagrams in Chapter 3 and Chapter 5.

Figure 14-1 shows the initial class diagram drawn during analysis for the example use case `GenerateBill`. In the example diagram, you can see that each `Room` has an ordered set of `Stays` (indicated on the diagram by the property {ordered} and the multiplicity *), and for each `Stay` and date, there is an associated `RoomRate`. A `RoomRate` can be for multiple `Rooms`, but for each combination of a `Stay`, a `date`, and a `RoomRate`, there is an association class `Lodging` that has some information about the specifics on that `date`, such as the number of occupants for that day.

For each `Stay` and `date` there is also a set of `RoomCharges` that can be applied — which might include things like room service or videos. We could have hooked the `RoomCharges` to the `Lodging` instead of directly to the `Stay`, but we felt that the `RoomCharges` are probably generated by different subsystems than the `Lodging` charges, so it's probably better to separate the responsibilities.

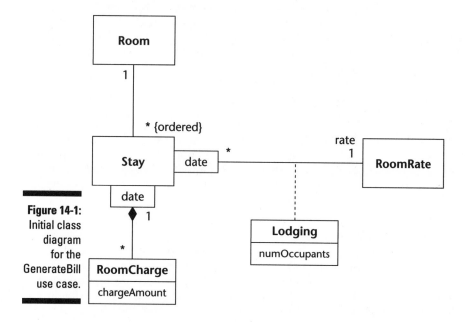

Figure 14-1:
Initial class diagram for the GenerateBill use case.

Focusing on a central class

A *central class* or *focus class* is the class that a use case appears to be most concerned with — usually creating, finding, or manipulating instances of that class or using it to find other information needed by the use case. You can see that the central class for this use case is `Stay`, as most items of information needed for the use case — in particular, the items on the bill — are available close to the `Stay` class. Though the needed information is accessible from the other classes, the distance from the `Stay` is the shorter. Of course, the measure here isn't the physical distance on the diagram, it's how many hops it takes to get to the information.

When you can identify the central class for a use case or operation, you have a head start in designing the collaboration. For example, as the interaction among the classes kick off, much of the behavior will need to be focused on how to find the correct instance of the central class. After it is found, this instance will probably be the correct place to assign most of the work. Knowing which class is the central class will allow you to focus your attention on the right place.

Now that we know that the central class is Stay, we need to design our approach to finding the correct instance of Stay as the use case runs. From the logic of the situation, it appears that the actor can be asked for the room number. To help find the correct instance of the central class (Stay), we create a HotelInventory class that acts as a container holding all the available rooms of the hotel. Its main behavior will be to find a particular Room object given a room number. (Refer to Figure 14-3 later in this chapter to see how this design-time container class is positioned.) The HotelInventory container uses the qualifier roomNumber as an index to the Rooms. If you know the roomNumber you can use the HotelInventory to find the Room you want. (The use of qualifiers as indices on associations is discussed in Chapter 4.)

From the correct Room, the use case then needs to find the correct Stay. We assume that the GenerateBill use case is normally started upon guest checkout, so we can use the latest Stay associated with the Room. It's possible to find the latest Stay from the Room, because the Stays are ordered from the perspective of the Room (back to the {ordered} property on the diagram).

Controlling a use case

Whenever you have a complex use case, you should consider which object controls and organizes the required behavior. Typically, no existing object from the initial class diagram will do. Though each object has its own natural responsibilities that are found by analyzing the use case and the problem domain, the control and organization responsibilities tend to be part of the solution and need to be added. Following good design practice of keeping our classes focused on doing one thing and doing it well, you shouldn't add these new responsibilities to any of the existing classes. Therefore, you need to design a new class — a use-case controller class that will initiate and coordinate the activities of the classes to meet the needs of the use case. Typically in these circumstances, you would name the use-case controller class with the name of the use case, GenerateBill, as you can see in Figure 14-3.

We recommend that you flag your controller classes with a special stereotype, such as «use-case controller» or «control» to remind the designer of the special features that controllers usually have. (We use «controller».) For example, a use-case controller typically requires its own active thread at run-time and is also ultimately responsible for the interaction with the actor.

As you progress, you'll often find other common design changes being made to standard modeling approaches. For example, when you see an association class, such as the Lodging class in Figure 14-1, you may need to convert it to a class that lies as an intermediate class between the ends of the original association (an *inline* class). You can see an example of how to do this in the sample diagram of Figure 14-2. This diagram shows the trick of keeping the promoted multiplicities correct. The outer multiplicities become inner multiplicities — they switch sides on the promoted class — and the outer multiplicities are replaced with 1.

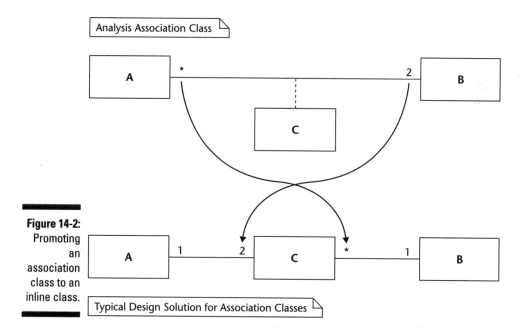

Figure 14-2:
Promoting
an
association
class to an
inline class.

Though there are other possible design/implementation approaches to association classes, the transformation shown in Figure 14-2 is the most common because it's easy to implement and easy to make the objects live in a database. We promote the association class Lodging in this manner in Figure 14-3.

Adding an output class

There is at least one more design class you need to add to the initial diagram shown in Figure 14-1. Because our use-case GenerateBill produces a bill, you must make sure that the Bill class is on the diagram. (Granted, that should be obvious, but the lack of it is a common error found in many diagrams.) For now, hang the Bill class off the use-case controller (as in Figure 14-3).

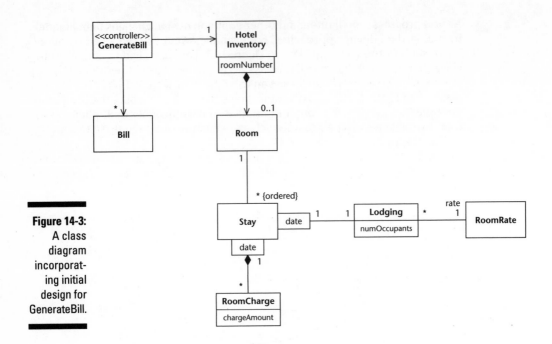

Figure 14-3:
A class
diagram
incorporat-
ing initial
design for
GenerateBill.

Preparing the participants

Using the class diagram as a guide to designing the collaboration, you need
to select the appropriate participants. We use a UML object diagram (as
described in Chapter 7) or a UML composite structure diagram (as described
in Chapter 5). In order to make such a diagram, you identify the objects
(instances) that need to participate, or you convert the classes to parts. (You
can treat the participating instances as internal parts of the collaboration in
the same manner as you treat internal parts of a class using the treatment
found on composite structure diagrams that we discuss in Chapter 5.) The
parts use the same syntax as those of lifeline references as described in
Chapter 12.

The basic name of the part/lifeline references for these purposes is as follows:

```
referenceName[selectors] : className
```

The component pieces of this syntax are as follows:

✔ referenceName is the handle you use to refer to the part. It may be
    the rolename of the participating object's class, the name passed in a
    parameter or local variable that contains the participating object. The

referenceName is optional, so you often see just the class name when there is only one object for that class in the collaboration.

✔ selectors is an optional field that selects a particular object or objects from a set. It may be a qualifier, an indexing subscript, or some Boolean expression. You don't need it if the referenceName refers to an object with a multiplicity of one.

✔ className is the class or type of the participating object.

Figure 14-4 shows the participating parts of the communication diagrams for the GenerateBill collaboration. In this diagram, the objects for the controller class GenerateBill (which controls the use case) and the container class HotelInventory (which contains and finds Rooms) don't need any referenceNames or selectors because they are unambiguous (there's only one of each of them). However, because there are many possible bills, you need to identify a specific Bill. In this model, the specific Bill being constructed is given the name of newBill.

There are also many rooms in the HotelInventory. To identify the specific Room, we've supplied a value rmNum as the selector. This corresponds to the value of the qualifier roomNumber off of the HotelInventory. (Refer to Figure 14-3.)

In the same manner, from the point of view of the [rmNum]:Room, there are still many possible Stays. When you generate a Bill, it's always for the most recent Stay, so a selector of [latest] is used. Selectors like *1st, 2nd, last, latest,* and *n*th are only allowed when the underlying association between the respective classes is an ordered or sorted association (as indicated by {ordered} or {sorted} on the diagram). If the association is not ordered or sorted, there's no way of asking for a positional element in effect, it's just a set of elements without an order.

From the point of view of the [latest]:Stay, there are many Lodging objects and RoomCharge objects. The [date] qualifier can address either type of object, so you can use a value for date or a dateRange as your selector. As either type of object can have multiple instances, you can also put the * multiplicity in the upper-right corner as a reminder.

Finally, the RoomRate class had a rolename of rate in the original class diagram (see Figure 14-1). Use this rolename as the referenceName for the part for consistency among the diagrams.

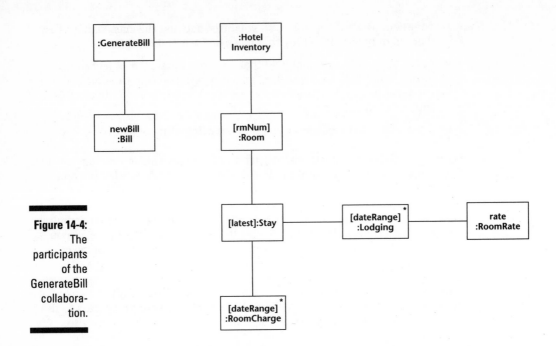

Figure 14-4:
The
participants
of the
GenerateBill
collabora-
tion.

Constructing the Communication Diagram

You place the messages used to perform the collaboration on the basic diagram of the participants. Each message, which is a communication between a sender object and a receiver object, is indicated on a line connecting the two of them.

The whole diagram is enclosed in a frame and you use the abbreviation sd to stand for your communication diagram.

You may be wondering why the abbreviation for a communication diagram is sd and not cd. We've wondered about that, too — and we've complained. Looks like this must have been one of those silly compromises that got made when the UML gurus got too tired. They wanted all the interaction diagrams to have the same abbreviation — to *simplify* things. And they didn't want to use id or int because they thought *those* would be confusing. That's why we have to live with sd as the abbreviation for *sequence diagram, communication diagram, timing diagram,* and *interaction-overview diagram.* The gurus can always justify using sd by saying that a communication diagram is a type of sequence diagram. With any luck, an early revision to UML 2 may yet fix it. In the meantime, if all that ambiguity bothers you, you may want to use cd as your abbreviation for *communication diagram* (provided your UML tool allows it).

The name of the communication diagram is the name of the use case or operation that you are diagramming. Because you are typically doing design when you make a communication diagram, you should consider taking a more formal approach to documenting the arguments and return values of the interaction. In Figure 14-5, we name the interaction based on the use-case name GenerateBill(rmNum:RoomNumber, out newBill:Bill).

With this as a name, you indicate that the GenerateBill interaction takes a RoomNumber as input argument — and that inside the interaction, this argument is called rmNum. There is also an output argument (of type Bill) that will be called newBill inside the interaction. Normally, if you create an object inside an interaction and it has to be visible outside, you also indicate it as an out argument or a return.

Numbering steps sequentially

Message syntax on a communication diagram is essentially the same as for the sequence diagram. (You can find more information on this syntax in Chapter 12.) The first key difference you notice is that on your communication diagram, the messages are numbered — and each message is executed in sequential order. By examining Figure 14-5, you can see that the following steps are executed in this order:

1. thisRoom=getRoom(rmNum): First, the GenerateBill controller asks the HotelInventory container class to find the correct Room object with the given rmNum. The correct object is returned and placed in an attribute within the GenerateBill controller named thisRoom. The HotelInventory object can find the correct Room because this relationship is indexed/qualified by roomNumber (See the Figure 14-3).

2. occFlag=isOccupied(today): Next, the GenerateBill controller queries the Room to see if it isOccupied(today). The GenerateBill controller can send the message to the room because the query is called on the Room object that is was returned from call #1.The notation thisRoom at the end of the message line reminds you of the way the GenerateBill controller knows about the object. The results from the query are returned and stored in an occFlag (short for occupationFlag), which is a local attribute of the GenerateBill controller.

   This is a good example of how designing the messages can cause structural changes to the class diagram. Because the GenerateBill now knows about a Room object, we may decide that there is a link between the two objects. We cover this and other approaches in Table 14-1.

3. **[occFlag] newBill = Bill(thisRoom, controller=self): Next,** the GenerateBill controller queries the Bill and tells it how to find the room by passing it the thisRoom argument. The controller has this value because call #1 returns it. But, before the call can be initiated, the controller checks the guard condition [occFlag], which was returned from call #2. If the call is performed, the Bill object is returned as newBill, which matches the return argument of the interaction.

The controller also creates a reference to itself and passes that to the Bill. This reference will be used in the next call (call #4) so the Bill can find the controller again. Self is a reserved keyword, representing the calling or executing object.

4. **billReady(self): Lastly, the Bill object calls the billReady() opera-** tion on the GenerateBill controller and passes a reference to itself back to the controller. The Bill is able to find the controller because the controller was passed in call # 3.

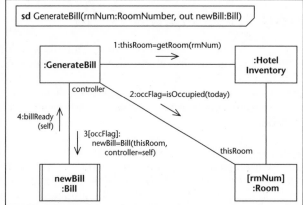

Figure 14-5:
Initial
commu-
nication
diagram.

Outlining procedural calls

Communication diagrams give you the numbering capabilities to display graphically the calls to operations — and then the calls from those called operations, and (in turn) the calls from the operations *they* call, and so on. If you can keep your head from spinning, you can identify as many levels of calls and operations as you need (or at least as many as will fit on the diagram).

This miracle is done by using a tool you've seen if you've ever examined a table of contents: an *outline-numbering* scheme. If an object gets a message to execute an operation that is numbered 3:, any messages it then issues (numbered

3.1:, 3.2:, or 3.3:) are *subordinate* messages because they're issued within the context of 3:. Accordingly, any message starting 3.x: must complete its business before the top 3: message can be considered complete. This follows the traditional outline numbering pattern shown below:

```
3:
    3.1:
    3.2:
        3.2.1:
        3.2.2:
    3.3:
    3.4:
4:
```

In Figure 14-6, we use some outline numbering of the messages. Examine (for example) message 2, where the GenerateBill controller asks the Room object if it isOccupied. To accomplish this work, the Room object also calls an operation on another object; in this case, it calls an operation on the latest Stay object ([latest]:Stay). Because this operation is subordinate, it needs a lower-level outline number. You would use 2.1, because this is the first (and only in this case) subordinate operation within operation 2. In the example, this operation on the Stay returns an occFlag to the Room if the latest stay included today. The Room, in turn, returns the occFlag back to the GenerateBill controller. When you use this outline-style technique of numbering, you can detail how each operation works and calculate results for its caller.

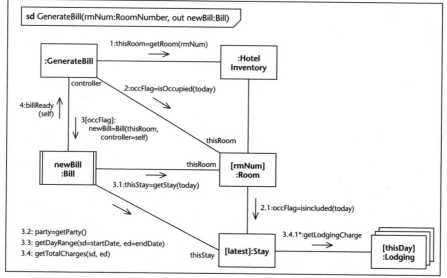

Figure 14-6:
A communi-
cation
diagram
with outline
numbering.

Message 3: also has some subordinate steps:

```
3[occFlag]: newBill = Bill(thisRoom, controller=self)
    3.1: thisStay = getStay(today)
    3.2: party = getParty
    3.3: getDayRange(Bill.sd = sd : startDate,
                     Bill.ed = ed : endDate)
    3.4: getTotalCharges(sd, ed)
        3.4.1*: getLodgingCharge()
```

This sequence of messages is governed by the guard condition on message 3. If the [occflag] is false, the whole sequence beginning with 3 is skipped. If [occFlag] is true, then message 3 is sent to create the Bill. Then (as the diagram says), the Bill sends message 3.1 to the Room and follows up with message 3.2, 3.3, and 3.4 to the Stay. As any number of levels can be used, message 3.4.1* getLodgingCharge() is sent by the Stay to the Lodging.

Looping

In Figure 14-6, you may see that there is a message with an * in the sequence number, 3.4.1*: getLodgingCharge(). This * indicates that many instances of that message are sent with that same number. We recommend thinking of this * as a multiplicity indicator, similar to that used on UML associations. If there's just a *, it indicates that the message is to be repeated as often as needed. If you repeat a message, then you also repeat all its subordinate messages.

If you want to have the message repeated a specific number of times, the syntax is as follows:

```
SequenceNumber*[iteration clause]:
```

The iteration clause has several common forms:

- **Boolean expression:** The expression repeats as long as the expression is True. A message such as 3*[isMoreNeeded] would continue until isMoreNeeded=False.

- **loopVariable=lowerLimit..upperLimit:** This expression initializes the loopVariable to the lowerLimit and sends the message. Then the loopVariable is incremented and tested against the upperLimit. As long as the loopVariable is in range, the message is sent again. These upper and lower limits may be integers or ordered enumerations of values. For example, the messages 4*[thisMonth=Jan..Dec] and 4*[thisMonthNumber=1..12] would both execute 12 times.

✔ **Codelike looping syntax:** UML allows you to write the iteration clause *using the target programming language*. Although there is some value to this practice, I wouldn't recommend tying your model to your programming language; after all, the language could change in the future. Also, your UML tool may not understand the syntax exactly — so it probably won't generate high-quality code.

In Figure 14-7, I've used the loopVariable approach in two locations. Look at message 3.3 from the Bill to the Stay. This tells us how the returned out arguments (sd and ed) are set and where their results go. Upon return, the two arguments, that of sd and ed, are set to the startDate attribute of the Stay and the endDate attribute for the Stay. Then, these values are saved in the Bill as Bill.sd and Bill.ed. Later, in message 3.4*, the Bill uses the sd and ed as (respectively) the lower and upper limit for a loop. The Bill sets up a loop with a loopVariable of thisDay and asks the Stay to retrieve the total charges for this day, via the call 3.4*[thisDay=sd..ed]: getTotalCharges(thisDay).

Message 3.4.1 is sent inside this loop to [thisDay]:Lodging, which illustrates that the loopIndex value, thisDay, (being passed in as a parameter in 3.4*) is being used by the Stay to find (or select) the correct Lodging. Within 3.4.1, the Lodging asks the RoomRate object for information on the rate. Every time the 3.4 loop iterates, you have message 3.4.1 sent, and then message 3.4.1.1 is sent.

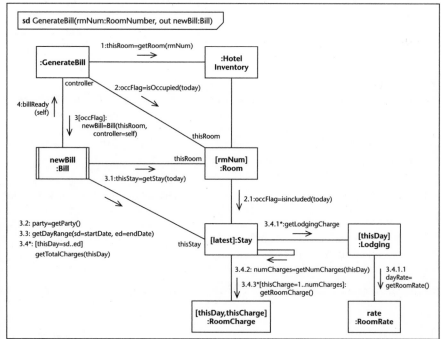

Figure 14-7:
A communication diagram with looping.

Looping or selecting?

Often an ambiguity can crop up when you send multiple messages to a specific lifeline (a part reference) on of a communication diagram. A lifeline refers to a participating instance, but the naming structure allows the reference to point to different instances in each loop iteration. Such a sending *could* mean that there are many messages, each sent to a separate instance, or it could mean that there are many messages, all sent to the *same* instance. Fortunately, you have several ways of trying to clear up this problem.

One common approach that was possible in UML 1.*x* was to indicate that the destination is a *multiobject*. Unfortunately, the UML gurus have eliminated this feature from UML 2, but many tools will still support it and it may be re-inserted

in UML 2.1. This technique involves making the target lifeline box look as if there's a stack of objects slightly offset. I've used this approach in Figure 14-6 on the Lodging. When you use this notation coupled with an * in the incoming message, you're indicating that the loop of messages is over different objects in the set.

A better solution, though only possible when you are using an explicit loop counter, is to make the loopVariable part of the selector of the lifeline. As an example, imagine that you want to create an array of the number of working days per month for a payrollCalculator. In the figure in this sidebar, there is a message that loops over the months and asks each month for the number of working days.

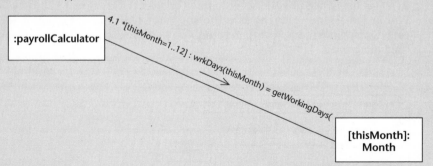

Note carefully that the loop index is used as the selector of the Month — and as the subscript of the return value from the call. This technique is very powerful; it allows specific identification of the elements of target lifelines, arrays, or any ordered collection. Of course, you can only use the loopVariable as a selector if the lifeline (in this case, the Month) is ordered in one of two ways:

✔ As an array, where the specific elements are indexed or referenced by a numerical value, such as 1..12

✔ Addressable by an *enumerated qualifier* that already has a defined order, such as the values, Jan, Feb, Mar, Apr, May, Jun, Jul, Aug, Sep, Oct, Nov, Dec

You may have to go back to the class diagram that contains the Month class and make sure that there is such a qualifier or an ordered relationship that you can traverse to find the correct month.

Messages 3.4.2 and 3.4.3 are also sent within the 3.4 loop. Message 3.4.2 is an operation call sent by the Stay to itself, to return the number of Charge objects associated with it for the current day getNumCharges(thisDay). The result returns as numCharge.

This result is then used to construct another loop — an inner loop that uses the index thisCharge and loops from 1 to the numCharges. As both loops — thisDay and thisCharge — are going on at the same time, you can use both loop indices to select the charge on which you want to operate.

Conquering Concurrency

Normally when you construct communication diagrams, the messages are all *sequential* — you can use a traditional, outline-style numbering scheme to indicate the order of the messages, and only one message is ever active at a time. Of course, in sophisticated multithreaded systems, you may have multiple threads running at once. If you refer to Figure 14-7, for example, you can see that the Bill object, when it has to return information to the GenerateBill object, does so with a call back to the GenerateBill rather than with a traditional return. We designed it this way because the Bill has lots of work to do that doesn't involve the GenerateBill. If we can free up the GenerateBill controller, it may be able to work with other guests to generate other bills while our Bill is busy. We treat Bill an active object that has its own thread of control distinct from that of the use case so the two objects can run independently.

Whenever you have a class or object that owns its own thread of control that it is able to run independently of its caller, you have an *active object.* You might want to use an optional notation on the Bill object to indicate that it is an active object. You indicate this by placing parallel, vertical bars next to the left and right sides of the class or object box (as in Figure 14-8).

We've been throwing the words *concurrency* and *concurrently* around a bit — and yes, you could run to the nearest dictionary and come up with a definition for them. Here, however, *concurrency* has a formal meaning in computer science and the world of UML — one that differs slightly from its everyday meaning.

If two events, A and B, are *concurrent,* the following must be true:

✔ There is no causal relationship between A an B (neither causes the other).

✔ A can occur before B, or B can occur before A.

✔ A and B can occur simultaneously (it's not logically impossible).

A and B don't have to run simultaneously — in fact, that's pretty rare, and it often has more to do with how precisely you record your time. And in single processors, A and B can't really run simultaneously, unless they swap in and out in a time-sharing way.

Looping concurrently

Whenever you indicate a loop in UML, the normal interpretation is that each iteration of the loop runs sequentially: The first iteration runs and finishes, and then next iteration runs and finishes, and so on until the last iteration. Often, however, this interpretation is overly restrictive — and not strictly necessary. If the results of the loop would be the same, no matter what the order of iteration (say, counting down instead of up), then you may be able to make all the iterations run concurrently. On some hardware, the compiler automatically detects whether the results of an iteration depend on the order — if they don't, the compiler forwards each iteration to a parallel processor.

If you want to have the loop iterations run independently and concurrently, use the following syntax:

```
3.4*||(loopIndex=lowValue..HighValue): msg()
```

Adding the two bars indicates that you want the iterations of the loop done concurrently (or in parallel — in which case, the bars are parallel). Adding the bars doesn't guarantee that the implementation will be done that way — after all, it's sometimes a platform consideration. For example, some platforms can't do parallel loops at all, and some can do no more than 255 at a time. But adding the bars does signal your intent that no loop iteration depend on any other — and that you *prefer* a parallel implementation. You can see an example of this concurrent looping in Figure 14-8 if you look at the following message:

```
3.4b.2*||[thisCharge=1..numCharges]:
          rc[thisCharge] = getRoomCharge()
```

The getRoomCharge() is a simple retrieval operation, so all the charges are retrieved at once (concurrently) and stored into a local array called rc[]. We show the assignment to rc[thisCharge] because we are using the lifeline/part notation and [thisCharge] is the selector (or qualifier) that indicates which object we are setting. (Ignore the b in the message number; it indicates a thread, which we explain later in this chapter.)

Identifying independent threads

If you work with multi-threaded systems, you may want to be explicit about concurrent processes. In UML, if you want to indicate that messages are to be sent concurrently, you have to give them the same sequence number. But to distinguish them, you give them individual names. For example, the following three messages would be sent concurrently, as they all share the same sequence number 4.1.

```
4.1cotton:       msg1()
4.1nylon:        msg2()
4.1polyester:    msg3()
```

All three threads run concurrently. Each of the different threads has a character string tag that can be used to identify it (cotton, nylon, or polyester). If you don't sew, you can use thread names like a, b, or c.

The thread names are useful because you still want to be able to identify subordinate messages on a communication diagram. For example, the following message executions have to obey the rules that govern subordinate sequence numbers:

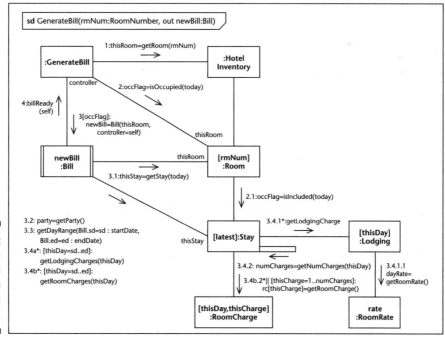

Figure 14-8:
A communication diagram showing concurrency.

```
4.1cotton:
4.1cotton.1:
4.1cotton.2:
4.1cotton.2.1:
4.1nylon:
4.1nylon.1:
4.1nylon.1.1:
4.1nylon.1.2:
4.1polyester:
```

These rules require that `4.1cotton.1:` finishes before `4.1cotton.2:` can start. And before `4.1cotton.2:` can finish, `4.1cotton.2.1:` must finish. To have `4.1cotton::` finish, `4.1cotton.2:` must finish also.

A similar ordering occurs with the `nylon` thread. However, because the two threads are concurrent, you can't say anything about the relative order of any cotton message or nylon message. You could have `4.1nylon.1.2:` running before `4.1cotton.1:` finishes or vice versa.

In Figure 14-8, there are two independent threads:

```
3.4a*[thisDay=sd..ed]: getLodgingCharges(thisDay)
3.4b*[thisDay=sd..ed]: getRoomCharges(thisDay)
```

In each thread, there is a loop over the number of days in the stay. Because each loop is a normal loop, each iteration of each loop occurs in order. But because the two loops are concurrent, the two loops are not in synch and could finish in any order.

In both threads, there are subordinate steps. In the `3.4a` thread, for each iteration of the loop there is a call to the `Lodging` and the `Lodging` then calls the `RoomRate`. In the `3.4b` thread, concurrent with the `3.4a` thread, each iteration of the loop has the `Stay` asking itself for the number of charges and then in a parallel loop, asking the `RoomCharges` for their values.

Capturing the Collaboration's Design

Each step you take to add detail and flesh out the steps in the communication diagram captures more information on how the collaboration works. Some of this design detail requires the underlying classes or associations to change their definitions. You have to go back to the class diagram and make sure that the features from the communication diagram map to the features of your class diagrams, as detailed in Table 14-1. Your tool may automate some of this mapping — updating one diagram may automatically update the others. You want to be sure that the communication diagrams and the class diagrams are consistent; they should be different views of the same underlying model. So in the table below we list several of the possible communication diagram design features, and we tell you what these features would be in the class diagram. By looking at Figures 14-8 and 14-9, you'll see how we did the mapping in practice.

Table 14-1	Mapping Communication Diagram Features to Class Design
Communication Diagram Feature	*Mapping to Class Design*
Message name	Target class must have an operation (or a signal reception) by that name.
Argument list	Argument lists on the class's operations/signals must match the communication diagram, in direction, type, number, name, and order. It's not required that the argument list be duplicated. Argument values may be used on the communication diagram if they can be matched directly and are compatible with the arguments of the class.
Return assignments	If you assign a named value, the results of a message return value must match the type of the return value from the operation. The named value must be an attribute or local variable of the calling class. If the named value is only used by that object within its current operation, you may use a local variable. If used in subsequent operations, or required to be persistent (live in a database), make it an attribute.
Selectors / qualifiers	Check to see if the relationship has a qualifier or is {ordered}.
Call direction	If during an operation on A, A invokes another operation on B, it must know about B. It can do this because of a link, or a parameter being passed to A that references B, a return value to A referencing B, or because B is in a well-known (global) location. If the knowledge about B needs to be remembered for other operations on A, or is persistent, the best solution is a link. Otherwise, it may be possible to store a reference to B locally for the duration of A's operation. When in doubt, use a link. Only a unidirectional link is needed from A to B. The reverse direction is needed only if B calls an operation on A.

In Figure 14-9, we've applied the guidelines of Table 14-1 to the details of the communication diagram shown earlier in Figure 14-8. Whenever there was a choice in identifying a feature as an attribute (as opposed to a local variable), we chose an attribute, primarily because it made it visible on the diagram. When you do this work of abstracting the design, you'll need to be more discriminating. You only need to use attributes if the knowledge of the value or reference is persistent across calls.

If you have multiple interactions or scenarios to describe for this collaboration, incorporate the features from all the communication (and sequence or timing) diagrams used to detail the interactions.

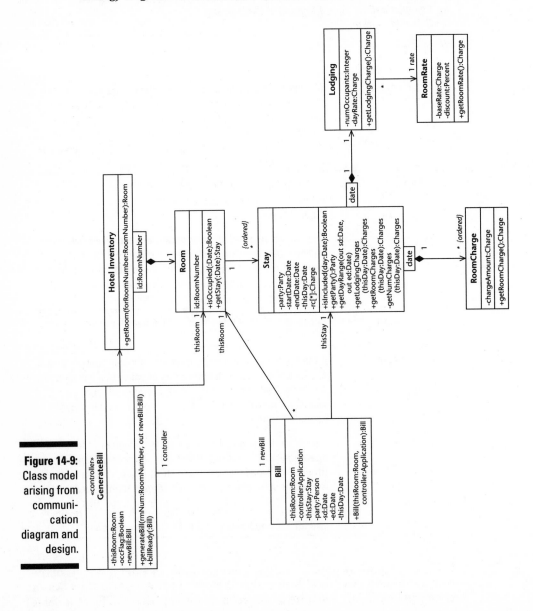

Figure 14-9:
Class model arising from communication diagram and design.

Chapter 15

Capturing the Patterns of Behavior

In This Chapter

▶ Defining patterns and frameworks

▶ Developing your own patterns

▶ Using UML to document your patterns

*Y*our object-oriented software succeeds because objects work together — they collaborate. Out of this collaboration emerges the functionality of your application. While developing applications, you've probably experienced déjà vu — you know, the sense that you've seen this program before. Many of your fellow practitioners capture these frequent programming solutions and call them *patterns* or *frameworks* — reusable solutions to common problems. In this chapter, we show you how to develop and document patterns and frameworks so you too can communicate your reusable models and designs.

Describing Patterns with Collaborations

You don't want to reinvent the proverbial wheel. In the old days, craftsmen built a physical template for a wagon wheel into the floor of a barn. They'd reuse the template or pattern to create a new wheel by bending wood to fit the framework etched in the floor. Builders, craftsmen, and engineers use the same basic approach to solving hard problems — they develop a pattern, using the following steps:

1. **Build ad-hoc solutions to a development problem.**

   The answer to a complex problem requires you to make a choice among competing alternatives. You build different solutions when you're not sure what works best or which solution offers the best results.

For example, suppose you must write software that constructs a complex assembly for a CAD/CAM (Computer-Aided Design/Computer-Aided Manufacturing) application. You must program two behaviors: the process of constructing the whole assembly (an air-filter unit) and the creation of each part in the assembly. The first thing you do is build several different software solutions to assemble air-filter units for the CAD/CAM application. These two bits of behavior can be programmed in many ways, and you need to try several solutions to see which one works best.

2. **Find the solution that works best in different situations.**

   In our running CAD/CAM example, the most successful solution to putting together a complex assembly is found by separating the two behaviors into different classes. You need a class that represents the assembly of an air-filter unit and a class that knows the process of constructing an air-filter unit.

3. **Abstract commonality out of your best solutions.**

   Find and extract the important common features (classes, attributes, operations, associations) of your solutions and make the solution as general as possible. Base your decisions on practice, not on theory. Look at balancing such competing factors as cost to build, time to build, and performance of the resulting solution.

   In the CAD/CAM software example, the common features of successful solutions are as follows:

   - **Provide a class that directs the construction of the whole assembly.** A `Director` class knows how to direct the assembly of air-filter units. The `Director` does not actually build each part, just knows which part to build in what order to build the parts making up the assembly.

   - **Define a common interface for building each part.** The interface must capture the operation signature (see Chapter 3) for building an assembly so we'll call the interface `Builder`.

   - **Supply a specific class that knows how to build individual parts for the whole assembly.** Since this class actually knows how to build individual parts for the assembly it gets the name `ConcreteBuilder`.

4. **Create a pattern that describes the abstractions you developed in Step 3.**

   Providing other developers with a pattern description helps you communicate clearly what works.

5. **Reuse the pattern in the appropriate situations to boost productivity and build high-quality solutions.**

Defining and classifying patterns

A pattern is basically a template solution to a problem. Patterns can be vital to the development process — but they're only effective if they're presented clearly and consistently.

When you describe a pattern, provide your fellow developers with the following information:

- ✔ **Pattern name:** Give your pattern a memorable name that matches its purpose.

- ✔ **Problem description:** You tell others just what problem this pattern solves. Provide your readers with information about the context of the problem, when to consider using your pattern, and how to recognize whether the problem they have is one to which your pattern provides an answer.

- ✔ **Solution description:** Here you describe the classes, how they collaborate, their associations, their constraints, and the job of each class.

- ✔ **Consequences of the solution:** Every one of your patterns has positive and negative aspects. Don't forget to tell other developers about any issues they must face as a result of choosing to use your pattern.

Patterns occur at many different levels of complexity. The three most important levels for complexity are given the following names:

- ✔ **Pattern:** A pattern is a solution to a small software problem that developers face over and over again in the construction of an application. A well-built application utilizes many patterns to solve modeling problems during analysis and construction issues at design time.

- ✔ **Framework:** A pattern for an entire application is known as a *framework*. Frameworks are "almost complete" applications; decisions about the structure of the application, specific classes, their behavior, and flow of control through the application are already made and in place. Just plug in a few of your own classes to employ the framework for your application's requirements.

- ✔ **Architectural framework:** A pattern for an entire system composed of many applications is known as an *architectural framework*. On a grand scale, you use architectural frameworks to bind many applications into a whole system of subsystems. An architectural framework could be a group of application frameworks, but it does not have to be. The important thing about architecture frameworks is that they describe how the individual subsystems work together. At this level, the architectural framework provides guidelines that specify responsibilities and interactions for each of your subsystems/applications.

For lots more information on patterns, check out the Hillside Group at
`http://hillside.net/`.

Using composite structure diagrams

You use a special *composite structure diagram* to describe a pattern. The composite structure diagram shows a "collaboration" and the parts that play different roles in the pattern. A *collaboration* is a group of objects interacting together to accomplish some functionality. (For more on composite structure diagrams, see Chapter 5.)

You show a pattern with a collaboration symbol and an internal structure:

- ✔ **Collaboration symbol:** A collaboration symbol is a large dashed oval shape. (Be prepared to make it large.) At the top of and inside the dashed oval, you place the name of the collaboration (that is, your pattern's name). Use a dashed line to separate the pattern's name from its internal structure.

- ✔ **Internal structure:** Place each element of your pattern inside the dashed oval. Be prepared to make the elements small if you didn't make the oval large enough. When illustrating a pattern, be sure to attend to the following issues:

  - **Draw a composite structure diagram:** When you show the elements of your pattern, you use a composite structure diagram. These diagrams consist of parts and connections. *Parts* are simply classes shown inside another class. *Connections* are special kinds of associations shown inside a class. See Chapter 5 for more details.

  - **Show each major class of your pattern as a part:** You draw each part as a box with the name of the part inside. I name the parts after the role each part plays in the pattern.

  - **Show connections between the parts:** If you have an association between the classes in your pattern, show them as connections between the parts. To show a connection, draw a line between the two parts that must communicate. Add any multiplicity constraints on the connection; put them between the parts. Don't forget to name the connection, just as you name associations. This helps others to understand what's going on.

  - **Decide whether to use an interface:** If your pattern calls for inheritance and abstract operations in a superclass, then use an interface. Instead of a superclass, you attach a provider interface to the subclass; the provider-interface symbol is a lollipop or a small circle attached to a line. The line joins up with whichever internal part provides the attributes and operations defined by the inter-face. For the part that actually invokes those operations, you show a required-interface symbol — half a circle attached to a line — and use the line to connect the required-interface symbol to the part that does the invoking. When that's done, you simply connect the required-interface symbol to the provider-interface symbol. When you're done, it looks like a ball-and-socket joint. (See Figure 15-1 for an example.)

Composite structure diagrams don't allow generalizations, so you can't use them to show an inheritance hierarchy. Use an interface symbol instead. (See Chapter 5 for more on composite structure diagrams and Chapter 6 for more on generalization and inheritance.)

UML 2 has a notation for expressing patterns. It's called a *composite structure diagram with collaboration.* If you're familiar with UML 1.*x*, don't confuse this diagram type with the old collaboration diagram. UML 2 doesn't actually have a collaboration diagram. Instead, UML 2 renames the old UML 1.*x* collab-oration diagram and calls it a *communication diagram.* (See Chapter 14 for more information on communication diagrams.) Collaboration means the structure depicted in a static diagram that shows the relationship among classes that serve as parts working together to accomplish some collective behavior, but the diagram doesn't specify *how* they collaborate.

Looking at a common design pattern

Figure 15-1 illustrates the design pattern known as Builder that developers frequently use. You see a large dashed oval with the name of the pattern at the top. The Builder design pattern consists of three primary classes and two interfaces — a provider interface and a required interface. The Director knows what to build and when to build it. The ConcreteBuilder knows how to construct a particular Product. The pattern also includes the Builder provider interface and the Builder required interface. An instance of the Director invokes operations on instances of a ConcreteBuilder defined in the Builder interface. The provider interface is shown with the Builder name above as a small closed circle attached to the ConcreteBuilder. The required interface is shown with the same Builder name above an open circle (socket) attached to the Director. An instance of ConcreteBuilder then invokes known operations on the Product class to construct instances of the parts that eventually make up the Product.

If you document design patterns and you have to deal with inheritance (gen-eralization), use an interface to capture the abstract superclass.

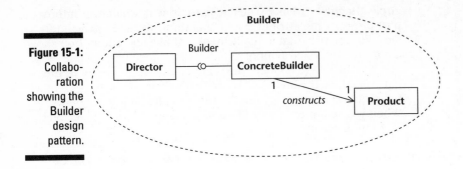

Figure 15-1:
Collabo-
ration
showing the
Builder
design
pattern.

Applying Patterns

The diagram in Figure 15-1 shows you who's involved in a collaboration, but it doesn't provide much detail about the attributes and operations of the individual classes you must construct before you can use the pattern for yourself. To help you and others with using patterns, you need to show a specific example fitting your own classes into the pattern or template. In UML 2, the example you build to show others how you are using a pattern is known as a *collaboration occurrence.*

You use collaboration occurrences to show details of how you apply a pattern to your specific application. You show a collaboration occurrence by placing the name of the occurrence and a colon in front of the name of the collaboration. For example, if you use the builder pattern to build air-filter units, you would name the collaboration occurrence as `AirFilterUnit:Builder`.

Instead of showing everything inside a large dashed oval, you can show a collaboration or collaboration occurrence as a *small* dashed oval, connected to each class via dashed lines. The role that each class plays in the collaboration appears on the dashed line, next to the name of the class playing the role. Use this form of collaboration to show details of the participating classes' attributes and operations.

Using the Builder pattern

Figure 15-2 shows you an example of the `Builder` pattern for building air-filter units. You notice the `AirFilterUnit: Builder` name in the small dashed oval indicates this is an example — a collaboration occurrence. The example uses the alternative form of a collaboration occurrence. The classes, important attributes, and operations for this use of the `Builder` pattern look like this:

✔ The `AirFilterConstructor` class plays the role of `Director` in the `Builder` pattern. To follow the `Builder` pattern, you must provide the class that plays the role of `Director` with a `construct` operation.

✔ Only a class stereotyped as an `interface` can play the role of `Builder` in the pattern. (Remember a class stereotyped as an interface is a special kind of class that specifies a contract that other classes must perform if they are to realize the interface.) Any class that supports the `Builder` interface must have an `assembly` attribute, along with a reference datatype that references an instance of the `Product` being built.

✔ The `Builder` interface also requires the implementation of a `buildPart` operation.

✔ The `AirFilterUnitBuilder` class plays the role of the `ConcreteBuilder`, thus providing a `getResult() : AirFilterUnit` operation. That operation returns an instance of the `AirfilterUnit` class, which plays the role of the `Product` in this pattern.

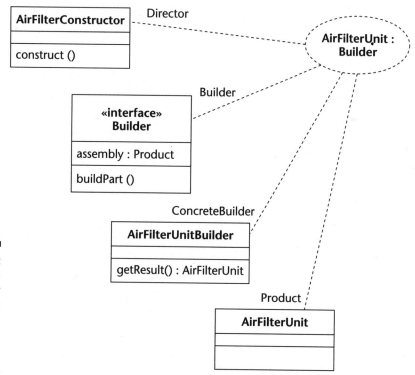

Figure 15-2:
Alternative
form for
showing
a collab-
oration
occurrence.

Showing object interaction

Whenever you document a pattern, you have to show how the objects playing various roles interact. You can use a sequence diagram or communication diagram to document the nature of the interaction between parts of a collaboration.

Figure 15-3, for example, is a sequence diagram that shows the `Builder` pattern interaction. Play by play, it looks like this:

1. the: `Client` creates an instance of `ConcreteBuilder` called `aConcreteBuilder`.

2. the: `Client` creates an instance called a of type `Director`, and passes it a reference to the `aConcreteBuilder` instance just made in Step 1.

3. The instance a: `Director` turns around and asks `aConcreteBuilder` to `buildPart`.

4. The sequence gets into a loop where the `Director` instance asks the `ConcreteBuilder` instance to build all the parts that are necessary until the assembly is complete.

5. After the assembly is constructed, the: `Client` invokes the `getResult` operation on `aConcreteBuilder : ConcreteBuilder`.

6. A constructed instance of the `Product` is returned to the: `Client`.

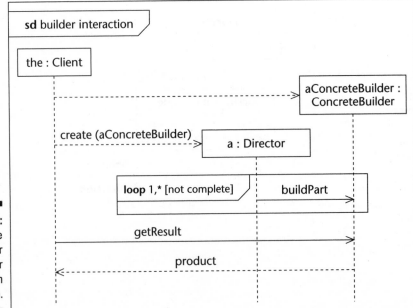

Figure 15-3:
Sequence
diagram for
the Builder
design
pattern.

Framing Frameworks

Patterns help you solve small problems when you develop an application. *Frameworks* provide you with an "almost complete" application. For example MacApp provides you with a framework for building applications on an Apple Macintosh machine. You'll notice some frameworks provide a solution for some important part of an application (frameworks that focus on the user interface design or a framework for accessing data in a relational database).

Frameworks also include special classes known as hotspots, which are the places in the framework that must change to bend the framework to your will. When you use a framework, you must develop classes and code for each hotspot. (For example, a reservation framework would have a hotspot for the specific commodity that a "reserver" can reserve.) You must provide the class definition that conforms to the commodity hotspot. For example, if you build a hotel-reservation system, then the commodity you provide is the room that a potential guest reserves.

Building your own application framework is hard to do. Many developers have tried and failed. Good application frameworks involve many classes, multiple use cases, various hotspots, and intricate interactions — all of which require lots of documentation. (For example, the MacApp documentation runs to almost 20 megabytes.)

Should you choose to develop a framework as the basis for your application, you have to document the following information:

- ✔ **Who's involved:** You need a class diagram to help others understand the details of each class involved in the framework.

- ✔ **Where you plug in to a hotspot:** Each hotspot of the framework must be described so you can build customized classes that conform to the framework.

- ✔ **Collaborations:** Instances of the most important classes collaborate to accomplish the job of the framework. You should provide composite structure diagrams that show the roles each major class plays in the framework.

- ✔ **How the collaborating objects interact:** At runtime, the objects of your framework must interact to accomplish the functionality of your "mini-application." Use sequence, activity, and communication diagrams to show the most important interactions.

- ✔ **Control mechanism:** If your framework uses events, interrupts, and other such ways of controlling the application, then your framework documentation must include these details. For example, if the framework is event-driven, use a state machine diagram to describe the timing and control of the major application-oriented events. (See Chapter 16 for more on the state machine diagram. See Chapter 17 for more on events and interrupts.)

Frameworks can be quite complex. The often involve patterns of patterns. For example, Figure 15-4 illustrates a simple ownership collaboration. Figure 15-5 shows a reservation pattern that incorporates the ownership pattern twice.

The ownership pattern itself is simple, incorporating only two parts — the part playing the role of owner and the part playing the role of the property owned. What we haven't shown in Figure 15-4 is the morass of details — any attributes, operations, and significant interactions between instances of the Owner class and instances of the Property class. You would see those in the alternative form of the collaboration, or in a simple class diagram.

Figure 15-4:
The ownership collaboration.

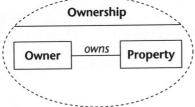

For our reservation example, the important classes in any reservation play the following roles:

✔ Reserver: This entity in the collaboration reserves the commodity by placing a reservation with the renter.

✔ Commodity: The item being rented such (as a videotape, a crash dummy, or a room in a hotel) is known as the commodity being reserved.

✔ Guarantee: The owner of the commodity must have some guarantee of payment. This guarantee often takes the form of a credit card or cash.

✔ Renter: The renter offers a commodity for reservation by a reserver.

Figure 15-5 shows the Reservation collaboration with all these elements. We also show you that the Reserver plays the role of Owner in the Ownership collaboration. Here the Guarantee is the Property of the Reserver in the Ownership collaboration. You can also see that the Renter and the Commodity play roles in their own Ownership collaboration.

Frameworks can be very complex. Even simple examples of frameworks involve collaborations involving other collaborations. Strive to keep your diagrams as simple as possible, while still communicating to other developers what they have to know when they use your pattern or framework.

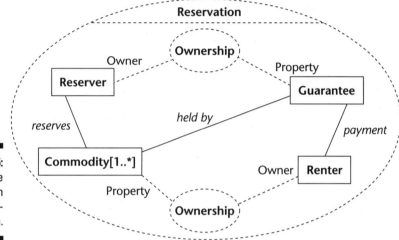

Figure 15-5:
The reservation collaboration.

Figure 15-6 applies the Reservation collaboration to the specific occurrence of reserving rooms in a hotel with a credit card. The Potential Guest class plays the role of Reserver, the Room plays the role of Commodity in hotel reservations, the Hotel plays the role of Owner, and the Credit Card plays the role of Guarantee.

If you want to make the Reservation collaboration a usable framework, then you also have to show the following:

- ✔ **A use-case diagram** with descriptions of each use of the reservations system for each actor.

- ✔ **A class diagram** describing each class in the framework, especially the key classes shown in the collaboration occurrence of Figure 15-6.

- ✔ **A component diagram** showing the components of your framework and their interfaces.

- ✔ **A series of sequence and communication diagrams** telling other developers how each major use case is accomplished through the collaboration of the classes in the framework.

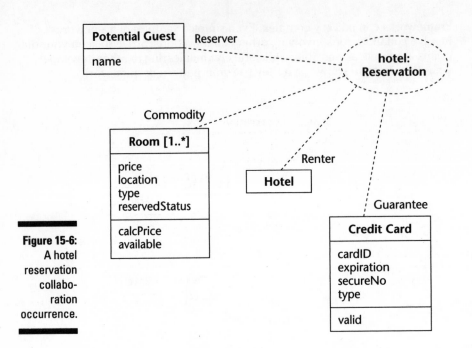

Figure 15-6:
A hotel
reservation
collabo-
ration
occurrence.

Part V
Dynamic Modeling

The 5th Wave — By Rich Tennant

"We're researching molecular/digital technology that moves massive amounts of information across binary pathways that interact with free-agent programs capable of making decisions and performing logical tasks. We see applications in really high-end doorbells."

In this part . . .

*I*t's alive! You create objects, let them live out their days, and finally delete them. Your objects are not simply data for some lifeless function to chew up. You need a way to describe the life cycle of objects contained in your system.

We cover how to explore and document your objects' lives by using state diagrams to show important moments — and what your objects do after those events. We also describe how to give your objects a memory of the past, use complex UML state notation, and avoid too much complexity in your depictions of dynamics. Although dynamic modeling can be perplexing, we help you get a handle on the needed notation with lots of tips and tricks.

Chapter 16

Defining the Object's Lives with States

In This Chapter

▶ Building state diagrams

▶ Giving objects a memory

▶ Working with different kinds of states

▶ Showing event transitions

▶ Relating sequence diagrams to state diagrams

*E*ach object in your system has a life. You create it, it interacts with other objects for a specified time, and then you remove the object from your system. This chapter shows you how to use UML to describe the life of an object — from its birth to its death. This chapter introduces you to the basic state-diagram notation for showing an object's internal states, transitions between states, and the timing of an object's behavior. To help make state diagrams less of a hassle, we provide steps for building them — and show how state diagrams relate to class diagrams and sequence diagrams (scenarios).

Showing the Life of an Object

Your objects are not just some data combined with a few functions that use the data. They are so much more — an object has life. For example, an order entry system has accounts that customers use to pay for the products they order. In this system you create an object such as `CustomerAccount` and then invoke operations like `open` to open the account. Sometime later you may have to remove that object. (For example, when a customer account is no longer active it gets deleted.)

The values for each attribute of an object are hidden inside the object. So, your objects have a memory. When you invoke a function in a programming language that isn't object-oriented, the function remembers nothing about the last time you called it. You must feed it all the data it needs to do its job. On the other hand, an object can remember what has gone before in its life. You cannot (for example) invoke the `withdraw` operation on `CustomerAccount` before you invoke the `open` operation. The `CustomerAccount` object must remember whether it's open or not before the withdrawal can be performed. Because a thorough modeling of your system should take this memory capability into account, you need a way to show the life of an object.

Documenting object behavior and events

We recommend that you use UML's state-diagram notation to keep track of what your objects are doing over time. A *state* is some major behavior that an object performs while time passes. A state diagram depicts the proper sequence of an object's behavior that result from some event over time. With UML, you use states to show what an object is doing and when it is doing it.

There's more to an object, however, than just the behavior it performs while in a state. You stimulate your objects' behavior with *events*. In general terms, of course, an event is a moment in time when something of importance happens. In UML, you use event notation to describe that important moment. When you stimulate an object by notifying it of an event, the object reacts to that notification according to its current state. For example, a customer account responds to the `open` event by validating its associated credit card. But it only does this when the object is first initialized — not at any other time. If you try to open an account after it's already open, nothing happens.

 An event describes a moment in time. From an object's point of view, an event is a stimulus that causes a change of behavior. A state (by contrast) describes some major behavior an object performs in response to an event. Time passes when an object is in a state, but events take no time at all.

As your objects become more complex, you describe their states — and the events that affect them — by using state diagrams. The notation is pretty simple:

- **States:** States are shown as rounded rectangles. Take a rectangle, round off its corners, and you have depicted a state. Place the name of the state in the middle of the top part of the rounded rectangle.

- **Events:** Any event that causes an object to make a transition from one state to the next is shown as a line with an arrow connecting the two states. Place the name of the event close to the line that represents the transition. The arrow on the line shows the direction of transition, from the original state to the next state. The line that connects two states as a result of an event is called an *event transition*.

You will almost always have to include a couple of other specialized states — the *initial state* (your object's starting point in life) and the *final state* (your object's final resting point).

Constructing state diagrams

Building state diagrams is all about considering *when* behavior happens within an object. State diagrams — including *events* that indicate the arrival of important moments and *states* that indicate what happens as a result of those moments — show the flow of control within your objects.

Here are the steps we use when building a state diagram:

1. **Choose one class and focus on the life cycle for all objects of that one class.**

   For example, choose `CustomerAccount`.

2. **Start your state diagram with an initial state in the upper-left corner of the state diagram.**

   Show an initial state as a large solid dot with an event transition coming from it. After you identify the first major state of your class you can connect the event transition from the initial state to that first major state.

3. **Identify events.**

   Think about what causes your object to change its behavior — to stop doing one thing and start doing another. You're looking for important moments in the life of your object.

   The `CustomerAccount` example has the following events: `open` (open an account), `validated` (the account has been checked to make sure everything is okay), `passed` (the trial period for the account is finished), `renew` (it's time to renew the account), and `close` (the account needs to be closed).

4. **Think of what the object spends its time doing in response to the events you identified in Step 3.**

   Develop a list of these major chunks of behavior (that is, put a name to these states) where time passes for your object.

   The `CustomerAccount` spends its time doing the following:

   - `Validating` its credit card.

   - Staying `OnTrial` while the customer maintains a positive balance and pays their bills on time.

- Staying `Established` while the customer may have momentary negative balances and stretch out the payment of bills.

- `Renewing` the customer's account on a regular basis.

- `Archiving` all information associated with an account that is closed.

5. **Order the list of states:**

   - **Initial state:** Ask yourself if there is a state that must come first before any others, such as `Validating` in the `CustomerAccount` example.

   Intermediate states: Look at the other states and see which ones must come before or after other states. In the `CustomerAccount` example, `OnTrial` comes after `Validating` and before `Established`. `Renewing` comes after `Established`. `Established` comes after `OnTrial` and before `Archiving`.

   Final state: Check to see whether there is a state that must come last, such as — `Archiving` in the `CustomerAccount` example.

6. **Place your states in the diagram, ordering them from top (initial state) to bottom (final state) as developed in Step 5.**

7. **Add the events identified in Step 3 as lines that connect the states.**

   Use arrowheads on the lines to indicate the directions of the transitions from one state to another.

8. **Determine when the object is removed from your system.**

   Ask yourself, *What state your object must be in before you can delete it? What event occurs to tell your object that it's time to go?*

   Our `CustomerAccount` must be `Archiving` before it can be deleted. When the account is saved, then the account can be deleted from the system.

9. **Place a final state on your diagram and show the transition that brings an object from other states to this final state.**

   Show the final state as a large bull's eye symbol. Draw event transition arrows from all the states where the object can be deleted (determined in Step 8) to the final state's bull's eye symbol.

   A state diagram does not have to have a final state. So, you may not have to perform Step 9 for your state diagram.

10. **Abnormal events: After you have a basic state diagram for your object, think about the times when things go wrong.**

   Ask yourself whether your object is notified, at some points in time, of any cancel, abort, or error events. Add the states that result from these abnormal events and provide the appropriate event transition. For example, while our CustomerAccount is OnTrial, the account may fail and have to make the transition to the Canceling state. After it's canceled, the account must move on to the Archiving state.

11. **Step back from your diagram and check to make sure it makes sense.**

    This is the life cycle of your object. Verify that the object performs its behaviors in the right order.

You use a state diagram for all the objects that belong to one class. So when you are building a state diagram for a class, consider the behavior of all possible objects of that class.

Figure 16-1 illustrates a simple state diagram for the CustomerAccount object. The following steps will help you trace through and understand the diagram:

1. We start off with a large dot known as the initial state.

2. When the open event happens, the CustomerAccount goes into the Validating state.

3. After the account is validated, then the object transitions to the OnTrial state.

4. At this point, if the passed event happens, the CustomerAccount becomes Established. However, if instead the fail event happens the CustomerAccount goes into the Canceling state.

5. If the CustomerAccount finds itself in the Established state, it can be renewed or archived.

6. Only when the renew event happens can the object then perform the Renewing behavior.

7. The renewed event is the only event that makes the CustomerAccount transition out of the Renewing state.

8. If the close event happens while the CustomerAccount is Renewing, then that event is ignored. The CustomerAccount will not transition to another state; it will continue doing the behavior of the Renewing state.

9. If the account is in the Established state and it receives the close event, the account performs the behavior associated with the Archiving state.

10. If the object is in the Canceling state and it receives the canceled event then the account will transition to the Archiving state and perform the archive behavior.

11. When the saved event occurs while the CustomerAccount is in the Archiving state, then the object moves to its final state. (The final state is shown as a bull's-eye at the bottom of Figure 16-1.)

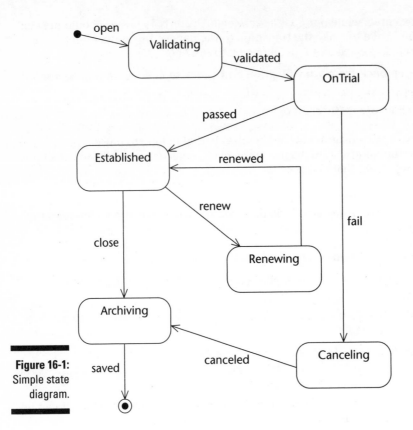

Exploring different types of states

The states you use for your objects come in several flavors — wait states, constraint-based states, ongoing-process states, initial states, and final states. Earlier in this chapter, we told you about a couple of especially important states — the initial state and final state, the starting and stopping points in an object's life.

The other three important kinds of states are:

- **Wait states:** In these states, an object simply waits for an event to happen. The object doesn't do anything really important while it's waiting for something to happen. A credit-card object (for example) waits until it's asked to either validate itself or handle a charge against itself.

- **Constraint-based states:** In these states, an object behaves in a certain way according to the values of its own attributes — or according to the links it maintains with other objects. The credit card is in the expired state when the value for its expired-date attribute is earlier than today's date.

✔ **Ongoing-process state:** This type of state occurs when your object is performing some behavior that is ongoing. The object leaves this state when some other significant event occurs. Otherwise, the object will continue doing this ongoing process. The credit card remains in the validating state until it's validated.

After your object has entered a particular state, it may perform some behavior that takes time. Such behaviors are known as *activities*. In UML, you show an activity inside a state with the word `do`, followed by a slash (/), which is in turn followed by the operation that denotes the behavior being done while in the state. For example, when an instance of the `CreditCard` class goes into the `Expired` state, the card must notify the bank that it has expired. The notation for this activity is `do / notify(Bank)`.

Name your states by using either an adjective phrase or a verb phrase. If your state is constraint-based, give it a name that describes the values for the required attribute and/or links. (`Expired` is just such a name — it describes the value for the `validDate` attribute.) For states that represent ongoing processing, use a phrase that has an "ing" verb in it. (`Debiting` and `Validating` describe ongoing processes for the credit card.)

Objects wait a lot. You will have objects that just wait around for some event to happen. After the event occurs, the object makes a transition to a separate state, performs some important job, and then makes the transition back to a state of waiting.

Transitioning from state to state

An event stimulates your object to make a transition from one state to another. When you show a transition, you can also specify some details as part of the event:

✔ **Information:** Sometimes, when your object is notified of an event, you also have to pass some information to the object as part of the event. You show this in UML by following the name of the event with the information being passed (and enclosing the information in parentheses).

For example, suppose a credit card is told it's time to make a charge to the card. At the same time the card must be told the amount to charge. The notation would look like *charge(amount)*, as shown in Figure 16-2.

✔ **Actions:** If you want your object to perform some very small operation when it receives an event, you can show that procedure on the event's transition line. Such a simple procedure is called an *action*. We use actions for simple counting, resetting variables, initializing some value, sending a message to another object, or performing a quick calculation. Use a slash (/) after the event's name and just before the action to indicate your procedure.

For example, suppose that when a credit card is checked to see whether it's valid, the card must keep track of how many times it has been checked. The notation for this example of an *event/action pair* looks like this:

```
valid / checkcount = checkcount + 1
```

✔ **Guards:** A *guard* is used to check some condition when an event happens. If the event happens and the condition is true, then the object transitions to the next state. However, if the event happens and the condition isn't true, then the object doesn't make the transition. Show guard conditions in square brackets on the respective event transition line right after the event name.

When the credit card notifies the bank that it has expired, the bank notifies the card of its status. If the status is `renewed`, the card goes back to a wait state. If the card status is `canceled`, then the card makes the transition to its final state. The UML notation that describes these two guard conditions looks like `notified[renewed]` and `notified[canceled]`.

Often your object sends an event to another object to notify it that some important moment has arrived. The sending of events is treated just like any action that takes place during a transition: You show the event's name followed by a slash (/), and then follow that with the name of the class and the operation taking place in that class. For example, after the an instance of the `CreditCard` class receives the event that tells it an amount is successfully `debited`, the card must tell the `Customer` how much was debited. The UML notation for sending this event looks like this: `debited / Customer.debitNotify(amount)`.

Events take no time. Therefore actions trigged by events take no time.

You might be thinking, *How can an event take no time when everything on a computer takes at least a little time?* Well, in practical terms, events do take a negligible amount of time. However, even if events (and their corresponding actions) take measurable time on some clock somewhere, they are not interruptible. No ongoing process or incoming event can occur that prevents these events/actions from completing. If, at some lower scale of the system, interruptions (such as clock ticks or screen refreshes) are going on, they are not noticeable, nor do they prevent the events/actions from completing.

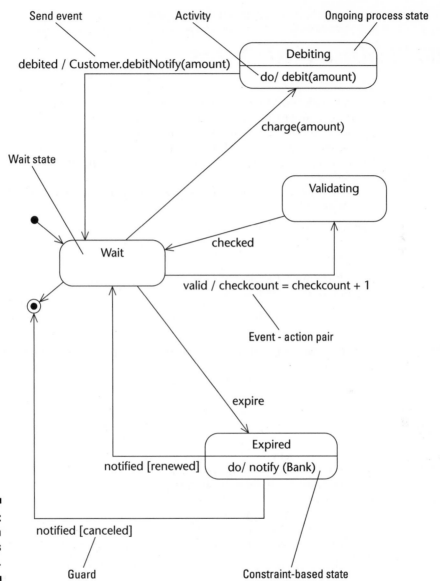

Send event

Activity

Ongoing process state

debited / Customer.debitNotify(amount)

Debiting

do/ debit(amount)

charge(amount)

Wait state

Validating

Wait

checked

valid / checkcount = checkcount + 1

Event - action pair

expire

Expired

notified [renewed]

do/ notify (Bank)

Figure 16-2:
Object with
three types
of states.

notified [canceled]

Guard

Constraint-based state

Programming an Object's Memory with State Attributes

Some of your objects have complex lifecycles. We use state diagrams like the one in Figure 16-1 to help us understand an object's life and what an object has to remember from one moment in its life to the next. The customer-account objects that make up our running example in this chapter are not simple data structures holding information about current customer balances. There are also rules they must obey to live life to the fullest:

- When a customer first opens an account, the customer's credit must be validated.

- After the account is validated, it is put on trial to see whether the customer always maintains a positive balance and always pays their invoices within thirty days.

- After the trial period is over, the account is established and can be renewed every three years.

- At some point, the customer account is archived — for example, when there is no activity in the account for a period of five years.

- Money can't be withdrawn from the customer account while it's being validated. Money can only be withdrawn when the account is in the trial period or when it's fully established.

Since the customer account is an object it can remember its current state and that is enough to help you program for all these rules. For example, you can program the `withdraw` method of the object to work only if the object has already been opened. This is easily done if you use an attribute to capture the current state of the object and then your `withdraw` method check that state attribute to see whether it's set properly. We use the following steps to give the `CustomerAccount` class memory of what it has done (using the Java programming language):

1. **Create several fixed attributes that represent each state of the class.**

   In this example, we need attributes representing the `Validating`, `OnTrial`, `Established`, `Renewing`, and `Archived` states. Each attribute representing a state gets initialized with a separate integer value.

2. **Next we provide an attribute to capture the current state and another attribute to capture the current balance of the account.**

   We use the following code to make this happen:

```
Public class CustomerAccount {
    private int accInitialized = 0;
    private int accValidating = 1;
    private int accOnTrial = 2;
    private int accEstablished = 3;
    private int accRenewing = 4;
    private int accArchived = 5;
    private int currentState = 0;
    private int beginningBalance = 0;
    private float currentBalance = accInitialized;
```

3. Set the current state.

Some of the operations change the `currentState`. For instance, the `open` operation that opens a customer account checks beforehand to make sure the `currentState` is set to its initial value. (It makes sense to not let you open an account that is already open.) Then the operation sets the `currentState` to the value of the attribute representing the validating state. Now the operation can ask the customer's credit card whether it's valid. If everything checks out, we set the `currentState` by setting the current state to the value of the `accOnTrial` attribute and the `currentBalance` of the account is set to the `beginningBalance`.

Each operation that causes a change in state must set the `currentState` attribute to the correct value. Why? So the object can remember what it's been doing. For example, the following code for the `open` operation first checks the `currentState`.

```
public Boolean open(Currency beginningBalance) {
    if (currentState == accInitialized) then {
        currentState = accValidating;       // validating
        if (myCreditCard.valid = True) then {
            currentState = accOnTrial;       // now on trial
            currentBalance = beginningBalance;
        }}}
```

If `currentState` is set to the value of `accInitialized` then the code changes the `currentState` to the value of `accValidating`. Next the `valid` operation is invoked on an instance of the `CreditCard` class — `myCreditCard`. If the `valid` operation returns `True`, then the `currentState` is changed to the value of the attribute representing the `OnTrial` state and the `currentBalance` is set to the value of the `beginningBalance` attribute.

4. Check current state.

Some of the operations can only execute if the object is in the correct state. You can also check to be sure state-based business rules are followed. When (for example) the `withdraw` operation is invoked on an instance of the `CustomerAccount` class, the operation must check to see whether the object is in the `OnTrial` or the `Established` state. If so, then the operation can reduce the `currentBalance` by the withdrawal amount. Given the rules for `CustomerAccount`, this operation needs to check to see if the withdrawal amount exceeds the current balance, which would yield a negative balance. If a negative balance is achieved while the `CustomerAccount` is in the `OnTrial` state, the operation fails and another object is notified of the failure.

The withdraw operation for `CustomerAccount` looks like the following code in the Java programming language:

```
public Currency withdraw (Currency amount) {
  if ((currentState == accOnTrial) or
      (currentState == accEstablished)) then
    currentBalance = currentBalance - amount;
  if ((currentState == accOnTrial) and
      (currentBalance < 0)) then {
onTrialManager.failure(this);
    currentBalance = amount + currentBalance;
    return currentBalance;}
  else
    return currentBalance;
  }}
```

This code first checks to see if the `currentState` is set to the attribute value representing either the `OnTrial` or the `Established` state. If so, the code then deducts the withdrawal `amount` from the `currentBalance` to come up with a new `currentBalance`. Next the code checks to see if the state of the account is equal to the attribute value representing the `OnTrial` state. If the `currentBalance` is less than zero, the `failure` operation of another object — an instance of the `TrialManager` class called `onTrialManager` — is invoked. Next the `currentBalance` is reset to the original amount. In other words, the customer account balance remains unchanged and no currency is withdrawn from the account. The old value for the balance of the account is returned. On the other hand if everything worked out correctly, the account balance is changed and the new current balance is returned.

Now you know that your objects not only have a life, they also remember what they've done during their lives. Your objects can get very complex.

Creating State Diagrams from Scenarios

One other way to build your state diagrams is to check your sequence diagrams to see which events are important to the more dynamic objects in your system. You see whether a sequence diagram shows one object sending an event to another — and whether a second object, stimulated by that incoming event, must make a transition from its present state to another state.

To illustrate the process of creating a state diagram from a sequence diagram, consider an example from the retail air-filter order system. Order clerks interact with the order-entry system to review customer accounts.

Figure 16-3 illustrates a scenario interaction between Jim (an instance of Order Clerk), the account reviewer, and myDB (an instance of the DatabaseAccessor class). You notice that we have inserted thin vertical oval shapes into the diagram. *These ovals are not part of UML.* We placed them on the diagram to show you where the AccountReviewer object is in some state. Each incoming event causes the object to transition to a new state. Each oval corresponds to a state in Figure 16-4.

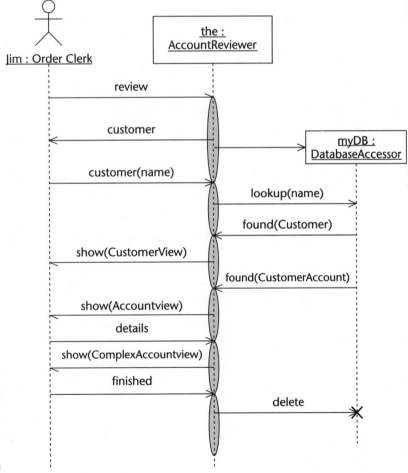

Figure 16-3:
Sequence
diagram for
reviewing
an account.

You can use the following process to create a state diagram from a sequence diagram:

1. **Look at your sequence diagram and choose objects for which you want to build a state diagram.**

   Look for those objects that have a lot of events going into them. They have the most state transitions. So, we have to diagram them in order to understand their life cycle. For example instances of the `AccountReviewer` class receives a lot of events.

2. **As always, start with placing an initial state in the upper left-hand corner of your new state diagram.**

3. **Get things started by adding a wait state.**

   This state will wait for the first event of your sequence diagram to arrive. Draw a simple transition line from the initial state to the wait state. You don't have to name this transition because it represents a completion transition. (A *completion transition* happens automatically after a state completes its behavior. See Chapter 17 for more information.)

4. **Find incoming events.**

   Look at the object lifeline (the dashed line) on the sequence diagram of your chosen object. Each event that comes into that object becomes an event transition in your state diagram.

5. **Locate an event pair, which consists of an incoming event and the next incoming event.**

   You look at the first and second events that come into your object. It doesn't matter where these events come from, whether from one or two other objects. In our example, `Jim` the order clerk sends the `review` event to the account reviewer. The second incoming event is `customer(name)`.

6. **Determine what your object is doing in response to the first incoming event.**

   Ask yourself, *What is this object doing between the time it received the first event and the time it receives the next incoming event?* Think of a name that captures this behavior of the object at this time.

   In our example using Figure 16-3, the `: AccountReviewer` sends the `customer` event to `Jim : Order Clerk`. Then the `: AccountReviewer` waits for `Jim : Order Clerk` to return the name of the customer they are interested in reviewing. At about the same time, the `: AccountReviewer` object is creating and instance of the `DatabaseAccessor` class called `myDB`. We choose the name `Wait for Customer Request` because the `: AccountReviewer` is waiting for a request to review a specific customer.

7. **Place a new state on the diagram**

   Give it the name you came up with in Step 6. In our example, you would add the `Wait for Customer Request` state to your diagram.

8. **Draw a transition with the name of the first incoming event between your wait state and the new state you just placed on the diagram.**

   In our example, you add a transition line between the `Waiting` state and the `Wait for Customer Request` state. Then you give this transition the same name as the incoming event: `review`.

9. **Add transitions and states:**

   In this step, you perform Steps 5, 6, 7, and 8 *for each pair* of incoming events. You take the second incoming event and pair it up with the third incoming event, assess the state, draw the next state, and show the second incoming event name as the transition between the previous state and the next state. The next pair of incoming events you look at is `customer(name)` and `found(Customer)`.

   The account reviewer is looking up the customer matching the name that comes from the database. It looks like the state is `Finding Customer`. The transition from `Wait for Customer Request` to `Finding Customer` is named `customer(name)`.

10. **Consider the last transition.**

    Your object ends up in some state after the last incoming transition. That state is often the final state (or the first wait state you placed in the diagram). Ask yourself, *What happens to my object's life after the last incoming transition?* If it's finished, then place a transition that leads to a final state. If your object starts all over again, then draw a transition that leads back to the first wait state. The account reviewer returns to its original wait state to wait for a clerk to ask it to review another customer account.

By following this procedure for converting a sequence diagram to a state diagram, we obtained the diagram in Figure 16-4. Notice that each transition has the same name as an incoming event on the sequence diagram (shown in Figure 16-3). The state names indicate what the account reviewer is doing as a result of the incoming event.

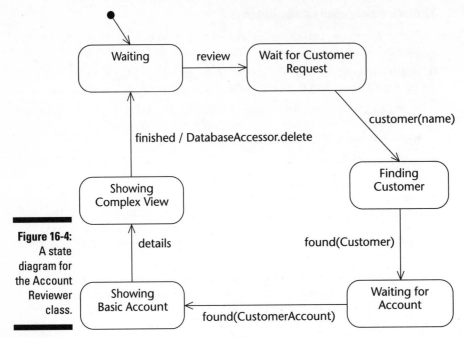

Figure 16-4:
A state
diagram for
the Account
Reviewer
class.

Sequence diagrams help you develop state diagrams for objects that have a lot of incoming events.

You can start a state diagram based on one sequence diagram that contains our object of interest. Then you should look at the other scenarios that the object participates in, examine their sequence diagrams and determine how our object behaves differently in each alternative sequence. Ask yourself the following questions: *Does the object receive different incoming events? Does it do different things?* You can apply the same process of creating new states when you see an incoming event pair, but be careful you don't come up with new names for existing states. You should do this until you've exhausted all the interesting scenarios that include your object of interest.

Chapter 17

Interrupting the States by Hosting Events

In This Chapter

▶ Relating event transitions to class diagrams

▶ Structuring many events using generalization

▶ Using different types of events

▶ Ordering behavior with events

▶ Using transition icons instead of text

*Y*our objects are constantly interrupted by other objects. Each interruption causes an object to stop what it's doing, consider the interruption, and then do something as a result of the interruption. In UML, these interruptions are called *events*. In this chapter we show you the ins and outs of using the different types of events that your objects deal with. You will also see how events on your state diagrams relate to operations on your class diagram. We explain a modeling technique to use when you have too many events. Since state diagrams illustrate flow of control inside your objects, we show you the correct order of execution of event actions and state activities.

UML 2 provides you with a new "transition" notation. Because this chapter focuses on the events that interrupt your objects, we show you the new icons UML 2 has for diagramming all the parts of a transition — events, guard conditions, and actions.

Making Use of Events

You draw state diagrams to understand the life cycle of an object. Each event received by one of your objects causes the object to change state — to change its behavior in a major way. So you work with events to accomplish the following:

✔ **Develop operations for your classes:** Events in your state diagram tell you when an object represented by that state diagram must perform some state-based behavior. When an object's behavior (specified as an operation on the object's class shown in a class diagram) is called, then the object performs the operation-based behavior. Because events cause an object to perform some behavior (state-based behavior) they make good names for operations for the object's class. For more on this see the section on "Operating your events" later in this chapter.

✔ **Understand parameters for operations on a class:** We make use of complex groupings of events in a technique that parameterizes and simplifies the number of events and operations you must contend with. Sometimes you can reduce the number of different operations in your classes by adding parameters to an operation on a class. We use events on state diagrams to help. For more on this see the section on "Objectifying your events" and "Parameterizing event hierarchies" later in this chapter.

✔ **Consider the sequence of behavior within an operation:** You can use events of different types to better control the behavior of your objects. For more on this see the section on "Holding special events" later in this chapter.

Operating your events

The only way anything happens in an object-oriented system is to have groups of objects work together. To get your system to perform a task, one object calls another object — which calls yet another and returns a result. Then still another object sends a message to an object, and so on. Each of your objects does a small piece of the overall task.

Figure 17-1 shows the state machine diagram for the objects of a simple `CreditCard` class. The life cycle of a credit card starts at the large dot (initial state) and immediately moves to the `Wait` state. If the event `charge(amount)` arrives, then the instance goes into the `Debiting` state. However, if the event `valid` arrives, then the instance moves on to the `Validating` state. If the event `expire` makes its way to the object (instead of `charge` or `valid`), then the object moves on to the `Expired` state. (See Chapter 16 for more details on state machine diagrams and using events to transition from state to state within an object.)

The *event transitions* (interruptions) that you place on a state diagram become operations performed on a class when you represent them in a class diagram. For example, when you send the `charge(amount)` event to an instance of the `CreditCard` class, that's the same thing as sending a message asking that some amount be charged to a credit card.

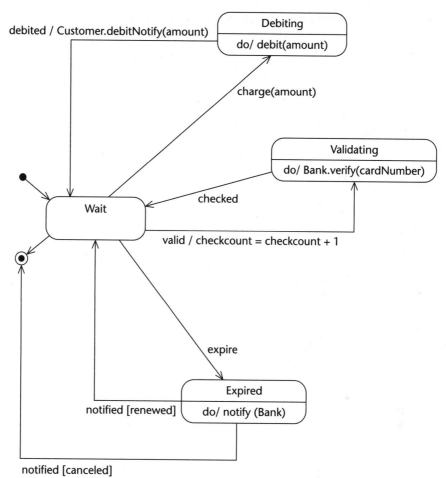

An event transition is the line that connects two states as a result of an event.

After you're satisfied with the state diagram for the objects of a class, then you can create operations in the class corresponding to each event transition on the state diagram that defines those objects. We took several of the event transitions in Figure 17-1 and placed them as operations in the `CreditCard` class shown in Figure 17-2. The following describes what we did:

✔ **Event valid:** The `valid` event becomes `valid(): Boolean`. From the state diagram in Figure 17-1 you see that along with the `valid` event is an action to add one to the `checkout` value and then to invoke the verify operation on an instance of the Bank class. If the bank verifies that the credit card number is okay, the operation is done. The method code for the valid operation looks like this:

```
public Boolean valid () {
    checkout = checkout + 1;
    if (bank.verify(cardNumber)) then
        return (true);
    else
        return(false);
}
```

✔ **Event charge:** The charge(amount) event becomes charge(amount : Currency): Boolean. However, after the charge event happens, the credit card must debit some amount from the bank and once debited, the owner of the card or customer must be notified. The method code for the charge operation looks like the following:

```
public Boolean charge(Currency amount) {
    if not canceled then
        if(bank.debit(amount)) then {
            Customer.debitNotify(amount);
            return(true);
        }
    else
        return(false);
}
```

✔ **Event expire:** The expire event becomes simply expire(). When the credit card is told to expire, the Bank is notified. The Bank, in turn, notifies the card whether it's renewed or canceled as a result of the expiration event. If the card is renewed, then the credit card goes back to its Wait state to wait for more valid and charge events. If the card is canceled, then it goes to its final state and is removed from the system. The method code for the expire operation looks like the following:

```
public Boolean expire() {
    String cardStatus;
    cardStatus = bank.notify(expired, cardNumber);
    If cardStatus == "renewed" then {
        renewed = true;
        canceled = false;}
    else if cardStatus == "canceled" then
        this.finalize   // clean up for the java garbage
                            //collector.
}
```

The code examples for the valid, charge, and expire operations represent just one way of designing the CreditCard class. If we're dealing with asynchronous calls in a multithreaded environment, we could choose to implement the code in any of several different ways.

Figure 17-2:
Class
diagram
showing
events as
operations
of the
CreditCard
class.

«Domain» **CreditCard**
- cardNumber : String - bank : Bank - expirationDate : Date - type : CardKind - renewed : Boolean - canceled : Boolean - checkout : Integer
+ valid() : Boolean + charge(amount : Currency) : Boolean + expire()

Objectifying your events

Modelers often run into the situation of having an object that receives so many events, that it becomes hard for you to get a handle on what is going on. For instance, consider the events that some relatively high-tech air-filter machines must deal with. The machine is set to on, off, or standby. Meanwhile the fan has a service limit. The air filter is notified when the fan has reached that time limit and needs replacement. A sensor tells the air filter whether the airflow from the fan is normal or too slow. The owner of the air filter can select one of several room sizes and fan speeds. The machine also has an ultraviolet light to kill germs — and that has a service life too. The really fancy air filters have motion sensors that send events to indicate whether dust is in motion in the room. Finally, the air filter has an air-quality sensor that sends events to the machine to help it control how long it should be running. (Confused by all this sending? We are.)

UML provides you with a way to make sense of this confusion of events: You can treat your events like classes and build a generalization (inheritance) hierarchy to organize your events. You see, events are really a lot like classes. Events have attributes called *parameters*. Events also have associations, which relate the event to the class that sends it — and to the class that receives it. When you treat an event like a class, you use the «signal» stereotype.

Figures 17-3 and 17-4 show what is called an *event hierarchy*. To create an event hierarchy, treat each event like a class — and give them the «signal» stereotype. (Be sure to consider *all* the different kinds of events being sent to the AirFilter class.) To complete the process, follow these steps:

1. Group your related events and form a generalized event.

In the air-filter example, the on, off, and standby events become PowerOn, PowerOff and PowerStandby classes, each of which is a specialization of the PowerEvent class. We looked for other groupings and modeled them as `FanSpeed`, `Airflow`, `MotionSensorEvent`, `RoomSizeSettingEvent`, `AirQualitySensorEvent`, and `ServiceEvent` classes.

2. Continue grouping the groups if necessary.

The `MotionSensorEvent` and the `AirQualitySensorEvent` are both kinds of `SensorEvent` class. The `FanSpeed` and `Airflow` are both kinds of the more generic `FanEvent` class.

3. Group the most generic events under one class.

Finally, we grouped the *most* generic events under one class called `AirfilterEvent`.

Now you can use the diagrams in Figures 17-3 and 17-4 to see the structure of all those events. Seeing the structure of all these events allows you to check whether any events are missing or out of place.

Figure 17-3:
The first half of the air-filter-event general-ization hierarchy.

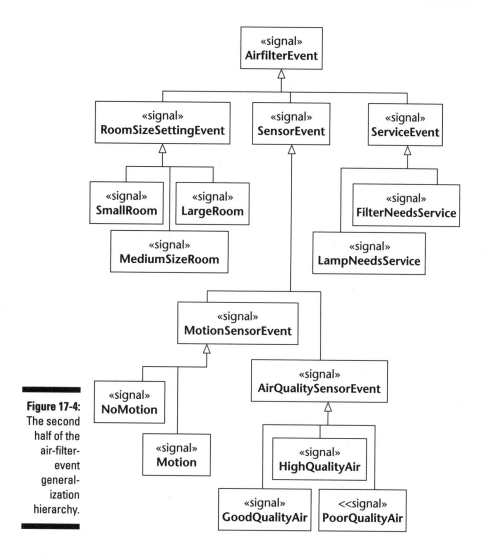

Figure 17-4:
The second
half of the
air-filter-
event
general-
ization
hierarchy.

Converting events into classes is a form of *reification,* which is the technique of taking something that isn't an object of some class (in this case, an event) and making it into one. Now that we've reified some events, we can give them attributes, invoke their behavior, and even store them away in a database for later use.

Parameterizing event hierarchies

Parameterization is another payoff you can get from generalizing events. You can reduce the number of events by changing the lowest event classes in your generalization hierarchy into parameters that exist in the more generic superclass. Use this technique when you want fewer events to deal with. Transforming events into parameters in a superclass reduces their complexity, making them simpler and easier to program.

Figure 17-5 illustrates the results of using the following steps to parameterize your event hierarchies:

1. **Identify the classes you want to turn into parameters.**

   First locate the leaf classes in your hierarchical tree of events. *Leaf classes* are the classes at the very bottom of the hierarchy that have no subclasses below them. Select all the leaf classes that can make up one superclass in your event hierarchy.

   For example, `PowerOnEvent`, `PowerStandby`, and `PowerOffEvent` are leaves in the event hierarchy shown in Figure 17-3. Each of these classes is a subclass to the `PowerEvent` superclass.

2. **Identify the superclass.**

   Select the generalized superclass of the leaf classes selected in Step 1. (See Chapter 6 for more on superclasses.)

   The superclass chosen is the `PowerEvent` class.

3. **Create an enumeration class.**

   This is a class with the «enumeration» stereotype. Its attributes hold values of a particular datatype used in some other class. In this case, your enumeration class holds each leaf event as an attribute.

   In the air-filter example, you would create a new class called `PowerKind`, give it the «enumeration» stereotype, and give the class three attributes — `on`, `standby`, `off` — corresponding to the three leaf classes chosen in Step 1 (which they now replace).

4. **Add an attribute to the superclass.**

   Add an attribute to the superclass you chose in Step 2. This attribute's datatype is that of the enumeration class you created in Step 3.

   In the air-filter example, you would add the `power` attribute to the `PowerEvent` class. The attribute has an initial value of `off`, and the UML notation for the attribute looks like this:

   ```
   - power : PowerKind = off
   ```

5. **Add a set operation to the superclass.**

   Add an operation to set the value of the attribute you added in Step 4, placing it in the same superclass.

   In our example, add the `setPower` operation. The UML notation looks like this:

   ```
   + setPower(p : PowerKind)
   ```

6. Add multiple parameters.

You can have a superclass whose attributes include more than one parameter. Just follow Steps 1 through 5, but place the attributes and operations in the superclass of the superclass.

The `FanEvent` class has two subclasses `FanSpeed` and `Airflow`. These classes, in turn, have subclasses that can be parameterized. The `FanEvent` class ends up with two attributes `fanSpeed` and `airFlow`.

The event-generalization structures shown in Figures 17-3 and 17-4 can help convey an understanding of all the events that effect one complex class such as an `AirFilterUnit` class. This generalization process helps you categorize your events. Finally, to simplify the diagram, you change those event classes into parameters in a superclass. Figure 17-5 shows the result of this process: an `AirfilterEvent` superclass with only four subclasses.

If your classes must handle a lot of events, another common technique for implementing them is to specify an operation such as `handle(event)`. Instead of having one operation for each event (as in Figure 17-2), you can have one operation that handles *all* the different events. For the `Airfilter` class, for example, you can provide the operation `handle(event:AirfilterEvent)`.

Holding special events

An *event* is a moment in time when something of importance happens. Events stimulate an object to make a transition from one state (of performing some behavior) to another state (with different behavior). When the new state is attained, the transition caused by the event is complete; event transitions are what happens between states.

Sometimes you want your events to occur *during* an object's state. These special events are shown inside the rounded rectangle that represents a state:

- ✔ **Entry events:** Every time your object changes state and starts a state, an entry event is generated. This is the moment in time when your object "enters" the state before it starts performing the behavior of that state.

  - • **Entry actions:** The action associated with each entry event — the *entry action* — is performed as soon as your object enters the state that includes this action. Entry actions are small chunks of behavior (like normal actions); what's different is when they occur. (See Chapter 16 for more information on actions.)

  - • **Notation:** Inside the rounded rectangle that represents a state, place the word `entry` followed by a slash (/) followed by the entry action.

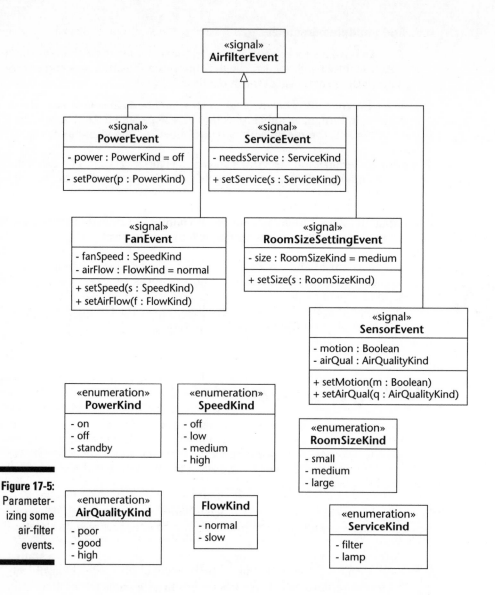

Figure 17-5:
Parameter-
izing some
air-filter
events.

✔ **Exit events:** Every time your object receives an external event and must change state, an *exit event* is generated. This is the moment when your object exits its current state, before it performs any actions associated with the external event that made it exit.

   • **Exit actions:** The action associated with each exit event — the *exit action* — is performed just before your object exits the state that generated the action in response to the external event.

- **Notation:** Inside the rounded rectangle that represents a state, place the word exit, followed by a slash (/), followed by the exit action.

✔ **Internal events:** If you have an event-and-action pair that occurs inside a state, you may have an *internal event*.

> **No entry or exit actions:** This type of event does not cause the object to exit the existing state. Nor does it cause a reentry into the existing state (which would trigger an entry action).

> - **Notation:** Inside the rounded rectangle that represents a state, place the name of the internal event, followed by a slash (/) followed by the action that your object should perform if the internal event occurs.

You can model queries as operations (requests for information from your object) that generate internal events.

✔ **Deferred events:** Sometimes you want to defer event actions — keep them from occurring until later. Such *deferred events* are recognizable as events that *can* occur while an object is in a particular state, but the execution of any associated action is specifically blocked for now. The notation for this type of event is to place the name of the deferred event followed by a slash (/) followed by the word defer inside the rounded rectangle that represents a state.

Figure 17-6 is a partial state diagram from the customer-account example that we used at the beginning of this chapter. The figure illustrates entry, exit, internal, and deferred events. On entry to the Validating state, an instance of CustomerAccount performs the entry action by sending the valid event to a linked instance (theCreditCard) of the CreditCard class. Upon exit from the Validating state, an instance of CustomerAccount performs the exit action by setting its own internal attribute, dateOpened, to today's date. If the deferred event statement should be received while an instance of the CustomerAccount class is performing the do activity (in this case, wait for validation), then the statement event is deferred to another state (OnTrial) that does not defer the statement event. The OnTrial state handles three internal events: statement, withdraw and deposit.

Other events you can use in special situations to model events between states include these:

✔ **Completion transition:** A *completion event* is generated when all entry, internal, and do behaviors within the state are complete. If the state is connected to another state by a transition that has no label, then the object automatically makes a transition to the state that comes after executing any exit action. Completion transitions used to be known as *automatic transitions* in earlier versions of UML.

✔ **The** when **event:** Use this kind of time event when your object must be notified of a *precise* moment in time. The notation for a when event is the word when, followed by the required absolute time condition (placed in parentheses).

✔ **The** after **event:** Use this kind of time event when your object must be notified of a *relative* moment in time. The after event begins after your object enters a specified state. The notation for an after event is the word after, followed by the required relative time condition (placed in parentheses).

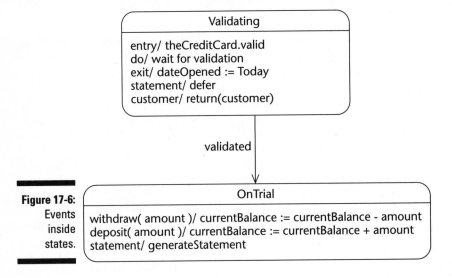

Figure 17-6:
Events
inside
states.

Figure 17-7 shows you examples of a when event, a completion transition, and an after event. Here's how they play out:

✔ **The** after **event:** Six months after an instance of the CustomerAccount class enters the OnTrial state, the instance stops any do activities and makes a transition to the Established state.

✔ **The** when **event:** When the renewDate attribute of an instance of the CustomerAccount class is equal to today's date, and the instance is in the Established state, then the instance stops any do activities and makes a transition to the Renewing state.

✔ **The completion transition:** After the renewing behavior (not shown) is finished, an instance of CustomerAccount follows the completion transition and automatically goes back to the Established state.

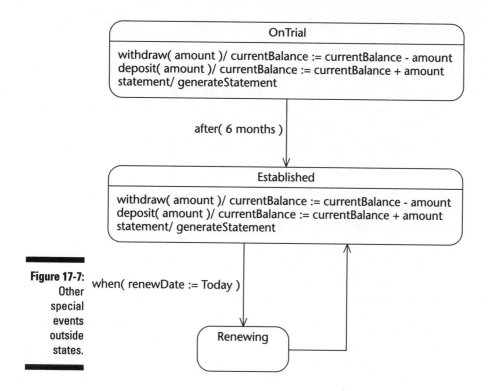

Indicating Order of Execution on a Diagram

You use state diagrams to indicate flow of control. As you develop state diagrams, you indicate what sequence of behavior is allowed for an object. When an event arrives at your object, the state diagram shows just what happens next.

Be careful how you put your state diagrams together. You want to make sure that operations happen in the right order. To help you determine the sequence of behavior, pay attention to the flow of control specified by the meaning of UML's state-diagram notation.

Figure 17-8 shows a small piece of the CustomerAccount state diagram. If an instance of the CustomerAccount is in the Idle state, and the open event is received by the instance, then the following sequence of actions occurs:

1. **An action on the incoming event:** `display("validating")`.

2. **An `entry` action:** `entry/theCreditCard.valid`.

3. **The actions of all deferred events:** none for the `Validating` state.

   Note, however, that when the object makes the transition to the `Cancel` state, the `statement` event may be handled then — provided it arrived during the `Validating` state.

4. **A `do` activity(the main behavior of the state):** `do/wait for validation`.

5. **Internal actions:** `customer / return(customer)`.

   The internal event interrupts the `do` activity and performs its action. Then control returns to allow the `do` activity to pick up right where it left off.

6. **An `exit` action:** `exit/dateOpened := Today`.

   The `exit` action is performed only after the object receives the `notValid` event, causing the object to make the transition out of the `Validating` state.

7. **Action on the outgoing event:** `display("Invalid Credit Card")`.

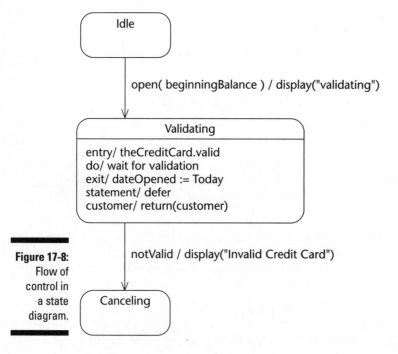

Figure 17-8:
Flow of
control in
a state
diagram.

Showing Transitions as Icons

Sometimes you want to emphasize the transitions of your state diagrams instead of the states. UML provides you with a notation that gives you a transition-oriented view of state diagrams. Instead of showing an event in text, you can use special icons. Each part of the event text has its own icon:

- ✔ **Signal receipt:** The name of the incoming event and its attributes is known as the signal received by your object. A signal-receipt icon looks like a small flag with the name of the event and its attributes inside. Some people describe the signal-receipt icon as a rectangle with a triangular notch in its side (either side will do).

- ✔ **Signal sending:** If your object must send an event off to another instance as a result of receiving the incoming event, then show the sending of the event with a signal-sending icon. This icon looks like a boxy arrow with the signal-sending event information shown inside the box. Others might describe it as a rectangle with a triangular point coming out of one side (again, either side will do).

- ✔ **Action sequence:** The action part of the incoming event is shown with an action-sequence icon (a box with the action text shown inside).

An example of this transition-oriented notation is shown in Figure 17-9. Instances of the `CustomerAccount` class have the following event that causes a transition from the `OnTrial` to the `Cancel` state:

```
nonpayment(Invoice) [Invoice.date < Today - 30 days] /
         customer.overDue(Invoice); display("Late Payment")
```

Use a choice-pseudostate icon to handle the guard condition `[Invoice.date < Today - 30 days]`. The choice-pseudostate icon is shown as a large diamond with the decisions shown in square brackets. The decisions are tested and the object makes the transition to the next icon, depending on which decision is `true`. (You can find more about this and other pseudostates in the Chapter 18.)

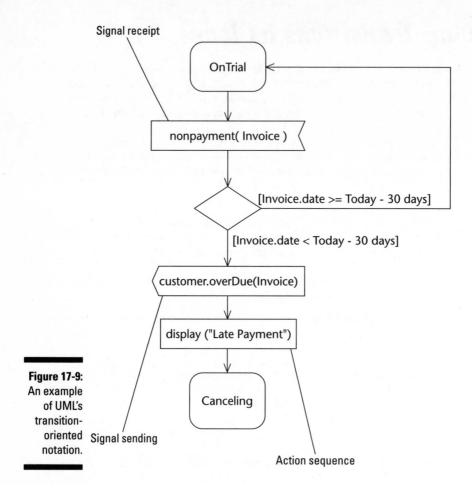

Signal receipt

OnTrial

nonpayment(Invoice)

[Invoice.date >= Today - 30 days]

[Invoice.date < Today - 30 days]

customer.overDue(Invoice)

display ("Late Payment")

Canceling

Signal sending

Action sequence

Figure 17-9:
An example
of UML's
transition-
oriented
notation.

Chapter 18

Avoiding States of Confusion

In This Chapter

▶ Avoiding overly complex state diagrams

▶ Handling concurrent states

▶ Using a shorthand notation to reduce diagram complexity

▶ Working with protocol state machines

▶ Steering clear of data-flow diagrams

S ome objects are really dynamic. They are expected to perform many different behaviors at many different times. The rules for what behavior your objects must execute — and just when to execute that behavior — can get really complex. To help you avoid your own state of confusion, this chapter shows you how to build complex state diagrams that really do the job — and can help maintain your sanity.

Simplifying Large State Diagrams

Creating a state diagram for an object with simple dynamics is easy. You usually have an `initial` state, a `wait` state, a few important event transitions to states with important behavior, and a `final` state. But, with more dynamic objects you may notice the following characteristics:

✔ The same entry, exit, and internal events are repeated in several different states.

✔ The same event transition is coming *from* several different states — but all going *to* the same state.

✔ A couple of different `do` activities can happen at the same time but completely independent of each other.

✔ There are very complex activities within a state that also depend on important events.

✔ Interruptions cause your object to stop what it's doing. Then the interruption must cause a complex method to execute without further interruption. And after the interruption is handled, allow the object to pick up with what it was doing before the interruption.

Don't be surprised if your state diagram tends to sprout an awful lot of lines, repeated event transitions, and many states that all do the same thing. Fortunately, you don't have to have all this repetition. You can solve these problems by employing the following techniques:

✔ **Generalize your states:** Arranging states to emphasize their commonality of events and behaviors helps simplify the diagram.

✔ **Build submachines:** Creating separate mini-state diagrams, which you can reuse in your state diagrams, makes your diagrams easier to understand and easier to maintain.

✔ **Utilize pseudostates:** Using a special shorthand notation reduces the number of states and transitions you have to depict for certain situations.

✔ **Show concurrency:** Illustrating concurrency — independent behavior — within an object by establishing separate regions inside the same state makes for a more compact diagram. (Some of your objects *can* walk and chew gum at the same time.)

Generalizing states

Each of your states has at least one activity that the object does when the object is in that state. An *activity* is some major behavior performed by an object that takes time. If this activity involves a complex sequence of behavior you can show that activity with a state diagram inside the larger state. The states shown within a state are known as *substates*. The "superstate" containing the substate is also known as the *generalized state*. When you have to describe an activity within a state as a state diagram, simply expand the surrounding state and place your substates inside. This type of UML diagram looks like someone's put a state diagram inside another state diagram.

Figure 18-1 shows an example of a simple state (Archiving) and its primary behavior (do / saveAccountData). If an instance of CustomerAccount is in the Established state and the close event occurs, then the object makes a transition to the Archiving state. Another way into the Archiving state is from the Canceling state when the canceled event occurs. (Note that these two distinct transitions have *one* destination.) Once in the Archiving state, the account data must be saved. When the saved event occurs, the object makes a transition out of Archiving and into the final state.

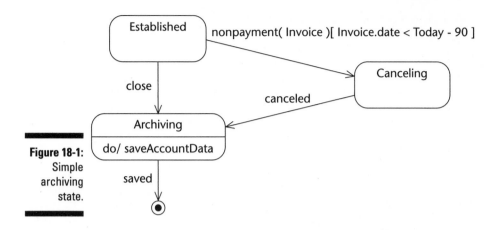

Figure 18-1:
Simple
archiving
state.

The process for saving account data is complex and involves some important events. To archive an account requires that all transaction processing come to a halt, then the account gets locked, then officially closed, and finally all the data associated with the account gets backed up. You can show the detailed sequences for the Archiving behavior as substates within the Archiving superstate.

Figure 18-2 demonstrates what this process looks like:

1. An instance of CustomerAccount, upon entering the Archiving state, makes an automatic transition from the initial state (the large black dot) to the Locking state.

2. As the object enters the Locking state, the entry action requestLock takes place. Transactions are halted and the object waits for the locked event to occur.

3. Upon receiving the locked event, the object makes a transition to the Closing state where it formally closes the account so no more transactions can take place on this account.

4. When the account is shut down and the object receives the closed event, the object enters the Backup state.

   In the Backup state, the object must log in to the database, and then insert account data into the database. When there is no more account data to insert, the object receives the lastTransaction event.

5. The lastTransaction event stimulates the object to exit the Backup state; the object performs the exit action and logs out of the database.

6. While the object makes its transition from the Backup state within the Archiving state, the saved event is sent to the object playing the role of self. (In effect, the object sends itself the saved event.)

7. When the `saved` event is received at the higher-level state (as diagrammed in Figure 18-1), the whole object to makes the transition to the `final` state.

Look out for repeating substates. Sometimes an object must do the same thing at several different points in its life. You could end up creating the same substate diagram for several different superstates. If this starts to happen to you, use submachines.

Using submachines

Submachines are really mini state diagrams you can include in other state diagrams. This ensures that you don't have to repeat yourself. For example, each instance of the `CustomerAccount` class has several states — `OnTrial`, `Established`, `Canceling`, and `Renewing` — that must handle the `statement` event. When the `statement` event occurs, the `CustomerAccount` object must perform `generateStatement`.

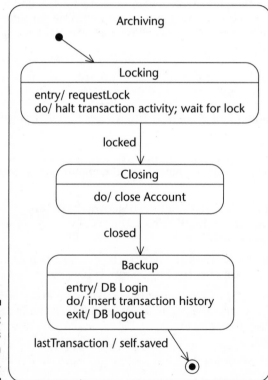

Figure 18-2: States within states.

However, `generateStatement` isn't a simple action. Generating a statement is dependent on customer information, transaction data, the day of the year, and whether there are any overdue invoices. To address this issue, you could create a substate diagram for generateStatement and place it inside the OnTrial, Established, Canceling, and Renewing states. However it's more efficient to create a submachine for generating a statement, and then *include* it in those four states.

Follow this process to make use of submachines:

1. **Recognize the need for a submachine.**

   You may want to create a submachine if either of the following is true:

   - You are repeatedly using the same group of substates inside several different superstates within the same object's state diagram.

   - You see a mini state diagram within the different state diagrams belonging to objects of separate classes.

   In our example, we recognize that a submachine is warranted because the states for generating a statement are reused in the OnTrial, Established, Canceling and Renewing states of CustomerAccount objects.

2. **Build a submachine.**

   Pull out the common mini state diagram and create a separate state diagram. This state diagram has one superstate with the common substates inside it. You have to give the superstate a name.

   We named the submachine's superstate GenerateStatementSM for the CustomerAccount example. Figure 18-3 shows the UML notation for the submachine GenerateStatementSM. The submachine contains the WaitForCustomer, ObtainingTransactions, Summarizing, TransactionFormating, and GenerateOverDueNotice substates. Every time you include the GenerateStatementSM in other states, the exact sequence for generating statements based on customer information, the day of the year and checking for overdue invoices is performed.

3. **Include the submachine.**

   Now that you have a submachine you can use it wherever you need it. This is done with a special include statement. In the state that has the submachine, place the word include followed by a slash (/) followed by the name of the included submachine.

   Figure 18-4 shows how we used the GenerateStatmentSM within the Canceling state of a CustomerAccount instance. We created a substate, Wait for Cancel, so the object can wait for the account to be canceled. If while it's waiting, a statement event should occur then the object transitions to the HandleStatement state. Because it "includes" a submachine, the GenerateStatementSM submachine is executed.

   When the GenerateStatementSM completes at its final state, the object will automatically transition back to the Wait for Cancel state.

You use submachines to describe common "event/action" sequences such as handling errors, providing help, reading data and writing data.

Inheriting events in substates

When you create substates within a superstate, your substates inherit flow of control from the superstate. An event that stimulates your object to exit a superstate also causes your object to exit any substate it may be in. If you have a transition that goes directly to a substate from outside the superstate, then the entry actions are executed in sequence from the outer most superstate to the inner most substate. The opposite is true for exiting a substate to another state outside an enclosing superstate. The object executes any exit actions in sequence from the inner most substate to the outer most superstate. Any internal events on superstates are inherited by the substates. They will interrupt the current substate.

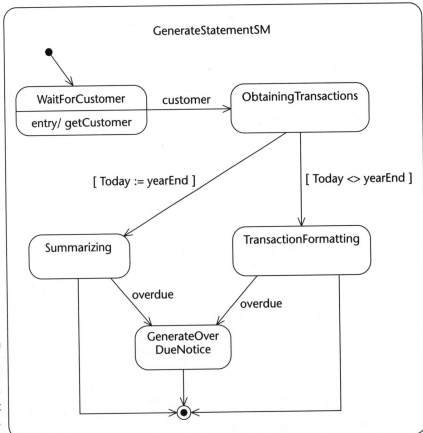

Figure 18-3:
The Generate-Statement submachine.

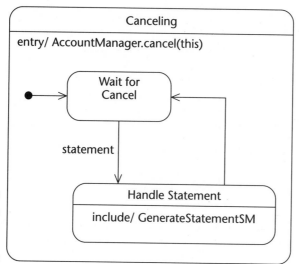

Figure 18-4:
Including a
submachine.

If you're an object-oriented programmer, this may sound familiar. This is parallel to how "new" operations are done when you create an instance of a subclass. First the new operation of the superclass is performed, followed by the new operation of the subclass. Your object performs the destructor operation of the subclass and then the destructor operation of the superclass.

Figure 18-5 shows a piece of the state diagram that describes instances of the CustomerAccount class. In this diagram, we have included the OnTrial, Established, and Renewing states as substates within the ManageTransactions superstate. When the object receives the validated event, it transitions directly to the OnTrial state. First the entry action TransactionManager.notify(this) is executed and then the entry action accountStatus := OK is executed because the entry actions are inherited from outermost to innermost actions.

Figure 18-5 also uses flow-of-control inheritance to reduce the complexity of the diagram. Instead of having individual transitions from OnTrial to Canceling, from Established to Canceling, and from Renewing to Canceling, you need only one transition. The ManageTransactions superstate has such a single transition — cancel — and it goes straight to the Canceling state. All substates inherit this same transition. Thus, when the object receives the cancel event — no matter what substate it occupies within ManageTransactions — it makes the transition to the Canceling state.

If you refer to Figure 17-7, you can see the OnTrial state and the Established state, both with the deposit and withdrawal internal events. If you use flow-of-control inheritance, you only have to show them once — as internal events in the superclass. (Because you cannot make a deposit or withdrawal when the account is being renewed, we had to "defer" those operations in the Renewal state.)

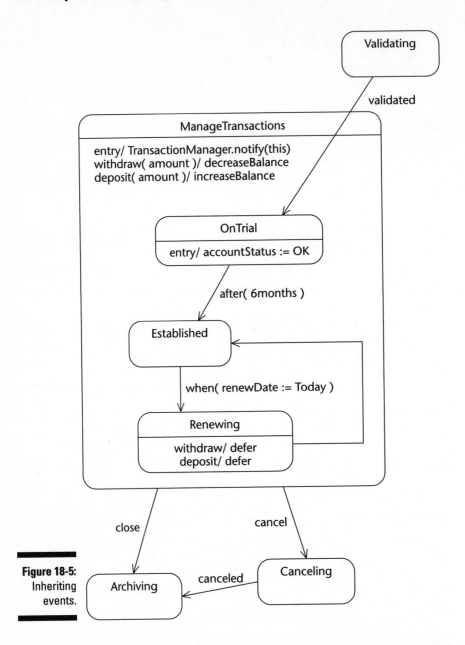

Figure 18-5:
Inheriting
events.

Utilizing pseudostates and saving history

As you build more complex state diagrams, you can make use of some short-hand notation we call *pseudostates* that provide you with common ways to hook transitions together. Chapter 16 introduces a couple of pseudostates —

the `initial` state and the `final` state. The initial state is indicated on a diagram; its large dot and transition to some other state serve as shorthand for *Start here when you enter this state diagram*. It's simpler than having a regular rounded rectangle represent a state with a name like `Please start here` (you'd have to get everyone who reads your state diagrams to know that the `Please start here` state where you always start your state diagrams). With more complex state diagrams you have to connect up many transitions to form complex paths through the different states in your objects. To help you, UML provides pseudostates for connecting these transitions.

Most of the time your objects are happy to be interrupted by some important event. The event stimulates your object to move on to some other state to do some other activity, happy never to return to its previous state. While a `CustomerAccount` object is in the `ManageTransactions` state, it's either in the `OnTrial`, `Established`, or `Renewal` substates. But, you have to interrupt the object so it can produce a statement. When the statement is produced, you have to get your object back to the substate it was in before the interruption. That means saving the history of what the object was doing so you can get back to it.

You save the history of a state so you can get back to it later with the *history pseudostate*. Actually there are two kinds of history pseudostates:

- ✔ **Shallow history:** UML shows this pseudostate with a capital *H* inside a small circle. The shallow history pseudostate captures information about the current state but not any of its substates.

- ✔ **Deep history:** When you want to capture information about the current state and all its substates, then you use the deep history pseudostate. This is shown as a capital *H* followed by an asterisk (*) inside a small circle.

- ✔ Your history pseudostate has a transition from the state that handles the important interruption to the history pseudostate. You can also include a transition from the history pseudostate to the *default state* within the superstate: Any incoming object that has never been in the superstate before makes an automatic transition to the default state. As an example, Figure 18-6 shows you how to handle the `statement` event when it happens during the `ManageTransactions` state.

Here's the play-by-play sequence shown in Figure 18-6:

1. A `statement` event stimulates the object into a transition from the `ManageTransactions` state to the `Handle Statement` state.

2. When the `Handle Statement` state is finished, control passes to the `history` pseudostate.

3. From there, the object continues in whatever state it occupied before the `statement` event interrupted.

4. If no substate of `ManageTransactions` was active at the time of the interrupt, then the default state pointed to by the `history` pseudostate (`OnTrial`) is activated.

Use internal events to handle simple interruptions to your object's behavior. These events occur while an object is doing some activity within a state — and they don't cause the object to exit that state. (See Chapter 17 for more information on internal events.)

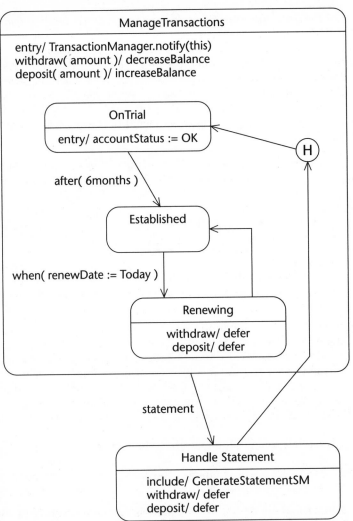

Figure 18-6:
Using the history pseudo-state.

Handling Concurrency with States

Some of your objects can (in effect) walk and chew gum at the same time. Think of the objects you have that are aggregations: They include the whole object (the aggregate), and all the individual part objects contained within the whole. The parts of your aggregate work independently of each other, a situation called *concurrency*. So you need a way to show that some states in your objects are concurrent — they don't depend on each other, and can (but don't have to) happen at the same time.

Concurrent objects have causally independent behavior; in object-oriented systems, *concurrent* doesn't mean "simultaneous." Concurrent independent behavior among concurrent objects *can* be simultaneous — but it doesn't have to be.

Diagramming concurrent states

As an illustrative example, consider an air-filter machine. It's composed of several parts, among them are the controller for the air-filter machine, the ultraviolet lamp, the filter to clean air, and the fan to move air through the filter. Figure 18-7 illustrates this aggregation relationship between the `AirFilterMachine` class and its parts.

The diamond shape in Figure 18-7 represents aggregation. If the diamond is filled in, that represents the stronger form of aggregation known as composition. For more details see Chapter 5.

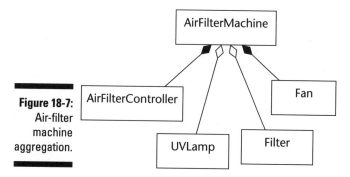

Figure 18-7: Air-filter machine aggregation.

When you want to show the concurrent states for the class playing the role of the whole in an aggregation, just show a state diagram for every part of the whole. Figure 18-8, for example, combines the state diagrams for the `AirFilterController`, the `Fan`, the `Filter`, and the `UVLamp`. The state of one instance of `AirFilterMachine` is a combination of current states — one for each of its parts.

You can also think of an object as having the state of being itself (as an instance of its class). Figure 18-8 shows the states of the object inside a superstate. Thus you see the superstate `AirFilterController` containing `Off`, `On`, and `Standby` substates.

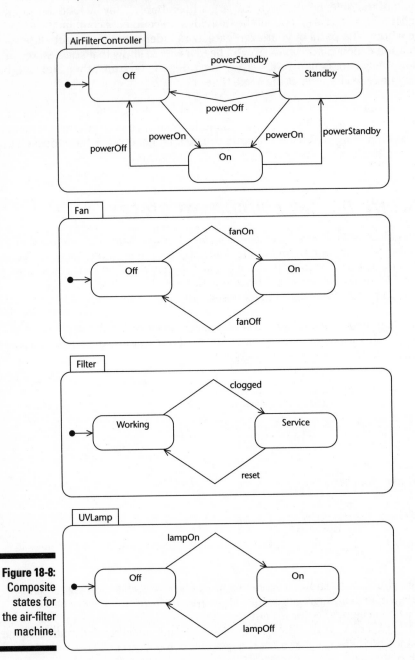

Figure 18-8:
Composite
states for
the air-filter
machine.

Notice that the superstates in Figure 18-8 have little tabs attached to them — that's just another minor variation on UML state-diagram notation: the name of a state in a small box attached to the top of the state.

You can also show concurrent states within an object. In the example of the air-filter machine, concurrent states across objects are all part of one aggregation. But some states have *concurrency* — independent behavior — within themselves. The `On` state for the `AirFilterController` (for example) is more complex that you might first realize. When you turn on the air-filter machine, you're telling an instance of `AirFilterController` to perform the following tasks, all at the same time:

- **Check sensors:** Keep an eye on all the sensors to make sure they're working properly. If a sensor isn't working, go into a service mode.

- **Monitor air quality:** Check the air quality through the air quality sensor. When the air quality is less than the desired level, increase the fan speed. When the air filter achieves the right level of air quality, decrease the fan speed and return to simply monitoring air quality.

- **Monitor motion:** Using a sensor, check for motion. If there is motion (such as a person walking by), go into cleaning mode: increase the fan speed and turn on the ultraviolet lamp. When there is no motion (or a certain amount of time has passed), return to simply sensing motion.

The `AirFilterController` must perform each of these tasks when it's in the on state and it must perform them independent of each other. To show concurrency within a state, divide the state into regions. Each region is separated from the others by a dashed line. a mini state diagram is placed into each region showing the concurrent behavior. Figure 18-9 contains the concurrent states for the `AirFilterController`'s `On` state. To keep this state diagram simple, we have not shown you the substates of the `CleaningAir`, `Servicing` and `Cleaning` states. (Details for the `CleaningAir` substate are discussed in the section "Using pseudostates with concurrent substates" later in this chapter.)

Using pseudostates with concurrent substates

A couple of handy pseudostates can help you construct states that have concurrent substates:

- **Fork:** The `fork` pseudostate enables you to take a single event transition and split it into several parallel control paths.

- **Join:** The `join` pseudostate merges multiple transition paths into one transition.

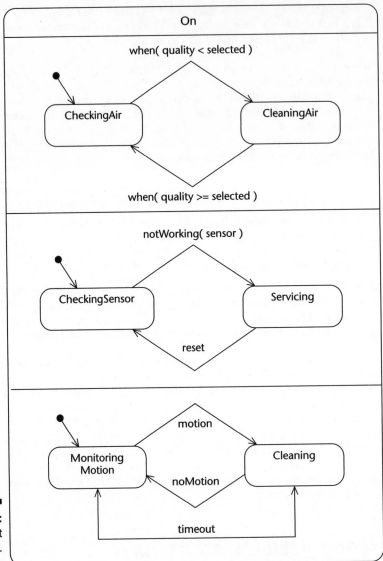

Figure 18-9:
Concurrent
substates.

The UML notation for a pseudostate (whether a fork or a join) is a short, thick line that shows transitions coming in or going out. Figure 18-10 shows an example of how to use the `fork` and `join` pseudostates.

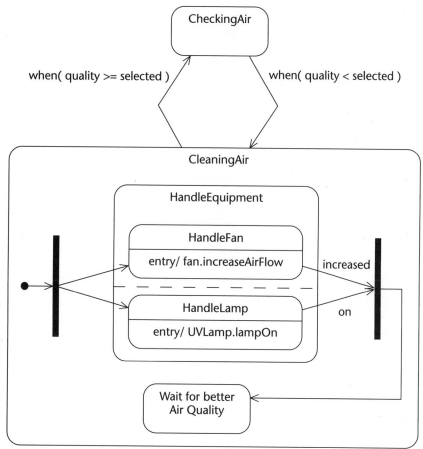

Figure 18-10:
Using fork
and join
pseudostates
to manage
complex
control
paths.

Here's what's happening in Figure 18-10:

1. If the `AirFilterController` is in the `CheckingAir` state and the `when(quality < selected)` time comes, then the object makes a transition to the `CleaningAir` state.

2. In the `CleaningAir` state, the `fork` pseudostate (the thick line at the left of the diagram) splits the just-completed `when` transition into two parallel control paths.

   Both control paths lead to the `HandleEquipment` substate.

3. `HandleEquipment` has two concurrent regions, to which control flows as needed:

- In one region, the HandleFan state is executed.

- In the other region, the HandleLamp state is executed.

- HandleFan and HandleLamp are independent of each other.

4. At this point, while control is in the HandleEquipment region, the object receives the next event:

- If the increased event is received, then the object leaves the HandleFan state and makes a transition to the join pseudostate (the thick line at the right of the diagram).

- If the on event is received, then the object leaves the HandleLamp state and makes a transition to the join pseudostate.

5. The join pseudostate makes no transition to the Wait for better Air Quality state until the object receives both the increased and on events.

These two events may arrive in any order. The object simply waits until both arrive before moving on.

Building Protocol State Machines

When you want to show the sequence of events an object reacts to — and the resulting behavior — you use the UML notation that creates *behavioral state diagrams* (also known as *machines*): Such state diagrams have event/action pairs, entry actions, exit actions, and do activities. Most of your state diagrams use these features; in effect, they are *behavioral state machines*.

Sometimes, however, you just want to show a specified sequence of events that your object responds to — and when it can respond — without having to show its behavior. Such a specified sequence is called an *event protocol*. In UML 2, you can show event protocols by diagramming *protocol state machines*. These differ from behavioral state machines and have special uses.

Normally we recommend using regular state diagrams to show internal sequences of behavior for all objects of a class. Sometimes, however, you want to show a complex protocol (set of rules governing communication) when using an interface for a class. For example, when you are designing classes that access a database for your application you need to use common operations like open, close and query a database. But, these operations must be called in the right order. You cannot query the database before you open it.

One solution to designing a simple database access class is to develop a DatabaseAccessor class with a DBaccess interface as shown in Figure 18-11. But, the DBaccess interface has a complex protocol that governs its use because of the rules governing communication between any other object and the DatabaseAccessor class implementing the DBaccess interface. To use the interface properly, you have to open the database and *then* set up a query. You can put these rules in a state diagram to indicate the protocol that must be followed when using the interface.

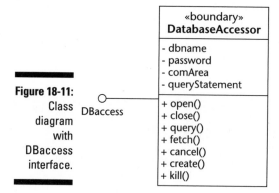

Figure 18-11:
Class
diagram
with
DBaccess
interface.

Regular state diagrams don't help you with interfaces because interfaces don't describe behavior implementation they just declare what operations the class must perform. It's up to the class to specify the implementation of an interface. On the other hand a protocol state machine enables you to declare what operations can happen and the order they can happen without having to say anything about behavior implementation.

Figure 18-11 shows the DBaccess interface attached to the DatabaseAccessor class; the DatabaseAccessor class must conform to the operation sequence (that is, the protocol) of the DBaccess interface: The open, close, query, fetch, cancel, create, and kill operations must be implemented in the order specified by the DBaccess interface's protocol (shown in Figure 18-12).

You draw a protocol state machine in much the same way you draw any other state machine. Remember, however, to follow a few special rules:

✔ States can have names but can't show entry actions, exit actions, internal actions, or do activities.

✔ Transitions show operations but not actions or send events (as regular state diagrams can).

✔ Transitions can have preconditions and postconditions shown in square brackets [ ], as in the following example:

```
[queryStatement <> null] query / [comArea set]
```

• A *precondition* states what must be true before the object can transition from one state to another. In this example, when an object that conforms to the DBaccessor interface receives the query operation, the `queryStatement` attribute is checked to see whether it's `null`. If the object is in the `Opened` state, and the `queryStatement` isn't `null` then the object transitions to the `Queried` state.

- A *postcondition* states what must be `true` once the object completes its transition and is now in a new state. In this example, when an object that conforms to the `DBaccessor` interface makes a successful transition to the `Queried` state, that means the postcondition must now be `true` — the `comArea` is `set`.

Avoiding data-flow diagrams

Many developers are used to thinking of the flow of data moving from function to function — so when they try to draw a state diagram, what they get is actually a good old-fashioned data-flow diagram: They draw lines between states that show data flowing from one to another. But a state is not some function that executes — and a data-flow diagram is not a state diagram. A data-flow diagram in disguise doesn't help you think of the life cycle of your objects.

To avoid this misuse of state diagrams, you have to be aware of two kinds of states:

✔ **Do-forever state:** Left to itself, this type of state performs its activity forever. It only stops doing its behavior when an event interrupts it, causing a transition to another state. The `WaitForCustomer` state, for example, is willing to wait forever. Only when it receives the `customer` event will the object make a transition to the `ObtainingTransactions` state.

✔ **Do-until states:** This type of state performs its activity until the activity is complete; then it makes an automatic transition to another state. You can easily find do-until states by finding transitions that *have no event* on the line-with-an-arrow that links pairs of states. The `GenerateOverDueNotice` state, for example, simply generates a notice and

then automatically makes the transition to a `final` state. The `GenerateOverDue-Notice` does not have to wait for an event to cause a transition.

You can check your state diagram to see what you're building. The key is the proper checking of how many do-forever and do-until states exist in your diagram:

1. Count the number of do-forever states.

   These are the real stuff of state diagrams.

2. Count the number of do-until states.

   Look for those automatic transitions without event names; they're a dead giveaway.

3. Evaluate whether the diagram you're building is really a state diagram.

   If the majority of states in your state diagram (around 70% or more) are do-until states, you probably have a data-flow diagram. On the other hand, if the majority of states in your diagram are do-forever states, then you have a solid, flow-of-control state diagram.

When you find your state diagram is really a data-flow-type diagram, then consider using an activity diagram instead.

✔ You draw your protocol state machine as a group of substates within one large frame, like the frames for sequence diagrams we show you in Chapter 12.

✔ You must name the protocol state machine as such; place the keyword `protocol` in curly brackets { } next to the name.

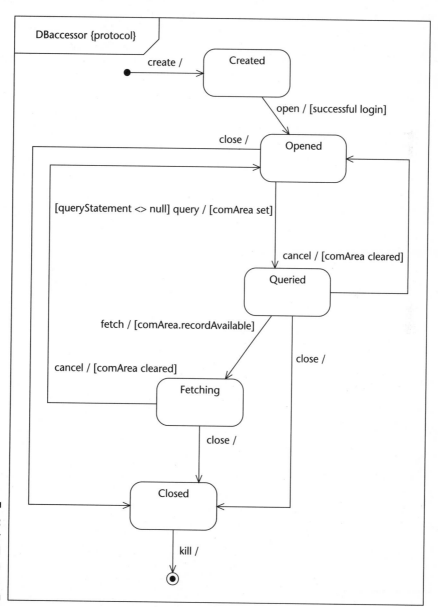

Figure 18-12: DBaccessor protocol state machine.

The diagram in Figure 18-12 shows a protocol state machine for the DBaccessor interface. Any class conforming to the DBaccess interface must implement the protocol state machine. You can show the implementation of the protocol state machine as a regular state machine with all the actions and activity behaviors thrown in. That way it's clear to other developers how you will implement the protocol for a specific class in your design.

State diagrams aren't meant to show the flow of *data* from one process step to another. Instead, they're supposed to show where the flow of *control* goes when some behavior happens. Don't let your state diagram mutate into a data-flow diagram. We've included a handy sidebar to help you hold the line.

Part VI
Modeling the System's Architecture

The 5th Wave   By Rich Tennant

In this part . . .

In the old days, when life was simple, you worried about software applications that ran on *one* computer. Today, your systems and software are far more complex. Your software is loaded on a server machine but run on a client machine. You may have multiple servers — each performing an important task in support of the whole system. Your data resides everywhere. Your software must account for network outages and system crashes. The life of a developer — your life — is not simple anymore.

This part helps you rein in your complex systems by providing you with proven system-design steps. We show you how to use UML to explore different architectures and document your design decisions. You want maintainable, flexible, and modular systems and software. We show you the techniques that we use to reach those goals — assembling components, decomposing systems, applying architecture patterns, and realizing subsystems — when we're faced with designing today's complex applications.

Chapter 19

Deploying the System's Components

．．

In This Chapter

▶ Stepping through a system's design

▶ Considering design priorities

▶ Breaking your system into subsystems

▶ Sorting logical and physical system diagrams

▶ Getting componentized

▶ Deploying hardware configurations

▶ Showing off artifacts

．．

So you know what you want to build, and you've got some requirements for your system, but there is just one little problem: Your system is spread out across several different computers and you must build pieces of software to run on each platform. You have to figure out a design for this complex system by thinking about what software goes on which piece of hardware. But there are so many choices. Ah, for the good old days when life was simple and our systems were applications that ran on a single user's computer.

When you build today's complex (dare we say *enterprise-wide?*) systems, you need a way to step back from the details and develop an overall strategy for how your system and its software application(s) are put together. There comes a time when you have to look at the big picture and describe how your system works. This chapter describes the steps for designing large systems and describe the UML diagrams you use to define your system. We help you get a handle on describing the relationships between the hardware and the software components that make up your system.

Defining Your System

Once you have some requirements, it's a good idea to start describing how your system is going to work. Gone are the days of simple applications that work on one computer. These days you're likelier to build applications that are split across many different computers. Take, for example, a hotel reservation system that works over the World Wide Web. In our travels, we often use a Web browser to access a hotel reservation system. We look for room availability, make the reservation and specify how we'll pay for the room. These reservation systems include our computer, its Web browser, an http Web server, server-side programs, the hotel's own reservation system, a database management system, and access to a credit card authorization system. In the face of this system complexity, you need a way to come up with the right design — and a way to describe that design using UML.

During design, we recommend you think about designing the total system first before diving into the details. When you build complex applications, make some high-level decisions before you focus on designing individual classes. By making decisions about architecture, hardware, networking, software interfaces, components, and databases, you limit the number of possible designs. By looking at the big picture first, you make sure your requirements are handled — and you end up adding classes that your users need, but could never tell you they need. Once you have your system organized and you know you have all the big pieces, then you can focus on the details of designing your classes.

The number of potential designs for the hotel reservation system is almost limitless. Just think of the many possible technologies, network configurations, hardware platforms, class definitions, programming languages, vendor software, middleware techniques, remote communications protocols, and database techniques you could use. (Stop! The room is spinning.) Let's consider the big picture first to "get our arms around" this system.

The process for designing the big picture involves the following steps and considerations:

1. **Consider the design priorities.**

    Of course you want to build a system that meets the needs of your users. But, there are other competing factors you must consider in your design, such as the following:

    - **Functional requirements:** Each use case represents required functionality of your system. (For more on use cases see Chapter 8.) Some use cases may be more important than others, and given your budget and schedule you may have to choose which use cases to implement and which to leave for another day. Perhaps the first version of the hotel reservation system implements the basics: making and canceling reservations. The next version will handle marketing features such as surveys and upgrading reservations with earned points.

- **Flexibility:** You can design your system to be modular. That way when users change their mind (never happens), your design is easy to change. However, the more flexible you make your design, the longer it takes to design — and the more it will cost to build. You could design the system to handle reservations for anything — trucks, videotapes, crash dummies, or theater tickets — not just rooms. But if you do so, don't be surprised if it takes longer to develop the complete reservation system.

- **The "ilities":** Really great designs consider scalability, reliability, and availability to name a few. A design for the hotel reservation system that handles one hotel in version one and can be expanded to handle a whole chain of hotels — *without* major design changes — is a *scalable* design. If your design consistently makes and cancels reservations — no matter how may users are connected — then it's considered a reliable design. If you decide to make the reservation system available 24-7, you must design in enough redundancy to make sure the system stays up even in the event of a failure.

- **Performance:** Your chosen design has an impact on system speed. If it's not fast enough, users waste time waiting. If the system is way too fast, you probably spent more money than necessary to develop it. To design the hotel reservation system, we have to ask, *How fast is fast enough?*

- **Cost:** Most, but not all, systems that we design have a budget. The design must not cost more than what the stakeholder is willing to pay for the system. For $100 million, we could build a fancy, fast, flexible, modular, scalable reservation system. But, the return on investment for that system would be a long time coming.

- **Schedule:** Like cost, schedule is a factor in our designs. Usually, market forces such as competition require that a system be designed and built by some date. Otherwise the competition wins with a product that gets market share. Building a hotel reservation system should not take so long that the company looses potential guests to other hotels.

Each of these priorities affects your design. First, we speak with project stakeholders about these design issues to get a sense of priority. If performance is the overriding design priority, then we design our system to achieve high levels of speed through hardware choices and parallel processing. If cost and schedule are the top priorities, we look for ways to minimize the required hardware (because that takes money) and the required functionality (because that takes time *and* money).

Unfortunately, these design issues are not compatible with each other. Designing to one will impede your design in another. For instance designing for performance usually increases your costs. Designing your system to meet the all the needs of users impedes your ability to meet your schedule. Because of these design trade-offs, we recommend you get these priorities straight first before launching into the hard work of designing a complex system.

2. **Review current system.**

If your new system is a replacement or an addition to some existing system, take a look at how the old system is designed. Choices that made sense for an older system (such as that of the database vendor) or for a specific hardware platform may limit your "new" design. In our reservation system example, the older hotel reservation system is built on a simple client-server model. We can reuse the hotel's current room reservation management server as part of the new reservation system.

3. **Decompose the system.**

Take your system and break it up into smaller subsystems. This is what engineers have always done — take a big problem and break it into lots of smaller problems. If we can solve each of the smaller problems, then combining the solutions should solve the bigger problem. We would break up the hotel reservation system into conceptual pieces such as user presentation, the business logic behind making reservations, persistent storage, and credit-card processing. Now, if we can define these simpler pieces known as subsystems, the new hotel reservation system is as good as designed.

4. **Define an architecture.**

Once you define your subsystems, you have to describe how those subsystems relate to each other — and the hardware that supports those subsystems. Our presentation subsystem runs on the machines belonging to potential guests who visit the Web site. The business-logic subsystem runs on a combination of hardware, including a machine running Linux as well as our existing reservation-management server. Credit-card processing starts on the same machine as the reservation management server and utilizes a B2B (business-to-business) server across the Internet.

5. **Choose object persistence.**

Some of your objects must persist. If your system is turned off, you have to preserve your objects so they don't get lost. During this step, you have to decide how you will preserve those objects. Some of your options include relational database management, object-oriented database management, and plain old files. Your choice has a significant impact on the design of a persistence subsystem, and on how other subsystems can use it. If a guest makes a reservation using the hotel reservation system today — and the system goes down tomorrow — that reservation had better be there when the system comes back up. Often designers use an existing relational database to hold hotel-reservation information.

6. Define subsystem interfaces.

Treat subsystems just like classes. Each subsystem is responsible for some major operations. During this step, you decide what those operations are and describe them as interfaces. The credit-card processing subsystem is responsible for checking the validity of a guest's card. And the subsystem must authorize any charges against a guest's credit card.

7. Select Components.

Building today's systems for maximum flexibility means designing with components. A *component* is a modular, self-sufficient, replaceable unit that works like a black box in your system. In this step, you select which parts of your system you want to act as replaceable or reusable units (that is, as components). The `CreditCardAuthorization` subsystem, the `Reservation` class, and the `Room` class are good candidates for modular components.

8. Pick system strategies.

You have to consider how your system starts up and how it shuts down. You must have a design strategy for handling errors and system failures. Regrettably (in this day and age), your system also must consider information security, data integrity, and customer privacy. These concerns may add use cases, classes, and subsystems to the overall systems design. The hotel reservation system must protect guest credit-card numbers and people's addresses from prying eyes. The system must not allow hackers to modify any reservations.

The first time you perform Steps 1 through 8 on a project, don't make any hard and fast design decisions. Just review the issues because each decision you make at each step has an impact on decisions you could make during the other system design steps. For instance, when you decide to use a certain vendor's relational database-management system, doing so imposes limits on how you define your interfaces — and on exactly how you could decompose your system into subsystems.

9. Iterate Steps 2 to 8.

Now, having visited the design issues presented in Steps 1 through 8, revisit each step and make some tentative decisions based on the design priorities you chose in Step 1. Use UML diagrams such as a package diagram and a deployment diagram to capture your design choices.

10. Iterate again.

We find that a good system design emerges after going through Steps 2 through 8 two or three times.

Designing your system involves a lot of steps. Luckily, UML provides you with notation and diagrams to help. Table 19-1 lists the major design elements that need defining during systems design and the UML diagrams that help you.

Table 19-1	Systems Design Diagrams	
Design Element	**UML Diagram**	**Description**
System Decomposition	Package Diagram and Component Diagram	Take your system and break it up into more manageable pieces known as subsystems. Show the subsystems and show their dependencies.
Interfaces	Class Diagram	Explore and then describe the contractual obligations of each subsystem. Treat each subsystem as if it were a class and describe the operations for that subsystem.
Hardware	Deployment Diagram	Describe the hardware you will use to run your software. And show how the hardware is connected together. Show the physical hardware architecture for your system as nodes with communication paths between them.
Components	Component Diagram	Show which parts of your system are really replaceable units also known as components. Show the structure of your system as black boxes with their interfaces, ready for replacement or reuse.
Deployment	Deployment Diagram	Indicate how your components and subsystems are realized as physical artifacts. In addition, show the hardware on which those artifacts are deployed.

Constructing Logical Pieces

Your first major step in designing a system is called "system decomposition." In this step you take the big-picture point of view and break your system up into "logical" pieces. You use a package diagram to group classes that must work together. (See Chapter 7 and Chapter 20 for more details on the package diagram.) You build component diagrams showing subsystems to present a consistent concept of how your system is put together. Later on you create real physical artifacts such as program code, Java scripts, or Web pages for each of these logical parts of your system.

Packing up your classes

You create subsystems to group classes together in a conceptual (logical) way for your design. The basic notation for a subsystem is a rectangle with the name of the subsystem at the top of the rectangle with a stereo type of «subsystem» and optionally a small fork icon in the upper-right corner of the rectangle. We use the fork icon to help the developer quickly pick out the subsystems from a complex diagram. Subsystems are a kind of package. The idea here is that just like packages that hold classes, subsystems can hold classes for your design. Take a look at Chapter 7 for more information on how and when you can put packages to work. Each subsystem in your system owns the classes within it. You cannot have the same class owned by two different subsystems. However you can import classes into a subsystem from another subsystem or package. (You can find more details on importing in Chapter 20.)

Figure 19-1 shows a simple subsystem labeled Reservations Business Logic. The subsystem contains the Person, Room, and CreditCard classes. The reservations business logic subsystem also contains the reserves association and the pays-with association. You can think of the Reservations Business Logic subsystem as a logical grouping with some of the classes required by the hotel reservation system.

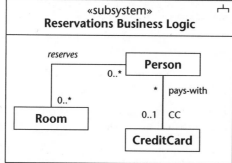

Figure 19-1:
A subsystem and its contents.

Your design classes should be owned by one — and only one — subsystem. The idea is to treat subsystems just as you would UML packages: Make sure you don't put the same class into more than one subsystem. If you do, you find their definition mutates into something different in the different subsystems, and confusion will follow. A frazzled developer may grab the wrong definition of the class, use it in an application, and break the system.

You don't have to put the same class in more than one subsystem, because a subsystem can import and reuse classes from other subsystems. (We explain importing classes in Chapter 20.)

Decomposing your system

You can think of your system as being one large package with all the classes contained inside — but that gets confusing. It's easier (and saner) to organize your system so that it's composed of groups of classes. You group your system's classes so that each group of classes must handle the behavior of only a part of your system — for example, realizing a use case or accessing a database. These groupings are what we've been calling *subsystems*. Each subsystem is capable of dealing with one important part of the overall problem your system is designed to solve.

We see projects get out of hand when they have just one package holding all the classes. The developers get confused and the system implementation is disorganized. You can get away with just one package if the software applications are small. If you build a large system, however (like a hotel-reservation management system), then sooner or later you'll have to break it up into smaller, more manageable pieces.

Use the following major techniques to identify subsystems and get started with system decomposition:

- ✔ **Establish subsystems:** Split your system into three major subsystems:

  - **Presentation:** The *presentation subsystem* is responsible for all interaction with the users.

  - **Application:** The *application subsystem* is responsible for handling all the business logic.

  - **Data:** The *data subsystem* is responsible for storing data making sure your objects persist.

- ✔ **Use aggregation:** If you have a large aggregation in your domain model, think about making a subsystem that contains the aggregate and all its parts.

- ✔ **Use case:** Create a subsystem that contains all the classes for your application that are necessary for making the use case work properly. You may want to combine several similar use cases into one subsystem. (You can find more details on grouping use cases into subsystems in Chapter 20. For more on classes that help your use case come alive see Chapter 7.)

✔ **Group domain classes:** Consider making a subsystem that holds all your domain classes. *Domain classes* reflect the domain or language of the user. These domain classes appear in various use cases in your application — and they must persist. Having all the domain classes in one place makes it easier to enforce a common definition and provide a common way to store these classes in a database.

Not all of these techniques mentioned above are compatible with each other. For example the three tier approach (group by presentation, application, and data) is not really compatible with use case approaches (group by functionality), although a very large system may use a combination of approaches.

If your system is really complex, you can break up any subsystem into lower-level subsystems. There are two ways you can show the subsystems inside your system:

✔ **Showing subsystems within a package:** Figure 19-2 illustrates the subsystem within a package technique for showing system decomposition. The Hotel Reservation System as a package contains three subsystems, Web Presentation, Reservations Business Logic, and Persistent Store(DB). Notice that each subsystem has the small fork icon. The Hotel Reservation System package could have also been shown as a subsystem with a «system» stereotype.

✔ **Membership notation:** You can also use membership notation to show system decomposition. You show the containing package at the top of the diagram. Attach a circle (with a plus sign inside) to the bottom of the package. Then draw a line from the circle-with-a-plus to each of the subsystems. Figure 19-3 shows this alternative notation using the package membership notation. The package diagrams in Figures 19-2 and 19-3 mean the same thing. Normally we prefer showing subsystems inside the main system package — that way it's easier to understand the containment visually.

Developing subsystem responsibilities

As you get these logical subsystems in place, you should ask yourself, *Just what is each subsystem responsible for?* Your subsystem is an aggregate or whole and the classes inside are the parts. Just as your system has major operations it must perform (use cases), each subsystem has a group of major operations for which it's responsible.

To help you understand what each subsystem must do, we recommend you create a simple class diagram that shows each of your subsystems as classes — and each subsystem's major responsibilities as operations.

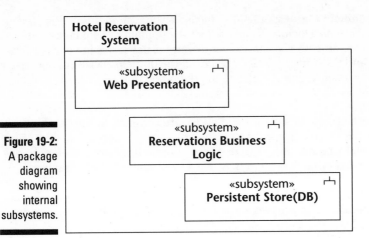

Figure 19-2:
A package
diagram
showing
internal
subsystems.

As an example, the hotel reservation system has a `Reservations Business Logic` subsystem. This subsystem is responsible for making room reservations, canceling reservations, guaranteeing a reservation, finding a room, checking its availability, and getting a price for the room. Figure 19-4 shows the major operations for the `Web Presentation`, `Reservations Business Logic` and `Persistent Store(DB)` subsystems.

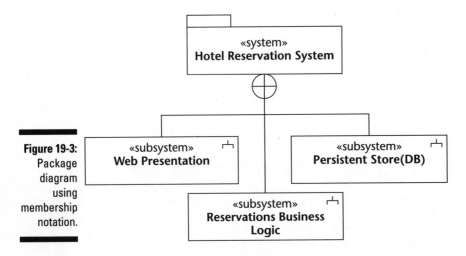

Figure 19-3:
Package
diagram
using
membership
notation.

You can focus on each subsystem, one at a time, and show its responsibilities as use cases and the other subsystems as actors. An example of this approach is given in Chapter 8.

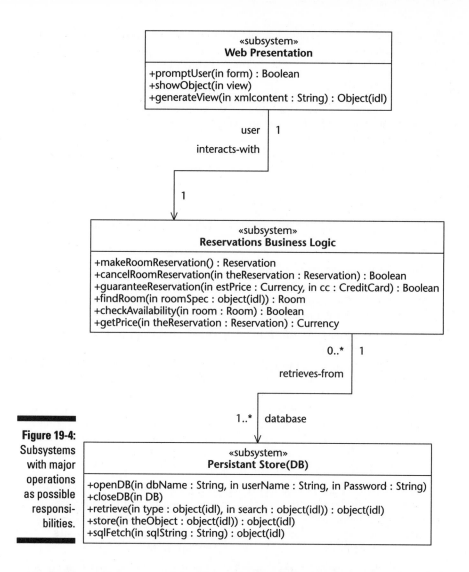

Figure 19-4:
Subsystems
with major
operations
as possible
responsi-
bilities.

Working with Components

You organize a system into subsystems. A standalone subsystem, autonomous and modular (relative to the bigger system), is known as a *component*. UML components are like replaceable parts — you take one out and fit another in its place. We like components because we can replace it without having to change anything else in my system. Components make your systems more flexible, maintainable, scalable, and reusable. Components come in many shapes and sizes. Subsystems are one example of a large component. A complex class with many internal parts and external interfaces could also be a component. (Remember a component is a replaceable part.)

When you construct replaceable components (parts), be sure to carefully define the boundary of the component. You define the boundary by clearly describing the responsibilities and interfaces of the component. Such parts are easy to make because everyone knows exactly what the component should do. This improves productivity and makes the component easier to test (the testing teams know exactly how the part is supposed to work), which improves quality. Also, the more a component is reused, the more trustworthy and reliable it becomes.

For your components to be replaceable parts they must have the following criteria:

- ✔ **Hide the inner workings:** The insides of a component are hidden from (and inaccessible by) objects outside the component. If you want to make a truly replaceable part, you can allow no dependencies to exist between the insides of the component and any other objects.

- ✔ **Provide interfaces:** An interface describes what operations you can invoke on a component — but, not how any such operation is performed. An object outside a component uses an interface without knowing which instance of a class is being invoked. All an outside object must know about a component is that it's using the appropriate interface (so it looks for the *signature* of the interface). That way the outside objects are kept in the dark about the inner workings of the component. Providing interfaces are a way of hiding the inside workings of a component from the outside. Components rely on the principles of encapsulation and information hiding. See Chapter 2 for more on these principles.

- ✔ **Make the inner parts independent:** You must make sure the objects internal to the component have no knowledge of outside objects. Otherwise trying to replace the component would break the system — there would be no guarantees that the appropriate outside objects would be available to the replacement component.

- ✔ **Specify the required interfaces:** Sometimes the objects inside your component must access objects on the outside. If the object on the outside has its own interfaces declared, then the objects on the inside use that common interface instead of accessing outside objects directly.

You can think of a component as a subsystem with internal classes that work together to realize the publicly stated interfaces.

Logical versus physical

The experts talk about logical data models, physical models, logical views, and physical elements. You needn't worry about all this babble. When the experts use the term "physical," they are referring to something in the real world that all of us experience. The experts use of the word "logical" simply means conceptual.

For instance a *physical table model* (also known as a physical data model) describes the tables of a relational database as they physically exist in a database. The actual names of the table and its fields are used in physical table model.

On the other hand, the *logical data model* describes the tables in a more generic or conceptual way — as *entities*. Entities are the concept behind the physical tables of a relational database.

The logical model for an object-oriented system consists of the conceptual pieces that make up the system: subsystems, components, and classes. The physical model consists of the real parts of a system: hardware, network connections, classes with design details specified, application code, scripts, and files.

Showing black boxes

UML 2 redefines the meaning of the "component diagram." In earlier versions of UML the component diagram defined components as the physical implementation of your software such as executable code files, dynamic link libraries, and source code files. The component diagram showed dependencies among the pieces of your software implementation and their hardware location. The experts who developed UML ran into a little problem: While they were busy defining diagrams, we object-oriented programmers were busy with our own meaning for the word *component*.

We needed replaceable parts for our applications. Classes were not replaceable. We needed an object-oriented part that provided not only behavior, but also interfaces independent of how the part worked. We needed better black boxes. So, during the mid-to-late 1990s, the practical development community came up with the idea of components. UML 2 catches up with developers and redefines the concept of *component* to bring it in line with the idea of an *autonomous replaceable unit*.

You show a component as a rectangle with the name of the component inside. The component has a stereotype of «component» and (optionally) a small icon in the upper-right corner that looks like a small box with a couple of tabs hanging off. (We're not making this up. Honest.) Because a component must hide its inner workings from the outside, it often has interfaces attached to the sides of the rectangle. Each interface that a component provides *to* the outside world looks like a "lollipop" (a circle on a stick) in the diagram. Each interface that the component requires *from* some other class or component in the system looks like a half-circle on a stick.

Figure 19-5 provides a black-box example of UML notation for a component called `PersistentStore`. Here it has the «component» stereotype and the small component icon on the right side. Our application component, `PersistentStore`, provides the following three interfaces:

- `DBAccess`: Another object in your system uses the `DBAccess` interface to open and close a database.

- `DBQuery`: If an object in your system wants to query an open database, that object uses the `DBQuery` interface. Then, in response to the query, the `PersistentStore` component then stores or retrieves objects as needed from a database.

- `DBTest`: Sometimes you have to test the connection between your system and an open database. An object in your system would use the `DBTest` interface for this purpose.

Our `PersistentStore` component also requires access to a relational database via a specific interface. Figure 19-5 shows this required interface with a half circle (socket) on a stick called `Rdbms`. The `Rdbms` interface must be provided by another class or component in your system. The `PersistentStore` connects its required interface to another component's provided interface — and both have the name `Rdbms`.

Figure 19-5:
Basic
component
with
interfaces.

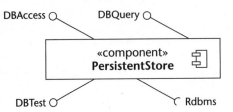

Figure 19-6 shows another black-box example of a component. Notice that UML doesn't make you use the circles-and-half-circles-on-a-stick notation; you can replace the lollipops with operations — showing the provided interfaces with the «provided interface» stereotype and the required interfaces with the «required interface» stereotype. The diagrams shown in Figures 19-5 and 19-6 have the same meaning.

Your components are, in effect, black boxes. Nobody can see what goes on inside them — but everyone can see their interfaces. The software components represented in your diagram have interfaces too, no less than the pieces of electronic equipment that have tangible interfaces for hooking up various cables.

«component»
PersistentStore

«provided interface» +DBAccess()
«provided interface» +DBQuery()
«provided interface» +DBTest()
«required interface» +Rdbms()

Describing the interfaces

You show components as black boxes when you want to wire them together
to make up your system. In the example of the PersistentStore component
in the previous section, you connect the PersistentStore to another component that provides the Rdbms interface.

But, if you're building the insides of a component for others to assemble into
their system, you have to show the interfaces' details. If (for example) other
developers want to use your PersistentStore component to retrieve data
from the database, they have to know the signature of the retrieve operation in the DBQuery interface, which may look like this:

```
retrieve(type : Object, search : String): Object(id1)
```

When you build a component, give the users of your component a special
interface specification using a component diagram. In this type of diagram
you show the component as a black box and the interfaces as classes. Each
interface has the «interface» stereotype, the name of the interface as the
name of the class, and the full operation signature for each operation with in
the interface. Connect up the provided interfaces to the component with a
realizes dependency. The *realizes dependency* shows that the component
implements the operations specified by the interface. Connect the required
interfaces to the component with a uses dependency. The *uses dependency*
shows that the component must use some other component that implements
that interface.

Your users of the PersistentStore component will appreciate the component diagram shown in Figure 19-7. This diagram shows users of the
PersistentStore component that if they want to store an object instance in
the database, they must invoke the DBQuery interface with store(theObject:
Object(id1)): Object(id1). Further, if they want to perform an SQL
query on the database, they would use the DBQuery interface with
sqlFetch(sqlString : String) : String. To keep the diagram simple,
we haven't shown the detailed signature of operations in the DBAccess,
DBTest, and Rdbms interface classes.

If you refer to Figure 19-6, you can see that it shows the PersistentStore
component with three provided interfaces and one required interface.

Figure 19-7 shows the same thing, only it uses dependency arrows instead of stereotypes:

- ✔ The dashed line with a large, closed arrowhead is the realizes dependency. That means an interface is realized by a component. For example the DBQuery interface is realized by the PersistentStore component.

- ✔ A dashed line that has a regular arrowhead and the «uses» stereotype means that the component uses the interface — in fact, that it *requires* the interface. For example, the PersistentStore component uses (requires) the Rdbms interface.

Looking inside the box

But wait a minute — you want to *build* components, not just assemble them. You need a way of showing the insides of your component. That's easy: just add a compartment below your component and put a class diagram there. Classes inside the component work together to accomplish the interfaces of the component.

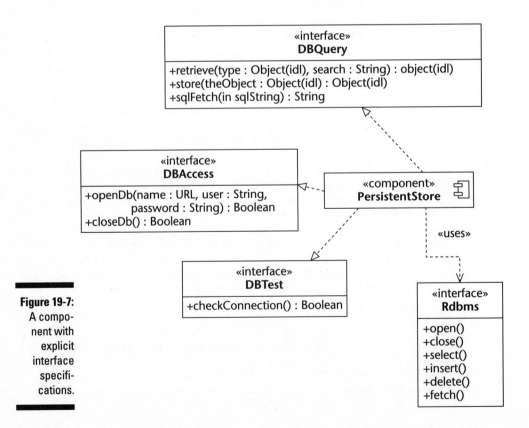

Figure 19-7:
A component with explicit interface specifications.

Because you must show how the internal classes are hooked up to the component's interfaces, UML provides some special terms and notation for the purpose:

- ✔ **Ports:** A port is a point of interaction between the inside and the outside of your component. Provided and/or required interfaces are attached to these interaction points. You show a port as a small square on the edge of your component. By attaching interfaces to a port, you're specifying the services that the component provides — or requires — through that port. One way to tell which port does what is to name it, putting the name next to the small square.

  Ports can be used on classes and subsystems as well as components.

- ✔ **Delegation:** When a request for service comes into your component through a port, you have to show who handles that request. Do so with a link between the port and one of the internal classes (or components) inside the larger component. Your connecting link should be a line with an arrowhead indicating the direction of the request. The line is also stereotyped «delegate».

- ✔ **Stereotypes for inner workings:** UML provides you with several stereotypes that help distinguish between the different parts inside your component. You can use the following stereotypes on the inner workings (classes and internal components) inside your component:

  - «focus»: A part with this stereotype executes some or all the business logic internal to the component.

  - «process»: A part with this stereotype executes a transaction. It must make sure that an important sequence of behavior — the transaction — completes. If the transaction fails to reach completion, this part must undo any behavior done to make the transaction happen — in effect, eating the evidence.

  - «service»: A service part has no states; it just computes a value. Such a part is really a function (sequential set of instructions) dressed up as an object.

  - «entity»: A part that persists. An entity's attribute values, behavior, and state carry on beyond the life of the application runtime environment.

  - «auxiliary»:A part that assists the focus part with implementing business logic for the component.

- ✔ **Ball and socket:** You can use the ball-and-socket notation to show assemblies inside your component. If you have one class that must have a particular interface and another class that *provides* that interface, then you can hook them up in the diagram: Just place the ball end of the provided interface into the half-open end of the required interface.

TIP

Whenever you design a component, create a component diagram to show its inner workings. You use such a diagram to help you explore, design, and document the best ways to wire your component. You should also create a component diagram that shows the component as a black box surrounded by `interface` classes, each with a detailed operation signature. Pass this second diagram out to all the developers who will be integrating your component into their system.

Figure 19-8 provides an inner structure example of the `PersistentStore` component. When an object outside of the `PersistentStore` invokes the `DBAccess` interface using the `openDB` or `closeDB` operation, the request is delegated to an instance of the `DBManager` class.

Incidentally, the `DBManager` is the focus of `PersistentStore` — so it makes sure any business logic for the component is handled properly. The `DBManager` creates an instance of the `checkConnection` class so the component can provide the service associated with the `DBTest` interface. Both the `DBManager` and the `checkConnection` must have interfaces on an internal component called `Connection`.

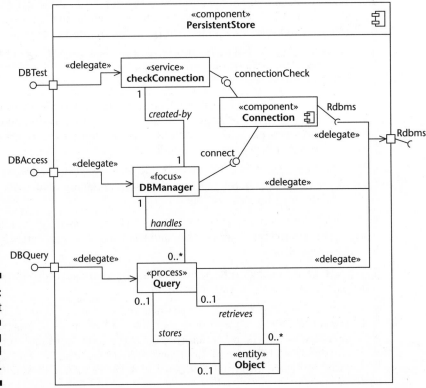

Figure 19-8: Component diagram showing internal classes.

You can see the use of the ball-and-socket notation in the example. The DBManager requires the connect interface that the Connection component provides. The Connection component, DBManager and Query all require the Rdbms interface. The Rdbms interface is external to the component; it must be provided by some other class or component in the system.

Deploying Physical Pieces (Implementation)

Before your design can see the light of day, you must plan the physical appearance of your system — describing the hardware, communication paths between devices, and the different types of files that run on that hardware. UML provides ways to show all such aspects of implementation on a deployment diagram.

Diagramming the physical architecture

Deployment diagrams show the physical architecture of your system — essentially a connected arrangement of hardware — as nodes (three-dimensional boxes). You draw lines between nodes to represent communication paths between your hardware components.

Nodes are very similar to classes. In fact, like the aggregate classes that contain parts, your nodes can contain other nodes. You can document detailed hardware configuration information by adding attributes and operations to your nodes. For instance we would specify that our user's Web-client hardware have the following attributes:

```
memory : Kilobytes = 256
diskCapacity : Gigabytes = 20
cpuSpeed : Mhz = 1.2
screenResolution: pixelRes = 1024 x 768
```

Some UML tools display this information right on the diagram. If not, the configuration information is still accessible in the definition of the node for later retrieval.

Any type of hardware that can execute software and talk to other hardware devices — for example, printers, modems, scanners, and external disk drives — are represented as nodes on a deployment diagram. Your communication paths represent such things as local area networks, the Internet, a USB cable, or (indeed) any mechanism that links one node to another. Use stereotypes to indicate the nature of the communication that goes on between your hardware components.

Communication paths between nodes are similar to associations between classes. You can show multiplicity, roles, and even qualifiers on the paths between the nodes. We like to show multiplicity to help developers understand how many nodes are in our design configuration.

You can use a number of stereotypes on the nodes and the communication paths of your deployment diagram. Some of the more common stereotypes are as follows:

✔ **Nodes:** Use these stereotypes to indicate the type of hardware node you're deploying:

«device»: Use this stereotype for a node that has processing capability.

- «application server»: A node of this type provides a remote service for an application.

- «client workstation »: A user's computer is often designated with the client workstation stereotype.

- «mobile device»: Laptop computers, cell phones, and other devices that use wireless communications are considered mobile devices.

- «embedded device»: Yes, developers of real-time embedded systems also have a stereotype.

- «execution environment»: This is a stereotype of a virtual node providing an environment for executing a program. A virtual node looks like hardware but is not actually hardware. An operating system or a Java virtual machine are examples of an execution environment.

- «container»: Enterprise-system development that uses Java also uses a "container" node to hold components. Designate that piece of hardware with the container stereotype.

✔ **Communication paths:** Use these stereotypes to specify types of communication links between hardware nodes:

- «serial»: Use this stereotype to indicate a serial-port connection between nodes — for example, a connection between a mouse and a computer via the serial port.

- «parallel»: Use this path to hook up nodes via the parallel port. Many printers and scanners are hooked up this way.

- «usb»: The Universal Serial Bus (USB) type of connection is used widely to hook up external devices (nodes) to computers.

- «lan»: Use this stereotype to indicate that two nodes are networked together.

- «internet»: Use the internet stereotype to indicate that the two nodes are using the vast resources of the Internet to communicate. If you have a Web application, you have an internet connection.

A deployment diagram that shows your hardware layout helps others understand how to build the system you have in mind. Keep it simple — show only the hardware architecture and its configuration. Such a diagram helps you to explore the dependencies among your hardware components. In large systems, this simplicity becomes especially important. Consider, for example, corporate data-warehouse configurations that involve many different types of nodes, including the following

- ✔ Online transaction-processing database servers

- ✔ Operational database servers

- ✔ At least one store server that provides *atomicity* (requiring each transaction to execute — or not — as a unit)

- ✔ Various metadata servers

- ✔ Multiple data marts

- ✔ Online application servers, load balancers, and users' desktop computers

All these nodes must utilize various corporate networks to communicate. We use a deployment diagram to organize these machines into an architecture. We look for communication bottlenecks in the diagram. We get consensus on the deployment and then publish the final version of the deployment diagram so all the developers understand the complexity of the data warehouse structural design.

Don't try to show everything on your deployment diagram; just show the major pieces of your architecture. You can show computers — or, for that matter, CPU chips — as nodes on a deployment diagram, and if necessary, you can show lots of detail — disk drives, memory cards, backplane communication buses, even specific wires. But these details are not important to most developers of software applications. Just show what's important to get the job done.

Figure 19-9 illustrates a simple deployment diagram for the hotel-reservation system. Potential guests use a Web Client and gain access to the reservation system through one of several hotel Web Server nodes. The Web Server passes information and requests between the user's Web Client and a single Reservation Server. The hardware sitting at the hotel's check-in desk as well as the manager's office is all one node — the Reservation Client node. This hardware also has access to the Reservation Server by using Java's remote method-invocation protocol (rmi). The Reservation Server uses the Database Server node for saving reservations and uses one of several available Credit Bureau nodes for credit authorizations.

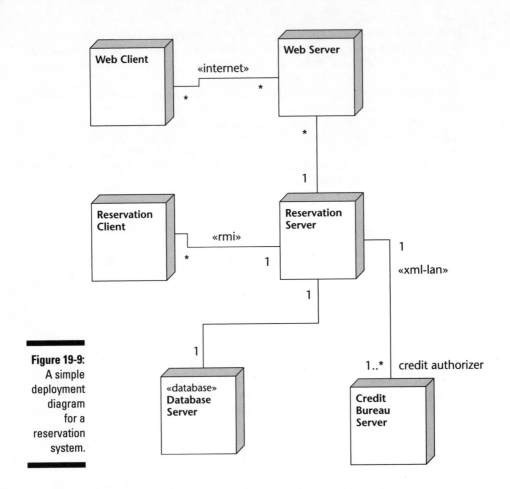

Realizing your system as artifacts

UML 2 introduces the artifact. We're not talking relics here. *Artifacts* are the physical files that make up your implemented system found running on various hardware nodes. Artifacts replace the UML 1.*x* definition of component.

Your system is logically composed of components, subsystems, classes, and functions. You realize these logical elements as physical artifacts or files. For example, a compiled file with executable code, a Java JAR file, a dynamic link library (dll) file, and a Web script are all artifacts. These are all physical manifestations of your work as a developer. You use deployment diagrams to show not only hardware nodes but also the artifacts that reside on them.

You show artifacts as a rectangle with the name of the artifact inside. The name is usually the filename with its extension, such as room.jar. You use the stereotype «artifact» and optionally a small icon that looks like a dog-eared page. On a deployment diagram, you can show artifacts in the following ways:

- **Inside the node on which they reside:** Just place the artifact inside the boundary of a node.

- **With a location property naming the node on which they reside:** The location property is shown below the name of the artifact as follows (replace *node name* with the actual name of the node):

  {location = *node name*}

- **Along with their dependencies to other artifacts:** You show dependencies among artifacts as dashed lines, each with an arrowhead indicating the direction of the dependency.

- **With a component property naming the component that the artifact implements:** The component property is shown below the name of the artifact as follows (replace *component name* with the actual name of the node):

  {component = *component name*}

- **As dependencies to the component(s) that they implement:** Show the artifact and the component it depends on in your deployment diagram. Then draw a dashed line with an arrowhead from the artifact to the component it depends on.

Artifacts are the physical implementation of components or subsystems. So every artifact depends on some component or subsystem, regardless of whether you show it on a deployment diagram.

Figure 19-10 provides an example of a deployment diagram for part of the hotel reservation system. Two artifacts residing on the Reservation Server node — ReservationLogic and Persistence.jar. ReservationLogic depends on the Persistence.jar file because at runtime instances in the ReservationLogic file must invoke instances in the Persistence.jar file. The Persistence.jar file depends on the Rdbms.exe executable file that resides on the Database Server node.

You may notice that the diagram shows two ways to indicate an artifact's dependency on a component. For the ReservationLogic artifact, the component dependency is shown as a property {component = Reservations Business Logic}. For the Persistence.jar artifact, the dependency is shown with a dashed line and an arrow pointing to the PersistentStore component.

UML provides you with a number of common stereotypes for your artifacts. Instead of using the plain «artifact» stereotype you can use any of the following to match your deployment situation:

✔ «executable»: This artifact can be executed as a program on a computer.

✔ «library»: You use this stereotype when you have a file that is a dynamic (or static) link library or DLL file.

✔ «script»: Script artifacts are source code files that get interpreted at runtime by some other program. If you have (for example) a Javascript file downloads to a Web browser, use this stereotype.

✔ «page»: Use the page stereotype to denote a single HTML page.

✔ «file»: This is a generic stereotype. Use this for any old file that is important to the runtime environment. You might use this for a profile or configuration-setup data file used by a program to start up an application.

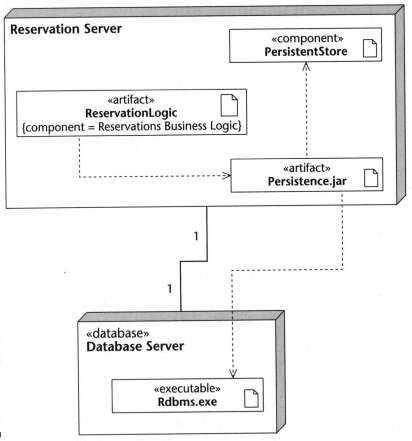

Figure 19-10:
Deployment
diagram
with
nodes and
artifacts.

Chapter 20

Breaking the System into Packages/Subsystems

In This Chapter

▶ Defining good packages

▶ Developing subsystems from packages

▶ Considering dependencies

▶ Specifying required subsystem services

▶ Realizing a subsystem

▶ Using architectural patterns to decompose your system

*E*ven the development wizards can get it wrong. This chapter shows you the tricks of the trade so you can avoid or at least contain the mess that can result when designing large systems. When designing these large systems, poor system decomposition — partitioning a system into smaller systems or *subsystems* — can exacerbate the confusion, and you can end up with a maintenance headache resulting from built in dependencies throughout the system. If this is the case, you may have a queasy feeling that the system is *brittle* — which means that every time you make a change to one part of the system, you end up having to make changes in lots of other places too. To help you head off such a scenario, this chapter shows you some measures you can take to avoid brittle systems. We talk about moving from analysis-time packages to design-time subsystems. You'll see examples of subsystem notation and architectural patterns that get you started building solid systems that stand the test of time.

Using Packages and Subsystems

Your requirements for a system start out as simple statements from a few users — and before you know it, you have many different types of users, lots of use cases, burgeoning domain terminology, and piles of business rules. As you develop your design solution, you must contend with users' machines, application servers, Web technology, networking, security, database performance, and a host of other issues. All this results in lots of diagrams and lots of classes to implement. To help you avoid confusion, UML provides packages and subsystems.

A *package* is an all-purpose way to group things such as classes, use cases, and/or diagrams together — and it's represented as a tabbed folder. Packages help you keep your development organized. Packages own what's inside them, and the internal contents of your packages are either *public* (visible outside the package), private (hidden inside the package), or *protected* (visible to package extensions, hidden from external packages).

A package can import the contents of another package and then use the imported package contents as if they were inside. You refer to an element like a class that belongs to another package with the `PackageName::ElementName` notation. For example, `Product::AirFilter` refers to the `AirFilter` class owned by the `Product` package.

You use packages to organize your requirements at analysis time. You use subsystems to organize your solution at design time. You can treat subsystems just like packages. In UML 2, subsystems and packages are not exactly the same thing, but they are close enough. (Subsystems are shown as a rectangle with a small fork icon in the upper right-hand corner.)

We use packages and subsystems during analysis and design as follows:

1. **Develop analysis packages.**

   During analysis, you can start grouping classes that must work together into the same package. You can also group your use cases by creating a package for each actor and placing the use cases initiated by that actor in the package.

2. **Reorganize packages for system design.**

   When you start designing your system, move classes and use cases around to group things together for your developers. Developers appreciate packages organized by important use cases, hardware, development schedule, or department ownership of the information. We'll give you more details on reorganizing packages later in the chapter.

3. **Convert packages to subsystems.**

   Change the packages into subsystems. The subsystems now hold and own, the contents that the packages did. The value of this step comes later when you design the details of each subsystem.

Not all analysis-time packages turn into subsystems. You might keep a package that holds common datatype definitions during design time. Subsystems in your system import the contents of the datatype package.

4. Consider dependencies.

Look at each subsystem and examine how it may (or may not) depend on the contents of other subsystems.

5. Reorganize subsystems.

Rearrange the contents of your subsystems to either increase dependencies (for performance) or decrease dependencies (for modularity) among your subsystems. At this stage, you use architectural design patterns such as façade or three-tier to reduce subsystem dependencies and increase the flexibility of your system's design. (You can find more about façade and three-tier patterns in the section "Using other architectural patterns," later in this chapter.) Doing so can often lead to a change in how you arrange your subsystems. If you reduce subsystem dependencies, you can have teams of designers work independently on each subsystem.

6. Design subsystem details.

After you're satisfied with the overall organization of your subsystems, then you begin designing their details. UML enables you to show the specification (requirements) and the realization (implementation details) for each subsystem.

If you organize your subsystems well, then teams of developers can design each subsystem without worrying about how the other subsystems are designed.

Creating analysis packages

The systems you analyze are probably large and complex with many different types of users, too many classes to remember, and lots of different behavioral interactions among the classes. To keep it all straight, we use packages during analysis. Here are some of the packages we find useful during system and software analysis:

- ✔ **Domain groups:** Group your domain classes (classes that reflect the terminology of the user, like hotel, room, or reservation) into a package. If you have lots of classes, then consider creating subpackages to further organize these domain classes. Look for a group of classes closely associated with each other and loosely associated with other classes in the domain. You can also look for classes that participate in any of the following:

- **Classification scheme:** You organize these classes into an inheritance hierarchy. Sometimes this makes for a good grouping.

- **Aggregation:** If you have an aggregate class that has a lot of parts, put the aggregate class and its parts into their own package.

- **Persistent class group:** If some (but not all) of your domain classes must *persist* (live beyond the life of the running application), place them in their own package.

✔ **Actors and use cases:** Each actor interacting with your system uses that system for its own purposes, which is a different from the purposes of other actors. Create a package for each actor and place the use cases for that actor in their respective package. If an actor has a lot of use cases (more than 5–9) consider creating subpackages to group the use cases more specifically for that actor.

✔ **Application class groups:** As you consider the classes required by your application, place them either in an appropriate use-case package or create a separate package to hold them. Such *application classes* are the control, view, and boundary classes that an application needs so it can make a use case work properly for an actor.

✔ **Common datatypes:** Often classes can represent enumerations (such as eye color), data classification (including units of measurement such as miles for distance and pounds for weight), and abstract datatypes (such as address, currency, or date). Place any such common datatype in a package so you have one definition of it that everyone can reuse.

You can continue to use packages during the design phase of your project as a general-purpose way of grouping elements from your UML diagrams together. However, we like to use subsystems during design because they allow you to show how specific requirements are realized by a group of cooperating classes.

Figure 20-1 shows some of the packages for an air-filter product business. The order clerk and the clerk's use cases are owned by the `Order Handling` package. The `Account Billing` package contains the accountant actor and use cases directly accessed by the accountant. A separate `Analysis Datatype` package holds several classes stereotyped as enumerations and a couple of abstract datatypes.

The domain packages for the air-filter business example are shown in Figure 20-2. To keep the diagrams simple, we don't show all classes and associations. You can see some of the classes owned by the `Customer Accounting` package, but we don't show the contents of the `Supplier Accounting`, `Airfilter Product`, and `AirEvents` packages. Call it an exercise of a handy UML feature: showing or hiding the contents of a package as needed.

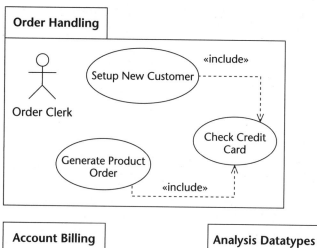

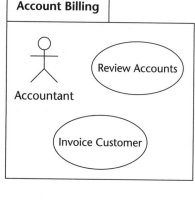

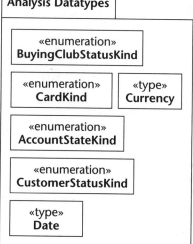

Figure 20-1:
Analysis
packages
for actors,
use cases,
and data-
types.

Creating subsystems

If your analysis results in a lot of classes and required behavior to make the system or software conform to what your users need, then you need to organize your design using multiple subsystems. During design, you can create subsystems according to the following criteria:

✔ **Use cases:** You can create subsystems that focus on a group of similar use cases. The analysis-time packages that you based on your use cases are good starting points when you're creating these subsystems. As when creating the analysis-time packages, you should look for use cases that have the same actor. The air-filter business example has two such subsystems: `Order Handling` and `Billing`.

When creating subsystem, keep use cases that depend on other "included" use cases in mind. You should ask yourself: *In which subsystem should I place the "included" use case?* There are a couple ways to answer this question:

- You can place an included use case in the subsystem where it's most often used — and let other subsystems import it if they need it. For the air-filter example, we chose to put the `Check Credit Card` use case in the `Billing` subsystem instead of the `Order Handling` subsystem because the accountant uses it more frequently than the order clerk does. The `Order Handling` subsystem will import the `Billing` subsystem. During design, you're allowed to move things around if it meets your design priorities.

- Alternatively, you can place the included use case in its own subsystem. Other subsystems that need the behavior of the included use case must import the behavior. We favor this approach if several other use cases in our system must access the included use case. If you chose this option for the air-filter example, you would create a subsystem, call it `Credit Check`, and place the `Check Credit Card` use case with in it. The `Order Handling` and `Billing` subsystems would depend on the `Credit Check` subsystem.

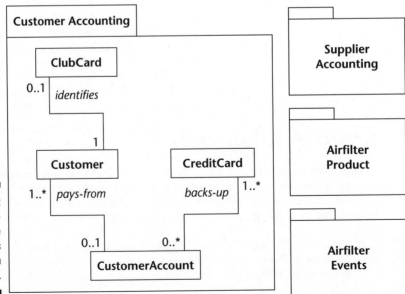

Figure 20-2:
Analysis-time packages for problem domain.

✔ **Hardware and software:** Your information system has software that runs on hardware. You can use this as a basis for creating subsystems. Consider the following examples:

  • **Hardware:** Create subsystems around the different kinds of hardware in your system. The `Order Handling` subsystem, for example, can be broken down into two more subsystems: `Web Orders` for handling orders placed over the Internet and `Clerk Orders` placed on standard-issue office equipment of the order clerks.

  • **Software:** You have three kinds of software in your system: new software you develop, old legacy software that you have to use for a while yet, and commercially purchased software (such as application programs, transaction managers, database-management systems, and office software suites). Create subsystems to contain each of these different types of software. (The air-filter business would need a subsystem for the commercially purchased database-management system.)

✔ **Schedule:** You don't always get the chance to build and deliver the required software for your system all at once. You have a schedule you must follow, rolling out specific pieces of the software over time. You can create subsystems that group related use cases (and the classes that implement those use cases) for each delivery deadline in the schedule. If you built subsystems according to the schedule in the air-filter example, you'd need a subsystem containing `Setup New Customer`, `Invoice Customer`, and `Check Credit Card` use cases for the first scheduled rollout. The second rollout would have a subsystem containing the `Generate Product Order` and the `Review Accounts` use cases.

✔ **Ownership:** If you have developers from different departments who must take ownership for a particular piece of the system, consider creating subsystems based on that ownership. If we have developers with accounting expertise, then we create a subsystem and place all accounting-oriented classes, use cases, and components in it. Similarly, the database department is responsible for (you guessed it) the database subsystem.

✔ **Deployment:** Today your applications are spread across the user's computer, Web servers, application servers, and database servers. You can create subsystems based on where you deploy the software. The air-filter business needs subsystems for the software that gets deployed on each of these different machines.

Figure 20-3 shows a group of subsystems based on the analysis-time packages for the air-filter business example. The two analysis-time use-case packages lead to the `Order Handling` and `Billing` subsystems. (The `Billing` subsystem contains the `Check Credit Card` use instead of `Order Handling`.)

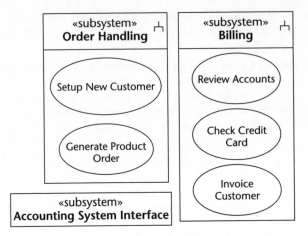

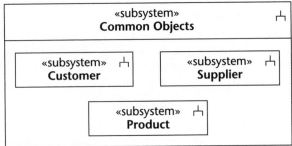

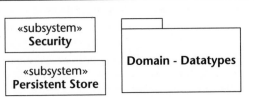

Figure 20-3:
Example of
design time
subsystems.

At analysis time, all the different domain packages lead to a subsystem that
holds all the *common objects*. The Common Objects subsystem contains several sub-subsystems — Customer, Supplier, and Product. The Persistent
Store subsystem provides an interface to a back-end relational database-
management system. The Security subsystem handles all login and user
authorization tasks. The Accounting System Interface provides access
to a legacy accounting system.

The Analysis Datatypes package is now called the Domain - Datatypes
package for the system design. Not all analysis packages convert to
subsystems.

Exploring Dependencies

Unless your system is simple, no one subsystem does everything. Each subsystem must rely on services supplied by other subsystems to get its own job accomplished. When one subsystem can't do its work without relying on another subsystem, you have *dependency*.

An example of dependency occurs in the air-filter business example: The Order Handling subsystem must rely on the classes inside the Common Objects subsystem to generate a product order. If you were to make a change to the operations of the AirFilter, Customer, or CustomerAccount classes, then you would have to change classes inside the Order Handling subsystem too.

The dependencies among your subsystems come in three flavors (Figure 20-4 illustrates these flavors):

- ✔ **Dependent:** If one of your subsystems depends on the contents or interfaces of another subsystem, but not the other way around, this is the simple case of *one-way dependency*. The Order Handling subsystem is dependent on the Common Object subsystem. (You hear experts refer to *client-supplier,* or *client-server dependency.* These are just other terms for one-way dependency.)

  Show one-way dependency as a dashed line that connects two subsystems; include an arrowhead that points from the dependent subsystem to the subsystem it depends on. You can show dependencies among packages in the same way.

- ✔ **Codependent:** Two subsystems are *codependent* or *two-way dependent* when they depend on each other. If a class in the Common Object subsystem must have access to a class in the Order Handling subsystem and some other class in the Order Handling subsystem needed access to yet other classes in Common Objects, then we have a two-way dependency (also known by its fancier name, *peer-to-peer dependency*).

  You show two-way dependency as two separate dependency lines that connect the same two subsystems but go in opposite directions. (A more informal notation for codependency is a single dashed line that has arrowheads at both ends.)

- ✔ **Independent:** If you have two subsystems that have no dependency between them, they are called *independent*. In the air-filter example, the Persistent Store subsystem and the Accounting Interface Subsystem have no dependencies between them.

  You show that two subsystems are independent by *not* connecting them with dependency lines.

If you want a maintainable system, avoid codependency among your subsystems. Dependency means that a change in a subsystem may lead to a change in the dependent system. But, codependency is worse. A change in one codependent subsystem may lead to a change in the other codependent subsystem, which in turn could lead to a change in the first codependent subsystem.

After you have your subsystems, consider the dependencies among them: Build a diagram that shows your design-time subsystems and packages, using dashed-lines-with-arrows to indicate each subsystem's dependency on other subsystems and packages. While you're exploring these dependencies, consider the degree of coupling and cohesion present in each subsystem:

- ✔ **Coupling:** A highly coupled subsystem has many dependencies.

- ✔ **Cohesion:** A highly coherent subsystem has all the classes it needs to meet its assigned responsibility.

To increase or decrease coupling and cohesion among subsystems, you move classes from one subsystem to another until you find the right balance.

Look for *codependent* (two-way-dependent) subsystems — and try to make them one-way-dependent. You can do this by moving classes from one subsystem to another or by creating a subsystem that holds only the common classes. Architectural patterns (discussed at the end of this chapter) can also help you break the cycle of codependency.

Every system you build has some amount of coupling and some degree of cohesion. But, the desired levels of coupling and cohesion depend on your design priorities and goals. Those goals relate to functional requirements, performance, cost, and schedule. You find more information on design priorities in Chapter 19.

Before you design your system, consider your design priorities. As you perform the design tasks, keep an eye on coupling and cohesion. Adjust your design to obtain the right level of coupling and cohesion to meet the design concerns.

Diagramming dependencies

Figure 20-4 illustrates a design diagram with subsystems, packages, and dependencies for the air-filter business example. We like to put the user-oriented (use case) subsystems at the top and low-level service-oriented subsystems at the bottom of our dependency diagrams.

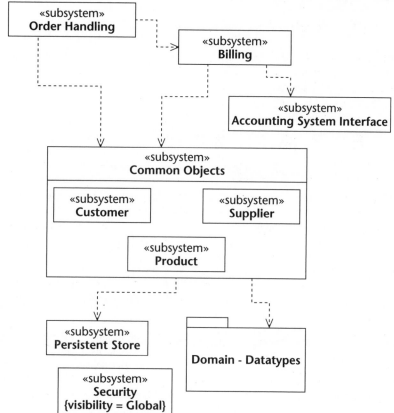

Figure 20-4:
Diagram
showing
dependen-
cies among
subsystems.

At the top of the diagram in Figure 20-4, you see the two subsystems that interface with the Order Clerk and Accountant actors — Order Handling and Billing. Order Handling depends on Billing because Billing contains the included use case Check Credit Card. Order Handling and Billing both depend on Common Objects. The Billing subsystem must access the Accounting System Interface subsystem, so there is a dependency there too.

All classes in the Common Objects subsystem — such as Customer, AirFilter, SupplierAccount, and CreditCard (not shown in the figure) — must be saved in a database. So, the Common Objects subsystem depends on the Persistent Store subsystem — and on the definitions of abstract datatypes and enumerations contained in the Domain-Datatypes package.

Notice that the Security subsystem has a property {visibility = Global}. That means that all the other subsystems may depend on the Security subsystem because it's globally available to all parts of the system.

Considering coupling and cohesion

There are many possible design solutions for your system. Each solution has good points and bad points. We use the concepts of coupling and cohesion to figure out how well any particular design solution meets our design priorities. In and of themselves coupling and cohesion are neither good nor bad — but they can tell you a lot about how your system approaches its work — and whether you want to change that.

The concept of coupling expresses how interconnected the parts of our system are — in effect, how interconnected such parts as classes or subsystems are. A class with six associations is more coupled than a class with two associations. A subsystem that depends on another subsystem is more coupled than a subsystem with no dependencies. Another way to think about coupling is to consider how much an instance of a class must "know" about its surroundings. The more an object must know about other objects' methods, the higher the coupling.

Cohesion, on the other hand, expresses how well all the internal parts of a class or subsystem work together. If a class must have every one of its attributes and operations in order to work, the class is highly cohesive. However, if a couple of attributes are only used with one operation and another few attributes are only in use by a different operation, the class has lower cohesion within the class. When all classes inside a subsystem work together to accomplish the tasks required of the subsystem, then the

subsystem is highly cohesive. However if a subsystem has several groups of classes where each group works independently of each other, then the subsystem is less cohesive.

Suppose you're designing a system to be flexible. A flexible design enables you to make changes in one subsystem without affecting or changing other subsystems. Flexible systems call for a modular design with high cohesion and low coupling. Subsystems with high cohesion are replaceable — and if they have a low degree of coupling, fewer changes are needed; the result is more modularity. If your subsystem exhibits high coupling, that means it's dependent on many other subsystems. In a highly coupled system, chances are that a change in one subsystem leads to changes in other subsystems.

But, if you're designing a system for performance, you tend to increase the coupling and lower the cohesion of your classes and subsystems. That way when an object must get data quickly, it goes directly to an object that can provide that data instead of indirectly through many interfaces. For example, you have an object that needs data from a database you have design options. You could have the object invoke the behavior of a generic database interface object. Or, you could write the access code right into a method in the object that needs the data. The second option ties your object directly to the database but, it performs faster.

 Instead of drawing a lot of dependency lines from just about every subsystem to just one commonly needed subsystem, use the global-visibility property instead.

Importing what you need

As you work on a subsystem, you come to a point at which you need the services of a class that resides in another subsystem or package. You have two choices:

- **Invoke an interface:** When you call an operation on the subsystem where the needed class resides, that operation invokes the needed class. Suppose (for example) you're using the façade design pattern (more on façade in the section "Using other architectural patterns," at the end of this chapter) to make this happen: When an instance of the Customer class changes, an update must be made to the database. You can design the Customer class to invoke the interface operation store(this) on the Persistent Store subsystem. The internal elements of the Persistent Store subsystem then get to work storing the data from the Customer instance in tables in the database.

- **Import the class:** You import the class right into the subsystem that must use the class, making it appear as if the imported class is inside the subsystem that needs it. The imported class is still owned by the package or subsystem from which you imported it, but you can use it directly. The AirFilter class needs the Pound (weight in pounds) abstract datatype that resides in the Domain - Datatype package. By importing the Domain-Datatype package into the Product subsystem, you can treat the Pound class definition as if it were inside the Product subsystem.

You import elements from other subsystems so that their visibility is either public or private. You make the contents of another package or subsystem public in another subsystem by using the «import» stereotype on a dashed dependency line. You make the insides of another package or subsystem private in another subsystem by using the «access» stereotype on a dashed dependency line.

Figure 20-5 illustrates what happens when you use the «import» and «access» stereotypes. On the left side of the figure, you import the contents of Domain - Datatypes into Product and make them publicly visible to other subsystems. So, when the Order Handling subsystem imports Product, it also imports the elements originally in the Domain - Datatypes package.

However, the situation is quite different on the right side of Figure 20-5. You "access" the contents of Domain - Datatypes and make them private — hidden from other subsystems. As a result, when the Order Handling subsystem imports Product, it does not import the elements originally in the Domain - Datatypes package and may not use them.

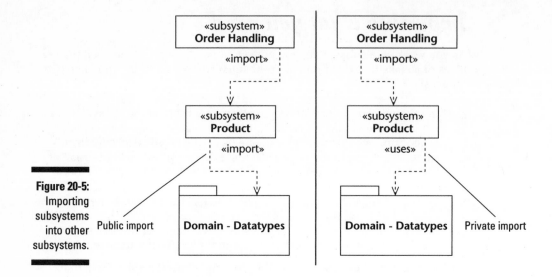

Figure 20-5:
Importing
subsystems
into other
subsystems.

Merging what you have

Suppose you realize that two subsystems are almost identical. They have about the same number of classes, the names of the classes are similar, and relationships between the classes are almost identical. To solve this problem, UML provides a special dependency called *merge* that works like inheritance. A package or subsystem merges the contents of another package or subsystem by inheriting its contents within its own scope. To indicate merging, attach the «merge» stereotype to the dependency line.

For example, in the air-filter business example we have similar subsystems — Customer and Supplier. Both subsystems have an account. In the Customer subsystem it's called CustomerAccount and in the Supplier subsystem it's called SupplierAccount. Each type of account is backed up by a line of credit. In the Customer subsystem, the customer's credit card provides the line of credit. The business sends invoices to customers and receives invoices from suppliers. In both cases, the invoice is paid through the respective account — Customer or Supplier Account. There must be a way to simplify this situation. Figures 20-6 and 20-7 illustrate one such solution: merge.

When you see common classes and associations in different subsystems, create a subsystem that contains their commonality. Figure 20-6 shows a new subsystem called ClientAccount. The ClientAccount holds generic classes such as Client, Account, LineOfCredit, and Invoice. The Customer and Supplier subsystems are shown merging the ClientAccount.

Figure 20-7 shows the classes internal to the Supplier subsystem as a result of merging the ClientAccount subsystem. The supplier contains its own

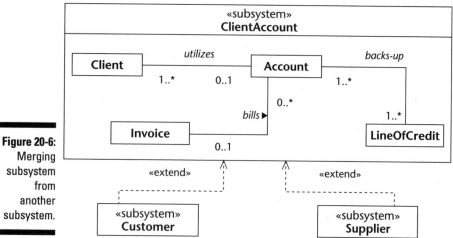

Figure 20-6:
Merging
subsystem
from
another
subsystem.

Invoice, Client, Account and LineOfCredit classes. These classes play specific roles in association with each other. The Invoice class plays the role of payable in this subsystem. In the Customer subsystem (not shown), the Invoice plays the role of receivable.

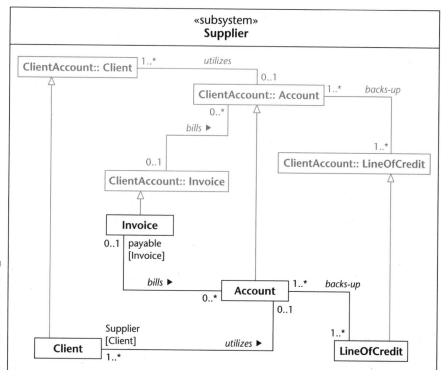

Figure 20-7:
Illustration
of merged
subsystems's
internal
classes.

Notice that Figure 20-7 shows some classes and associations as gray. We did that to illustrate how the merge dependency leads to inheritance. (You would not show those gray elements in your diagram. When you merge another subsystem or package those gray elements are implicitly there.) For example, the `Invoice` class owned by the `Supplier` subsystem is a subclass of the `Invoice` class owned by the `ClientAccount` subsystem — `ClientAccount::Invoice`.

You add attributes and operations specific to the classes in the `Supplier` subsystem and inherit the generic attributes and operations from the classes defined in the `ClientAccount` subsystem. The associations are also inherited. You see the `bills` association inherits from the gray `bills` association. As a consequence the `bills` association inherits the multiplicities (`0..1` and `0..*`) and role names (`Invoice` and `Account`). We have changed the role name from `Invoice` to `payable`. UML allows us to indicate that we're redefining the role name by showing the new role name as `payable` and the old (inherited) role name as `[Invoice]`.

Patterning the Relationships

If you build systems, you may experience déjà vu — the same kinds of subsystems appear in different system architectures. You're not losing your mind. Many systems display similar architectural patterns when you structure their subsystems. You make use of these patterns to solve common design problems when you start putting your system together. An architectural pattern gives you a reusable template to base your systems design.

Utilizing the three-tier architecture pattern

Three-tier architecture is a common pattern for systems. This pattern separates your system into three distinct areas of behavior found in almost every system (presentation to the user, business logic, and object persistence). It also separates subsystems by technology (for example, user interface, application, database) and machine location (user-client machine, server machine, database machine). What you get (ideally) is a consistent user interface across multiple applications. But not all related behavior is confined to the same subsystem. For example, handling an instance of the `Order` class is done in several different places.

Using the three-tier architecture pattern you decompose your system into three subsystems:

✔ **Presentation:** The subsystem that plays the Presentation role is responsible for all interactions with the user of the system.

✔ **Business Logic:** This subsystem must perform calculations and make sure the application adheres to business rules. This is where the real work of the application takes place, independent of any user interfaces.

✔ **Database:** The back end of the system is the subsystem that plays the role of the database. This subsystem is responsible for storing any data or objects that must persist beyond the runtime of the application.

Modeling architectural patterns

You use a collaboration to diagram an architectural pattern. If you're showing just the pattern, draw a dashed oval with the name of the collaboration at the top. Draw a dashed line to separate the name of the collaboration from the elements depicted as involved in the pattern collaboration. In the main body of the oval show a simple diagram with the subsystems that interact to form the pattern. You name the subsystem in such a way as to indicate the role they play in the pattern. You can also show connections between the subsystems and any other dependencies between the subsystems that make up the pattern. (See Chapter 15 for more on collaborations.)

Figure 20-8 illustrates the three-tier pattern. The basic idea is quite simple, three subsystems labeled Presentation, Business Logic, and Database are contained inside a named collaboration oval. The dependencies between the three subsystems are also show to further clarify the pattern. If you use this pattern your three subsystem must follow the pattern of dependencies shown in the diagram.

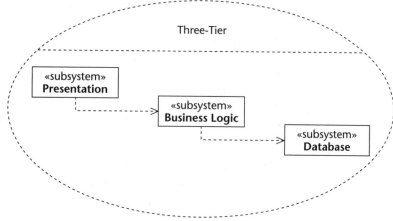

Figure 20-8:
Three-tier
architec-
tural
pattern.

When you want to show a specific "occurrence" of a pattern, you draw a *collaboration occurrence* — a small, named collaboration oval — and don't forget the dashes. To show each your specific subsystems that participate in the pattern, use a dashed line to connect each subsystem to the collaboration oval. Then, at the end of the dashed line next to each subsystem, show the role that subsystem plays in the pattern. Role names come from the generic pattern description.

Figure 20-9 shows an occurrence of the three-tier pattern for the air-filter business example. A subsystem called `OrderViewClient` plays the role of the Presentation subsystem. The `OrderViewClient` is responsible for presenting screen views of order and customer information to the user. The `OrderHandlingServer` subsystem performs all the business logic of the order-handling application. It, in turn, depends on the `PersistentStore` subsystem to play the role of the `Database` part of the pattern. `PersistentStore` is responsible for all storage and retrieval of order and customer information.

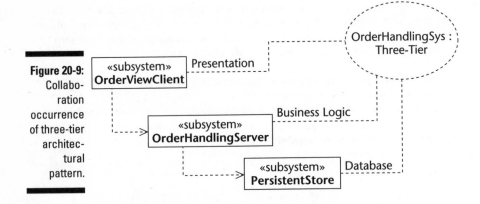

Figure 20-9:
Collaboration occurrence of three-tier architectural pattern.

Using other architectural patterns

It can be especially helpful to use architectural patterns to get you started with decomposing your system into subsystems. You may want to consider the following other architectural patterns:

✔ **Façade:** You provide a simple interface, the *façade,* to hide complex internal details, such as the system's *subsystems, components,* and/or *classes.* Many complex subsystems use this pattern to hide their complexity from other subsystems.

✔ **Adapter:** You want to convert the interface of an existing system or sub-system, the *adaptee,* to an interface more easily used, the *adaptor.* This pattern serves to "wrap" legacy systems and hide the old interface to the legacy system.

✔ **Master-slave:** You have to have one subsystem, the *master,* in complete control of other subsystems, the *slaves.* The master issues commands and accepts responses from the slaves. Command and control systems tend to use this pattern.

✔ **Pipe-filter:** When you want a system that must perform a step-by-step sequence based purely on data input, you actually have two tasks:

  • Create a pipeline architecture with subsystems that perform *each step.*

  • Create a subsystem to hold the *data.*

The subsystems that perform each step can also filter the data passing through them. Signal-processing systems and batch-oriented systems (for example) use this pattern.

Part VII
The Part of Tens

In this part . . .

In this part, we get to make several lists of stuff that help you model with UML while still being fun, informative, and useful — such as common UML pitfalls and mistakes to avoid, Web sites full of additional UML information to surf, UML tools that make pretty pictures easy to draw, and a selection of the best UML diagrams — complete with instructions on when to use them.

Chapter 21

Ten Common Modeling Mistakes

In This Chapter

▶ Avoiding diagram pitfalls

▶ Checking for problems

We've been teaching modeling for the analysis and design of systems for more than a decade. During this time, we've witnessed many of the same modeling mistakes over and over. As you learn to apply UML to meet your needs, keep in mind these pitfalls (which we hope to help you avoid). This chapter lists ten of the most common blunders made by modelers. Use it to check your work as you and your co-developers construct UML diagrams.

Splitting Attributes and Operations

We see developers create some classes with attributes but no operations, and other classes that have no attributes — *only* operations. (We don't know about you, but every object-oriented class we ever met had both attributes *and* operations.)

The developers making this mistake are really thinking about data structures and the functions that act on the data. They translate that idea into the object-oriented world by using the steps much like the following:

Blunder 1:   Equate data structure only with class attributes.

Blunder 2:   Equate a function that manipulates data structures only with class operations.

Blunder 3:   Create one instance of the class with operations.

Blunder 4:   Create one instance of the class with attributes.

Blunder 5:   Use the class with the operations to change the values of the class with attributes.

Do *not* follow the five steps we've just outlined (but you knew that). They lead to splitting up attributes and operations. Big mistake.

Make your classes whole by putting the attributes and operations that need each other together in one class.

Figure 21-1 shows classes with attributes and classes with operations — separately (and confusingly). The Vehicle class works with the Truck class. The Tools class is similar to the ToolKit class. The Person class is another name for the Employee class. Figure 21-2 shows a better model, with the attributes and operations put together.

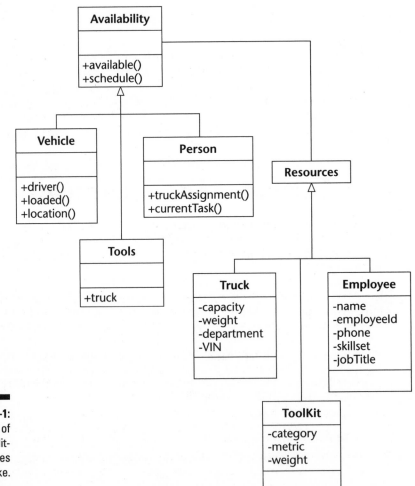

Figure 21-1:
Example of
a split-
classes
mistake.

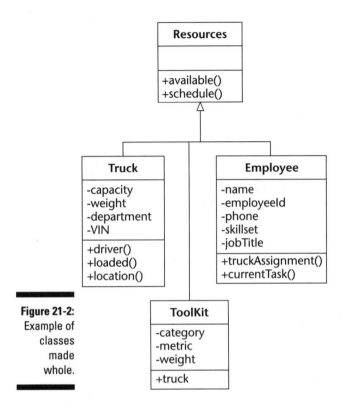

Figure 21-2:
Example of
classes
made
whole.

Using Too Few or Too Many Diagram Types

We've observed some developers use just one diagram for every situation. They forget that other UML diagrams are there to help them understand, communicate, analyze, design, and implement. They build class diagrams to capture classes (and their static relationships), but also try to represent object interactions, data flows, and system decompositions with those same class diagrams. Unfortunately, the class diagram was never meant to capture that other stuff very well — but use-case, sequence, state, and activity diagrams seem foreign to these experts.

Some developers produce only class diagrams because that's what translates most easily into object-oriented programming code. Alas, the code they produce is not dynamic enough (because the developer didn't consider state diagrams) or even what the user wants (because the developer never thought about the use cases for the application).

Other developers seem compelled to use every single UML diagram whether they need to or not. Some people pride themselves on their knowledge of UML notation. They show off their abilities by using every diagram on every project. You waste valuable time trying to decipher these extra diagrams without making any progress toward completing the project.

Every UML diagram has a purpose and value, but not every diagram is necessary on every project. Your project is unique; some — but not all — UML diagrams will help you get the job done. If your project involves maintaining an existing system (for example), then some class diagrams, a couple of sequence diagrams, and a deployment diagram may be all you need. However, if you build real-time embedded systems, you need state diagrams along with sequence diagrams (because you want the team to understand timing issues), *and* some class diagrams. Every project is different.

Check out Chapter 24, where we list ten useful diagrams to get you started. Our aim here is to avoid getting stuck on just one diagram — but also to spare you the confusion of trying to use all the possible UML diagrams.

Showing Too Much Detail

One team of developers we worked with proudly showed us over one hundred sequence diagrams they had constructed. Each diagram was like the one in Figure 21-3 — only worse. There were twenty to thirty instances shown at the top of some of these diagrams. The team used really big pieces of paper to print out their masterwork. We asked them a couple of questions: "Do you *maintain* these diagrams — as the requirements change, do you update their details?" Their answer was a simple "No." (Yikes.)

Often developers start drawing UML diagrams because they want to build a program. Each event line in our client's sequence diagrams (for example) might become a method call from one object instance to another. Rather than clarify the interaction requirements for their software application, the team bogged down in unnecessary programming details before they even knew what to program.

If you think to yourself, *I could have written the program in less time than it took to create this diagram,* then you have too much detail.

You can avoid too much detail by thinking about whether a risk to the project exists if you *don't* show the detail on your diagram. Often there is none. If you do find some risk to the progress of the project, than add a *little more* detail to the diagram.

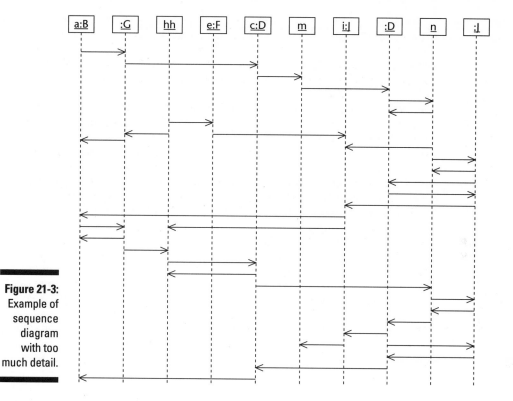

Figure 21-3:
Example of
sequence
diagram
with too
much detail.

Using Vague Terminology

To keep the peace, some modelers give their classes vague names. One modeler, for example, had a diagram with the `Tuple` class on it — and the developers were confused about its meaning. When we asked the modeler about it, we found out the modeler was avoiding a political fight. You see, the developers had strong opinions about the meaning of specific data items. Instead of clearly defining `Tuple` to be a grouping of either abstract or concrete data items and named functions, used as metadata in the process of extracting data from a source data set, the modeler choose to stay out of trouble by using vague class names. No one could accuse the modeler of choosing sides in the "data item" battle, and the modeling work could still go forward.

Now the whole point of using UML notation is to foster communication. Often users and developers are not precise about what they mean. For example, you may find that the same term, `Tuple` — as applied to abstract-versus-concrete data elements — has different meanings to different people. Work with each person to find out precisely what he or she is talking about. Then use UML to communicate the different meanings accurately *to each group*. You become the hero because you help overcome conflict among developers by clarifying what they mean when they use similar terminology.

Defining the Same Thing Twice

The users you talk to have their own language and UML diagrams help you understand that language. But as you carefully build class diagrams that define the terminology of your users, the unthinkable happens (in fact, rather frequently): Two users use different words to mean the same thing. For example, in the insurance world *hazard* and *peril* can mean the same thing. We asked one user the meaning of *hazard* and were told, "When a hazard occurs, we must pay an insurance claim if the policy handles that hazard." Another user told me, "A peril is a description of an incident for which we write coverage." We used UML to model the meaning of *hazard, peril, insurance policy, claim,* and *coverage.* As this model matured, The `Hazard` and `Peril` classes had almost identical attributes, operations, and associations with the `Policy` and `Coverage` classes. After we discussed the meaning of *hazard* and *peril* with both users, they agreed the two words meant the same thing.

Look through your diagrams to find classes with similar attributes, operations, and associations. If you find a couple of similar classes, question your users and the other developers. Ask for examples of these similar classes from your users. If they turn out to be the same, you should choose a single name for the class and stick with it. (You might use the other name for some other purpose — say, as a role name on an association or the name of a common superclass.)

Linking Everything Together

Developers often get used to feeding a function with all the data it needs — and (just as often) apply this same thinking to classes. These programmers create a class and connect it (via associations) to all other classes that have any data the first class might need in one of its operations. For instance, an `AutoPolicy` class is associated with `Claim`, `MedicalCoverage`, `LiabilityCoverage`, `ComprehensiveCoverage`, `Auto`, `Agent`, `Premium`, `Payment`, and `Person` classes. The developer forgets that one class (`AutoPolicy`) can ask another class (`Premium`) for information about yet another class — the dollar value from the `Payment` class — without having to associate the `AutoPolicy` class directly to the `Payment` class.

Class diagrams — where most classes connect to most other classes — can be the royal road to maintenance nightmares. Any time you associate one class to another class, you have a dependency between those classes. If you change one class, the other may change too. The more associations between classes, the more dependencies you must worry about.

When you see class diagrams with every class connected to every other class, remove some of those associations. You should find out which associations are really necessary and which associations exist simply to get data from one class to another class.

Creating Too Many Use Cases

Some business analysts go use-case crazy. Before they know it, they have an unruly plethora of use cases. This happens when the business analyst creates — CRUD. Yep, CRUD. For example, the user needs to **C**reate addresses, **R**ead addresses, **U**pdate addresses, and **D**elete addresses. So the analyst creates *four* use cases to handle the Address class. Then, with a flourish, the Read Address use case is included by putting «includes» in the Create, Update and Delete Address use cases. (By the way, this analyst is just getting started. *Every class known to the user* must be created, read, updated, and eventually deleted — which means dealing with *thousands* of use cases.)

When you see lots of use cases, check to see if they are CRUD. Check the following to identify CRUD:

- ✔ **One class:** Several use cases all center around just one class.

- ✔ **Not a major class:** The use cases deal with a relatively minor class in your application.

- ✔ **CRUD:** The use-case names are similar to Create X, Read X, Update X, and Delete X, where X is the minor class.

- ✔ **Simple interaction:** Each use-case description is short and simple to describe.

- ✔ **Include Read use case:** Several of the use-case descriptions include the Read X use case. In other words several use cases have an «include» relationship to a use case named Read X.

If you recognize CRUD use cases, combine them into one use case and call it Maintain X. However, if the CRUD use cases really represent different goals to the users, then they should be separate.

You should be careful not to fall into the opposite trap of creating a diagram with one use case that seems to do everything. You can recognize this situation by looking at the use-case description. If it has sprouted many complicated alternative paths, replace that overburdened use case with several simpler ones.

Completing One Diagram Before Moving On

Some modelers get stuck because they want to "complete" one diagram before they work on another diagram. For example, a team of developers can easily get fixated on use cases. They complete the use-case diagram and fill out every single use-case description, down to the last alternative scenario. Only then do these developers feel ready to move on to building a class diagram that defines the terminology that crops up in those use-case descriptions. There's just one problem: They discover that the terms used in the use-case descriptions are inconsistent because various users expressed the same word to mean different concepts and different words mean the same thing. As a result, the single-minded developers must go back to every use-case description and change them, one at a time, to make them consistent with the class diagram.

The work you perform on one diagram can help you with other diagrams. Consider developing your UML diagrams in parallel. For example, when you start your work on use cases, at the same time start building a class diagram as you talk with users. Defining the meaning of the users' language as you go can help keep your use cases in sync with your class diagram throughout the project.

Cycling Around Class Diagrams

Modelers are not always careful with the multiplicity they show on class diagrams. However, you can discover multiplicity inconsistencies easily if there are *cycles* in the class diagram. You have a cycle if you find a path that starts at a class, goes along a series of associations and connected classes, and comes back to your starting class. Figure 21-4 illustrates a cycle from Person to Policy to Vehicle back to Person.

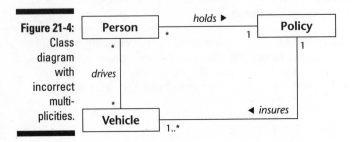

Figure 21-4: Class diagram with incorrect multiplicities.

To check for inconsistencies of multiplicity, work through the following steps:

1. **Select one of the classes in the cycle as the starting point.**

   In the example in Figure 21-4, start at Person.

2. **Follow the association from the starting class to the next class in the chain.**

   This takes you to Policy because Person connects to Policy through the holds association.

3. **Take a look at the multiplicity at the end of the association you just followed next to the class you found in Step 2.**

4. **Make a mental note of what that multiplicity means for the two classes.**

   A person can hold exactly one policy.

5. **Now go back to the starting class and follow the chain of classes in the opposite direction until you get to the class you found in Step 2.**

   In the running example using Figure 21-4, you have Person to Vehicle to Policy.

6. **Take a look at the multiplicity at the end of the last association you just followed to get to the class you found in Step 2.**

   In this example, this multiplicity is also exactly 1.

7. **Consider the meaning of the indirect relationship between the starting class and the ending class via this other route.**

   A person can drive zero or more vehicles and each vehicle can only be insured by one policy.

8. **Check to see whether the meaning you got from the diagram in Step 4 squares with the meaning you got in Step 7.**

   If it doesn't, then you have a potential inconsistency in multiplicity — and it must be fixed. If you are to believe the diagram in Figure 21-4, an instance of the Person class can only hold one policy, and a policy insures one vehicle. But that same person can drive more than one vehicle (where each vehicle is insured by exactly one policy).

   Those two statements are inconsistent under most circumstances. How can a person hold *only one* policy (if you follow the holds association) *and* hold *more than one* policy if he or she drives several vehicles and each of those vehicles can have a different policy?

Check all the cycles in your class diagrams for contradictions by using the eight steps given here.

Not Listening to the User

Many of the modeling mistakes we see are traceable to someone's poor listening skills. Rather than listen to what a user needs from a software application, some developers are too busy thinking about how they are going to write their next program. These developers dream up terminology like `QualifiedEditableAccount`, `Tuple`, and `Xref`. In the end, the software does not meet the needs of the user. That's partly because those arcane terms aren't much help when the original developers are no longer on the project. When users ask for a better system, the new developers get completely confused because they can't relate what the user is saying to anything in the program code.

Users provide you with a wealth of information for your software application. Here's a strategy for making the best use of it:

1. **Listen to your users carefully.**

2. **Convert the users' terminology into classes.**

    For example, in the insurance domain, define `Policy`, `Customer`, `Vehicle`, `Coverage`, and `Claim`.

3. **Convert the users' required interactions with your software into use cases and sequence diagrams.**

    Capture what it means to the user to "generate a policy," "handle a claim," and "bind a policy."

4. **Design your system and write the code based on what the user told you.**

    For example, implement a `Policy` class that uses the same terminology as that of your users.

5. **Listen to the user after you deliver the software.**

    Now, when the user talks about changing something related to an insurance policy, you know right where to go in your design the make changes. You will not be hunting down `Tuple` and `Xref` to see whether that's where to change your code.

Recently, while serving on a "panel of experts" at a conference, one of your authors (Jim, in fact) was asked, "How can you tell a good modeler when you see one?" His response was, "The best modelers are the ones who really listen."

Chapter 22

Ten Useful UML Web Sites

In This Chapter

▶ Finding more information on UML

▶ Utilizing the Web as a UML resource

We'd like to believe that after you read this book on UML 2, you'll never need to look at another UML resource — but we know that's not true. UML is so big and vast (with new approaches to using it arising all the time) that it's likely you'll need to find more information on UML some time in the future. We've constructed this chapter to recommend some useful Web sites that should help you with your future UML needs.

Before you go any further, when you first find that you need something more on UML, you should go to your friendly neighborhood bookstore, or if you prefer the Web, go to Amazon.com at `www.amazon.com` and spin through the capsule reviews of books on UML. And if you (ahem) happen to find some more of ours. . . . (Well, okay, we know our books aren't the only ones out there, but why break up a beautiful relationship?)

Weave a Tangled Web

The Web is a good source of information, but it's not a perfect source. You'll find three main problems with using the Web as a source of information:

✔ **If it costs nothing, it may be worth nothing.** The quality of the Web sites is notoriously uneven. Examine every Web site with a challenging eye. Is the information on this site accurate and useful? Not every one who publishes on the Web is an expert. This chapter helps you select trustworthy sites — but never suspend your judgment while surfing.

✔ **Nothing's where it used to be.** The Web is ephemeral. Sites appear and disappear, change their names, or quickly get out of date. You may have to be a skilled sleuth to find the latest incarnation of a site.

✔ **You can't surf a million waves at once.** The Web is so big that you'll quickly be inundated with information. A simple search for UML on Google, www.google.com, results in over 1,390,000 hits.

With these limitations in mind, you may wonder why you should bother with the Web at all. Well, the Web's advantages stem from the same properties as its disadvantages:

✔ **The price is right.** While the highest-quality material will be from traditional books, almost all material on the Web is free.

✔ **Quick and up-to-date.** Not only is it quicker to find a Web site than buying a book, the Web is often the only place to get up-to-the-minute material. In a fast-moving field like system development with UML, you'll be able to hear about something first on the Web. (Of course, afterward you'll probably want to buy the book.)

✔ **Diversity of opinion and expression.** The Web is so large that you're more likely to find someone who has an answer for your specific question, or for your domain, or expressing a point of view similar to yours. That's a big help when you're doing something fairly different or have a problem understanding the standard examples.

UML Home Page

As OMG is the owner of UML, you should first go to OMG for the official information about UML.

OMG is located at www.omg.org, but you'll probably want to go directly to their UML home page at www.uml.org. From this site, you can find pointers to the official UML 2 and UML 1.x published specifications and official works-in-progress. For example, the official UML 1.5 specification is found at www.omg.org/technology/documents/formal/uml.htm.

The UML 2 official Request For Proposal (RFP) documents are also there. If you work for one of the over 800+ members of OMG, you'll also be allowed to look at ongoing works-in-progress.

This site has additional useful background information on UML and some pointers to other informative UML sites.

UML Forum

UML Forum (www.uml-forum.com) is a virtual community and knowledge portal containing pointers to some official and semiofficial information.

We particularly like the set of UML tutorials written by key UML developers such as Cris Kobryn, Gunnar (gunnaro@morfeus.it.kth.se), Bran Selic (karin.palmkvist@enea.se), Morgan Björkander (morgan.bjorkander@telelogic.se), and J.Warmer@klasse.nl. You'll also find pointers to tool vendors, UML books, and conferences.

UML 2 Submitters

There are several groups submitting UML 2 proposals to OMG. While the winner's site will be the most useful, the other submitters' sites will have useful information on how they see UML 2 being used — and some alternative approaches to modeling:

- ✔ **UML 2.0 Partners:** The leading group, called U2P (UML 2.0 Partners), has a Web site (www.u2-partners.org) where you can download their latest proposals, catch the latest news, and make comments on their Yahoo! group.

- ✔ **Community UML:** One of the proposing groups, the communityUML (yep, one word), maintains a Web site of all the various proposals, including their own proposal called 3C (Clear, Clean, Concise). See http://community-ml.org/submissions.htm.

- ✔ **2U Consortium:** A specific Web site for the 2U Consortium (Unambiguous UML) can be found at www.2uworks.org.

- ✔ **pUML:** A specific Web site for the precise UML group (pUML) can be found at www.cs.york.ac.uk/puml/uml2_0.html.

OCL Center

OCL is an important part of UML whose use is increasing with the growth of Model-Driven Architecture and model-consistent business rules. You'll also need to understand OCL if you want to understand the formal UML 2 specifications. This Web site (www.klasse.nl/ocl) keeps you informed about the status of OCL, OCL 2.0, and several OCL-dedicated tools.

Magazines and Information Portals

These sites usually have copies of their latest articles from their magazine or for-fee services. They're often controversial, but are full of insightful opinion and advice.

- ✔ **Software Development Magazine:** Software Development Magazine has a Web site for their influential articles on UML. Always interesting. Take a look at their UML Design Center at `www.sdmagazine.com/uml/`.

- ✔ **DevX:** DevX has an excellent set of recent articles on UML in their UML Zone. Some of their best stuff requires a paid-up membership. Take at look at what they have at `www.devx.com/uml`.

Search Engines

Searching for UML is a tricky business. First of all, UML doesn't only mean Unified Modeling Language. You'll probably find hits for User Mode Linux, University of Massachusetts Lowell, and Unified Marxist Leninist (the Communist Party of Nepal). Together these hits may outnumber the hits on UML sites. Use the advanced search forms when possible to eliminate the extraneous hits.

You have several options when choosing a search engine:

- ✔ **Google:** The most popular Web-search engine appears to be Google (`www.google.com`).

- ✔ **Tech search engines:** You'll probably be best searching with more technically focused search engines from Northern Light (`http://nlresearch.northernlight.com/research.html`), Overture (`www.overture.com`) or Teoma (`www.teoma.com`).

- ✔ **Zeal.com:** Another good search engine is `www.zeal.com`. In this site, users can suggest sites and write reviews. The quality of the hits is very good, and you can be become one of their Zealots.

Tool Sites

Many UML tool vendors offer good UML sites in addition to their tools. Here are some of the best:

- ✔ **Rational's UML Resource Center:** Lots of good material, especially some early stuff on UML (`www.rational.com/uml`).

- ✔ **Popkin's UML Resource Center:** Several papers and book recommendations (`www.popkin.com/customers/customer_service_center/enterprise_architecture_resource_center/uml.htm`).

Training Sites

Several companies make a living by offering training, consulting, and mentoring in UML and other related topics. Their Web sites offer online course catalogs and often articles and other reference material. We could start, of course, by recommending our company, the Advanced Concepts Center, LLC, and its Web site (www.acclearning.com) for discussions on UML, a complete list of UML tools, great courses, and (harrumph) a highly knowledgeable staff of instructors/mentors. But if you happen to be on another continent or planet, then by all means look around for a nearby UML guru.

Forums and Groups

Participating in a community forum is sometimes the best way to get up to speed. Members share their questions, opinions, and experience. Often there's a resident expert or two who helps the group. The quality of the answers may vary, and the quantity of traffic can be large, but here are some of the best. Visit them and you may (virtually) bump into one of us as we stop by to give some advice:

- **UML-Forum:** With over 1000 members, this is one of the largest groups; Cris Kobryn, the leader of the U2P team, moderates it. (http://groups.yahoo.com/group/uml-forum/)
- **The OOAD_UML group:** This group is probably even more active than the UML-Forum. (http://groups.yahoo.com/group/OOAD_UML/)

Miscellaneous Sites

Here are some interesting specialty UML sites that might be worth visiting:

- **Define a term:** If you need to look up a UML term, try Kendall Scott's UML Dictionary at www.softdocwiz.com/UML.htm.
- **Ask a question:** If you want an interactive Ivar (a chatterbox in the form of a virtual simulacrum of Ivar Jacobson) to query about UML, try Jaczone's Cyber Ivar at www.jaczone.com/cyberivar.

Chapter 23

Ten Useful UML Modeling Tools

In This Chapter

▶ Knowing which tool to use just in CASE

▶ Choosing a UML modeling tool

*N*o matter how good you are at drawing, even if you're an artist, you're not going to do a lot of UML by hand on paper or even on a whiteboard. Maybe for a few high-level diagrams, it'll work. But the more complex diagrams are difficult and hard to draw, and the cross-diagram consistency quickly gets out of hand, even if you're handy with a drawing tool. Many different UML tools are vying in the market for the privilege of helping you with drawing. Most of these tools will do more than drawing, even more than modeling — they'll do consistency checking, generate code, write reports, reverse-engineer existing code into models, and a host of other things. The full-featured tools are often called *CASE tools*, where CASE, in case you didn't know, stands for **C**omputer-**A**ided **S**oftware (or sometimes **S**ystem) **E**ngineering. Some don't like the CASE tool moniker and prefer Modeling tool because the CASE tools got a bad name in the early nineties when they weren't quite the silver-bullet solution they were claimed to be. But whatever name you call them, reach for these tools when you want to do UML modeling.

Picking a Tool

Pick a tool that meets the following requirements:

✔ **Up to date:** Does your tool support UML 2 (or have plans to do so within your timeframe)? Some of the smaller tools don't have the time or money behind them to stay updated. On the other hand, sometimes the larger tools are burdened with a large user population that must migrate to any new version. Look for the UML 2 features that you need — and consider how soon you can get them up and running.

✔ **Affordable:** Buy the best tool that you can afford, considering not only the price of the tool but also the price of any support or maintenance that you'll need. Look for a tool that fits your checkbook.

✔ **Understands XMI:** *XMI* (XML Model Interchange) enables you to get your model out of one tool and into another tool. If your tool supports XMI, you're less likely to get stuck with the limited modeling capability of a tool that you've outgrown. XMI is also essential for getting the best-of-breed in tools. Many vendors specialize in enabling specific parts of the development solution (for example, modeling, metrics, or code generation). With XMI as the glue, you can pick one tool as the best for modeling and another as the best for generating code. Look for a tool that speaks XMI.

✔ **Stable:** The fancier the tool, the more unstable it may be. Look for a tool that foregoes too many bells and whistles so that it won't blow up on you.

✔ **Supported:** The UML tool market is an exciting and dangerous place; companies come, and companies go. Look for a tool from a company that you trust.

✔ **Checks consistency flexibly:** Most tools have some ability to check consistency among the models. This is good. However, you'll often find that the tool's idea of consistency may be too strict for your purposes. Look for a tool that enables you to control checking at the lowest level possible.

✔ **Has an MDA approach in mind:** With the growing popularity of the OMG's Model Driven Architecture approach, a good tool should be able to support this initiative by handling platform independent and platform-specific modeling. Look for a tool that supports MDA.

✔ **Scalable:** Many tools are great solutions for single users but won't scale up to many users as the same time. So consider: How many of your users can be modeling at the same time? Look at the tool's strategies for locking, providing concurrent updates, and managing configurations. See whether it meets your team's needs; look for a tool that grows with you.

✔ **Works in and for your environment:** The tool has to run on your development platform as well as generate code suitable for your target platform. Look for a tool that works where you want it to.

✔ **Supports the diagrams that you need:** It's unlikely you'll need every diagram that UML 2 has, certainly not equally. For example, some tools make the best class diagrams, some make the best state diagrams, and some make the best use cases. They differ in the amount of detail that they support, and in whether they generate code from that diagram. Look for a tool that knows how to do what you want.

At our last count, there were over 128 UML-capable tools to choose from — a tool for every user, purpose, and price range. In fact, it's been said that any developer who acts as his or her own tool has a fool for a tool. So take a look at some of these tools and pick what works for you.

We selected ten representatives that should simplify your choices, but if you don't find what you need, there are plenty more out there.

Argo/UML

> ✔ **Produced by:** Tigris
>
> ✔ **Web site:** argouml.tigris.org

Maybe you don't want to pay a lot — or you want to get a good tool for free. Well, with Argo/UML, you tap into the Open Source community. Argo/UML is a fast-growing and improving tool, with support for OCL and automated design wizards. Choose Argo/UML when you want to go open source.

Cittera

> ✔ **Produced by:** CanyonBlue
>
> ✔ **Web site:** www.canyonblue.com

The Internet is supposed to change everything. Cittera uses a Web-based repository for your models and will host your models. Their collaborative development approach enables users from all over the Internet to work on the same model — complete with audit trail and version control. Choose Cittera if your development is distributed, mobile, and flexible.

Ideogramic UML

> ✔ **Produced by:** Ideogramic
>
> ✔ **Web site:** www.ideogramic.com/products

So maybe you really *want* to use your hands and not the point-click-drag idiom. This tool is gesture-based — specialized (but easy-to-remember) gestures enable you to draw UML diagrams that can be saved and transferred to any XMI-capable tool. Hook it up to something like Mimio to draw diagrams on the whiteboard. Your squiggles are straightened, and correctly formed boxes appear. Chose Ideogramic UML if you want to draw great-looking diagrams on a whiteboard with almost no effort.

Objecteering

- **Produced by:** Softeam
- **Web site:** www.objecteering.com

Every tool has its own strengths. Objecteering is strong in many areas but is probably the most powerful UML tool for constructing profiles. This means that if you want to use one of the UML dialects — such as SPEM (Software Process Engineering Modeling), CWM (Common Warehouse Modeling), or EDOC (Enterprise Distributed Object Computing) — you may want to use Objecteering. This tool is also especially handy if you want to make modifications to support your special methodology.

Rational Rose Suite

- **Produced by:** IBM
- **Web site:** www.rational.com

You probably can't go wrong with the most popular tool. It's certainly strong in many areas and has a full suite of tools to support your development, especially in areas such as requirements management and configuration management. Rational has other UML tools, such as Rose R/T and Rational XDE, that are also worth looking at. With IBM owning Rational, things may change, but for now, it's the market (and marketing) leader. Choose Rational's tools if you're conservative or need the full software development environment.

Rhapsody

- **Produced by:** i-Logix
- **Web site:** www.ilogix.com

If you're a real-time or embedded-systems developer, you'll need a special tool. There are several out there, but Rhapsody is one of the most popular. Choose Rhapsody if you're *embed* (so to speak) with real time.

System Architect

- ✔ **Produced by:** Popkin
- ✔ **Web site:** `www.popkin.com/products/system_architect.htm`

This popular tool offers you something UML-and-beyond: It also supports Enterprise Frameworks such as the Zachman Framework and the Department of Defense Architecture Framework (DoDAF, formerly C4ISR Framework). These frameworks are gaining wide acceptance in the commercial and government sectors for capturing information on entire businesses. (*Frameworks* are templates for capturing the who, what, why, when, where, and how of the entire business at various stages of development.) UML is integrated with support for traditional business process, as well as functional, organizational, and relational data modeling — all of which provide great legacy-environment support. System Architect also supports system-engineering environments. Pick System Architect if UML isn't enough for you.

Tau

- ✔ **Produced by:** Telelogic
- ✔ **Web site:** `www.telelogic.com`

Here's another leader in UML and software development. Telelogic is noted for higher-end technical tools that are attractive to large-scale aerospace, communication, and manufacturing projects (among others). Tau offers good real-time and multiuser capabilities as well as a powerful suite of associated tools. Telelogic's latest version, Tau, Generation 2, was the first to claim UML 2 support. (See `www.taug2.com`.) Pick Tau if you need the power.

TogetherSoft

- ✔ **Produced by:** Borland
- ✔ **Web site:** `www.togethersoft.com`

Sometimes you want to be agile. TogetherSoft's powerful tool attracts the eXtreme Programming developers and is probably the tool with the fastest-growing market share. When you change the diagram, the code changes before your eyes — and vice versa. Borland has a whole bunch of other great UML tools, and it is assembling a powerful suite, but it has an integration challenge ahead. Choose TogetherSoft if you want to be streamlined and agile, or if you like a *powerful* underdog.

Visio

✔ **Produced by:** Microsoft

✔ **Web site:** www.microsoft.com/office/visio

Not just a drawing tool, Visio includes code generation, reverse engineering, and good notation coverage. Microsoft has been quietly building up Visio to be a complete tool tailored for its .NET environment. We expect to see more from Microsoft as the competition in the tool market heats up. Choose Visio if you buy the complete Microsoft line or like the flexibility of having a good drawing tool.

Chapter 24

Ten Diagrams for Quick Development

*T*his book provides you with a basic reference to the Unified Modeling Language — but you also have to know why particular diagrams are important, when to use them, and what each diagram can do for you. This chapter gives you a tour of our ten favorite ways of using the basic UML diagrams — as well as a few tips along the way. You will find more detailed examples of the basic UML diagrams and how we use them throughout the rest of the book.

Context Diagram

The first diagram that you need on any project is a *context diagram*. UML does not have a context diagram per se. We use the use-case diagram of UML to show the context of the system or software that we are developing. So, we give this special use-case diagram a solution-oriented name: *context diagram*. If you already have one, that's great. But in our experience, most software- or systems-development projects start out without a context diagram, blissfully unaware that they need one.

For your system or software development to be successful, you have to know the answers to the following questions:

✔ Who uses your system?

✔ What data must go into your system?

✔ What information and objects must your system produce as output to users and other systems?

A context diagram answers these questions because it shows your system in a setting (context) defined by its interactions. The diagram helps define the boundaries of your system or software application by showing all the users and systems that your application must interact with.

A context diagram provides a good starting point for your work on use cases. In fact, you build a context diagram based on the use-case diagram provided by UML. Use the following steps to construct such a diagram:

1. **Place a large rectangle in the center of the diagram.**

   This represents your system or software application.

2. **Place the name of the system at top-center, just inside the rectangle.**

3. **Identify and name each of the actors that you expect to interact with your system.**

   Actors can be human users, other systems, hardware, or the clock.

4. **Place the actors around the outside of the rectangle representing your system.**

   Use "stick figures" (including the name of each actor) for human users. If the actor is not a human, use class notation that uses the name of the actor as the class name and give the class the «actor» stereotype.

5. **Draw a line between the actor and the system rectangle.**

   This shows that the actor interacts with your system.

6. **Show the information, data, and/or objects that flow into your system from an actor above the line connecting that actor to the system.**

   You show this as text with a small arrow pointing from the text toward the system rectangle.

7. **Show the information, data, and/or objects that flow out of your system to an actor below the line connecting that actor to the system.**

   Again, you show this as text with a small arrow pointing from the text toward the actor receiving the system output.

8. **Repeat Steps 6 and 7 for each actor that sends data into the system or receives data from the system.**

The context diagram helps you set boundaries for the scope of your project. You know from the context whom your system must satisfy, what data your system must accept, and what data your system must generate.

Use-Case Diagram

To understand your system's requirements from the users' perspective, build a use-case diagram. A quick way to create one is to start with the context diagram. If you remove the data input and output from the context diagram and simply add a use case for each of your actors, you have a use-case diagram.

The use-case diagram helps you understand the major functionality that your system must provide for each type of user. That's vital information when you want to organize the requirements imposed on each group of users (that is, on each actor). Each use case tells the requirements story from the user's perspective.

Don't try to complete your use-case diagram with all the use-case descriptions (textual description of the details of the user's use of the system) at once; instead, follow these steps:

1. **Develop a basic use-case diagram and just supply the name, summary, and actor in each use-case description.**

2. **Model the user's domain in a domain class diagram for your use cases.**

   For more information, read the section "Domain Class Diagram" later in this chapter.

3. **Return to your use-case descriptions and fill in the pre- and postconditions.**

   You might also want to provide a (simple) example of a user interaction.

4. **Add details that you found while discussing user interaction (in Step 3) to your domain class diagram (in Step 2).**

5. **Consider adding alternative and error scenarios to your use-case descriptions.**

Creating careful, thorough use-case diagrams, and use-case descriptions can help you achieve the following goals:

✔ **Easier communication:** Use cases are written in the language of the user. Your users and project stakeholders understand what you're talking about because you use their words. You understand what the users are saying because you focus on their needs.

✔ **Better-educated users:** Users often don't know exactly what they want in a new software application. You will educate your users because you understand their goals, develop use cases to meet those goals, and describe back to the users (in a language that they understand) what the use cases does to help them. As you help users to focus on their job goals, they in turn tell you what they need from your system to meet those goals.

✔ **Closer focus on requirements:** Developers find it hard to focus on requirements. All too often they think about how to make a program work. Developers focus on technology and implementation details because that is their training. Use cases help you stay focused on users' needs (requirements).

✔ **Natural stages for incremental development:** Each use of the system is geared toward one group of users. You don't have to build an entire application; all you need is one that does just a few use cases. Then, incrementally, design and build a few more use cases — and deliver them in the next increment to your system. You can get away with this incremental approach because use cases don't depend on each other. What one group of users may need is different from what another group needs. In our experience, each use case has its own classes. If the user requirements (for example) change for one particular use case, they don't cause changes in other use cases.

Use interview notes and use-case descriptions to help you build a domain class diagram. User interactions (part of your use-case documentation) can help illustrate the dynamics of your system or software. You capture the dynamics of text descriptions in sequence diagrams.

Domain Class Diagram

Your users work with objects all the time. They talk about the objects and their relationships in their *domain,* which is a fancy term for the group of objects that your users deal with. The insurance domain has objects such as policy, policyholder, claim, coverage, covered item, and hazard. Finance has its own domain language, including items such as equity, fund, portfolio, account, and trade. To build a system or a software application that your users understand, we recommend that you capture the language of the user in a class diagram that we like to call the *domain class diagram.*

If you take a look at the applications that you build, you find some of the same classes in each application. If you work in the insurance domain (for example), you need a policy class for applications such as policy generation, underwriter review, claims handling, and premium billing. You can also use the domain class diagram to define specialized terms and other user jargon. That's because there's one thing that computers can't handle — vagueness. Every term, class, attribute, operation, and association must be nailed down — precisely.

A domain class diagram must accomplish the following:

✔ Precisely define user terminology

✔ Provide common classes that are useful in many different applications

✔ Allow you to work with users to understand how they structure the world

So take the time to build a class diagram that accurately reflects what your users mean when they talk about their "domain."

Start building a domain class diagram early in your project. We begin our own domain diagrams at the same time that we're working with users to develop use cases.

Sequence Diagram

We use sequence diagrams to show interactions between objects related to our system or software application. You can use these diagrams to detail the scenarios for each use case. The sequence diagram shows a small group of objects and the *events* (important moments in time) being passed between the objects. As time passes, you show each event in sequence, moving down the page of the diagram.

Don't try to show how your objects collaborate by using a sequence diagram during analysis. Some developers use the sequence diagram to show how their programs work *before* they clearly understand the requirements. You can avoid this mistake by showing when an object must notify another object that an important moment has arrived.

Don't try to show thirty-object instances across the top of a sequence diagram. We've seen this done — it isn't pretty. You should have between two and eight objects on a single sequence diagram — no more. That way, the diagram doesn't get too cluttered.

We like to build two levels of sequence diagrams during analysis:

- **High-level sequence:** To focus on a use case, we show a sequence diagram with just the actor objects and an object representing the system. These diagrams, each showing no more than two or three objects, are a graphical way of relating the text of a use-case description. This type of sequence diagram gives a high-level view of events and of the order in which they come into and go out of our system.

- **Application-level sequence:** For each use case, we build application-level sequence diagrams. For each high-level sequence diagram, we substitute the actor objects with application objects such as view, boundary, and device objects. These are the objects that the users will actually interact with. We replace the system object with some kind of controller or manager object.

If you want to show object collaboration during design, use a communication diagram and not a sequence diagram.

State Diagram

State diagrams show the internal workings and life cycles of your objects. For instance, each software object is born into the runtime environment, lives a life interacting with other objects, and then dies out. State diagrams capture these important moments in time, including the event transitions for your objects. The states themselves capture what your objects are supposed to do after an important event.

We build state diagrams for objects that are dynamic. In other words, they change a lot during their life. In general, you can build a state diagram for the following kinds of objects:

- ✔ **Controllers:** Those objects that control the timing and behavior of other objects are called *controllers* — the objects that know when to get things done to meet the goals of your system. This type includes objects that make each use case work properly as well as objects that must start up and shut down your system. Each of these objects exhibits complex behavior that must be done in the right order at the right time.

- ✔ **Event handlers:** If an object must receive events and then (as a result of the events) ask another object to actually *perform* the needed work, the object that has this job deserves a state diagram. Use the state diagram to show the allowable sequence of events and the resulting behavior.

- ✔ **Aggregations:** When you have an aggregate with many parts, the object that represents the aggregate has an interesting life. At first, the aggregate must create instances of its parts. It then must receive requests from the outside and pass them off to the appropriate part(s). When the aggregate is deleted, it must first delete its internal parts in the right order and then (and only then) delete itself. You should capture the complex life cycle of an aggregate with a state diagram. (See Chapter 5 for more on aggregates.)

- ✔ **Dynamic domain:** Every user domain has at least two or three dynamic objects. For instance, an insurance policy goes through many states in its life — open, established, claim processing, canceling, archived, and closed (to name a few). Look at each of your domain classes and think about their life cycles. If those look interesting, build a state diagram that describes them.

Application Class Diagram

There comes a point in your project when you have to understand requirements imposed by your application. To gain that insight, we build an application class diagram for each use case. The *application class diagram* is simply a UML class diagram that shows the classes that work together to accomplish all the scenarios of a particular use case.

A domain class diagram defines the requirements imposed on you by the user's language. The application class diagram defines the requirements imposed on you by the very application that you're building.

If your users interact with a graphic user interface (GUI), you need classes that know how to paint the GUI in a way that offers a view of some domain classes. For example, if a user wants to see a policy object, you need a `view` class that extracts the data out of an instance of the `policy` class and shows that data in a GUI window — complete with text boxes, radio buttons, and drop-down lists.

If any use cases require your application to do things in a specific order, create a `controller` class. This class is responsible for remembering what the user has done and what comes next. For example, in the insurance scenario, when a user generates a policy, he or she must create the policy first — and *then* assign coverage to it, assign covered items, and indicate who owns the policy. When the user has done these tasks, all this information must be complete and correct before the policy goes to the underwriter for review. In this case, we create a `policy manager` class that controls the other objects at runtime, making sure that the use case works properly.

Other than a `controller` class and `view` classes, you may have to create the following application classes:

- ✔ **Boundary class:** This is a class that hides the details of one part of a system from another part. We use a separate class that knows how to access the database as a boundary between our domain objects and the database.

- ✔ **Device class:** A device class usually represents a physical device (such as a barcode scanner) or the software driver for a physical device. Working much like a boundary class, a device class isolates a physical device for our domain objects.

- ✔ **Surrogate class:** We use surrogate classes to stand in for our use-case actors. *Actors* are those things outside our system that interact with the system. *Surrogates* are classes inside our system that stand in for the actor outside the system. If our application must store and track information about users (for example), we create surrogate classes inside our system to hold that data.

You may find that other developers use different terminology for these classes. Instead of using *controller,* they use *control.* Instead of the word *boundary,* they use the word *view* or *interface.* Instead of calling the diagram an *application class diagram,* they call it a *robustness diagram.* ("You say *tomayto,* I say *tomahto.* . . .") No wonder people get confused.

Don't try to give your domain classes all the knowledge of the following:

✔ How to display themselves in a GUI window

✔ How to display themselves over the Net in a Web browser

✔ When to display different attribute values

✔ How to store and retrieve data from a database

Let your domain classes know how to be themselves. Let other classes have the responsibility of showing your domain classes as pictures in a GUI or of handling their interactions with a database.

Package Diagram

Your systems or software applications start out as one big design problem. Like all good engineers, you take that problem and break it up into smaller problems. If you can solve each of the little problems, you solve the big problem. You can use the package diagram to help break a big problem into smaller problems — and show that decomposition.

We use the UML package notation to show our application as a large package. Inside the large package, we show smaller packages — one for each subsystem. After our subsystems are set, we convert the packages into subsystems. Then we draw dependency lines to indicate which subsystems must rely on other subsystem(s) — and which ones they rely on. (For more details on this process, see Chapter 20.)

At the start of your systems design phase, draw a simple package diagram showing the decomposition of your system into subsystems. Then consider all your system design issues such as layering, subsystem interfaces, database access, and networking. As you make your strategic design decisions, modify the package diagram to reflect those decisions. Finally, give a copy of this big picture system diagram to each of the subsystem design teams. By using the package diagram, they can understand how their subsystem fits into the overall system.

Deployment Diagram

Your system or application has two crucial structures that exist in the real world — hardware deployment and software artifacts. Too often developers get lost in the details of their code without ever understanding how their work fits into the deployed application. We use a deployment diagram to document our hardware-and-software layout.

During system design, show the hardware architecture of your application with a deployment diagram. Then, as you develop your software for each subsystem, show the software as artifacts on your deployment diagram. That way, you gain an understanding of where each piece of software runs and on which piece of hardware. Finally, show the reliance of one artifact on another by means of dependency lines.

Use deployment diagrams to look for places in your design where there may be too much interdependence among the pieces of hardware and software.

Communication Diagram

In your object-oriented system or software application, objects working together make the application work. Use communication diagrams to show this all-important object collaboration; they should show the following aspects of that cooperation, all at the same time:

- ✔ Instances of parts linked together for a specific collaboration

- ✔ Flow of control by showing the numbered sequencing of messages being sent to each part

- ✔ Flow of data by showing the parameters being passed along with the messages and the return data assigned to the results of a message

Use communication diagrams at design time to explore exactly how your objects work together — and then document your design for programmers to implement.

We use communication diagrams both at systems design time and detailed design time. The system communication diagrams show how the subsystems cooperate to accomplish the system's use cases. Communication diagrams showing subsystems as objects help us understand the interfaces that each subsystem must provide. At detailed design time, we build communication diagrams to show how the objects inside a subsystem will work together to accomplish the major operations required of the subsystem.

Activity Diagram

When you want to focus on the flow of control *across* objects and the flow of data from object to object — but not on the relationships *between* objects — use the activity diagram. This diagram allows you to show sequences of behavior over time among objects — but (unlike the communication diagram) it doesn't show linkages between objects. This diagram is especially useful when you're showing workflow among people in a business process.

Instead of building lots of sequence diagrams to show all the possible ways that events happen in parallel for a single use case, you can use one activity diagram.

Index

Symbols & Numerics

* (asterisk), in multiplicity specification, 69
{} (braces), enclosing constraint, 56, 63
^ (caret), for bottom to top association, 65
: (colon)
  between object and class name, 53–54
  between part name and class name, 90
. (dot operator), in OCL, 187
<<>> (double angle brackets), for
  stereotype, 55, 137
:: (double colon), between class and
  operation, 50
Φ (Golden Ratio), for class box size, 52
«» (guillemets), for stereotype, 55, 137
- (hyphen)
  for irrelevant message argument, 197
  for private visibility, 57
  for role name, 72
< (left angle bracket), for right to left
  association, 65
( ) (parentheses), enclosing operation
  arguments, 51
+ (plus sign), for public visibility, 57
# (pound sign), for protected visibility, 57
"" (quotes), for literal message, 198
> (right angle bracket), for left to right
  association, 65
/ (slash)
  for an action or activity, 267
  for derived attribute, 55
  for event actions, 285–287
[] (square brackets)
  for multiplicity, 47, 90
  for preconditions or postconditions, 310
~ (tilde), for package visibility, 57
2U Consortium Web site, 373
3C (Clear, Clean, Concise) proposal, Web
  site for, 373

• A •

abstract class, 106–107
abstract operation, 106
abstract use cases, 167
abstraction. *See also* encapsulation;
    information hiding
  definition of, 10–11, 20, 21–23
  in text-based behavior specification, 183
«access» stereotype, 351–352
accessor operations, 56
acronyms, in class and object names, 43
Action Semantics, 188
action sequence icon, 291
actions, 214. *See also* activities
active objects, 241–242
activities
  concurrent, 220
  definition of, 214
  within a state, 267
activity diagram. *See also* interaction-
    overview diagram
  constructing, 216–220
  definition of, 213–216
  partition names in, 224, 226
  showing responsible parties in, 224–226
  swim lanes in, 224–225
  uses of, 14, 179, 216, 391–392
«Actor» stereotype, 137
actors. *See also* use cases
  analysis packages based on, 342
  clocks as, 136
  customers (clients), 132–133
  defining use cases based on, 139, 142
  definition of, 133
  devices as, 135–136
  diagramming, 137–138, 139–141
  generalized, 138, 165
  identifying, 133–136
  as internal design elements, 144

actors *(continued)*
  naming, 137
  nonhuman (proxy), 134–136, 138
  paired sets of, 134
  primary, 139, 141
  responsibilities of, in activity diagram, 224–226
  roles of, 136–138
  secondary, 139, 141
  transparent, 136
  users, 133, 370
adapter architectural pattern, 357
Advanced Concepts Center Web site, 375
after event, 288
aggregation. *See also* composition; encapsulation; information hiding; internal context diagram
  analysis packages based on, 342
  behavior of, 85–86
  in class diagrams, 114, 115
  composition compared to, 25, 88–89
  definition of, 20, 24–25
  external associations of, 84
  internal structure of, 84
  naming, 86
  representing as association, 83–84, 86
  sharing parts of, 87–88
  state diagram for, 388
  subsystems and, 322
  transitive property of, 89
Agile methodology, 36
algorithms, in behavioral specification, 187–188
alt operator, 206, 209, 211
alternate courses of use case, 155–160
analysis packages, 340–343
angle brackets
  double (<<>>), for stereotype, 55, 137
  left (<), for right to left association, 65
  right (>), for left to right association, 65
application class diagram
  definition of, 122–125
  uses of, 388–390
application classes
  analysis packages based on, 342
  definition of, 122–123
«application server» stereotype, 334

application subsystem, 322
application-level sequence diagram, 387
applications. *See* software and system development; tools for UML modeling
architectural patterns, 354–357
architecture, system. *See* system architecture modeling
Argo/UML tool Web site, 379
arguments
  for event hierarchies, 283–285
  for interactions, 204–206
  for methods, 196–198
  for operations, 49–51
arrow
  on dashed line, from object to class, 54–55
  for directional navigation of association, 63, 79
  filled in, for direction of association name, 65
  hollow, for generalization, 94
  for messages sent and received, 196, 199–201
«artifact» stereotype, 336–337
artifacts, 336–338
assembly connector, 90
assert operator, 211
association end name. *See* roles
associations. *See also* aggregation; links
  aggregation as type of, 83
  in application diagram, 123–124
  classes as, 75–76, 231
  constraining, 75
  definition of, 62–63, 64
  diagram of, converting to code, 80–81
  diagramming, 64, 65, 68–69, 74, 77, 79
  generalization compared to, 95
  inheriting, 101–102
  multiplicity of, 62, 67–71, 102
  naming, 62, 65–66
  navigation of, 78–79
  not naming, 66
  qualified, 63, 77–78, 102
  reflexive, 73–75
  symmetric, 89
  too many of, 366–367
  transitive, 89
asterisk (*), in multiplicity specification, 69

asynchronous call, 200–201
asynchronous messages, 196
attributes
  of association, 75–76
  base, 56
  composition parts as, 91–92
  default values for, 46–47, 103
  derived, 55–56, 103
  diagramming, 55–56, 59–60
  identifying for a business, 44–45
  identifying from knowledge
    responsibilities, 48
  inheriting, 101, 103
  multiple values for (multiplicity), 47–49
  name of, inheritance and, 103
  naming, 45–46
  omitted (null) values for, 48
  state, 269–272
  static, 58–60
  type of, 44–45
  visibility of, 57–60
  without operations, 361–383
automatic transition. *See* completion
  transition
automating development with UML.
    See MDA
«auxiliary» stereotype, 331
availability, system design
    requirement, 317

● *B* ●

balking call, 201
ball and socket, for assemblies in a
    component, 331, 333
base attributes, 56
behavior of actors. *See* use cases
behavior of class. *See* operations
behavioral diagrams, 13, 14. *See also*
    specific diagrams
behavioral specification, 179, 183–188
behavioral state diagram, 308
behaviors, modeling.
    See functional modeling
binary relationship, 98
black box components, 327–329

Booch, Grady (original developer of
    UML), 18
Booch methodology, 35
Boolean datatype, 45, 46
Borland, TogetherSoft tool, 381
boundary class, 123, 389
boxes. *See also* rectangle
  for actors, 138
  for classes and objects, 52, 55–56, 59–60
  with parallel vertical bars, for active
    objects, 241
  for qualifiers, 77
  small, for component parts, 331
  stack of, in communication diagram, 240
  three-dimensional, for nodes, 333
  with two small rectangles, for
    components, 327–328
braces ({}), enclosing constraint, 56, 63
brackets, square. *See* square brackets
break operator, 209, 211
brittle systems, 339
bull's eye, for final-activity nodes, 215
business logic subsystem, 355
business objects, parallelism with software
    objects, 40
business rules, in use case scenarios, 160
«business» stereotype, 143
button names in messages, 198–199

● *C* ●

CanyonBlue, Cittera tool, 379
caret (^), for bottom to top association, 65
cascading operations, 85
Catalysis methodology, 36
central class, for use case, 229–230
circle. *See also* socket
  filled in (large dot)
    for initial nodes, 215
    for initial state, 263
  half circle, on a stick, for interfaces, 327
  labeled, for connectors, 215–216
  with plus sign inside, for
    membership, 323
  on a stick, for interfaces, 327
  with X inside, for final-flow nodes, 215
Cittera tool Web site, 379

class diagram. *See also* hybrid class/object diagram; object diagram
breaking into hierarchical levels, 114–116
communication diagram evolving from, 228–232
communication diagram mapped to, 244–246
constructing, 113–119
content of, 116
context diagrams for, 120–121
cycles in, 368–369
definition of, 111–112
for frameworks, 257
for functional modeling, 181–182
for internal classes of components, 330–333
number of classes in, 115
object diagram compared to, 72–73
project-oriented, 119–127
for subsystem responsibilities, 323–325
time period for, 118–119
uses of, 11, 13, 15, 113, 179, 320
using for every purpose, 363–364
«class» stereotype, 143
classes. *See also* attributes; objects; operations; subclasses; superclasses
abstract, 106–107
application, 122–123, 342
as association, 75–76, 231
associations between, 62–63, 64–66, 366–367
associations with themselves, 73–75
as attribute type, 45–46
boundary, 123
central, for use case, 229–230
composition parts as, 90–91
concrete, 106
containing only attributes or operations, 361–383
controller, 123, 230–231
definition of, 20, 40
device, 389
diagram of, converting to code, 79–80
diagramming, 52–56, 59–60
distinguishing from types, 46
domain, 121–122
duplicates of, 366
events treated as, 281

as friend, 58
generalization and, 21, 25–26, 93–97
grouping into subsystems, 318, 321–323
hotspots, 255
identifying for a business, 40–41
importing into subsystems, 351–352
multiple, wrapping into packages, 125–127
naming, 42–43, 365, 370
roles of, 71–73
specialization and, 21, 25–26, 97–98
surrogate, 389
view, 123, 389
visibility of, 57–60
classification scheme, analysis packages based on, 342
class-scope. *See* static attributes; static operations
«client workstation» stereotype, 334
clients. *See* customers
client-server dependency, 347
client-supplier dependency, 347
clocks as actors, 136
code. *See* software and system development
codependency, 347–348
cohesion
in subsystem, 348, 350
in text-based behavior specification, 183
collaboration. *See also* communication diagram
for architectural patterns, 355–356
definition of, 227
diagramming, 250, 355–356
in frameworks, 255–258
in patterns, 250–252
showing object interaction in, 254
UML modeling tools supporting, 33–34
collaboration diagram. *See* communication diagram
collaboration occurrence, 252–254, 356
colon (:)
between object and class name, 53–54
between part name and class name, 90
colons, double (::), between class and operation, 50
COM (Microsoft), 30

common objects, subsystems based
  on, 346
communication diagram
  class detail in, 245–246
  class diagrams consistent with, 244–245
  class diagrams in preparation for, 228–232
  constructing, 234–241
  for frameworks, 257
  looping in, 238–241, 242
  messages in, 235–241
  naming, 235
  operation calls in, 236–238
  participants of, 232–234
  sd abbreviation for, 234
  uses of, 15, 179, 391
communication paths between nodes,
  334–335
communication standard for
  components, 30
communityUML Web site, 373
completion event, 287
completion transition, 274, 287
component diagram
  for frameworks, 257
  for interfaces, 329–330
  uses of, 14, 15, 320
component environment, 30. *See also* EJB
«component» stereotype, 143, 327
component-based development, 29–31
components
  black boxes, 327–329
  choosing, 319
  communication between, 30
  definition of, 28, 325–326, 327
  delegates for, 331
  diagramming, 327
  icons for, 327
  interfaces for, 326–330
  internal classes of, 330–333
  ports for, 331
composite structure diagram
  constructing, 250–252
  definition of, 89–92
  uses of, 14, 16
composite structure diagram with
  collaboration, 251
composition. *See also* aggregation
  aggregation compared to, 25, 88–89
  as association, 86–87

as composite structure diagram,
  89–92
  definition of, 25, 86
  inheriting parts of, 101
  transitive property of, 89
conceptual types, 48
concrete class, 106
concrete use cases, 167
concurrency
  of activities, 220
  definition of, 241–242
  identifying threads in, 243–244
  looping and, 242
  with states, 303–308
  of use cases, 140–141
connectors, 90, 215–216, 224
constraint-based state, 266
constraints. *See also* invariants;
      postconditions; preconditions
  on associations, 63, 75
  inheritance of, overriding,
    103–104
  inheriting, 101
  OCL used to define, 185–187
construction elements, 40
constructor operation, 85, 97
«constructor» stereotype, 60
«container» stereotype, 334
context diagram
  constructing, 120–121, 384
  definition of, 11
  for use cases, 145
  uses of, 383–384
control flow, 214
control nodes, 215
controller class
  application class diagram for, 389
  definition of, 123
  state diagram for, 388
  for use case, 230–231
«controller» stereotype, 230
CORBA (Object Management Group), 30
cost, system design requirement, 317
coupling, in subsystem, 348, 350
«create» stereotype, 194–195
CRUD test for use cases, 367
curly brackets. *See* braces
customers (clients), 132

• D •

dash. *See* hyphen
dashed line
  with arrow, from object to class, 54–55
  for dependencies, 76, 125, 347
  dividing concurrent substates, 307
  for included use cases, 162–163
  for lifelines, 190
dashed oval, for collaborations, 250, 252–253
data flow. *See* object flow
data slots. *See* attributes
data subsystem, 322
database subsystem, 355
databases
  as actors, 134–135
  internal compared to external, 135
  for object persistence, 318
  terminology, compared to classes and objects, 44
  UML modeling tools for, 32–33
Data-Description Language. *See* DDL
data-flow diagram, avoiding, 309. *See* activity diagram
datatypes
  analysis packages based on, 342
  for arguments, 49–50
  for attributes, 44–45
  implementation compared to conceptual types, 48
  inheritance and, 103
  intrinsic, 45
  of qualifiers, 77
data-validation rules, in use case scenarios, 160
DDL (Data-Description Language), UML modeling tools supporting, 33
decision node, 215
decomposition of system
  creating subsystems, 318, 321–323
  definition of, 318, 320–321
  process for, 322–323
deep history pseudostate, 301
default values, attribute
  definition of, 46–47
  inheritance and, 103
/defer, for deferred events, 287

deferred event, 287
«delegate» stereotype, 331
delegates, for components, 331
delegation connector, 90
Department of Defense's Architecture Framework. *See* DODAF
dependencies
  dashed line for, 76, 125, 347
  with diagrams, 12
  with interfaces, 329–330
  with merged subsystems, 352–354
  with subsystems, 341, 347–350
deployment, subsystems based on, 345
deployment diagram
  artifacts in, 336–338
  constructing, 333–335
  uses of, 14, 15, 320, 390–391
derived attributes
  definition of, 55–56
  inheritance and, 103
design class diagram, 228–232
design pattern. *See* patterns
design phase
  package diagram for, 390
  sequence diagrams for, 202
  subsystems for, 342
designers, 17
design-time boundary objects, 199
«destroy» stereotype, 195
destructor operation, 85, 97
developers. *See* implementors
development. *See* software and system development
device class, 389
«device» stereotype, 334
devices as actors, 135–136
DevX Web site, 374
diagrams. *See also* shapes and symbols in UML diagrams; *specific diagrams*
  abstract classes represented in, 107
  actors represented in, 137–138, 139–141
  aggregation represented in, 83–84, 86
  alternative categories of, 15
  architectural patterns represented in, 355–356
  artifacts represented in, 337
  association classes represented in, 76
  associations represented in, 64, 65, 68–69, 74, 77, 79

choosing using modeling frameworks, 15–16
classes represented in, 52–56, 59–60
collaborations represented in, 250, 355–356
completing in parallel, 368
components represented in, 327
composition represented in, 86–87, 89–92
converting to code, 79
dependencies represented in, 76, 125, 347
diagram of, 12
events represented in, 262, 285, 290–292
generalizations represented in, 94–96
generalized use cases represented in, 167–168
interfaces represented in, 327
level of detail in, 364–365
lifelines represented in, 190–193
links represented in, 63
list of, 13–15
multiple inheritance represented in, 108
multiple, wrapping into packages, 125–127
multiplicity represented in, 68–69
nodes represented in, 333
number of elements in, 3
objects represented in, 52–56
point of view for, 11
preconditions and postconditions represented in, 186
roles represented in, 71–72
specialization represented in, 97–98
spelling and grammar checking for, 43
states represented in, 262
subsystems represented in, 321
transitions represented in, 290–292
use cases represented in, 139–141, 167–168
uses of, 13–15, 31
using too many or too few, 363–364
diamond
    for decision and merge nodes, 215
    filled in, for composition, 86–87
    hollow, for aggregation, 84, 87–88
direction of argument, 50
discriminator. *See* generalization sets
do/, for activity in a state, 267
DODAF (Department of Defense's Architecture Framework), 15

do-forever state, 309
domain class diagram
    definition of, 117, 122
    uses of, 122, 386–387
domain classes. *See also* use cases
    analysis packages for, 341–342
    definition of, 121–122
    dynamic, 388
    responsibilities of, 390
    subsystems for, 323
domain groups, 341–342
domain language, 121
dot
    for initial nodes, 215
    for initial state, 263
dot operator (.), OCL, 187
double angle brackets (≪≫), for stereotype, 55, 137
double colon (::), between class and operation, 50
do-until state, 309
dynamic diagrams, 15
dynamic domain classes, 388
dynamic modeling. *See* events; state diagram; states

• E •

EJB (Enterprise Java Beans), 30
elide. *See* information hiding
≪embedded device≫ stereotype, 334
embedded systems, UML modeling tools for, 32
encapsulation, 20, 23–24
Enterprise Java Beans. *See* EJB
≪enterprise≫ stereotype, 143
≪entity≫ stereotype, 331
entry/, for entry actions, 285
entry action, 285
entry event, 285
enumeration datatype, 46
≪enumeration≫ stereotype, 217, 284
error handling, for aggregation, 85
event handlers, state diagram for, 388
event hierarchy
    creating, 281–283
    parameters for, 283–285
event protocols, 308–312

event transition, 262, 267–269, 278–279
events. *See also* states
  actions performed during, 267
  completion, 287
  definition of, 262, 277
  generalizing, 281–283
  guard checking condition during, 269
  handling all with one operation, 285
  icons for, 290–292
  identifying, 263–265
  inheriting, in substates, 298–300
  internal, 287, 302
  occurring during object's state, 285–289
  operations corresponding to, 278–281
  organizing into an event hierarchy, 281–285
  passing information to object, 267
  time taken by, 269
  uses of, 277–278
«executable» stereotype, 338
«execution environment» stereotype, 334
exit/, for exit actions, 287
exit action, 286
exit event, 286
«extend» stereotype, 169–174
extension use cases, 169–174
external context diagram, 120
eXtreme Modeling methodology, 36
eXtreme Programming methodology, 36

• F •

façade architectural pattern, 356
«file» stereotype, 338
files. *See* artifacts
final state, 263, 264
final-activity node, 215
final-flow node, 215
flexibility, system design requirement, 317, 350
focus class. *See* central class
«focus» stereotype, 331
fork icon, for system or subsystem, 181, 321
fork node, 215
fork pseudostate, 305–308

framework
  definition of, 29, 31, 255
  developing, 255–258
  diagrams for, 257
  pattern compared to, 31, 255
friend class, 58
functional diagrams, 15
functional modeling. *See also* activity diagram; collaboration; patterns; sequence diagram
  algorithms in, 187–188
  class diagrams for, 181–182
  list of diagrams used for, 179
  preconditions and postconditions for, 184–187
  text-based behavioral specification for, 183–188
  use-case diagrams for, 180–181
  use-case specification for, 183–184
functional programming
  comparing to object-oriented techniques, 177–178
  splitting attributes and operations, 361–363

• G •

generalization. *See also* classes; inheritance
  of actors, 138
  association compared to, 95
  definition of, 21, 25–26
  diagramming, 94–96
  of events, 281–283
  identifying superclass and subclasses with, 93–97
  of states, 294–300
  of use cases, 166–169
generalization sets, 98–100
GET operation. *See* accessor operations
global visibility, 349–350
Golden Ratio (Φ), for class box size, 52
Google Web site, 374
grammar-checking diagrams, 43
guard conditions, for events, 269
guillemets («»), for stereotype, 55, 137

• H •

H*, for deep history pseudostate, 301
H, for shallow history pseudostate, 301
Happy Path of use case, 154
hardware. *See also* physical architecture, modeling
hiding information. *See* information hiding
high-level sequence diagram, 387
Hillside Group Web site, 250
history pseudostates, 301–302
hotspots, 255
hybrid class/object diagram, 113
hyphen (-)
  for irrelevant message argument, 197
  for private visibility, 57
  for role name, 72

• I •

IBM, Rational Rose Suite tool, 380
icons in UML diagrams. *See* shapes and symbols in UML diagrams
icons used in this book, 4–5
Ideogramic tool UML Web site, 379
i-Logix, Rhapsody tool, 380
implementation datatypes, 48
implementors (developers), 16, 17. *See also* software and system development
«import» stereotype, 351–352
«include» stereotype, 161–163
included use cases
  definition of, 161–163
  delivering with base use case, 174
  documenting, 163–164
  generalizing actors in, 165
  subsystems for, 344
independency, 347
indexing, with qualifiers, 78
information hiding, 11, 20, 23–24
information systems, UML modeling tools for, 32
informative messages, 196
inheritance. *See also* generalization
  in class diagrams, 114, 116
  code reuse with, 109–110

definition of, 21, 27, 95, 101–102
enforcing with abstract classes, 106–107
of events in substates, 298–300
list of items inherited, 101
multiple, 108–109
overriding attributes of, 103
inheritance hierarchy
  for events, 281–285
  for generalization, 95–96
  for specialization, 97–98
initial node, 215
initial state, 263, 264
initializing attributes. *See* default values, attribute
input devices as actors, 135
instance. *See* objects
«InstanceOf» stereotype, 55
integer datatype, 45
interaction diagrams. *See also* communication diagram; interaction-overview diagram; sequence diagram
  constructing, 203–211
  definition of, 13
  list of, 14–15
  multiple or repeating paths in, 206–211
  referencing from other diagrams, 203–206
  sd abbreviation for, 234
  timing diagram, 15
  uses of, 15, 189
interaction occurrences, 203, 221, 223
interaction-overview diagram. *See also* activity diagram
  constructing, 221–223
  definition of, 220–221
  dependency on activity diagram, 12
  uses of, 14
interactions. *See also* scenarios of use case
  definition of, 190
  multiple or repeating paths in, 206–211
  parameters for, 204–206
  referencing from other interactions, 203–206
  sequence diagram for, 190–192
«interface» stereotype, 329
interfaces
  for components, 327–330
  definition of, 29, 30
  diagramming, 327

interfaces *(continued)*
  inheriting, 101, 106–107
  invoking from subsystems, 351–352
  specification for, 329–330
  for subsystems, 319
internal context diagram, 120–121.
    See also aggregation
internal event, 287, 302
internal transition, 195
«internet» stereotype, 335
interrogative messages, 196
«interrupt» stereotype, 201
intrinsic datatypes, 45
invariants, 184–187
italics, for abstract classes or
    operations, 107
iterative development life cycle, 35
Ivar Web site, 375

• J •

Jacobson, Ivar
  original developer of UML, 18
  Web site with virtual simulacrum of, 375
join node, 215
join pseudostate, 305–308

• K •

knowledge responsibilities for objects, 48

• L •

«lan» stereotype, 334
language development, UML modeling
    tools supporting, 33
language of the user. *See* domain language
left angle bracket (<), for right-to-left
    association, 65
«library» stereotype, 338
life cycle
  of aggregation, 85
  definition of, 29
  methodology compared to, 35
  types of, 34–35

lifeline of object
  definition of, 189, 193
  diagramming, 190–193
  references for, 232–233
line
  dashed
    with arrow, from object to class, 54–55
    for dependencies, 76, 125, 347
    dividing concurrent substates, 307
    for included use cases, 162–163
    for lifelines, 190
  solid
    for associations, 62
    for links, 63
  thick
    for fork or join nodes, 215
    for fork or join pseudostates, 306–307
links, 62, 63–64. *See also* associations
logical models, 327
lollipop icon, 327
loop operator, 206, 208–209, 211

• M •

machines. *See* behavioral state diagram
main course of use case, 154
master-slave architectural pattern, 357
MDA (model-driven architecture)
  definition of, 16
  UML tool support for, 378
member variables. *See* attributes
membership notation for subsystems,
    323–324
merge dependencies, 352–354
merge node, 215
«merge» stereotype, 352
messages
  arguments in, 196–198
  asynchronous, 196
  button names in, 198–199
  in communication diagram, 235–241
  definition of, 195–196
  informative, 196
  interrogative, 196
  literal, quoting, 198
  methods used to send, 199–201
  naming, 196–199
  procedural, 196

methodology
  basic steps for, 34
  choosing, 35–36
  definition of, 29
  history of, 18
  life cycle compared to, 35
  types of, 35–36
  UML not as, 17
methods. *See also* events; operations
  definition of, 101
  inheriting, 101, 104–106
  operations compared to, 28
Microsoft COM. *See* COM
Microsoft Visio tool, 381–382
«mobile device» stereotype, 334
model-driven architecture. *See* MDA
modelers, 17
modeling. *See specific types of modeling*
modeling frameworks, 15–16
modeling tools. *See* tools for UML
    modeling
multiple inheritance, 108–109
multiplicity
  of aggregation association, 84
  of arguments, 50
  of association, 62, 67–71, 102
  of attributes, 47–49
  of composition parts, 90
  for concurrency in use cases, 140–141
  diagram of, converting to code, 80
  diagramming, 68–69
  inconsistencies in, 368–369
  reduced by qualifiers, 77–78
  time period relevant to, 118
multithreaded systems. *See also*
    concurrency
  invariants and, 184
  threads in communication diagram,
    243–244

• N •

name-direction arrow, 65
naming
  actors, 137
  aggregation, 86
  associations, 62, 65–66

attributes, 45–46
classes, 42–43, 365, 370
communication diagram, 235
identical names for the same class, 366
messages, 196–199
objects, 43–44
operations, 50–51
use cases, 142, 143
vague names, 365
navigation arrow, in association, 63, 79
neg operator, 211
no cycles constraint, 75
nodes, 333–335
Northern Light Web site, 374
nouns, using to define objects and classes,
    40–41
null values, for attributes, 48

• O •

object diagram. *See also* hybrid
    class/object diagram
  class diagram compared to, 72–73
  definition of, 111–112
  uses of, 14, 113
object flow, 215
Object Management Group. *See* OMG
Object Management Group, CORBA.
See CORBA
object modeling. *See* associations; classes;
    generalization; inheritance; objects
object node, 214
object-constraint language. *See* OCL
Objecteering tool Web site, 379–380
object-oriented development, 18, 24,
    177–178. *See also* software and system
    development
object-oriented principles used in UML,
    19–28, 39–41
Objectory methodology, 35
objects. *See also* classes
  active, 241–242
  aggregation and, 20, 24–25
  creating during interaction, 193–195, 201
  definition of, 20, 39
  destroying during interaction,
    193–195, 201

objects *(continued)*
  diagramming, 52–56
  encapsulation of, 20, 23–24
  generalization and, 21, 25–26
  identifying for a business, 40–41
  information hiding and, 11, 20, 23–24
  inheritance and, 21, 27, 95, 101–102
  knowledge responsibilities for, 48
  life of, 261–263
  lifeline of, 189, 193
  links between, 62, 63–64
  messages sent and received by, 195–201
  name of, underlining in diagram, 53–54
  naming, 43–44
  persistence of, 318
  polymorphism and, 27–28
  public, breaking encapsulation and
    information hiding, 24
  singling out important aspects of
    (abstraction), 10–11, 20, 21–23
  specialization and, 21, 25–26
  as a variable, 43–44
OCL (object-constraint language)
  for behavioral preconditions and
    postconditions, 185–187
  for pseudocode, 188
  UML modeling tools supporting, 33
  for use case preconditions and
    postconditions, 154
  Web site for, 373
OMG (Object Management Group)
  original development of UML, 18
  owns UML, 17
  Web site for, 372
OMT methodology, 35
one-way dependency, 347
ongoing-process state, 267
OOAD_UML group Web site, 375
operation call, 199
operations. *See also* events; methods
  abstract, 106
  accessors (GET/SET), 56
  activity diagrams for, 216
  for aggregation, 85
  arguments of, 49–51
  cascading, 85
  constructor, 85, 97
  converting use cases to, 181–182

defining (signature of), 49–51, 106
  destructor, 85, 97
  diagramming, 56, 59–60
  events corresponding to, 278–281
  extending, 105
  inheritance of, 101, 104–106
  naming, 50–51
  optimizing, 106
  private, 182
  public, 181–182
  restricting, 105
  return type of, 49
  signature of, 106
  static, 58–60
  visibility of, 57–60
  without attributes, 361–363
operators in interaction diagrams, 206–211
opt operator, 206–208, 211
ordered constraint, 75
output class, for use case, 231–232
output devices as actors, 135
ovals
  dashed, for collaborations, 250, 252–253,
    355–356
  for use cases, 140, 146
Overture Web site, 374
overview diagram. *See* interaction-
    overview diagram
ownership, subsystems based on, 345

• P •

package diagram
  definition of, 125–127
  uses of, 14, 320, 390
packages
  definition of, 125–127
  subsystems compared to, 340
  for system design, 339–343
  for use cases, 146
  visibility of, 57
«page» stereotype, 338
par operator, 211
«parallel» stereotype, 334
parameters. *See* arguments
parentheses (()), enclosing operation
    arguments, 51

partition names, in activity diagram, 224, 226

patterns
applying to a specific application, 252–254
composite structure diagrams for, 250–252
defining, 249–250
definition of, 29, 31
developing, 247–248
framework compared to, 31, 255
showing object interaction in, 254
for systems, 354–357
Web site about, 250

people. *See* actors; customers; stakeholders; users

performance
high degree of coupling for, 350
as system design requirement, 317

persistence
analysis packages based on, 342
of objects, choosing, 318

Petri net, activity diagrams compared to, 216

physical architecture, modeling, 333–338

physical models, 327

PIM (Platform-Independent Model), MDA and, 16

pipe-filter architectural pattern, 357

Platform-Independent Model. *See* PIM

Platform-Specific Model. *See* PSM

plus sign (+), for public visibility, 57

point of view for diagrams, 11

polymorphism, 27–28

Popkin, System Architect tool, 380–381

Popkin's UML Resource Center Web site, 374

ports, 331

postconditions
for activities, 219
for text-based behavioral specification, 184–187
for transitions in protocol state machines diagram, 310
for use-case specification, 154

pound sign (#), for protected visibility, 57

precise UML group Web site, 373

preconditions
for activities, 219
for text-based behavioral specification, 184–187
for transitions in protocol state machines diagram, 310
for use-case specification, 154

presentation subsystem, 322, 355

primary actors, 139, 141

Principle of Least Surprise, 28

private operations, 182

private visibility, 57–58, 182, 340

procedural messages, 196

process modeling, activity diagrams for, 216

«process» stereotype, 331

programs. *See* software and system development; tools for UML modeling

project-oriented class diagrams, 119–127

property. *See* attributes

protected visibility, 57, 340

protocol state machines diagram
constructing, 310–312
definition of, 308–310
uses of, 14

«provided interface» stereotype, 328–329

proxy actors, 134–136, 138

pseudocode, for algorithms, 188

pseudostates
with concurrent substates, 305–308
definition of, 300–302

PSM (Platform-Specific Model), MDA and, 16

public operations, 181–182

public visibility, 57–58, 182, 340

pUML Web site, 373

qualifiers
on associations, 63, 77–78, 102
diagram of, converting to code, 80
indexing with, 78
reducing multiplicity, 77–78

quotes (""), for literal message, 198

• R •

Rational Rose Suite tool Web site, 380
Rational Software, UML development and, 17, 18
Rational Unified Methodology, 36
Rational's UML Resource Center Web site, 374
realizes dependency, 329
real-time systems, UML modeling tools for, 32
ReceiveEvent event, 195
rectangle. *See also* boxes
  action sequence icon, 291
  for components, 327
  for interaction-overview diagram, 221
  rounded
    for activities, 214
    for events during states, 285
    for states, 262
  with triangular notch, signal receipt icon, 290
  with triangular point, signal sending icon, 290
ref operator, 211
reflexive associations, 73–75
region operator, 211
reification, of events, 283
reliability, system design requirement, 317
«required interface» stereotype, 328–329
return call, 199–200
return type of operation, 49
Rhapsody tool Web site, 380
right angle bracket (>), for left-to-right association, 65
robustness diagram. *See* application class diagram
roles
  of actors, 136–138
  of classes, 71–73
  diagram of, converting to code, 80
  inheriting, 102
RTF. *See* UML Revision Task Force of OMG
Rumbaugh, Jim (original developer of UML), 18

• S •

scalability, system design requirement, 317
scenarios of use case. *See also* sequence diagram
  definition of, 155–160
  list of diagrams for, 179
schedule
  subsystems based on, 345
  system design requirement, 317
«script» stereotype, 338
sd abbreviation, 191, 234
search engines, 374
secondary actors, 139, 141
semaphore message, 201
«semaphore» stereotype, 201
SendEvent, 195
sequence diagram
  application-level sequence, 387
  constructing, 190–192
  constructing state diagram from, 272–276
  creating and destroying objects in, 193–195
  for design phase, 202
  for frameworks, 257
  high-level sequence, 387
  multiple, summarizing in activity diagrams, 216
  for object interaction in a collaboration, 254
  sd abbreviation for, 191, 234
  sending messages in, 195–201
  uses of, 15, 179, 189, 202, 387
«serial» stereotype, 334
«service» stereotype, 331
SET operation. *See* accessor operations
shallow history pseudostate, 301
shapes and symbols in UML diagrams
  ball and socket, for assemblies in a component, 331, 333
  box
    for actors, 138
    for classes and objects, 52, 55–56, 59–60
    with parallel vertical bars, for active object, 241
    for qualifiers, 77
    three-dimensional, for nodes, 333

box icon, with two small rectangles, for components, 327–328
boxes, stack of, in communication diagram, 240
bull's eye, for final-activity nodes, 215
circle
 filled in (large dot), for initial nodes, 215
 filled in (large dot), for initial state, 263
 labeled, for connectors, 215–216
 with plus sign inside, for membership, 323
 on a stick, for interfaces, 327
 with X inside, for final-flow nodes, 215
diamond
 for decision and merge nodes, 215
 filled in, for composition, 86–87
 hollow, for aggregation, 84, 87–88
folder, tabbed, for packages, 126, 146, 340
fork
 for fork or join nodes, 215
 for fork or join pseudostates, 306–307
fork icon, for system or subsystem, 181, 321
half circle, on a stick, for interfaces, 327
history of choices for, 53
line, dashed
 with arrow, from object to class, 54–55
 for dependencies, 76, 125, 347
 dividing concurrent substates, 307
 for included use cases, 162–163
 for lifelines, 190
line, solid
 for associations, 62
 for links, 63
ovals
 dashed, for collaborations, 250, 252–253, 355–356
 for use cases, 140, 146
rectangle
 action sequence icon, 291
 for components, 327
 for interaction-overview diagram, 221
 rounded, for activities, 214
 rounded, for events during states, 285
 rounded, for states, 262

with triangular notch, signal receipt icon, 290
with triangular point, signal sending icon, 290
small square, for component ports, 331
socket, in pattern, 251–252
shell generation, UML modeling tools supporting, 33
signal receipt icon, 290
signal sending icon, 290
«signal» stereotype, 281
signature of operation, 50, 106
slash (/)
 for an action or activity, 267
 for derived attribute, 55
 for event actions, 285–287
socket
 ball and socket, for assemblies in a component, 331, 333
 in patterns, 251–252
 on a stick, for interfaces, 327
Softeam, Objecteering tool, 379–380
software. *See also* tools for UML modeling
software and system development.
 See also system design
 automating from UML models, 16, 17, 378
 component-based, 29–31
 converting diagrams to code, 79–81
 design phase, 202, 342, 390
 diagrams for, 31
 functional, 177–178
 life cycles for, 34–35
 methodologies for, 34–36, 129
 object-oriented
 benefits of, 177–178
 encapsulation and information hiding used with, 24
 history of UML and, 18
 patterns in, 31
 reusing code
 with domain classes, 121–122
 with frameworks, 255–258
 with inheritance, 109–110
 with patterns, 247–254

software and system development
(continued)
  terminology used for, 28–29
  types of systems being developed, 32–33
  UML tools improving productivity of, 32–34
Software Development Magazine Web site, 374
source of association, 78–79
specialization
  definition of, 21, 25–26
  identifying superclass and subclasses with, 97–98
spell-checking diagrams, 43
«spin-lock» stereotype, 201
spiral life cycle, 35
square. *See* boxes
square brackets ([])
  for multiplicity, 47, 90
  for preconditions or postconditions, 310
stakeholders, 132
state attributes, 269–272
state diagram
  avoiding data-flow diagram for, 309
  complex, simplifying, 293–302
  concurrent states in, 303–305
  constructing, 263–266, 272–276
  creating operations from events in, 278–281
  definition of, 262–263
  events as icons in, 290–292
  order of execution defined in, 289–290
  protocol state machines diagram, 308–312
  uses of, 14, 15, 179, 312, 388
state transition, 195
state-machine diagram. *See* state diagram
states. *See also* events
  activities or actions within, 267
  attributes of, 269–272
  concurrency with, 303–308
  definition of, 262–263
  diagramming, 262
  do-forever, 309
  do-until, 309
  generalizing, 294–300
  initial, 263, 264

pseudostates, connecting transitions with, 300–302
  submachines for, 296–298
  substates of, 294–296
  transitions between, 267–269
  types of, 266–267
static attributes, 58–60
static diagrams, 15
static operations, 58–60
stereotypes
  for actors in use cases, 137–138
  for artifacts, 337–338
  for communication paths, 334–335
  for components, 327
  for constructor operation, 60
  for creating and destroying objects, 195
  for enumerations, 217, 284
  for events treated as classes, 281
  for extended use cases, 169–174
  for importing subsystems, 351
  for included use cases, 161–163
  for instance of object, 55
  for interfaces, 328–330
  for internal parts of components, 331
  for merging subsystems, 352
  for messaging mechanism, 201
  for nodes, 334
  for subsystems, 321
  syntax for, 54–55
  for use-case controller, 230
  for use-case levels, 143–144
  for use-case packages, 146
stick figure. *See* actors
string datatype, 45
structural diagrams, 13–14. *See also specific diagrams*
structure of class. *See* attributes
subclasses
  basis for discrimination between, 98–100
  identifying with generalization, 94–97
  identifying with specialization, 97–98
submachines, 296–298
substates
  concurrent, pseudostates and, 305–308
  definition of, 294–296
  inheriting events in, 298–300
«subsystem» stereotype, 143, 181, 321

subsystems. *See also* components
  aggregation and, 322
  application, 322
  cohesion in, 348, 350
  as components, 325
  converting packages to, 340–341, 343–345
  coupling in, 348, 350
  creating during decomposition, 318, 321–323
  definition of, 321
  dependencies in, 341, 347–350
  diagramming, 321
  for domain classes, 323
  importing classes into, 351–352
  interfaces for, 319
  invoking interfaces from, 351–352
  membership notation for, 323–324
  merging, 352–354
  in a package, 323
  packages compared to, 340
  relationships between, 318
  responsibilities of, 323–325
  types of, 322
  for use cases, 322
superclasses
  abstract operations for, 106
  identifying with generalization, 94–97
  identifying with specialization, 97–98
superstates, 294
surrogate class, 389
swim lanes, in activity diagram, 224–225
symbols in UML diagrams. *See* shapes and symbols in UML diagrams
symmetric association, 89
System Architect tool Web site, 380–381
system architecture modeling. *See* subsystems; system design
system design. *See also* software and system development; subsystems
  architecture, physical, 333–338
  architecture, system, 318
  brittle systems, 339
  categories of systems, 32–33
  components for, 319, 325–333
  current system, reviewing, 318
  decomposition of system, 318, 320–325
  deployment for, 333–338
  interfaces for, 319, 327–330, 351–352

  list of diagrams for, 320
  object persistence for, 318
  packages for, 339–343
  patterns in, 354–357
  priorities for, 316–318
  process for, 316–319
  strategies for, 319
  subsystem interfaces for, 319
  users' terminology for, 370
system development. *See* software and system development
«system» stereotype, 143, 181
systems modeled by UML, 32–33

• T •

tabbed folder, for packages, 340
target of association, 78–79
Tau tool Web site, 381
Telelogic, Tau tool, 381
Teoma Web site, 374
text-based behavioral specification, 179, 183–188
thick line
  for fork or join nodes, 215
  for fork or join pseudostates, 306–307
threads. *See* multithreaded systems
Three Amigos, 18, 36
3C (Clear, Clean, Concise) proposal, Web site for, 373
three-tier architecture pattern, 354–355
Tigris, Argo/UML tool, 379
tilde (~), for package visibility, 57
time period for class diagram, 118–119
timed call, 201
timing diagram, 15
TogetherSoft tool Web site, 381
tokens, in activity diagrams, 216
tools for UML modeling
  definition of, 29
  features of, 33–34, 377–378
  systems modeled by, 32–33
  uses of, 32
  Web sites about, 374, 379–382
transitions
  completion, 274, 287
  event, 262, 267–269, 278–279

transitions *(xontinued)*
 icons for, 290–292
 internal, 195
 in protocol state machine diagrams, 310
 pseudostates connecting, 300–302
 state, 195
transitive association, 89
transparent actors, 136
2U Consortium Web site, 373
two-way dependency, 347–348
types. *See* datatypes

• U •

UML (Unified Modeling Language). *See also*
  tools for UML modeling; UML 2, new
  features in
 automating development with, 16, 378
 definition of, 1, 9–10
 history of, 18
 level of detail to describe with, 23,
  364–365
 methodologies for, 18, 29, 34–36
 misconceptions about, 17–18
 object-oriented principles used in, 20–28,
  39–41
 people using, 17
 Principle of Least Surprise for, 28
 training for, 375
 uses of, 9–11
 Web sites about, 372–373, 375
UML Dictionary Web site, 375
UML Forum Web site, 372–373
UML Revision Task Force (RTF) of OMG, 18
UML 2, new features in. *See also* UML
 Action Semantics, 188
 activity diagrams, 216
 artifacts, 336
 association end name, replacing role, 71
 behavioral state diagram, 308
 communication diagrams, 227, 228
 component diagram, revisions to, 327
 composite structure diagram, 90, 121
 composite structure diagram with
  collaboration, 251
 interaction frame and heading, 191
 interaction occurrences, 203

 interaction-overview diagram, 220
 MDA and, 16
 operators in interaction diagrams, 206
 package diagram, 126
 transition notation, 277, 290–292
UML 2, proposals for, 373
UML 2.0 Partners Web site, 373
UML-Forum Web site, 375
underlining
 for button names in messages, 198
 for link name, 62
 for object name, 53–54
 for static attribute or operation, 58–59
"Underlining the Nouns" technique, 40–41
Unified Modeling Language. *See* UML
«usb» stereotype, 334
use cases. *See also* domain classes;
  functional modeling
 abstract, 167
 activity diagrams for, 216
 alternate paths for, 171–172
 analysis packages based on, 342
 application classes for, 122–125
 central class for, 229–230
 changing capability of, 169–171
 class diagram for, 228–232
 concrete, 167
 concurrency of, 140–141
 context diagrams for, 145
 controller class for, 230–231
 CRUD test for, 367
 customers of, 132–133
 defining, 139, 141–143
 definition of, 131
 diagramming, 139–141, 167–168
 domain classes for, 121–122
 extending, 169–174
 generalizing, 166–169
 including other use cases in, 161–165, 174
 interaction-overview diagram for, 220–223
 levels of, 143–145
 naming, 142, 143
 optional goals for, 173
 output class for, 231–232
 packaging, 146
 priorities of, in system design, 316–317
 subsystems for, 322, 343–344
 too many of, 367

too many paths in, 367
when to use, 16
«use-case controller» stereotype, 230
use-case diagram. *See also* context diagram
  application class diagram for, 123–124
  constructing, 139–141, 143–144, 385
  converting to operations in class
      diagrams, 181–182
  definition of, 11, 139
  for frameworks, 257
  for functional modeling, 180–181
  uses of, 14, 15, 179, 385–386
use-case modeling. *See* use cases; use-case
      diagram; use-case specification
«use-case package» stereotype, 146
use-case specification
  alternate courses for, 155–160
  definition of, 147–149
  description for, 150
  design details omitted from, 151–153
  flow of events for, 153–154, 156–159
  for functional modeling, 183–184
  for included use cases, 163–164
  main course for, 154
  multiple scenarios for, 155–160
  narration (story) for, 149–153
  preconditions and postconditions
      for, 154
user-defined types, 46
users
  definition of, 133
  designing system for, 370
  interaction with application, showing,
      122–125
  verification of domain classes by,
      121–122
uses dependency, 329
»uses» stereotype, 330

• V •

v, for top-to-bottom association, 65
variable, object used as, 43–44
view class, 123, 389
visibility, 57–60, 182, 340, 349–350
Visio tool Web site, 381–382

• W •

wait state, 266
waterfall life cycle, 34–35
Web sites
  magazines, 373–374
  about OCL, 373
  about patterns, 250
  search engines, 374
  as source of information, 371–372
  about UML 2, 373
  UML Dictionary, 375
  UML forums, 372–373, 375
  UML home page, 372
  for UML questions, 375
  about UML tools, 374, 379–382
  about UML training, 375
Web-based systems, UML modeling tools
      for, 33
when event, 288
workflow diagram. *See* activity diagram

• X •

X, for destroyed object, 193, 201
XMI (XML Model Interchange), 378

• Y •

Y2K date problem, encapsulation and, 24

• Z •

Zachman modeling framework, 15
Zeal Web site, 374

FOR DUMMIES®

The easy way to get more done and have more fun

PERSONAL FINANCE & BUSINESS

Investing
0-7645-2431-3

Home Buying
0-7645-5331-3

Grant Writing
0-7645-5307-0

Also available:

Accounting For Dummies
(0-7645-5314-3)

Business Plans Kit For Dummies
(0-7645-5365-8)

Managing For Dummies
(1-5688-4858-7)

Mutual Funds For Dummies
(0-7645-5329-1)

QuickBooks All-in-One Desk Reference For Dummies
(0-7645-1963-8)

Resumes For Dummies
(0-7645-5471-9)

Small Business Kit For Dummies
(0-7645-5093-4)

Starting an eBay Business For Dummies
(0-7645-1547-0)

Taxes For Dummies 2003
(0-7645-5475-1)

HOME, GARDEN, FOOD & WINE

Feng Shui
0-7645-5295-3

Gardening
0-7645-5130-2

Cooking
0-7645-5250-3

Also available:

Bartending For Dummies
(0-7645-5051-9)

Christmas Cooking For Dummies
(0-7645-5407-7)

Cookies For Dummies
(0-7645-5390-9)

Diabetes Cookbook For Dummies
(0-7645-5230-9)

Grilling For Dummies
(0-7645-5076-4)

Home Maintenance For Dummies
(0-7645-5215-5)

Slow Cookers For Dummies
(0-7645-5240-6)

Wine For Dummies
(0-7645-5114-0)

FITNESS, SPORTS, HOBBIES & PETS

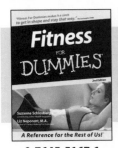

Fitness
0-7645-5167-1

Golf
0-7645-5146-9

Guitar
0-7645-5106-X

Also available:

Cats For Dummies
(0-7645-5275-9)

Chess For Dummies
(0-7645-5003-9)

Dog Training For Dummies
(0-7645-5286-4)

Labrador Retrievers For Dummies
(0-7645-5281-3)

Martial Arts For Dummies
(0-7645-5358-5)

Piano For Dummies
(0-7645-5105-1)

Pilates For Dummies
(0-7645-5397-6)

Power Yoga For Dummies
(0-7645-5342-9)

Puppies For Dummies
(0-7645-5255-4)

Quilting For Dummies
(0-7645-5118-3)

Rock Guitar For Dummies
(0-7645-5356-9)

Weight Training For Dummies
(0-7645-5168-X)

Available wherever books are sold.
Go to www.dummies.com or call 1-877-762-2974 to order direct

FOR DUMMIES®

A world of resources to help you grow

TRAVEL

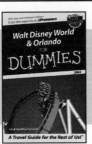

0-7645-5453-0

0-7645-5438-7

0-7645-5444-1

EDUCATION & TEST PREPARATION

0-7645-5194-9

0-7645-5325-9

0-7645-5249-X

HEALTH, SELF-HELP & SPIRITUALITY

0-7645-5154-X

0-7645-5302-X

0-7645-5418-2

Available wherever books are sold. Go to www.dummies.com or call 1-877-762-2974 to order direct

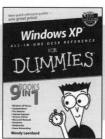

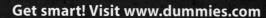